Nabi Misdaq has a rare blend of skills. As an anthropologist he studied contemporary Afghan society and then worked for many years as a journalist with the BBC's Overseas Service in which capacity he met and interviewed most of Afghanistan's leading politicians. Combining these skills with a profound knowledge of Afghan history, he has produced an enthralling study which reveals the fundamental problems encountered by generations of Afghan rulers in attempting to create a legitimate, centralised Afghan state, problems which, as Misdaq also shows, still confront Afghanistan's present-day leadership.

Ralph Grillo, Emeritus Professor of Social Anthropology,
University of Sussex

Dr Nabi Misdaq has described in this book how the Afghans defended their identity and country, Afghanistan, in odd conditions throughout history, with a special focus on the last 300 years. The publication of this book, considering the current conditions Afghanistan, is by itself an example of such defense. This is a thoroughly researched and compassionately argued work. I will recommend this book as a must for all those who have an interest in the geo-politics of Afghanistan.

Dr Farouq Azam, former Afghan Minister of Education

Afghanistan: Political Frailty and External Interference is a timely book. At a time when the focus of the world is on the region, it is one of the few anthropological commentaries by a well-known native. Nabi Misdaq's book is detailed and insightful. He has established himself as an authority on Afghanistan. I strongly recommend the book.

Dr Akbar S. Ahmed, Ibn Khaldun Chair of Islamic Studies
American University, Washington, DC

Afghanistan

Afghanistan provides a discourse on two and a half centuries of Afghan sociopolitical disquiet, outside interference and the resilience of the Afghans.

This book explains the clashes, reconciliations and bargaining between the central government and the tribes. The tribes are the corner stone of the present state and therefore it is not surprising to see a continuous struggle between the tribes in preserving their autonomy and the state that wants to usurp it. The author also investigates the effects of foreign invasions over the past two and a half centuries, in order to highlight the unique nature of the Soviet, and most recently, American invasions. *Afghanistan* also includes a discussion of a 'post-America' Afghanistan that will probably see many years of revenge and hostile ethnic tensions due to external interference. The issues covered include:

- Afghan history
- The role of Islam
- Contemporary theories of state
- Nationalism
- Ethnicity
- Tribalism

This book is essential reading for those with research interests in Afghanistan, Middle East Politics and History, as well as for the general reader wishing to learn more about this strategically located country.

Dr Nabi Misdaq, who came to England from Afghanistan on an academic scholarship, graduated from LSE before taking Masters and PhD degrees at the University of Sussex. The Soviet invasion took him from academia to the BBC, where he worked for almost two decades as a radio journalist, producer and as head of the Pashto section of the World Service, which he established in 1982. Since 2001 he has been residing in the USA where he taught Pashto at George Mason University, before beginning work on a major forthcoming Pashto–English dictionary as well as other language resources, in response to the dearth of reference materials available in the quintessential language of Afghanistan.

Routledge studies in Middle Eastern history

1 **The Boundaries of Modern Palestine, 1840–1947**
   Gideon Biger

2 **The Survey of Palestine under the British Mandate, 1920–1948**
   Dov Gavish

3 **British Pro-Consuls in Egypt, 1914–1929**
   C.W.R. Long

4 **Islam, Secularism and Nationalism in Modern Turkey**
   Who is a Turk?
   Soner Cagaptay

5 **Mamluks and Ottomans**
   Studies in honour of Michael Winter
   Edited by David J. Wasserstein and Ami Ayalon

6 **Afganistan**
   Political frailty and external interference
   Nabi Misdaq

Afghanistan
Political frailty and external interference

Dr Nabi Misdaq

LONDON AND NEW YORK

First published 2006
by Routledge
2 Park Square, Milton Park, Abingdon, Oxon, OX14 4RN

Simultaneously published in the USA and Canada
by Routledge
270 Madison Ave, New York NY 10016

Routledge is an imprint of the Taylor & Francis Group, an informa business

Transferred to Digital Printing 2008

© 2006 Dr Nabi Misdaq

Typeset in Baskerville by Wearset Ltd, Boldon, Tyne and Wear

All rights reserved. No part of this book may be reprinted or reproduced or utilised in any form or by any electronic, mechanical, or other means, now known or hereafter invented, including photocopying and recording, or in any information storage or retrieval system, without permission in writing from the publishers.

British Library Cataloguing in Publication Data
A catalogue record for this book is available from the British Library

Library of Congress Cataloging in Publication Data
A catalog record for this book has been requested

ISBN10: 0-415-70205-4 (hbk)
ISBN10: 0-415-47024-2 (pbk)
ISBN10: 0-203-09933-8 (ebk)

ISBN13: 978-0-415-70205-8 (hbk)
ISBN13: 978-0-415-47024-7 (pbk)
ISBN13: 978-0-203-09933-9 (ebk)

To all those who have given their precious lives for the unity, freedom and independence of Afghanistan.

Contents

List of illustrations   xiii
Preface   xiv
Acknowledgements   xviii
Acronyms   xix

Introduction   1
  Aims and objectives 1
  The scope of the book 2
  Population and society in Afghanistan 6
  Tribe and Pashtunwali 9
    Pashtunwali 10
    Afghanistan in history and anthropology 11
  The Afghan state 19
    The patrimonial state 19
    The segmentary state 22
  Nation and nationalism 24
  Ethnicity 29
  Islam 30
  Conclusion 32

PART I
A state in the making   33

  1 **Formation of the Afghan state: 1747–72**   35
    Introduction 35
    Struggle against the Moghuls: the Roshani movement 36
    Initial attempt in forming the state: the Ghilzai uprising, the Kandahar state 39
    The conquest of Persia: Mir Wais' family wrangles, the Hotak downfall 40

The 1747 Jirga: election of Ahmad Shah in Kandahar 42
Ahmad Khan as king: final attempt to form the state 44
Declaration of independence 44
Ahmad Shah: from king to emperor 45
State formation 48
Conclusion 50

2 State to nation: 1773–1973 — 52

Introduction 52
The fragility of the Afghan state 52
    Rivalry between Abdali (Durrani) confederacies 53
    The segmentary state 54
Attempts at modernisation 56
    Amir Abdur Rahman: the second Anglo–Afghan war (1879–81) 56
    Internal 'nationalisation' policy 59
    External policy 60
    Amanullah the Great Reformer: 1919–29 62
    Revolt at home 64
    Nader Shah: 1929–33 66
The geopolitical position of Afghanistan: its vulnerability to external forces 67
Conclusion 71

PART II
Sowing the seeds of turmoil — 73

3 Daoud's republic: 1973–78 — 75

Introduction 75
Pashtunistan 77
The decade of constitution 79
    Experiment in democracy 80
    Assessing the decade of constitution 81
Daoud's comeback 82
Daoud's Soviet connection 84
Why Daoud came to power 85
Daoud in office 87
Daoud's u-turn on the communists 90
Murders, assassinations and Daoud's overthrow 93
Conclusion 95

4 Afghan communist parties and personalities 97
Introduction 97
Leftists and nationalists come of age 98
The entry of the communists 99
Strife among the communists 103
Key communist leaders 107
   Nur Mohammad Taraki 107
   Hafizullah Amin 109
   Babrak Karmal 113
Conclusion 115

5 Events leading to the Soviet invasion 117
Introduction 117
PDPA internal tensions play into Soviet hands 118
   Khalq vs. Parcham 118
   Tension within the Khalq leadership 121
Soviets prepare the grounds for invasion 126
Soviets taking stock of uprisings and discontent 126
Amin's 104 days in office 130
Conclusion 138

PART III
Battleground of superpowers 141

6 Afghan resistance: 1975–92 143
Introduction 143
Manning, finance and the organisation of resistance 144
The Islamist movement in Afghanistan 146
   Phase 1: resistance against Daoud 149
   Phase 2: resistance against the communists 152
   Phase 3: resistance against the Soviets 155
   World reaction 156
   Afghan reaction 157
   The Kabul government's counter resistance 161
   The Kabul government and the Soviet expenses of war 163
   Phase 4: resistance against the Soviet surrogate
      government 164
Conclusion 166

7 From common cause to internal war and the rise of the Taleban   167

Introduction 167
The struggle for power 168
The Kabul communists, the Loya Jirga and the king 169
A new anti-Pashtun alliance 171
The struggle for political power 172
The urban guerrilla war 173
The Taleban 175
   The rise of the Taleban 176
   Taleban conquests 179
A closer look at the Taleban movement 189
Conclusion 194

8 Post-communist ethnicity   198

Introduction 198
Ethnicity in the pre-state era 199
Ethnicity in the Afghan kingdom 199
Post-communist ethnicity 201
The ethnic divide 202
Dividing Afghanistan on ethnic lines 211
Ethnicity revitalised 213
Harmony and provocation 217
Conclusion 221

Conclusion   224

Introduction 224
Continuity and discontinuity 224
   Terrain 224
   Tribe as a cornerstone of governance 225
The emergence of the modern Afghan nation-state 227
Resistance to modernity 228
The decade of the constitution 229
Ethnicity and ideology in contemporary Afghanistan 230
Comparative and theoretical issues: tribe and state 233
Islam 234
The way ahead 236

Epilogue: America's and Afghanistan's 9/11   241

Introduction 241
Background to the US occupation: the Osama bin Laden affair 241
   American bombing and occupation 244

Karzai and the new government 248
  Karzai as America's leader for Afghanistan 251
Winning hearts and minds? 253
Long-term consequences of American occupation 266
Conclusion 269

Appendix 1: categorising books on Afghanistan — 271

Appendix 2: the institutions of Pashtunwali — 273
  Islam and Pashtunwali 275

Appendix 3: state and Islamic jurisprudence — 277

Appendix 4: struggle against Persians in the West — 280

Appendix 5: Abdali uprising, intrigue and deception — 281

Appendix 6: the early life of Ahmad Shah, king in waiting — 283

Appendix 7: Nader Shah's assassination, formation of the Afghan state — 285

Appendix 8: Britain's Forward Policy and the 'great game' — 287

Appendix 9: British and Soviet/Russian interest in Afghanistan — 290

Appendix 10: the Pashtunistan issue — 293
  1. *Why was the Durand Agreement signed? 294*
  2. *The British drawing of this line did not incorporate all the tribes 295*
  3. *Could partition of British India legally pass on these tribes to the successor state of Pakistan? 296*
  4. *What constitutes the claim over this territory and its people by the two disputing countries, Afghanistan and Pakistan? 297*

Appendix 11: the initial months of communists in power — 300

Appendix 12: Mujahideen resistance parties — 302
  A. *Islamist 302*
  B. *Moderate parties 303*
  C. *Shi'ah parties 305*

Appendix 13: Geneva negotiations 306
Background to the talks 306
The mechanism for the talks 307
The agenda for negotiation 309

Appendix 14: Russian designs on Afghanistan 310

Notes 311
Bibliography 335
Index 344

Illustrations

Tables

I.1	Percentage of major Afghan ethnic groups	7
2.1	The conquests of Abdur Rahman, the Iron Amir	58
3.1	Parties and ideologies from 1966	80
4.1	Khalq and Parcham recruitment and political leanings	100
5.1	Afghan Sunni parties based in Peshawar	151
5.2	Afghan Shi'ah parties	151

Maps

1	Moghul and Safavid empires: farthest extents	xxi
2	Empire of Ahmad Shad Durrani at the end of his reign	xxii
3	British retreat route from Kabul, 1842	xxiii
4	Afghanistan and its six neighbours	xxiv
5	Two centuries of southward advance by Imperial Russia and westward of Imperial British India, coming to a halt on the Afghan borders	xxv

Preface

Writing a socio-political history of Afghanistan with the view of explaining the consequences of the Soviet invasion, in the context of Afghan history and politics, has been in my mind since the Red Army's march into Afghanistan in December 1979. Now that Afghanistan is over-run by yet another superpower, the United States of America, the publishing of a well documented and researched book is even more urgent. So when I decided on the shape and the context of the book, I was fortunate to have had more sources at my disposal than I could cram into such a book. Not knowingly, I have been collecting material to such an end for over twenty years.

In 1976 I undertook fieldwork in Afghanistan for a Sussex University DPhil thesis in Anthropology under the supervision of Dr Brian Street. That research was based in a Pashtun district of Zazi, out of nearly 260 such districts in the country. I was then working on the Timber Merchants of Zazi and how timber, as a cash item was important for their gradual relocation from their rural area to Kabul over the last one hundred years. My write-up of that thesis was at an advanced stage when the Soviet Red Army invaded Afghanistan in December 1979 and I decided to halt my study and to make myself useful to my people by working for the BBC, in my new capacity as a radio-journalist. I knew that Afghans would not tolerate the Soviet invasion and it would be a matter of two to four years before they would withdraw. I was right about the resistance the Afghan people mounted that forced the Soviets to retreat, but wrong on the timescale. If I could have gauged correctly how Afghanistan might have become a global geopolitical issue and how because of it the invasion would last for a decade and lead to further complications amongst ethnic and resistance groups, I probably would have continued with my studies.

Since leaving the BBC in 1996 I decided to return to university with the view of completing that thesis. However, because of the scope and shape of the thesis looking into the consequences of the Soviet invasion and related issues, I was unable to use or include my data on the Zazi. Also the war against the Soviets, the communists and amongst the resistance parties has totally changed factors on the ground. The forests were burnt by the Russians to deprive the resistance from taking shelter in the Zazi mountains; the climate has become dryer and much hotter; the people of Zazi have been scattered not just in Pakistan, India and Iran but to all parts of the world; the Zazi countryside is infested with mines and very few people have returned to an uncertain future. Under these circumstances it was not easy to bring the material up to date. Neither did I feel enthusiastic about writing a PhD from a frozen picture, though it could be the basis for a book in the future.

During my years at the BBC, I collected agency reports, BBC talks and commentaries, radio monitoring reports, newspaper cuttings and interviews that I had conducted myself with key figures, on an almost daily basis. There are also historic, political and anthropological books and manuscripts that were at my disposal. It was with such abundance of multi-sited material that I undertook to write a new thesis. The methodology of that thesis was therefore based on the evaluation of such sources and my own experience of living through it. It therefore has turned into an archival reflexive research, enriched with my own reading of events. The method I devised was a simple one. I would try to use different sources to tell the story and then analyse and comment on facts presented in order to clarify the issue at hand. This had worked well for me whether I was tackling physical environment or theoretical issues on nation, nationalism, ethnicity and so on.

I visited Afghanistan on numerous occasions during the Soviet occupation (1979–89) and the Mujahideen chaotic infighting years (1992–96) and had the opportunity twice to go back during the Taleban years (1996–2001). My previous visits were to report for the BBC about the on-going events amidst the war and the gathering of material for programmes to be broadcast later on. My two visits to Afghanistan took place in July–September 1997 and September 2000. During these last two visits I met with the Taleban leadership at all levels from their leader, Mullah Muhammad Omar, to cabinet ministers, commanders and their supporters in most parts of the country.

Afghanistan is an ongoing and developing story. I stopped my research in about June 2001 while the Taleban were still in power in Kabul. In October of that year the US attacked Afghanistan in retaliation for September 11, New York trade towers and Pentagon building in Washington. After thirty-four days of carpet bombing Taleban positions around Kabul and in the north, the Taleban withdrew from the capital and more than 8,000 of their troops laid down their arms and gave themselves up to Uzbek, Tajik and Hazarah warlords. But it was Kabul, the capital city that was important and who should control it. As I document in the Epilogue to this book, despite President George Bush's request that the Northern Alliance not enter Kabul, the followers of Ahmad Shah Masoud and his Shura-i-Nezar, from amongst the Northern Alliance, marched into Kabul and the killing of their opponents and stealing of private property started once again. It was a replay of the years 1992–96 when these groups committed major human rights violations.

Elsewhere, the US Special Forces and CIA agents recruited former warlords by giving them hundreds of millions of dollars in cash to help them capture or eliminate Taleban and al Qaeda leaders. Thus, once again the chaotic years of April 1992–September 1996 were repeated, when Mujahideen bands played havoc by killing, raping and stealing and the warlords and their militias were 'ruling' supreme in areas under their 'control' and not paying much attention to what the American installed government of Mr Hamed Karzai may say or ask them in Kabul. Three years on the American forces are guided by warlords and their militias, who were one by one defeated by the Taleban since October 1994. The Taleban being predominantly Pashtuns are considered to have represented or to have had the consent of the Pashtun majority and are now considered 'enemies' by the Americans who have killed over ten thousand of them in their homes, villages, at wedding parties and while holding *jirga* (local assemblies), as is their tradition to settle internal disputes and wrangles. In fact all Pashtuns never were Taleban and all Taleban never were al-Qaeda. While the followers and supporters of the present warlords poured on Kabul and the provinces to help and work with them, not a single Pashtun intellectual or former technocrat went to join the Taleban government when they were in power. Pashtuns, like others, had reservations about the Taleban system of government and their foreign policy. Yet the American military in three years of its presence so far (July 2004) in Afghanistan have not understood this simple fact. They are busy creating enemies from the Pashtuns for themselves instead of treating them as major players in Afghan war and politics over the centuries.

The delay in publication of this book also coincided with the US occupation of Afghanistan and the overthrow of the Taleban. In order to bring the work up to date, I have added an Epilogue at the end in which I discuss the occupation of Afghanistan, by the only one remaining superpower in today's world. Two key books have come out since '9/11', events in New York and Washington: Bob Woodward's *Bush at War* and Richard Clarke's *Against All Enemies*. Woodward is an editor of the Washington Post and interviewed Bush for three hours and Clarke was America's National Security and Counterterrorism expert both under Clinton and under George W. Bush till March 2004. Woodward also interviewed people in the Pentagon, the US National Security and other US military establishments. Both are insiders and so I have liberally quoted them in the Epilogue.

There are numerous Mujahideen to whom I owe thanks for looking after me, in all my visits during the Soviet Red Army Occupation and taking care of me while bullets were sometimes whizzing above our heads. Special thanks to the late Mullah Yar Mohammad who rescued me in Kandahar in 2000, to Hamid Karzai's father, the late Abdul Ahad Karzai, a former deputy speaker, who lent me and my colleague, Rahimullah Yosufzai, a pickup in Quetta, with a driver so that we could interview the Taleban and Dr Farooq Azam for inside information about the *Jihad* years. I am also grateful for the help and guidance of Professor Ralph Grillo who meticulously supervised my research, one result of that is the publication of this book. I am also more than thankful to Dr Michael Johnson who went through some of this material and made valuable suggestions and comments. I want also to thank my son Omar J. Misdaq for proofreading the final parts of the manuscript with a fine-toothed comb. I thank my wife Arian and my younger son Yusuf J. Misdaq for being patient with me, becoming a student once again. Also, special thanks are due to Clare Rogers, the Anthropology Secretary at the Department of Anthropology at Sussex University who always made sure I had access to rooms, computers and resources.

In this book, a prominent part is inevitably played by Afghans of Pashtun origin who form the majority of the country's population. As a Pashtun myself, I clearly have my own biases, but I have tried as best I can to set aside my own predisposition, and to approach the discussion in this work, more in sorrow and compassion than in anger, using a wealth of evidence at hand. It will be left to the reader to judge whether or not I have succeeded.

Acknowledgements

We would like to thank Princeton University Press for allowing us to use material from the following publication: Dupree, Louis; Afghanistan. © 1973 Princeton University Press, 2001 renewed PUP. Reprinted by permission of Princeton University Press.

Acronyms

AGSA	*De Afghanistan de Gato de Satelo Adarah,* Office Guarding Afghanistan's Interests
AIC	Afghan Information Service
Amir	Islamic ruler
APC	Armoured Personnel Carrier
CC	Central Committee
CPI	Communist Party of India
DRA	Democratic Republic of Afghanistan
DWOA	Democratic Women's Organisation of Afghanistan
DYOA	Democratic Youth Organisation of Afghanistan
FBIS	Federal Bureau of Information Service (USA)
FSB	Security Bureau of Russian Federation (Successor to the KGB)
GHQ	General Head Quarters
GRU	Intelligence Directorate (of Soviet General Staff)
HEI	Revolutionary Islamic Movement
HHDC	Homeland High Defence Council
HI	Harakate Islami
HI	*Hezb-i-Islami Hekmatyar*
HI	*Hezb-i-Islami Khales*
HW	*Hezb-i-Wahdat*
IIA	Itehade Islami Afghanistan
ISI	Interservice Intelligence Service (Pakistan)
JI	Jamiat Islami
KAM	*Kargari Atla'ti Mo'sesah* Workers Information Institute
KGB	Committee for State Security of Soviet Union
KhAD	*Khedamate Etla'te Dawlati* State Secret Police
NATO	North Atlantic Treaty Organisation
NFF	National Fatherland Front
NIFA	National Islamic Front of Afghanistan
NLF	National Liberation Front
NWFP	North West Frontier Province
PDPA	Peoples Democratic Republic of Afghanistan
SAM	Surface to Air Missiles

SAVAK	The Shah of Iran's Secret Police
SWB	Summary of World Broadcast (BBC)
Umma	The Community of the Believers
WAD	*Wezarate Etla'ate Dawlati* Ministry of State Intelligence
WAKFA	Wak Foundation for Afghanistan

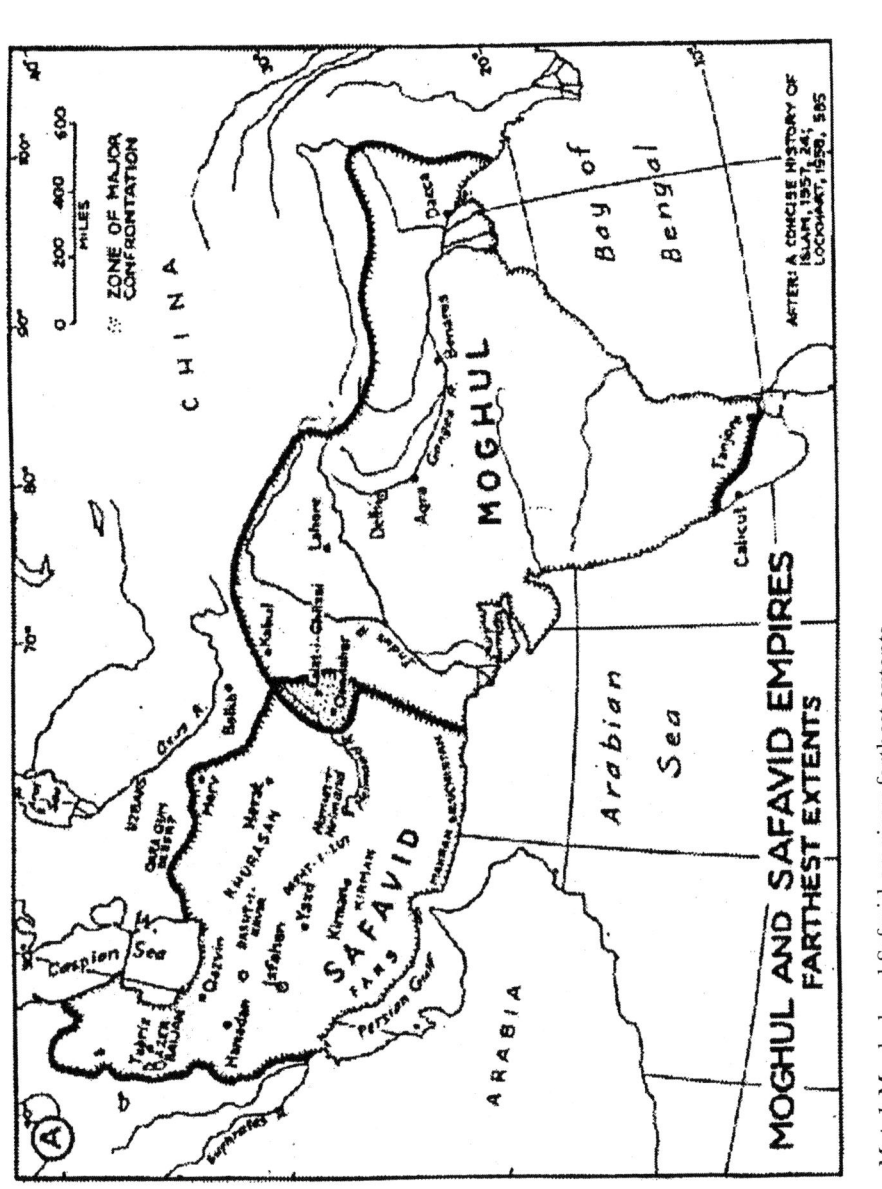

Map 1 Moghul and Safavid empires: farthest extents.

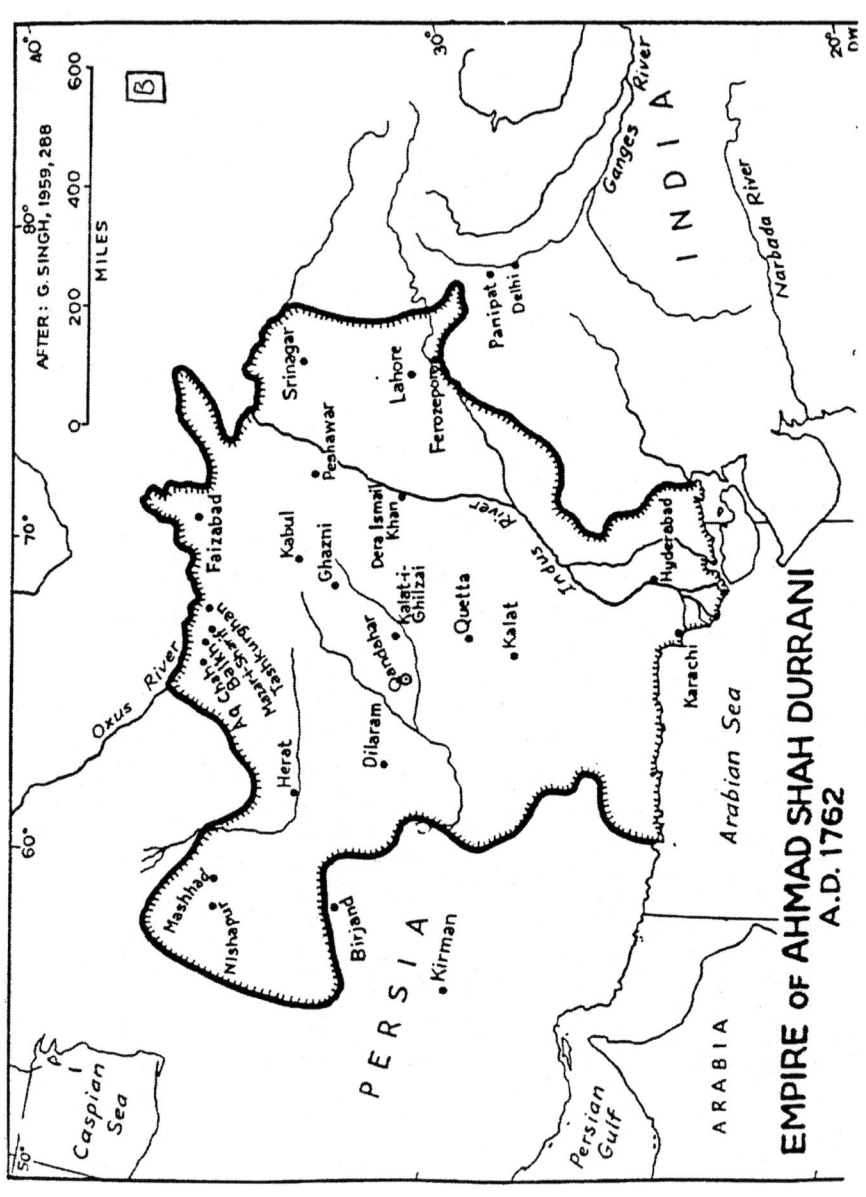

Map 2 The empire of Ahmad Shah Durrani at the end of his reign.

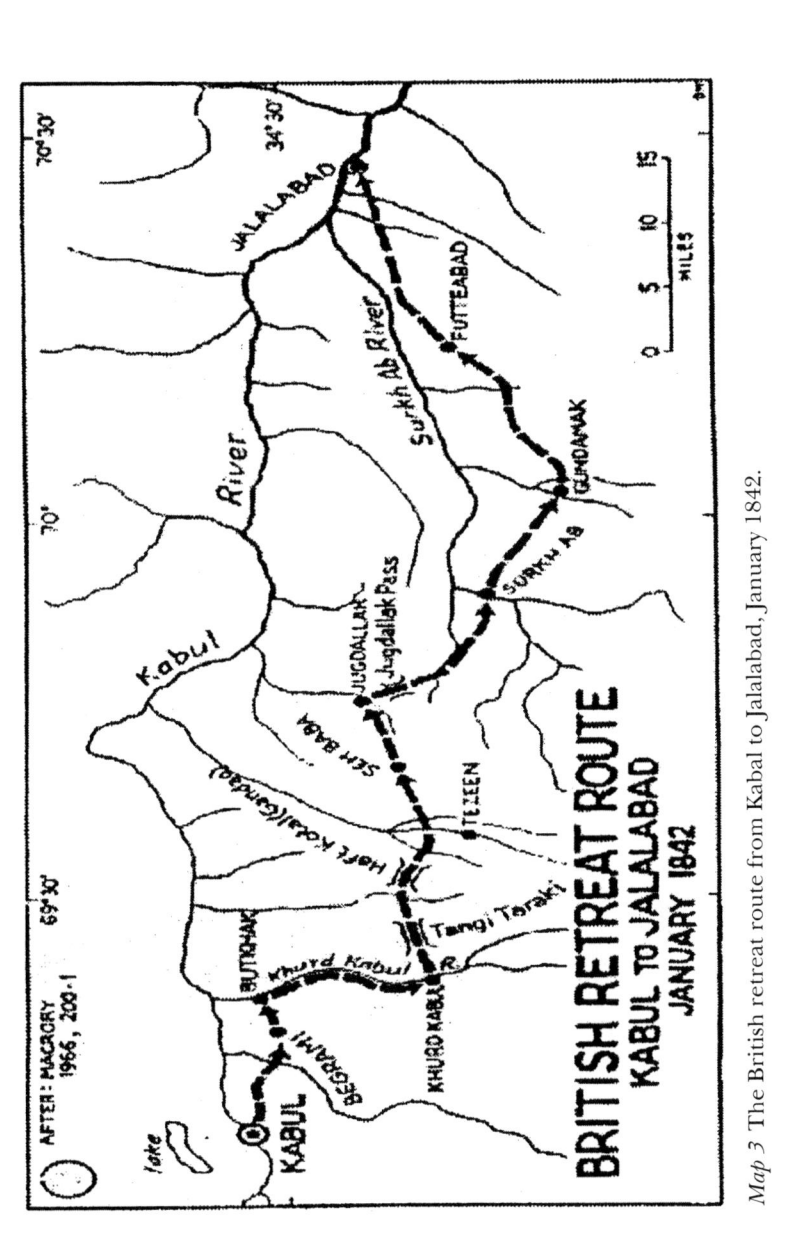

Map 3 The British retreat route from Kabul to Jalalabad, January 1842.

Map 4 Afghanistan and its six neighbours.

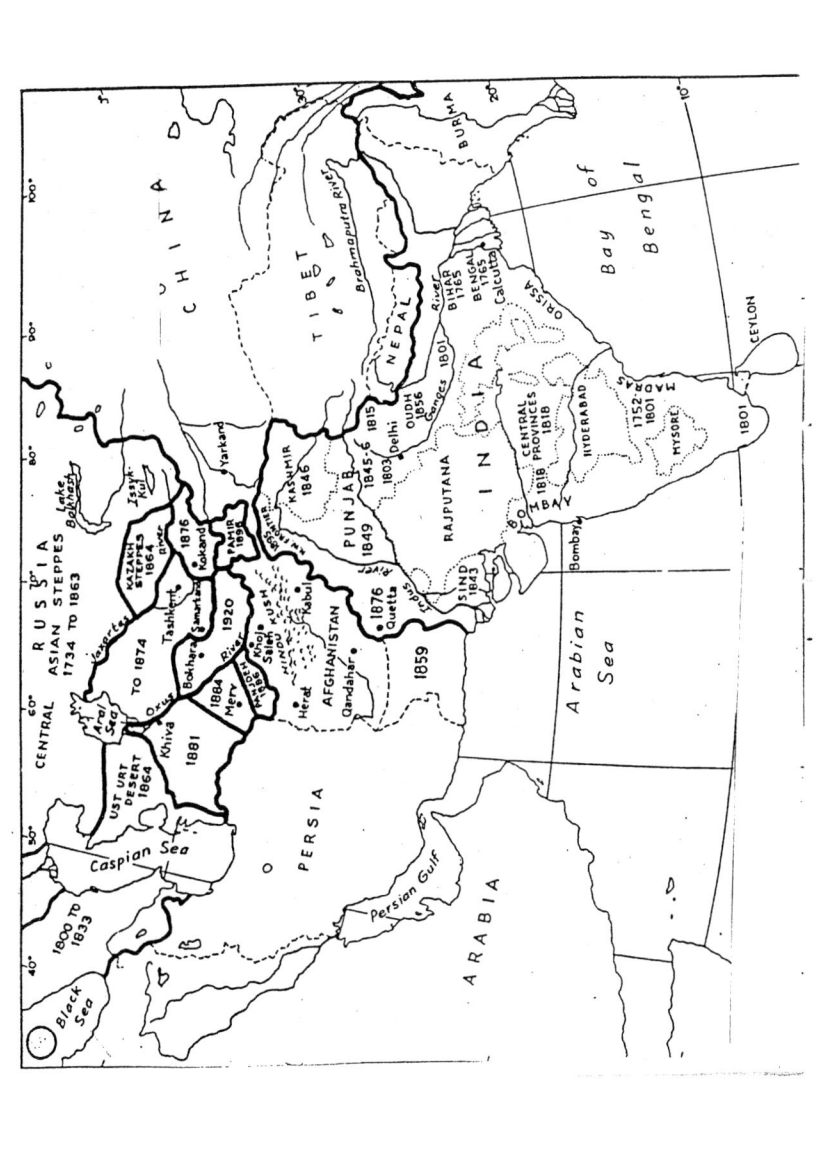

Map 5 Two centuries of southward advance by Imperial Russia and westward of Imperial British India, coming to a halt on the Afghan borders.

Introduction

Aims and objectives

Afghanistan has been in the limelight since the Soviet invasion in December 1979 when it became a geopolitical issue in the Cold War between the Soviet Union and the USA. Both superpowers fought their proxy war at costly expense to the Afghans. After the disintegration of the Soviet Union (1991), the US abandoned Afghanistan. Neighbouring powers like Iran and Pakistan, who had their own axes to grind, stepped in to fill the vacuum by supporting their favourite warlords. The ten-year war and national uprising against the Soviet and local communist forces thus turned into an on-going twelve-year civil war fought on ethnic, linguistic and religious grounds. After the rise of the Taleban in 1994, other regional powers, such as the Russian Federation and the newly independent countries of Uzbekistan and Tajikistan, also joined in. India, Saudi Arabia, Turkey and Western intelligence followed them, aiding the opposition warlords against the Taleban with arms, international publicity, food and medicine.

My contribution in this book to the general knowledge and understanding of these events is to draw on existing historical and scientific writings for my story line and to illuminate, add and complement this work through my research on tribe, ethnicity, nationalism, state and Islam. I also draw on my personal experience of following Afghan events closely in the last quarter of a century, by working and heading the Pashto Section of the BBC World Service. During this time I collected, almost on a daily basis, published materials such as news agencies reports, radio monitoring reports, BBC despatches and commentaries, newspaper cuttings and my own interviews with influential Afghan and non-Afghan experts on the war and its consequences. At first I was interested in working entirely from my collection of material. I soon realised that I would not be doing justice to political events since the overthrow of the monarchy in 1973, if I did not go back in history, at least to the founding of the present Afghan state in the middle of the eighteenth century, to assess if what has happened since is unique or whether there are examples and precedents in recent history for such occurrences. The approach in this book has, therefore, inevitably become a multi-disciplinary one, reviewing existing published material on history, politics and in the social sciences, and complementing them with recent research, theories and my own comments and analysis of these events and their root causes.

The scope of the book

Afghanistan has been described by historians of the region as the 'crossroads' of Asia. Many empires from Alexander the Great in the fourth century BC to Genghis Khan (thirteenth century), Timur-e-Lang, the Limping Timur or Tamerlane (fourteenth century), the Moghuls (sixteenth/seventeenth century), the Persians (seventeenth/eighteenth century) and the British (nineteenth/twentieth century), the Soviets in the 1980s and lastly the Americans in the beginning of the twenty-first century have traversed the length and breadth of the land, leaving their mark on the country and its population. A lasting sign of some of these, especially earlier invading forces is the people they left behind, which is the main reason for the heterogeneity of Afghanistan's population with their ethnic links across international borders. Looking over two and a half centuries of Afghan history, the heterogeneity of the people has been both the strength and weakness of the Afghan state. The state and its apparatus have always been potentially important for power. In Afghanistan, however, the political, tribal or ethnic composition of the groups, once they capture the prestigious seat of government, find difficulty in handling it. The state apparatus (with the exception of nine months in 1929) has been in the hands of different Pashtun dynasties since its foundation in 1747. Though from 1978–92 the state fell to the communists, three out of four of their leaders were also Pashtuns. In April 1992 it was first captured by the heterogeneous Mujahideen resistance groups, and in September 1996 by the Pashtun Ghilzai dominated Taleban, who took control of the capital, Kabul, and of over 90 per cent of the rest of the war-stricken country.

This book also provides the ground for a discussion of the long-term factors characteristic of Afghan history. These are terrain, environment, tribe, state, religion, language and the perennial weakness of the state, and the balance that is kept between the centre and the periphery. As to this last point, the two and a half centuries of Afghan history under discussion shows that whenever the equilibrium between centre and periphery is lost, the state intrudes on the tribe and vice versa. Such a state of flux shows that Afghanistan, more than most developing states, has often found it extremely difficult to come to grips with the forces of change and modernisation. Stubborn resistance to such forces has toppled monarchs and successive regimes. In nearly all the historical, sociological and anthropological works to date on Afghanistan, only passing references are made to change and modernity. And yet, looking at the root causes of uprisings and rebellions, I find that the conservative Afghan tribal and ethnic leadership has again and again rebelled and protested because of their disapproval of what they see as challenges to their customs, norms and traditions.

The book is in three parts. Part I: The Afghan state and its people 1747–1978. In this long period from the formation of the state to the takeover by the communists, the state expanded under its founder, Ahmad Shah Durrani, and since his death the borders contracted until just before the turn of the twentieth century. There were four dynastic changes, the first the founding Sadozai, the second in 1826 from the Sadozai to the Popalzai, followed by two further ones (1880 and 1929) all within branches of the same Durrani confederacy. The discussion in Part I is concerned with the long historical period and political processes, which have a bearing on events since the 1980s.

Part II: Political turmoil and Soviet invasion, 1973–79. This is the period of rapid social and political change and upheavals. In 1973 an influential member of the royal family toppled the 226-year-old monarchy and declared a republic. In 1978 the communists in turn overthrew the republic and its founder. Soon the whole country rose against the communists and they had to bring in the Soviet Red Army, with the result that 1.5 million Afghans of all ages, mostly Pashtuns, were killed, some five million made refugees, with twice that number becoming internally displaced. After nearly ten years of war and devastation, the Red Army failed to subdue the Afghans and left, leaving behind a surrogate communist government and upwards of ten million mines, dotted on footpaths, roads, farms and inside empty houses.

Part III: Ethnicity and power politics, 1975 to date. After the break-up of the Soviet Union, the communist government in Kabul was left 'high and dry' and fell in April 1992. Its leader, Dr Najibullah, was stopped by his own Uzbek militia at the airport, telling him 'you started the fire and now want to go leaving us to burn', and was prevented from joining his family in Delhi and forced to take shelter in the UN building in Kabul. His government handed over power to a hurriedly put together exile government that was formed from the leaders of the Mujahideen in Pakistan. After the Mujahideen president's first two months in office, a civil war of the most atrocious kind ensued in a struggle for power between resistance groups. After five years of the almost total devastation of Kabul City and the killing of over 60,000 of its citizens, and the forcing out of nearly one million more refugees, the Taleban came on the scene. They eliminated warlord after warlord, took Kabul in 1996 and the rest of over 90 per cent of the country in less than four years.

The period 1747 to the late mid-twentieth century shows how Afghanistan, time and again, went to the brink of disintegration and then was saved. This was a period of internal strife and civil war, with different parts of the country being ruled by different petty rulers and warlords, some belonging to the same ethnic and tribal configuration, others to different ones. The points that emerge are the weakness of the state, its propensity to factionalism (including ethnic factionalism), its susceptibility to external forces and the difficulty of modernisation.

From the time of the inception of the Afghan state, unlike many other countries in the region such as Iran, China and India that have been controlled from their respective strong centres, the centre in Afghanistan has always been weak or ineffective. That is why the centre has always lived in the shadow of the tribe at its periphery. The tribe precedes the state in that it was the tribes who set up the state. While the tribe's territory and boundary were fixed and known to its members, the state and its borders always shifted, expanding in the first quarter of a century after 1747 then remaining constant for the next quarter century and finally contracting until 1893. Since then the borders of the state have remained fixed and internationally recognised.

Another feature of the Afghan state is that, despite being in the shadow of the tribe, it has been a modernising force. But in order to attain the consent of the tribe, *amirs* and kings had councils of tribal representatives who were consulted on all state matters. This tradition in one form or another continued till the reign of Amir Abdur Rahman (1880–1901), who, in order to raise a modern army and establish civil servants and a judiciary, embarked on large-scale centralisation and modernisation. 'The reforms carried out by Abdur Rahman were not based on any reformist ideology. His conception of modernisation was purely pragmatic' (Roy 1986: 15).

Externally, the two imperial forces of Tsarist Russia and imperial Britain, competing with one another, stood on the borders of Afghanistan, one from the north and the other from east (see Map 5). This 'great game' was played at the expense of the people they overran, with only the Afghans in the region playing their 'game' as a tactic of survival and independence, skilfully and determinedly striving to keep their country intact, though losing land to both empires.

After the first civil war ended in 1826 and a loose central authority was established under Dost Muhammad, Amir Abdur Rahman, the 'Iron Amir', spent sixteen of the twenty-one years of his reign (1880–1901) fighting rebel forces in different parts of the country (see Table 2.1). Only then was he able to bind all parts of the state to his central authority. He created the modern system of taxation, the army, intelligence and the police. The uprisings in the periods 1801–26, 1880s/1890s and 1929 bear striking similarities to those of the warlords of the 1990s, continuing over the turn of the century and the rise of the Taleban. These periods of civil war (the first amongst different royal contenders that eventually led to dynastic change, the second against the power of central government, and the third against what appeared to be excessive modernisation) have their equivalent in the recent chaos that could be traced to the transfer of power (1973) in a royal coup in which the monarchy was overthrown. Subsequently the intervention and invasion of the Soviet forces (1979) led to a drastic socio-political and economic overhaul in Afghan society. The eventual outcome of the upheavals in the 1880s and 1990s were for strongmen and groups to appear, endeavouring to restore a semblance of normality. Thus, in both these situations, though a century apart, those at the forefront of the struggle were committed to bringing the whole country under one strong central rule by waging bloody wars to achieve this. In both cases those who resisted the disintegration of the country and fought for the restoration of law and order belonged to the same Pashtun majority in Afghanistan. But while Abdur Rahman was from the royal line and had a claim to the throne, the Taleban were from a neglected sector of Afghan society coming to prominence as a religious movement, using Islam as the basis of their legitimacy and campaign.

Another topic that needs investigating is why Afghan ethnic nationalism has become an issue. All published evidence indicates that it was men from minority ethnic groups who had been effectively running the country as civil and military leaders, mainly because of their skill and education. The Pashtun Persianised kings were at the top of the hierarchy as monarchs and presidents, but the remaining bureaucracy was run by non-Pashtuns. Why was this the case? Why, despite such a favourable position of the minorities in the country, have they built such an aversion to anything Pashtun? How is it that despite their overt differences with the Pashtuns, they have been influenced by and have accepted some characteristics of Pashtun culture? Is a feeling of mistrust between the various minorities on the one hand and the Pashtun majority on the other confined to political activists amongst these groups or is it common amongst the rank and file of both Pashtun and non-Pashtun? In either case what are the real motives behind such alienation? Is there a history of colonialism and exploitation of the minority by the majority or are there some external, economic and political factors that are unique to the last part of the twentieth century? These questions are addressed and commented on in Chapters 7 and 8.

The elaboration of these periods for the purpose of understanding the recent war allows me to concentrate the discussion on terrain, environment, ethnicity, tribe, state, modernisation and Islam, which are my core issues. The discussion of the past two and a half centuries will also underline the *longue-durée* of Afghan history. Throughout Afghan history there are what can be called long-term patterns, or *longue durée* as Fernand Braudel called it. These are:

1. physical terrain and its ecology;
2. the socio-political and economic situation that comes of it.

The study of the first is a kind of historical geography 'of man in his relationships to the environment', which Braudel calls 'geo-history' (Burke 1990: 36). Afghanistan's mountainous terrain has set limits on the modes of inter-group communication. There is also the added difficulty of movement over its high mountain passes, with the limited means of traditional transport: donkeys, mules and camels. The rearing of these beasts of burden and local agricultural produce are normally confined to their localities. Thus the socio-political and economic system encompassing nation, state, religion and physical environment are all factors that have a bearing on geography and history. Braudel in *The Mediterranean* saw this in three stages. First, the 'almost timeless' relationship between 'man' and his 'environment', then the gradual change in socio-economic and political structure and lastly the fast-moving history of events. Of these three, he regards the history of events, 'though the richest in human interest' as also the most superficial. He is concerned to place 'individual and events in context ... but he makes them intelligible at the price of revealing their fundamental unimportance' ... as 'surface disturbances, crests of foam that the tide of history carry on their strong backs' ... 'We must learn to distrust them' (Braudel 1995: 115–43).

In Afghanistan, the environment has shaped the people, for example the Pashtuns, over many centuries to be tough and uncompromising. Political historians, journalists and others reading modern Afghan history blame foreign invaders for not taking into account Afghanistan's terrain and the will of its ferocious people to resist outside intrusions. An American sociologist reviewing the history of nineteenth-century Afghanistan comments: 'Afghanistan was and would remain a singularly wild and anarchic place that could only be managed (if at all) by men of ruthless violence and ambition' (Edwards 1996: 3). But what these men of 'violence' have been doing to one another and to outside invaders changed the course of their and their invaders' history. These events have reinforced and added to their experience of how to react to forces from outside. These phases of historical 'reactive' movements and uprising, under the rubric of Braudel's 'events' have contributed to structural changes in Afghan socio-political outlook.

Population and society in Afghanistan

The population of Afghanistan is composed of diverse groups, speaking different languages, representing in a microcosm the macro-world of the people in the region. Locally, in nearly every province and even most districts within the provinces, different ethnic groups have intermingled, some over centuries and others relatively recently. Regionally, major ethnic groups with their other kinsman, often in larger communities, live across international borders. Thus:

All Pashtun, for example, are not Afghan citizens. Almost an equal number live in the Tribal Agencies and the North West Frontier of Pakistan. Tajik, Uzbeks, Turkmen and Kirgiz have their own ... republics in the [former] Soviet Union. Most inhabitants of the extreme western part of Afghanistan, geographically and culturally an extension of the Iranian Plateau, are simply Persian speaking Farsiwan farmers. Baluch live in the south-western corner of Afghanistan ... (Dupree 1980: 57).

There has never been a proper governmental census for Afghanistan's population. The historical records show that successive waves of Aryans from about the second millennium BC headed for Afghanistan. They found Dravidian and some even older occupants in the mountains and valleys of the great mountain barrier Hindu Kush. Those who settled forced the original inhabitants onto higher ground, while others continued on their trek to India. After the Aryans came Greeks, Sakas, Yuehchis, Kushans, Hephthalites, Arabs, Mongols, Turks and Persians. Most of the present inhabitants of the country are the descendants of these waves of immigrants and invaders.

World population, 1977 estimates the population of the two largest groups in the country: Pashtun 52 per cent, Tajik 19.8 per cent.[1] For the first time a proper scientific census of Afghanistan has been published by the WAK Foundation For Afghanistan (WAKFA), a non-governmental organisation. This nearly six-year survey (May 1991–December 1996) gives figures for all ethnic groups in the country both as 'ethnic' and 'linguistic' groups. Thus out of a total population of about twenty million Table I.1 shows the major ethnic and linguistic percentages.

Previous Afghan governments, the United Nations and individual scholars using partial surveys or sample surveys or even just ethnic or linguistic compositions of their own, have all given different and often contradictory

Table I.1 Percentage of major Afghan ethnic groups

No.	Name	Ethnicity	Language
1	Pashtun	62.73	55:00
2	Tajik	12.38	33:00
3	Hazarah	9.00	[9.00]
4	Uzbek	6.10	5.80
5	Turkmen	2.69	1.40
6	Aimaq	2.68	2.68

Source: WAKFA 1999: 47–8.

Note
The 9 per cent Hazarah, who speak their *Hazaragi* dialect of Farsi (Dari), are also part of the 33 per cent Dari [Tajik] speakers listed under Language; other smaller groups are not included in the table.

figures for the population of the country and its ethnic groups.[2] Table I.1 shows the number of 'Tajik speakers' are three times their actual 'ethnic composition'. The reason for this is that Farsi/Dari has been the formal language of the government since 1747 and 7.5 per cent of Pashtuns and a small number of Uzbeks, Turkmen and other groups have over the years adopted Dari as their language. The second reason is that 9 per cent of Shi'ah Hazarahs, whatever their original language, speak their own *Hazaragi* dialect of Dari. Third, the historic, cultural and political position of Tajik Dari speakers has been the main reason for their language extending to other groups. The Aimaq are another group, who because of their favourable agricultural and grazing position in central and Western Afghanistan, have not only maintained their ground but have attracted Pashtuns, Uzbeks, Turkmen and some other smaller groups to adopt their language and dialects. Dari, because of its long attachment to Persian Courts, has been the formal language of the government. Pashto, on the other hand, because of the sheer number of its speakers, was regarded as the national language. This is not very different from India or Pakistan where Hindi and Urdu are respectively the national languages with English being the formal and governmental language. However, the 1964 constitution elevated Dari making it, with Pashto, the formal and national language of Afghanistan, while committing the country to developing Pashto further. But in the long run the formal status of a language entails prestige and also prospects for education and jobs. Therefore, Dari's formal language status despite its numerical inferiority proved to be as strong and powerful as English is vis-à-vis Urdu/Hindi in Pakistan and India.

The economy of Afghanistan remains dependent on local agricultural produce and the import and export of such items, and on a small amount of industrial goods. Local produce includes food cereals, fresh and dried fruits, and raw cotton. Of the local produce fur, wool, hides and skins, carpets and rugs, medicinal herbs, seeds and spices were major export items. Sugar, tea, petroleum products, textiles and footwear were the main import consumer products. Thus in the 1950s when development and modernisation plans were incorporated in the country's First Five Year Plan, 72 per cent of income came from agriculture, while 5 per cent came from industrial employment, cottage industries and crafts (Yosufzai 1958–59: 10). The remainder came from services including local taxes and tax on imports and exports, to give the gross national product of 38.5 billion Afghanis for the year 21 March 1958–20 March 1959.

The economy of Afghanistan, after loans for the two five-year plans of 1956–61 and 1962–66 from the Soviet Union, the USA, Germany, Japan and some European countries and the export of Afghan natural gas to the Soviet Union, changed dramatically. Natural gas became Afghanistan's major export item, but it was of little relevance to the general economy for two reasons. First, its export was almost entirely confined to the Soviet

Union, who placed even the meters on their side of the border and paid below the international rate. Second, whatever the earnings on the gas, the Russians cancelled these against the cost of the import of arms and of loans outstanding on Soviet development projects.

Afghanistan in the 1970s remained one of the poorest countries in the world with $130 per capita annual earnings, an average life expectancy of forty years, a literacy rate of less than 10 per cent and agriculture continuing to be the main occupation of at least 75 per cent of the population. The economy that had improved after the Second World War collapsed after the Soviet invasion. The resistance groups' main aim was to bring the economy to a standstill making it costly for the Soviet occupation. Thus they attacked military and civilian centres. The Communist Prime Minister, Sultan Ali Keshtmand, admitted this in April 1983:

> The country's financial situation is ... seriously affected by political and economic problems ... counter-revolutionary bands sent from abroad have destroyed 50 per cent of the country's schools, more than 50 per cent of hospitals, 14 per cent of the state's transportation vehicles, 75 per cent of all communication lines, and a number of hydro-electric and thermal electric stations. About 24 billion Afghanis damage has been done to the country. This is one half of the total amount set for developing the country's economy during the 20 years before the April (1978) Revolution.
> (FBIS *South Asian Daily Report*, 12 April 1983)

After the departure of the Soviets and the communists, the Afghans were left counting the cost of the damage to their country. With the lessening of interest of the United States and the continuing civil war largely waged as a result of incitements by the neighbouring countries, the Afghan economy went from bad to worse. There was little chance of improvement especially when America, for its own political reasons, from being a supporter of the Afghan *jihad* during the war against the Soviets, had turned into an opponent. The US joined Russia in exerting influence at the UN and its Security Council by imposing sanctions (1999 and 2000) making it difficult for the Taleban government to obtain loans from the IMF, the World Bank or investments from other sources for Central Asian gas and oil pipelines across Afghanistan, which is considered a major regional project.

Tribe and Pashtunwali

In anthropological literature about Afghanistan, the tribe refers to a group of people who are nominally independent of the state, live in their own area, believe in the same descent ideology and share a common language and culture. Thus any Pashtun tribe is a local community, nominally independent, occupying its specific region, believing itself to be related to other Pashtuns through extensive patrilineal genealogies, ultimately tracing their descent to the same Aryan ancestry or their putative father, Qays. Qays Abdur Rashid is supposed to have gone to Arabia from the central province of Ghore, the then Pashtun stronghold, to have converted to Islam and to have married the daughter of Islam's greatest general, Khalid bin Walid. Qays had three sons from this marriage, Sarban, Bitan and Gherghasht. All Pashtun tribes from the border of Iran to the Indus River, and those settled in India, trace their genealogy to one of these sons of Qays.

Pashtun tribes speak their common language Pashto (though with different dialects). They mostly belong to the Sunni Hanafi school of Islam and uphold their common 'ideal type' culture of *Pashtunwali* and its code of honour and shame (see section below). Thus a common ideology of descent, belief in Islam and a code of behaviour are the integral unifying factors of Pashtun society. Despite their common genealogy some of these tribes, like those in Paktia, southern Afghanistan, are further divided into the two *gwand* blocs of *towr* or black and *spin* or white. These blocs are political structures used in tribal matters. Thus an intra-tribe dispute is settled through one's own *gwand*, but in inter-tribal affairs, or when the aid of the whole of Paktia province is required, it is the representatives of the two *gwand* who adjudicate on the issue at hand.

Pashtun tribal society is not pre-literate or oral. There is extensive literature and written poetry that predate most regional languages. The first Pashto poem by Amir Koror (p. 120) dates from AD 730. This poem's structure, skilful rhyming, parable and word usage indicate that poetry must have been composed and written many years before this first example which is available to us.

Pashtun tribes and ruling dynasties have not confined themselves to their localities. They have ruled over non-Pashtuns in the Himalayan foothills, Bengal, Delhi, Kabul and Iran. 'The historic role of warrior king is part of Pathan [Pashtun] consciousness' (Ahmed 1976: 6). Pashtuns form one of the world's greatest tribal groups, occupying extensive and varied lands, and are endowed with a particular warrior upbringing and history that has been a challenge to many armies and empires throughout recorded history. An important part of being Pashtun is to be aware of and adhere to Pashtunwali.

Pashtunwali

Pashtunwali is the code of honour and shame embedded in Pashtun custom and law. Although the tribal Pashtuns have changed with time and some no longer live in the tribal area, this tribal code still remains an ideal-type of upbringing and socialising. 'Throughout the Pashto-speaking area it is virtually impossible to find even a child – male or female – who is not keenly aware of the main elements of pashtunwali' (Spain 1962: 26). Even those Pashtuns who have settled in northern Afghanistan amongst other ethnic groups for over a century, though not admitting to the values of pashtunwali and regarding it as the way of life of the tribal Pashtuns, are keenly aware of it and uphold its major institutions.[3] 'Pashtunwali ... sets ... limits of acceptable behaviour within the community and governs the relations between tribes' (Gregorian 1969: 41). Pashtunwali on the one hand sets down the requirements and the conduct of the tribes and on the other the relationship of the individual to elements within his tribe such as *koranay* family, *kahole* household, *taber* lineage and *qawm* tribe. The institutions of pashtunwali (Appendix 2) are *melmastia* or hospitality, *badal* or revenge, *badragah* or escort and *nanawatai* or refuge and asylum.

Pashtunwali through these institutions lays down the rules of conduct in Pashtun tribal environments. It emphasises *turah*, literally the sword, but also meaning zeal in honourable success, *ghairat* or `*azat*, honour, as opposed to Islamic spiritual principles of *iman*, steadfastness of belief, *isteqamat* or *sobat*, tenacity and perseverance. The spirit of pride in oneself, one's family, tribe and nation is also very strongly felt amongst the Pashtuns. At the level of province and nation, pashtunwali forms a part of what could be termed 'Pashtun nationalism'.

Afghanistan in history and anthropology

The body of literature on Afghanistan is considerable in the local languages of Pashto and Dari and in the foreign languages of English, Russian, German and French. Here I cite those works that I have used and consider important contributions to the understanding of Afghans/Pashtuns and Afghanistan. One of the earliest books on Pashtuns and Afghanistan is Mountstuart Elphinstone's *The Kingdom of Caubul* (1814). Elphinstone was appointed as the first British Envoy to the Court of Kabul and paid his first and only visit to Peshawar, the winter capital of Afghanistan, to meet the Afghan King Shah Shuja in 1809.

> Elphinstone spent less than six months (7th January to 20th June) beyond the Indus, of which less than four (25th February to 14th June) were in Peshawar. Yet he came away with the knowledge of the country and people which less gifted men have not gained in a lifetime on the Frontier. Though he did not go beyond Peshawar, his instinct and research gave him a balanced picture of the whole of Kabul itself set in its valleys and gardens ... later he was to reject offers of the highest place and honours ... for the life of scholar and historian.
> (Caroe 1965: 279)

Elphinstone's *Caubul* has over the decades turned into one of the most popular and most widely read works for scholars. Olaf Caroe, who spent a lifetime as political agent on the frontier amongst Pashtuns, considers *The Kingdom of Caubul* as,

> the most precise and compassionate, appreciation of the frontier scene and manners. This man has every locality right, every tribe in due place, he sets his scene in correct and convincing perspective ... king or noble, tradesman or merchant, priest or peasant – all seems to him men deserving of appraisal, even their faults are worth a smile and loveable.
>
> (1965: 278)

For my purpose, Elphnistone's book lacks detailed discussion of what ordinary people said and did about the turmoil of times still remembered and talked about: the overthrowing of the Safavid Persians; the end of the Ghilzai rule; the start of the Durrani kingdom and empire and any details of the debates of the two key *Loya Jirgas* or tribal councils of 1709 and 1747. However, what snippets of Ghilzai reaction regarding the Durrani and vice-versa there are, I have quoted. His work on the genealogies of Pashtuns and their socio-political organisation is to this day regarded as important source material. In Book II, Chapter XII he also briefly accounts for other ethnic groups but his main aim was to provide a detailed account of the Pashtuns.

Leaving aside primary sources, such as manuscripts, periodicals and radio monitoring reports by the BBC and the United State's FBIS, I divide the major body of written books into seven categories (Appendix 1). Of these the first six categories are concerned with the description of the country, its people and environment with a wealth of romantic portrayal of the people and their prowess, accounting for their legend and/or romanticising their bravery and valour. They do not tell us much about how a tribal and ethnically dominated society has come to terms with the requirements of a plural society, or how the ethnic groups coexisted, or what were the bases of their co-operation and how they differed amongst themselves. Their approach was more general concerning themselves with epochs, mentalities and collective representations. Issues such as how people make sense of the past or that people's perception of their past is a retrospective product of their present are never presented. Nor is the general concern about social change, dynamism, decision-making and strategising amongst the Afghan ethnic or tribal groups discussed.

For many historians of Afghanistan the conception of time is 'linear'. The past is 'lineally and causally related to the present and the present is understood to be the result of the past' (Silverman and Gulliver 1996: 34). One author, echoing other writers' 'static' view of the Afghan past, even states that 'social and economic factors have had less importance in Afghan history than in other countries, since up until thirty years ago they were relatively static' (Fletcher 1995: vi). In fact Afghan socio-political development in the nineteenth century was anything but 'static'. The country had gone through important socio-economic and political changes. Afghanistan lost most of its foreign dominions, there were four dynastic changes, three Anglo-Afghan wars including a number of skirmishes with Tsarist Russia, the establishing of a nation-state and the ending of disputes over monarchical rule. Such changes were also taking place in the region and so, even if Afghanistan had wished, it could not have kept its immunity from wider changes outside its borders. For Afghanistan such changes arose at first as much as the result of British and Russian imperialism as from the desire to improve its economic and social wellbeing. Thus, in the first decades of the nineteenth century when Afghanistan faced the Sikh incursion into Peshawar, the Persian assaults on Herat and the Bukharan Amir's interference in the north, the Afghan monarchs, with the approval of the tribes, acquired some European military technology to fight these intruders. Later when they faced two wars with British India (in 1839 and 1879) and the Russians' occupation of Panjdeh (1886), Zolfeqar and Pamir (1896), the Afghans started making their own weapons, though on a small scale. In the meantime the public's hatred of the *kuffar* unbelievers or infidels in the north and east led to the strengthening of Afghan nationalism. Thus by the 1880s and 1890s the centralisation of power, the creation of a standing army of 142,000 men, the emphasis on 'Afghan' rather than on tribal or ethnic identity, and a policy of self-sufficiency were regarded as important steps in safeguarding the country's independence.

In the twentieth century, imitating European industrial, educational and economic processes became a prevalent preoccupation of the Afghan kings. This challenged Afghan social and economic values and gradually eroded customary patterns of social behaviour. This process of modernisation, which has been the root cause of social upheaval and a consistent policy of all monarchs throughout the nineteenth and twentieth centuries, has hardly been mentioned in historical writings as a way of understanding Afghan society. Only two scholars (both American) discuss modernisation: Leon Poulada (1962; 1973) and Gregorian (1969) repeatedly return to the issues of reforms and modernisation and their implication for Afghan society. From my reading of Afghan history, modernisation involves the import of new products and ideas and the attempts to consciously integrate these throughout society. In other words it involves the psychological and conscious preparation of one's society to internalise ideas and values that are foreign but necessary in the hope of raising living standards. It also involves the development of trade, communication and the expansion of government and other related institutions at the expense of tribal and ethnic values. 'Modernization involves passage through something like a colossal mill-race, in which a multigenerational struggle between the rural past and the urban-industrial future is fought out ... where one global mode of experience perishes to make way for a successor' (Nairn 1997: 104). Modernisation also means that secular rational and scientific thinking over time replaces religious, tribal and ethnic 'superstitious' values. Thus modernisation was presented by successive Afghan monarchs in such a way as to give the impression that change is good, and progress through such change is desirable and inevitable. As I discuss in this book, those in charge never prepared the ground for the introduction and implementation of such changes. They never realised that even in the heartland of the industrial West, the rural past's fading was a slow process. They never understood why people again and again rebelled, fearing challenges to their own social and religious beliefs.

Afghan nationalism and xenophobia that had been officially promoted by the rulers, while playing an important role in guaranteeing Afghanistan's independence, had the negative impact of keeping the country isolated for most of the nineteenth and twentieth centuries. This isolation was imposed, when Britain after its second war in 1879 took control of Afghan foreign policy. She thereafter acted on foreign policy matters for Afghanistan and Afghanistan had no embassies or trade missions of its own abroad, nor did other countries have representation in Afghanistan. King Amanullah, who challenged Britain, ended this isolation and after a short war, Britain agreed in 1919 to hand over Afghan foreign policy decision-making to the king.

The other negative effect of such isolation was the intentional or unintentional dropping of Afghanistan from most studies of the Middle East, Central Asia and South Asia. Even in the atlases of the region, Afghanistan is sometimes shown as part of Central Asia, in others part of South Asia or worse over a split page between these regions. Hence funding for such groupings never benefited Afghan Studies and this is the main reason for lack of more specialised scholarship on Afghanistan.

One of the earliest and most influential works on the Pashtun is *The Swat Pathan* (1959) by Fredrik Barth. This work has laid the ground rules for understanding a Pashtun society like Swat through the ongoing power game in the rival bloc system of Khans and Saints. The Khans basing their support on their tribal followers and peasant farmers, and the Saints on their religious, tribal and non-tribal followers. Barth's view of Swat was influenced by his previous research in his native Norway, explaining that society through the activities of its entrepreneurs. Barth spent nearly a year in Swat and his *Swat Pathan* study has been much commented on by other anthropologists such as Akbar Ahmed, Talal Asad and Brian Street. Barth in a letter to *Man* (1992) complains of 'a cottage industry' that seems to have sprung up amongst some anthropologists in re-assessing others' works.

Though Ahmed considers *The Swat Pathan* as thin on ethnography, but Barth's study is a brilliant theoretical examination of the complex Swat society. His attempt to explain this in terms of political leadership and the forces at work to make 'blocs' is also of relevance to other acephalous groups. Ahmed's *Millennium and Charisma* (1976) is also a contribution to the debate at that time on 'methodological individualists' and 'methodological holists' and he develops his objection to Western models applied to an eastern society, such as Swat. His models of *nang/galang, nangwali* (code of honour) and *terborwali* (paternal cousin rivalry) is relevant to Pashtuns in Afghanistan. Ahmed also traces the history of the Islamic Sufic order and its genesis to explain the influence of saints and religious personalities in Swat.

Ahmed's other book is *Religion and Politics in Muslim Society* (1983), which is an examination of Wazirestan's two Pashtun tribes, Wazir and Mahsud in NWFP, in order to explain unrest in terms of the interplay of power, authority and religious standing. The leaders he identifies are the traditional elders of tribes, representatives of the state, and religious functionaries. From the interplay of these three authorities he constructs his 'Islamic district paradigm' to analyse contemporary society in Wazirestan. All three are represented at the district headquarters: the Khans' distinct houses with their towers, the district commissioner's office, flying the government flag, and the mullah's central mosque and its towering minarets, as the symbol of each one's presence. All three 'vie for power, status and legitimacy in society. The competition is further exacerbated by the fact that all the major participants are Muslims; there is no simple Muslim versus non-Muslim category to fall back on...' (1983: 6). Ahmed's 'paradigm' therefore is Islamic in a sociological sense. It is about an Islamic society not Islam. Depending on the situations, these groups historically form and shift their alliances to face new situations, like invasion from outside, encroachment by central government or its local administrative representative – a leftover of the colonial structure in Wazirestan. Thus in Wazirestan, sometimes,

> choices are deliberately made in spite of being seen to lead to confrontation, conflict and disaster. In the end, the Wazir sacrifice the material symbols of prosperity, market and trade, in an attempt to uphold group honour, unity and loyalty ... an understanding of the complex and close interaction between administration and tribal groups is fundamental to the Islamic district paradigm.
>
> (1983: 9)

The study of Ahmed's Wazirestan and its encounter with the government or its local agent has relevance to my study of the centre/periphery interplay. The three types of leadership in Wazirestan are also present in my study of Pashtuns, with the difference that the equivalent of the colonial 'political agent's' function is carried by ordinary central government civil servants.

A major contribution in understanding the interplay of the centre and the periphery was the publication of a collection of papers presented at a conference in 1979 at London University, at the School of Oriental and African Studies (SOAS), to pull together historical and anthropological works on tribes and states in Afghanistan and Iran. These were subsequently edited by Richard Tapper in the volume, *Conflict of Tribe and State in Iran and Afghanistan* (1983) with a long introduction by him, tracing the common link between tribe and state in Afghanistan from 1700 to 1980 and in Iran from 1800 to 1980. Tapper first clarifies the 'notoriously vague' term 'tribe' which like 'race' has 'almost ceased to be of analytical or comparative value. The issues are conceptual, terminological and to some extent methodological'. He then asks 'Are tribes the creation of state? ... is it useful to contrast "tribalism" with "feudalism", or with "state"' (1983: 1). 'Tribal groups' in both countries are historically regarded as 'inveterate opponents of the state. They were notorious as makers and breakers of dynasties' (1983: 2).

He then defines tribe as a kinship group whose members in terms of language, culture and origin regard themselves as distinct. He refers to the acephalous '*nang*' Pashtuns as 'republican'. The lack of chiefdom and statehood amongst them is due to economic poverty, not being able to 'produce surplus necessary either to support a class of leaders or to attract revenue seeking administrators', and to 'their inaccessibility' (1983: 59–60). For a larger tribal grouping he uses the term 'confederacy' whose members are 'heterogeneous in terms of culture, presumed origins and perhaps class composition, yet are politically unified, usually under a central authority' such as the Iranian Khamseh, Qashqai and some Kurds (1983: 9). Thus he implies that Pashtuns and Turkmen too are 'confederacies' because they are not normally politically unified, while their smaller subdivisions like the Durrani, Ghilzai and Wazir, he calls 'tribes' (1983: 9–10). I argue that Pashtuns, Turkmen and Baluchs are three distinct groups in Afghanistan that could be described as 'tribal' because of their common descent, language, culture and religion. They are also nations because of their size, occupying large areas stretching over international borders. In my view it is their subdivision that forms confederacies, for example, amongst the Western Pashtuns the Durrani and Ghilzai and amongst the eastern Pashtuns the Wazir, Mohmand, Shinwari and others. Political unity, as one of Tapper's defining terms, is an ephemeral matter of convenience.

> In the eighteenth century, the tribes participated in the Afghan Empire by giving their support in return for subsidies, maintenance, recognition and continual autonomy. That is why in the nineteenth century the British, alternating between inactivity and forward policy, sought control, whether through conquest or subsidy, ... but the tribes who had not accepted even fellow-Pashtuns as rulers, had no intention of recognising the hegemony of outsiders.
>
> (1983: 60)

Even at other times, when all Pashtuns tribes have not joined in a war because of their geographical distances or had not felt the threat from peripheral events or for other such reasons, nonetheless, have never denied being part of the rest of their nation.

Tapper then turns to define 'state' as: '...a territorially-bounded polity with a centralised government and a monopoly of legitimate force, usually including within its bounds different social classes and ethnic/cultural groups' (p. 10). Afghanistan, despite varying limits of central control over its tribes, has been a territorially bounded polity with a central government and heterogeneous population and can thus be described as a state (p. 11). Tribe and state are, in terms of their nature as conceptually opposed tendencies, modes or models of organisation, not just analytically distinct but consciously articulated as cultural categories by and within the groups. 'As bases of identity, political allegiance and behaviour, "tribe" gives primacy to ties of kinship and patrilineal descent, while "state" on the loyalty of all persons dwelling within a defined territory, whatever else their relation to each other' (p. 66).

'Tribe' stresses ties of blood, culture and ascribed factors, while 'state' is impersonal and recognises contract, transaction and achievement. The division of labour in the 'tribal' model is 'natural'; in the 'state' model it is complex. 'The "tribal" model is socially homogeneous, egalitarian and segmentary, the state is heterogeneous, egalitarian and hierarchical. "Tribe" is within the individual, "state" external to him' (p. 66).

In his paper in the same volume, Rob Hager writes that unlike tribe and state,

> Relations between tribe and empire are based on paradoxes. The empire requires tribal unity through the mechanism of tribal leadership in order to create the hierarchy required for indirect rule and to promote its legitimating ideology, yet it also exploits tribal fission as a means of maintaining its control over the tribe ... tribe and empire are structurally complementary, just as state and tribe are structurally dis-congruous.
>
> (1983: 96)

Hager summarises the imperial British and Russian competition and the relation of the Afghan tribes towards them as follows:

> empire, tribe and state have all been important factors in the politics of Afghanistan in the nineteenth and twentieth centuries. Since the breakdown of the tribally based Sadozai empire in the first quarter of the nineteenth century ... Afghanistan has been the scene of nearly continuous imperial rivalry.
>
> (1983: 110)

This imperial interest, the 'great game', determined the environment in which the local Amirs 'acquired fixed territorial boundaries within which they began to assert a more comprehensive state-type jurisdiction' (ibid.,

p. 110). The competing empires realised that 'advance through Afghanistan means hard fighting' and also the Afghans understood that technically and economically they were not the equals of these empires. 'This mutual recognition of the power balance set the stage for establishing normatively-based relations, turning on the Afghans' desire for autonomy and subsidies on the one hand, and the ideologies and interest of their neighbouring empires on the other' (ibid.).

The Afghan tribes would see Hager's model of balance in perhaps slightly different ways. They regarded the toll they collected on their highways and the subsidies from these imperial forces as '*jaziah*' tax levied on non-Muslims. The Pashtun view of the British and the Tsarist neighbouring empire was succinctly explained to Ahmed by a Mahsud tribal elder: 'We are like men with two jealous wives – both pulling us in different directions; sometime we prefer the one, sometimes the other' (1983: 194). It is clear from such a commonly held opinion that the tribes never saw themselves playing the imperial 'game'. Ahmed adds:

> ...they were simply playing their own game. It may not have been on the same scale as the 'great game' ... but it was certainly played with the brilliance of born tacticians, and enabled them to remain independent at a crucial period in one of the most important regions of Asia.
>
> (ibid., p. 193)

Thus in the nineteenth century the tribes maintained their autonomy, with some funds coming to them from the imperial forces, regardless of how it was viewed by either side. The Afghan state kept its independence in the nineteenth and twentieth centuries, subsidised by the British until the third Anglo-Afghan war in 1919, and from then on it was subsidised by Soviet aid until 1992. The super-powers of the nineteenth century satisfied themselves by creating Afghanistan as a buffer zone between them. The British, who had a much longer experience of the Afghans, went about setting up yet a second buffer zone, that of the autonomous tribal belt of the North West Frontier Province (NWFP), along the Durand Line between themselves and Afghanistan.

A great many writers have written about Afghanistan and its people as a nation, a state or a nation-state. The volume on *Tribe and State* pulled together the research on tribes to see how they fared vis-à-vis the state (and empire). But little if any attention was paid to nationalism and the formation of the early states or how the Afghan example could be compared to them. However, this criticism is not completely well founded as most of the theoretical research on nationalism and the early states that I mention in this work was not then available. What was available was Weber's work on patrimonial states and also Southall's on the segmentary state. In this work I use the research on *Tribe and State* and complement it by seeing the Afghan state to have been similar to Weber's patrimonial state of medieval Europe, and as an almost perfect example of a segmentary state, as seen by Southall in his Alur research. I also take the argument of *Tribe and State* further by talking about nation, nationalism, ethnicity and Islam from the Afghan and the Western perspective. I assess what Gellner, Anderson and others say on these issues and discuss how the Afghan example could be evaluated in the light of their comments.

The Afghan state

The state is a political concept identifying a geographical territory under a single rule. The state is a territorially bounded polity with centralised power and a monopoly of legitimate force, including in its bounds different social, ethnic/cultural groups. This centralised political power is concentrated in its government, which can legitimise force to regulate the affairs of its citizens and its relation with other states. The state, unlike the tribe, despite giving an aura of strength and permanence is prone to instability, transience and disintegration. Whether or not a tribal and ethnic society like Afghanistan can be described as a state has been the subject of much discussion amongst historians, political scientists and anthropologists:

> Some scholars have declared modern concepts of the state to be inapplicable to pre-modern Iran and Afghanistan, in terms of degree of central control and the forms, function and ideology of government; but for our purpose the existence of territorial frontiers (however vaguely defined), a central government (however weak and limited in its aims) and a heterogeneous population, are enough to define a state. In these terms some confederacies constitute states, while some states operate on the basis of tribal ties, or, in the form of empires, recognise the autonomy of other states and tribes within their territories.
> (Tapper 1983: 10–11)

Accordingly, the Afghan state founded by Ahmad Shah Durrani in the eighteenth century was territorially bounded, although in his attempts to build an empire the frontiers were expanding. It had its centre in Kandahar; it had control over its territory, although revolts and opposition to the central government were rife; and like the majority of states around the world, it also included a heterogeneous population within its borders.

The patrimonial state

The Afghan state's tribal origin and tradition fit into Weber's view of the 'patrimonial' state, where the leader's 'authority is primarily oriented to tradition but in its exercise makes the claim of full personal powers' (Weber 1964: 347). Why should members of the tribe accept such authority? Weber goes on to say that these 'patrimonial retainers' receive tangible support in one of the following ways:

> (a) By maintenance at the table and household of his chief; (b) by allowance from the stores of goods or money of his chief, usually primarily allowances in kind; (c) by right of use of land in return for services; (d) by the appropriation of property income, fees, or taxes (1964: 351).

Traditionally, the Afghan king was looked on as a father figure, who shared the booty of war with all those who participated. He fed them and looked after his Pashtun tribesmen, in ways comparable to looking after his own family members. Afghan kings granted usufruct right of land for exceptional services and collected taxes to maintain their armies and to run their governments. The Afghan King, Amir Koror, in his poem (a short part of which I quote here, the earliest recorded (AD 730) in Pashto literature, illustrates his patrimonial position.

> ...There is nobody stronger than me.
> I am kind and magnificent to my subjects.
> With confidence I protect and nourish them.
> I strike for their well being.
> There is nobody stronger than me.
> My orders are carried by the lofty mountains.
> The World is mine, and my praises are sung from every pulpit.
> Days, nights, months and years,
> There is nobody stronger than me...

The Afghan modern state is polyethnic and stratified. The rulers were drawn within the myriad of Pashtun tribes. They were from 1747 to 1826 from the Sadozai branch and then till the end of Daoud's republic (1978) from Popalzay, the opposite segment of that confederacy. Within this patrimonial order, there were various levels of relationships from the ruling clan vis-à-vis its other close agnates, the Durrani and Ghilzai confederacies, and ultimately the wider Pashtun ethnic groups and those other non-Pashtun minorities. While within the Pashtuns the question has always been who should form the ruling group and dynasty and who should not, for the non-Pashtun, on the other hand, such differences were immaterial and they regarded all Pashtuns as part or segments of one and the same whole. Such simmering under the surface came to the boil after the withdrawal of the Soviet forces in 1989 and led to lengthy civil war, taking the country to the brink of disintegration. However, within the Pashtun tribes there was no differentiation on linguistic, cultural, religious and genealogical grounds. They travelled freely to one another's areas although, except in urban areas, it was not possible to settle easily on others' tribal land, as tribal land cannot be sold to outsiders without the consent of the tribe, and this itself is an expensive and lengthy process. Such limited fluidity and flexibility was even harder for non-Pashtuns, trying to settle amongst the Pashtuns because of cultural, linguistic or religious differences.

Within the Afghan patrimonial system the relationships of the rulers were often much closer to some non-Pashtun groups than to their own kith and kin. These were the Dari-speaking bureaucrats that ran the day-to-day business of the government. Successive governments from Ahmad Shah Durrani to Muhammad Daoud favoured such non-Pashtuns for their skills in literacy, administration and discipline in the army. These comprised in the main Dari-speaking Qizelbash, Farsiwan/Tajik and Uzbek. These groups never posed any challenge or threat to the rulers. Thus from the reign of Timur Shah (1772–97) onwards, the political corporate loyalty of the king to his Pashtun kinsmen was gradually replaced by his personal ties and links with his non-Pashtun subjects. Hence, the offspring of the founder of Afghanistan and the successor Popalzay dynasty were not so much concerned with their tribal or Pashtun origin, as with making sure they maintained their power and rule. This is one reason why there were so many wrangles amongst the ruling families, as other Pashtun royal claimants from opposite segments, who also had their clients among the skilled non-Pashtuns, supported contesting rulers.

The Afghan patrimonial system came to terms with such different ethnicities, both within and outside of their Pashtun lineages, by adopting the Persian term 'Afghan'. The name 'Afghan' was recorded on stones in Behistun and Susa (in Persia) and on the tomb of Darius the Great in Naqsh-e-Rustem in the fifth century BC as 'abagon'. The Persian usage of 'Abagon', 'Afghan' or 'Affaghanah' was their name for the Pashtuns. To this day, inside Afghanistan, 'Awghan' or 'Afghan' is also used by other ethnic groups to refer to the Pashtuns. They refer to themselves and are called by others as 'Afghan' when travelling abroad. Within Afghanistan they are usually known after their locality.

Since Afghanistan is home to many different ethnic groups, rulers hoped that in the long-term the dominant Pashtun culture and language, and Dari as the official language, would coexist and influence all citizens thus achieving concord in the Afghan multiethnic state. But in a region where most ethnic groups have much larger kin-groups across international borders, the integration into an 'Afghan culture' and 'Afghan identity', has proved hard to achieve. The pull of the Shi'ah religion for the Hazarahs, and the pull of the Farsi language, arts and literature for Dari-speakers, were factors tending more to the greater influence of Iran than to ethnic integration in Afghanistan. This was despite two-and-a-half centuries of interaction within the framework of a unitary state, and of intermarriage, especially between Dari-speaking Farsiwan/Daigon and Tajiks and Pashtuns, which became normal in towns and areas of mixed settlement in central and northern Afghanistan. The Pashtuns are tribal with long and elaborate genealogies and speak Pashto, while the Dari speakers are known after the area of their residence, such as Herati, Kabuli and Andarabi. However, in cities for pragmatic reasons the latter would link themselves either patrilineally or matrilineally to those in positions of power and authority. Even the term 'Tajik' as a reference to their ethnicity was confined to those Dari-speakers who remember Tajikistan as the place from where their fathers migrated. Most of the rest only began to think of themselves as 'Tajik' because of its usage by Dari nationalist and separatist groups (Parcham, Jam'iat, *Shura-i-Nezar*, Setam) after the invasion of the Red Army.

The Afghan kings, in safeguarding their own patrimonial position, attempted to create flexibility and fluidity in the domain under their rule, by making it possible for all their subjects to move freely and settle where they wished. Thus, from the late nineteenth century, Pashtuns, Hazarahs, Dari-speakers and others moved about and resettled, mostly in the under populated north. But when neighbouring governments covertly assumed responsibility for safeguarding the future of their ethnic kinsmen or co-religionists, and started aiding them in the 1980s, they turned Afghanistan into a battlefield.

The segmentary state

The concept of the 'segmentary state' was devised by Aidan Southall (1956) based on his fieldwork (1949–52) on the Alur of north-west Uganda and the Congo (Zaire).

The Alur occupied a large territory stretching between British Uganda and the Belgian Congo, now Zaire, with a population of a quarter of a million. The ecology of this land varied from forests, the fertile higher agricultural land used for grazing cattle to the tsetse-infested midland and the even more unhealthy lowland areas by Lake Albert, where the Alur specialised in mineral salt production and fishing (1956: 10–14). The Alur had migrated for some four and half centuries to what is now Alur country (1956: 18–20). 'The Alur system constituted a "segmentary state" similar to those found throughout the region among neighbouring people' (Grillo 1998: 37). Like other people in the region the Alur were patrilineal, tracing descent to a common ancestor. Lineage 'fission' is a common feature of such segmentary societies. John Middleton (1960) described the concept of 'fission' in great detail. The process of 'fission' among the Lugbara of Uganda, according to Middleton, occurs when a local agnatically related descent group on reaching a certain size, economic and sociological status breaks away, founding its own separate homestead. Alur lineages functioned in much the same way (Southall 1956: 38ff).

Southall's Alur material led him to conclude that the division by Fortes and Evans-Pritchard in their introduction to *African Political Systems* (1940) of African societies into two groups was oversimplified. Fortes and Evans-Pritchard defined their groups as follows:

One group, which we refer to as Group A consists of those societies which have centralized authority, administrative machinery, and judicial institutions – in short, a government ... the other group, which we refer to as Group B, consists of those societies which lack centralised authority, administrative machinery, and constituted judicial institutions in short which lack government – and in which there are no sharp divisions of rank, status, or wealth.

(1940: 5)

Southall observed that within the Alur, 'specialised political power is exercised within a pyramidal series of segments tied together at any one level by the oppositions between them at a higher level, and ultimately defined by their joint opposition to adjacent unrelated groups' (1956: 260). This he called a 'segmentary state', which in effect combines elements from both Group A and Group B. Southall further explained the difference:

group A, between a 'unitary state', where there is a strong, centralized authority ... and segmentary states where 'specialised' political power was exercised within a pyramidal series of segments ... by oppositions between them ... from an analogy of fission within and fusion, with complementary opposition between segments, occur[ing] in (non-centralized, acephalous) segmentary lineage systems.

(Grillo 1998: 33)

Southall does not want to restrict 'segmentary states' to societies, which have segmentary lineage systems. He writes that in a broader sense patrimonial states may frequently be described as 'segmentary'. But the 'fission' process amongst the Alur leading to the creation of new 'chiefs' and 'chieflets' follows the principle of lineage segmentation.

This description of the Alur has striking similarities to the patrileneal descent ideology of the Pashtuns who have a common language, Pashto, and an alleged collective descent from Qays.

Ever since the first Pashtun states of 1709 and 1747, the Afghan state could be characterised by Southall's principles of the 'segmentary state'. A centre is always there, though sometimes weak, with limited claim over power, thus enfeebling its monopolistic authority. A crucial balance is normally kept between the centre and the tribal periphery. This relation of balance between the centre and the periphery, whenever disrupted, either leads to intolerant rule from the centre or rebellion from the peripheral tribes. In the Pashtun segmentary lineage system, which is similar to the Alur and other acephalous societies, the *kor* or family, *kahol*, household, *taber*, clan (also ancestry), and *qawm*, tribe, are all in opposition at each and every level with those of their opposite segments at similar levels. At the top of the pyramid, the king's monopoly of power is limited and restricted to the centre and its immediate environment. The power of his specialised administrative staff cannot reach to all parts of the Pashtun tribal land. The central government has been there since the middle of the eighteenth century, but between the centre and the peripheral extremities there are various foci over which the centre has been unable to exercise power, except for a restricted authority. Generally, the further the periphery, the less it is disposed to the exercise of power from the centre. Even in the twenty-first century, the governments in Kabul and Islamabad have only nominal authority over the mostly acephalous tribes on both sides of the Durand Line dividing the Afghan and Pakistani states. As for the various segments of the Pashtuns, it is the relationship of these peripheral foci that reflect their position in the pyramid vis-à-vis others of their opposites in the segmentary ladder. Such flexibility and agility epitomises the segmentary nature of the Afghan state.

Nation and nationalism

In today's world the number of nations is put at some 5,000, while at present there are only some 187 states. 'What makes each one of these a nation is that its people share a language, culture, territorial base, and political organisation and history' (Haviland 1997: 615). Anthony Smith connects the rise of nationalism in Europe to 'the impact of the triple western revolution ... These were a revolution in the sphere of division of labour, a revolution in the control of administration, and a revolution in cultural co-ordination' (Smith 1986: 131). The first stems from a transition from feudalism to capitalism. The second from the linking of economic centres within the territory and the binding of the regional and urban elite to a common economic fate. The third stems from ecclesiastical authority and tradition, which was replaced by a sovereign state promising practical salvation in creating a community of citizens and equals (ibid., pp. 131–3). By contrast Hugh Seton-Watson after a 'thorough study' of the nation admits that no convincing definition of nation could be put forward. 'Thus I am driven to the conclusion that no "scientific definition" of the nation can be devised: yet the phenomenon has existed and exists' (Anderson 1983: 13).

Benedict Anderson sees the nation as an 'imagined community' and defines this 'imagined' concept 'in an anthropological spirit'. 'It is *imagined* because the members of even the smallest nation will never know most of their fellow-members, meet them, or even hear of them, yet in the mind of each lives the image of their communion' (1983: 15). This imagined community took shape following the development of print capitalism after the fifteenth century and also to an extent following the decline of religion and the dynastic powers in Europe. The development of the printing press and vernacular languages in Europe made people aware of the extent of their imagined communities. In addition to 'sacred communities, languages and lineages, a fundamental change was taking place in the modes of apprehending the world which, more than anything else, made it possible to "think" the nation' (ibid., p. 28).

Ernest Gellner analyses nation through the phenomenon of nationalism. 'Nationalism is not the awakening of nations to self-consciousness: it invents nations where they do not exist' (Gellner 1964: 169). Gellner writes that nationalism is purely a modern phenomenon and a product of industrial society. For him, pre-modern 'agro-literate' societies had no place for nation and nationalism. The division of these societies into elites and food-producing masses, separated on cultural lines, was unable to generate an ideology, which would overcome this division. Other historians and social scientists also regard nationalism as a modern phenomenon and date it back to the Enlightenment and the eighteenth-century French and American revolutions. Gellner's emphasis on modernity forecloses too abruptly on the past. Anthony Smith takes issue with the modern view of nationalism.

> If the system of European states came into being at the Treaty of Westphalia in 1648, it was not until the nineteenth century that these states began to be converted into 'nation-states' ... yet there are ... difficulties with this view ... even in the ancient world, striking parallels to the 'modern' idea of national identity and character, in the way Greeks and Romans looked on people who did not share their cultures ... in the way ancient Egyptians looked upon Nubians and Asiatic; and Mesopotamian and Biblical distinctions drawn between different people. In the ancient world, we find movements that appear to resemble modern nationalism in several respects, notably a desire to liberate territories conquered by aliens, or to resist foreign encroachments, like the Ionian resistance to Persian expansion in the late sixth century BC or the Gallic resistance to Caesar's campaigns.
> (Smith 1986: 11)

Anthony Smith emphasises that people will make a stand for what they regard to be theirs and are prepared to make sacrifices for their beliefs. He poses these questions. 'Are we then justified in regarding nations and nationalism as purely modern phenomena? If not, must we return to the older view that national ties and sentiments are the 'stuff of history' and a universal attribute of humanity?' (ibid., p. 12).

Pashtun 'nationalism' does not really fit into the European concept of nationalism. Pashtun nationalism is connected with *pashtunwali*, the code/way of Pashtun, *terborwali*, cousin rivalry, and *qawmwali*, tribal ways/rivalry. Afghan writers use *nayshnalism* to mean adulation of one's country. Thus Pashtun uprisings against invading forces and dominating empires are all seen by Afghan writers as aspects of nationalism, drawing on the Pashtun ethnically superior identity and experience in fighting, for the purpose of defending *meli `azat*, national honour.

Nationalism for my purposes is a movement by a community of people for the achievement of specific goals. Pashtun ethnic identity that subsequently became known by the English term *nayshnalism* was not a blindfold act for the Pashtuns. They knew of their rulers, and their dynasties in the Indian Subcontinent, central and south western Afghanistan. They knew that to get a free and independent state they had to struggle and fight for it and to be prepared to die, as many thousands had perished fighting the Persian and Moghul dynasties and imperial Britain in the past two centuries. This nationalism, expressing national sentiments and aspirations, was aimed at establishing their state. For the Pashtuns this nationalist aspiration was based on tribal factors, often at a confederate level, with the aim of achieving statehood by force if necessary. They saw themselves historically, demographically and culturally capable of achieving this especially when the state and nation were seen as the only source of achieving political power. They went about it not claiming merely that 'we are Pashtuns and our Pashtun ways dictates to us', but whenever possible with the consent of the elders of other groups, where their representatives would participate in the *jirga* or tribal council to this effect.

Nationalism has been defined as a watermark 'between older agrarian societies and modern industrial societies' (Banks 1996: 126). This view of nationalism has little bearing on the Afghan tribal, ethnically conscious nationalist movements, either of 1709, 1747 or of the centuries of struggles after. Afghanistan remained mostly tribal and was minimally affected by modern industrial processes. However, Gellner is nearer to the point when he says that nationalism does not arise out of the thinking of 'nationalist' thinkers: their thought merely serves to describe and identify the social conditions that give rise to nationalism. The social condition of servitude to Shi'ah Persia on religious grounds, and the grudge against the excesses of their governors over taxes and the mistreating of Pashtuns, were the main reasons for nationalist fervour and uprisings against Persia. The Pashtun were ready to die for their *millat*, nation, in order to do away with Persian, Moghul and British suzerainty. If this were not the case, the people of Kandahar would not have risen, under Mir Wais's leadership, slaying some 23,000 Persian occupying troops, and again would not have succeeded in eliminating a further army of 17,000 between 1709 and 1711. Similarly, they would not have joined the forces of Ahmad Shah to subdue local potentates in the north and north-east of present-day Afghanistan, as a first step in unifying the Afghanistan which existed in the minds of all concerned. Nor would they have embarked with Ahmad Shah to retake Khorasan from Persia and to conquer parts of India, on eight separate occasions, as moiety of previous Afghan rulers' domains.

Anderson's techno-educational qualifications for nationalism are also not applicable to Afghanistan. In his view, through printed works in the vernacular individuals gain a sense of being part of the imagined community of their nation, not so much by reading about the great events of national importance, but rather by reading about the conjunction of the general and the specific (1983: 45). In Afghan society where there is a predominant inability to read and write, the equation of the printing press and education does not add up to nationalism. However, its people, especially the Pashtuns, have a strong sense of genealogy, culture and religion. It is these that have been fuelling the Pashtun/Afghan sense of nationalism. Substituting 'Pashtun' for 'American', a quote from Anderson reads: 'A [Pashtun] will never meet, or even know the names of more than a handful of his fellow [Pashtuns]. He has no idea of what they are up to at any one time. But he has complete confidence in their steady, anonymous, simultaneous activity' (Anderson 1983: 31). Pashtuns have been ready, on numerous occasions throughout history, to shed blood and die if necessary, to avert danger to their 'Pashtun' ethnic identity, and since 1747 for their 'imagined' Afghan nation.

Ernest Gellner identifies crucial factors for the formation of nationalism as culture, power and education (Gellner 1983: 94). To Gellner nationalism is 'about entry to, participation in, identification with, a literate high culture which is co-extensive with the entire political unit and its total population' (1983: 95). From an Afghan viewpoint this is an Eurocentric view. The Afghan state, which came out of centuries of resistance against foreign domination, was not 'a literate high culture' or 'co-extensive with the entire political unit' or 'its total population'. The state was formed mainly through the consensus of the majority Pahtuns.[4] In 1747 and before, when we speak of nationalism we mean 'Pashtun nationalism' more than 'Afghan nationalism'. The name 'Afghan' has come to mean all those who live in Afghanistan, though 'Afghan' is in fact a Persianised version of Pashtun.[5] But the state that was formed in the middle of the eighteenth century was apparently acceptable to the non-Pashtun minorities and certainly they did not rebel against it. Meanwhile the Pashtuns because of their sheer number and ferocious independent nature have maintained hegemony over the other ethnic groups. So though the state is segmentary it is fashioned by the dominance of one ethnic group – the Pashtun.

But within that group there are many that are vying for power as in the Europe of the Middle Ages. The Roshanid movement against the Moghuls of the sixteenth and seventeenth centuries though spearheaded by *ulema* was a nationalist Pashtun movement by modern standards. The Roshanid for a short time succeeded in setting up their own state, comprising several eastern tribal areas. Meanwhile another persistent and continuous attempt to rally the Pushtun tribes in the Indian frontier area to a common fight for independence from the Moghuls was made by the warrior-poet Khushal Khan Khattak in the latter part of the seventeenth century (Wilber 1962: 41). Khushal Khan Khattak, through his poetry and prowess, has come to be regarded as an icon of Pashtun nationalism. He grew up within the Roshani milieu and as a man of letters, was also influenced by other Pashtun rulers such as the Suri and Lodi dynasties of the Delhi Sultanate. In one of many of his nationalistic couplets he says:

> Pashtuns, in matters of honour and shame
> are one from Amu[6] to Attak.[7]

In another famous couplet he says:

> I raise my sword for the honour of Afghan.
> I am the proudest of time Khushal Khattak.

As a tribal elder who fought the Moghuls on many a battlefield, Khattak wanted to see Pashtuns more prudent and united:

> More skilled in the swords are the Pashtuns than the Moghuls,
> Would only more intelligence was theirs.
> Were the tribes but of agreement amongst themselves,
> Emperors would prefer to bow before them.
> Every deed of the Pashtun is better than that of the Moghul,
> Concord is what they lack, how pitiful that is.

In another poem he laments their discord and friction. Unable to put an end to it he appeals to God and prays:

> Oh God! Grant them but concord, sweet refrain,
> And old Khushal will rise a youth again.

Pashtun nationalism uniting the tribes against Moghuls, Safavids and others in the eighteenth century was never tested, whether or not the minorities were, as Gellner put it, 'co-extensive with the entire political unit' created by the Pashtuns. Such yardsticks were not the norm then. However, the people of this part of the world, now known as Afghanistan, time and again in the past were often ruled by the same rulers. So over the centuries, despite their overt heterogeneity there is, as in most other countries, a certain level of homogeneity of national culture and norms. This close contact over a long period had given them the ability to communicate with one another. It is because of this that Afghan nationalism reifies the cultural similarities of all the people within its political boundaries. Hence the relation of all Afghans, through the medium of nationalism and the Afghan identity, to the Afghan state. Such a nationalistic relationship with the state excludes any ethnic group from demanding sole command or authority over the state, but when that happens the ethnic group(s) turn 'nationalist' with their own agenda. This is precisely what has been happening in the post-Soviet withdrawal period amongst the armed groups claiming to represent their own ethnic groups.

The debate in the West about nation and nationalism has set standards to which other countries have been compared. I have shown how this could be applied to Afghanistan and where the limitations are. Pashtun nationalism is not a product of a movement spearheaded by Western educated men. Rather it is intertwined with tribal practices going back for centuries with a proven track record of raising a *Lashker* or army for such occasions.

Ethnicity

One of the most basic features of Afghan ethnicity is that, locally and regionally, it is a diverse ethnic reality. Locally, in nearly every province and even in most districts within the provinces, different ethnic groups have intermingled, some over centuries and others relatively recently. Regionally, major ethnic groups have their other, often larger, ethnic kin across the international borders. Thus, some of the Tajik-speaking people in the northeastern provinces have emigrated from Tajikistan, as have some of the Uzbek in the four northern provinces from Uzbek Central Asia and the Turkmen from Turkmenistan. The smaller Baluch group came from British Indian territory and Iranian Baluchestan. The Shi'ah Hazarah and Qizelbash on religious grounds look to Iran. The Qizelbash are eighteenth-century immigrants from Persia.[8] On the other hand, the larger Pashtun tribal groups origin cannot be traced to any other country. Those Pashtuns in today's Pakistan are the creation of British colonial policy dating from 1893.

The civil war that was unleashed by some armed minority political groups was aimed at joining their ethnic groups with those of the newly independent republics of the former Soviet Union, thus making them part of the majority there. They wanted to achieve this by turning the Afghan unitary state into a federal state. This was regarded as a first step in dismantling Afghanistan and, therefore, the Pashtuns rejected it. Further, this was an unlikely proposition since the population of the country has been intermingled to such an extent that an ethnic cleansing of the most savage type would be necessary to carry it through. Also logistically these activists knew that they were neither the only armed groups nor even the majority in most of the provinces where they operated. Members of other ethnic groups also lived amongst them, intermarrying between themselves and with other groups, and have been burying their dead for decades in the same cemeteries and consequently are unlikely to accept such ethnic nationalist agendas. An indication of this was the recapture of 90 per cent of land from these ethnically based nationalist groups by the Taleban (1995–98), where the populace, with some exceptions, were relieved and co-operated with the Taleban with a view to remaining within the present political borders of Afghanistan.[9] This point was also made by the anthropologist Brent Glazer in his sample survey of refugees fleeing the fighting in Afghanistan to Peshawar, Pakistan.

> 100 peasants, artisans, traders, and students ... recently came from different parts of Afghanistan to Peshawar and intended to return soon ... All of them without exception stressed the importance of Afghan national unity incorporating all ethnic minorities. A partition of Afghanistan be it on ethnic or other lines, was seen as a terrifying prospect to be avoided by all means.
>
> (Glazer 1996: 180)

After the Second World War, many social theorists were of the opinion that as a result of modernisation and industrialisation the importance of minority cultural groups would gradually fade away. This stage of social development, if ever possible, is nowhere in sight in Afghanistan. If anything, ethnic attachment or what Weber calls the 'sentiment of prestige' (1947: 171ff) is revived in times of war and other emergencies. But the war against the communists and the Soviets and then the civil war have led a large number to be internally and externally dislocated. Even those who had forgotten their ethnic roots had to retrace their origins by joining their 'ethnic groups' as a guarantee for security. Such revivals of ethnic ties and dependence on them, in the post-communist era have exacerbated the civil war.

Ethnic conflicts and strife are not peculiar to Afghanistan. 'Thirty-five of the thirty-seven major armed conflicts in the world in 1991 were internal conflicts, and most of them – from Sri Lanka to Northern Ireland – could plausibly be described as ethnic conflicts' (Erikson 1993: 2). Ethnicity is then the relationship between groups whose members consider themselves and each other to be distinct on grounds of culture, language and sometimes religion. But 'when we talk of ethnicity, we indicate that groups and identities have developed in mutual contact rather than in isolation' (Erikson 1993: 10). It is this contact between ethnic groups that makes Afghanistan, like so many countries, a distinctly ethnic society. Afghan ethnic groups, especially in the post communist era, have been reifying their common origins, language and culture. Such ethnic emphasis has served to undermine Afghan identity, the authority of central government and to jeopardise the legitimacy of the state.

Islam

Apart from nationalism, that has been holding the country together since its founding, another factor that has played an important role in upholding such an identity is Islam. While 62.73 per cent of the population is Pashtun, the country is nearly 100 per cent Muslim. Of these 91 per cent are Sunni and 9 per cent Shi'ah (WAKFA: 1998).

'Islam' in Arabic means the voluntary surrender to the will of Allah and obedience to His commands. The Islamic way of life is based on total obedience to the Creator. There are three fundamental beliefs and five principles, also known as pillars, in Islam. The three fundamental beliefs (in Pashto) are *yowalay*, monotheism, or belief in one God; *paighombary*, prophethood, or belief in Muhammad and all the past prophets, and *qiamat/akherat*, or the day of judgement. The five pillars are: *shahadat*, professing that there is no god but Allah and Muhammad is His Prophet; *lemonz*, the five daily prayers; *zakat*, the 2.5 per cent annual contribution on profit, cash and jewellery for welfare; *rozhah*, one month a year's fasting; and *hajj* the pilgrimage once in a lifetime to Makkah, if one can afford it. Islam through the Quran and Sunnah provides man with *hedayat* or guidance to lead a balanced and purposeful life to avoid *dozakh*, hell, and earn a place in *janat*, paradise in the hereafter. In short, Islam tells man about the purpose of his creation and existence, his ultimate destiny and his place in the world amongst other creatures.

> Islam is all-encompassing in its scope, placing people both in the universe and in society, providing answers to the existential and historic questions, defining both their (inclusive) membership of the *umma* as well as their (positional) interrelationship to fellow humans. In most, if not all Muslim societies, the Islamic heritage constitutes the main shared cultural identity, both at the philosophical level and in the popular tradition.
>
> (Olsen 1995: 6)

Further to these religio-ethical teachings, as Islam expanded from the small cities of Makkah and Medinah (then Yathrib) to North Africa, the Middle East and the rest of Asia, social reforms through the application of Quranic and Sunnah principles formed legal enactment as the core of Islamic teachings (also see Appendix 3).

Islam, as a *deen*, is a total way of life and does not allow a division between religion and state. All state institutions are considered as religious, with the Shari'ah as their constitution. Social and political systems such as feudalism, class and various forms of political systems, over the centuries have come and gone, but Islam's continuity stands in contrast to these transient discontinuities.

Islam sees *millat*, nation, and *dawlat* or state, differently. According to Islam, the nation is the *umma*, the religious community, which amongst Muslims has no frontiers. The state, *dawlat*, is a geographically defined part of a section of the *umma*. While the *umma*, since the death of Prophet Muhammad (AD 633) till 4 March 1924 when the last of the Ottoman Caliphs was replaced by Mustafa Kemal of Turkey, was always headed by a *khalifa*, caliph, the *dawlat* was always headed by individual *amirs*.[10] While the *umma* comprises all approximately 1.2 billion Muslims from the USA to Indonesia, the *dawlats* are confined to geographical localities under separate rulers. This is how nation and state are seen in Islam and have also been understood for centuries by the Afghans.

Afghans by any Islamic standard are devout and conservative Muslims. Islam throughout the centuries has been the rallying power across the whole spectrum of Afghan society, especially when faced with foreign aggression. But internally, in the tribal Pashtun lands for example, there are other alternative forces and institutions that sometimes take precedence. Pashtunwali is a case in point, where its various institutions are used to settle disputes. Even in tribal matters Islam is present either by taking the Quran as an oath or placing the holy book in the middle, to ensure truthfulness and sincerity while discussing an issue.

Externally, whenever the country is faced with danger and aggression, popular Islamic and Pashtun traditions join in forming a new and relatively effective politico-military alliance, articulating a discourse to face the challenge. This was the case when the communists came to power in 1978, and again much more effectively eighteen months later when the Soviet forces invaded the country. After 1994 the Taleban used such a two-pronged approach to fight the warlords, while pointing to the machinations of regional and neighbouring governments who would have liked to see the disintegration of Afghanistan. Thus, the Islamic approaches in Afghanistan, whether it is leading or contributing, has always been to articulate a political discourse with the tribes and ethnic groups.

Conclusion

In this introductory chapter I have constructed my story line from historical and anthropological works for the discussion of tribe, state, ethnicity, nation, nationalism, nation-state and Islam. These are major areas in today's scholarship, which pre-occupy anthropologists, social historians, sociologists and political theorists. My work, because of its introductory nature of evaluating Afghan society through such concepts, cannot be exhaustive in its approach. Thus, I hope this book will be regarded as a systematic analysis leading to the understanding of Afghan society and its constraints in attempting to develop a modern nation-state, through the discussion and evaluation of such concepts and issues.

Having shown how my own material complements and extends existing anthropological and other works on Afghanistan, in the next chapter I take the period leading up to the formation of the Afghan state.

Part I
A state in the making

1 Formation of the Afghan state: 1747–72

Introduction

For millennia the area called Afghanistan has been the crossroads of invading empires, a network of trade routes and a centre or meeting place for cultures. The great civilisations of the Asian continent, in particular the Indian and Chinese, were inter-linked by various trade routes crossing through Afghanistan. An art historian of the region summarises in the following words: 'No land, in ancient times, was more thoroughly traversed in every direction. Doubtless no other was so well situated geographically to act as a link between east and west' (Auboyer 1968: 9). Perhaps because of this, Afghanistan has gained the title, 'cross-road of Asia' (Gregorian 1969: 21–4). This area nearly always has been a battleground of different invading armies, sometimes ruled by one, at other times by others, and yet most of the time disputed between them.[1] This violent and continuous change is part of the turbulent history of the Pashtuns or Afghans. An anthropologist of law writes:

> For at least a millennium, the Pashto-speaking people have preserved their independence and flourished through a tribal political organisation in their own homeland straddling the present Afghanistan-Pakistan international border. The tribal organisation of the people – more commonly called Afghans to the west, Pathan in the east, and Pushtuns/Pakhtuns on both sides of this border – today provides them not merely with a distinct cultural or ethnic identity, but especially for those in the central homeland nearest the border, with a form of polity alternative to that of the state.
>
> (Hager 1983: 83)

In the sixteenth and seventeenth centuries, the area known as Afghanistan was divided three ways between the Shabanid Uzbek empire in the north, the Safavid Persian empire in the west and the Moghul Indian empire in the east, with some cities like Kabul, Kandahar and Ghazni often disputed between them.

36 *A state in the making*

   This chapter first presents the historical background of how the state was formed. I write about the Roshani religious revivalist movement as an example of an early nationalist movement battling with the Moghuls. Another empire that stood in the way of Afghan national unity was the Persian Safavid. Hence the sixteenth to eighteenth centuries were a period of struggle against the Moghuls in the east and the Persians in the west with the aim of safeguarding their identity and attempting to set up an indigenous Pashtun/Afghan state, like the earlier Afghan states of Lodies, Suries and Ghories – the Delhi Sultanate. These struggles were spearheaded not by Uzbeks in the north against the remnants of the Shabanids or Tajik in the west against the Safavid, but by the various tribes of the Pashtun within the Roshanid movement in the east; Ghilzai and Abdali (Durrani) as two of the largest confederacies of tribes in the west. A tribal confederacy in the Pashtun sense means an ethnic identity that cannot be divided politically even along tribal lines.[2] Of the two, the Ghilzai dominant nomadic mode of life has been responsible for their spread all over the country, although a large proportion of them remain to this day in Kandahar and southeast and southwest Afghanistan.[3]

Struggle against the Moghuls: the Roshani movement

Afghans have been active in the Indian subcontinent, as traders, merchants and rulers for a long time (Gommans 1995: 4–5). Afghans from eastern Pashtun tribes had established ruling dynasties in India such as the Lodies (1451–1526) and Suries (1539–55) (Rahim 1961). These Delhi Sultanates preceded Zahir ud-Din Mohammad Babur, the founder of the Moghul Empire.[4] Other Pashtuns, locally known as Rohillas, for nearly a hundred years from the turn of the eighteenth century established their principalities in the foothills of the Himalayas, Rohilkand, Kaisur and Farrukhabad. These and the Delhi Sultanate were early Pashtun states and provided ample experience to establish a native state later on in Afghanistan itself. The above dynasties, though established on Indian soil, considered themselves culturally and linguistically Pashtuns/Afghans.

   With the precedents of Afghan rule in the subcontinent, the eastern Pashtuns, headed by a spiritual leader, Bayazid Ansari (1525–85?) started a supra-tribal uprising, called the Roshani, the illuminated or the enlightened movement, from amongst the tribes of the North West Frontier Province (NWFP).[5] Bayazid who became known as Pir Roshan, the apostle of light, aimed at creating ethnic and sectarian solidarity and therefore cast his net much wider than the localised tribe and ethnic groups. The Roshanid movement was in essence an emancipatory movement wrapped up in Pashto garb (Gommans 1995: 110). Pir Roshan through his preaching united the hill tribes and also the Shi'ah and Isma'iliah factions with the majority Sunni. He also sent da'wa or missionaries to places as far away as Balkh and Badakhshan in northern Afghanistan, Bokhara and Khiwa in

Central Asia and Delhi in India. Bayazid, and his sons and grandsons after him, worked to strengthen tribal solidarity through religious fervour to achieve autonomy and statehood. His descendants and followers on more than one occasion declared their independence from the Moghuls, minting their own money and calling on other Pashtuns to rise. Gregorian researching into the former Soviet Union's scholars' work on the Roshanids concludes that 'Soviet scholars see in the Roshani movement the first manifestation and the foundation of an Afghan national struggle for independence' (Gregorian 1969: 421, n49).

The local Yosufzai land-owning khans who were losing control over their tribes came to regard the Roshani movement as a threat. Therefore, with the aid of Moghul money and influence they stood behind a local religious and literary figure, Akhund Derwaza, as a challenge to Pir Roshan. Derwaza criticised Pir Roshan's heterodoxy, calling him Pir-e-Tarik, the apostle of darkness, and thus tried to convert his followers back to orthodox Islam. However, amongst the poor peasants, ethnic minorities and acephalous Pashtun, Pir Roshan's movement had spread with great vigour since its introduction in the early 1540s. The main reason for its success was the hefty tax system of the Moghuls, coupled with their policy of divide and rule over the tribes. Also the Moghul emperor Akbar, assuming a semi-papal position by placing himself above criticism, became the focus of religious discontent and this was another issue against which Muslim orthodoxy took exception. Thus according to Mount Stewart Elphinstone in 1630, when Bayazid's great-grandson, Abdul Qadir, launched an attack on the Moghul troops in Peshawar, fighting men from the tribes of the Afridi, Orakzais, Bangash, Mohmands, Yosufzai, Mohammadzai, Gigiani, Tarklauris, Baluchis, Turis and Zazis, numbering over 40,000, all took part (Elphinstone 1969: 209–11). However, despite such a united stand, the lack of a central command, tribal jealousy, and the unclear allocation of functions in this attack led to their major downfall against the Moghuls (Caroe 1965: 228–9). But this dynamic Pashtun movement continued to harass the Moghuls throughout the sixteenth and seventeenth centuries, despite the Moghuls' grant of land and donation of money to local khans, in the hope of inflaming inter-tribal warfare so that they could continue to reach their outposts in Kabul and eastern Afghanistan.

Another Pashtun figure of this time was the celebrated poet, writer and tribal leader, Khushal Khan Khattak (1613–89) of the Khattak tribe. Khushal Khan, as a literary man, knew more than most about Afghan/Pashtun history and politics. Afghan writers see his life-long struggles against the Moghuls as a wakeup call to national consciousness that could be described in today's political vocabulary as ardent 'nationalism'. The epitaph on his tomb bears a poem that is known to all Pashtuns:

> I bound on the sword for the pride of Afghan
> I am Khoshal Khattak, the proud man of this age

Elphinstone writing in 1814 saw his poems as 'intended to animate his countrymen to the defence of their independence, and to persuade them to concord and combination, as the only means of success' (1969: 192–3). Despite the Moghuls' grant of land to his great-grandfather in return for policing the road, he rose against the Moghul rulers and through his poetry and oratory became a formidable foe. 'In 1664 ... at the age of fifty-one [Khoshal] was dispatched in chains and under escort to Delhi ... to spend over two years in prison' (Caroe 1965: 233). Those Pashtun leaders whose loyalty was bought by Moghul money disgusted him. In one of his many Pashto poems, he expressed his revulsion in this way:

> What worthless creatures Pashtun are
> Without a scrap of sense
> They act like every dog and cur
> Haunting the butchers yard
> Their sovereignty they have renounced
> Preferring Moghul gold
> They seem to have but one desire
> To seek for Moghul titles
> (Mackenzie 1965: 147)

The Yosufzai tribe, who had settled in the fertile valley of Swat, is mocked in one poem for not joining him against the Moghuls:

> I alone am concerned for my nation's honour
> The Yosufzai are at ease, tilling their fields

However, after the middle of the seventeenth century, as a result of resistance from within some of the tribal leadership and the sophistication of the Moghul administration, it proved too difficult for the Roshani movement to overthrow Moghul rulers. Some Roshani leaders, true to Khushal Khan's above observations, ended up becoming Moghul Mansabdar officers, and others were appointed as Jagir land revenue collectors (Gommans 1995: 111). But the movement continued to flourish even within India, so much so that the Bangash Pashtun tribes, who were followers of the Roshani, established their own principality to the south of Rohilkand in Farrukhabad.[6] Towards the end of the seventeenth century the Roshani seem to have lost much of their rallying and fighting power. However, the movement continued to retain much of its spiritual vigour as a recruiting network for Afghans in the subcontinent.

This religious movement has similarities to the Taleban movement who recruited from madrassas, seminary schools, and operate across the tribal and ethnic divide. Taleban leaders, unlike the Roshanis Pirs saints, were *ulama* religious scholars, graduates from the madrassas and did not claim pir saint/holy men ranks as did the Roshanid leadership, including the son and grandsons of Bayazid. Pirs and other hereditary functionaries did not play any significant role amongst the Taleban. The Roshanis also compromised with Shi'ah and Isma'iliah. Taleban told me 'we can not deviate from mainstream Sunni orthodoxy'.

It is clear then that Pashtuns in the east since the sixteenth century used both the sword and Islam to achieve statehood. Though they were unsuccessful at dislodging the Moghul Empire their desire for an independent Afghan state was not weakened. Eventually it was the Ghilzai and Durrani in western Afghanistan, who in the eighteenth century succeeded in setting up their independent states. Some historians have called the Roshani movement a millenarian movement in the guise of Islam, while others see it as 'pure and naked nationalism'. Their saying, 'Pashtun seeks freedom, not slavery' is indicative of their nationalistic sentiments.

Pashtuns were familiar with the Persian and Indian methods of governing. They also had the examples of their own Lodies, Suries, Rohilah and the Afghan Turkik Ghaznawids, whose governments they helped establish and served as their own administrations.[7] So when Ahmad Shah came to power in the middle of the eighteenth century and went to conquer India, he found all these eastern Pashtuns ready and willing to help him avert 'the Hindu threat' and to achieve greatness for his own Durrani state.

Initial attempt in forming the state: the Ghilzai uprising, the Kandahar state

The struggle against Persian rule was started in Kandahar in 1709 by an important sub-tribe of the Ghilzai – the Hotak, led by Amir Khan, known as Mir Wais. Mir Wais was the kalanter, representative or spokesman of the Pashtuns in Kandahar. The Persian governor, a Georgian, re-named Shah Nawaz Khan, known to Afghans as Gorgin, bent on eliminating Pashtun resistance to the Safavid rule, massacred and committed atrocities against the Durranis in Kandahar (Appendix 4). Mir Wais spoke against these atrocities and wrote to the Persian Court about what the governor was doing. When Gorgin heard about it, he was taken prisoner and sent in shackles to the Persian capital. Mir Wais was well spoken and by the standard of the time a wealthy man. He soon worked out his strategy of bribing the Safavid officials and before long gained the confidence of the Persian king (Al-Afghani 1938: 18–19). Mir Wais then requested to go on a pilgrimage to Makkah and was given permission to do so. There he met the Imam of Makkah and the *ulema* of the Hijaz, informing them of the cruelties of the Shi'ah Persians in Kandahar. The Makkan *ulema* gave him a letter, saying that Afghans as Sunni were under no obligation to live under Shi'ah rule and also that, if a Muslim king acts contrary to the Islamic teachings, the subjects are not obliged to obey him (ibid.: 18). Keeping his meeting with the Arabian religious leaders a secret and having already won the Persian court over to his views, on his return to

Persia, he was allowed to go to Kandahar. In Kandahar he succeeded in convincing the governor that he was a changed man and 'thus lulled Gorgin into a sense of false security' (Ganda Singh 1959: 7). Gorgin once again restored him to his former position as kalanter of the city of Kandahar. Meanwhile Mir Wais called a secret *Loya Jirga*, a grand tribal meeting, of all regional Pashtun and some non-Pashtuns. At that meeting, after the *jirga* heard Mir Wais and had seen the letter of support from the Makkan *ulema*, they decided to get rid of the Persians once and for all.[8] The Baluch and the Kakar tribes volunteered their refusal to make further tax payments and so it was decided that once the bulk of Gorgin 23,000 forces were despatched after these rebellious tribes, Mir Wais and his insurgents would then take on Gorgin himself.

For this purpose a party was arranged in a garden outside Kandahar for the Persian governor and his entourage. The Persian governor walked straight into the trap. Mir Wais attacked Gorgin killing him and all his bodyguards and troops. The insurgents, then put on the uniform of the Persian officers, entered their headquarters in the city and captured the remaining forces. The Baluch and the Kakar tribes also rounded the troops that were sent after them. All this happened in 1709. Mir Wais without losing any time declared the independence of Kandahar on that very day (Ferrier 1858: 28–9; Malleson 1879: 225–6). 'Three powerful armies, one after the other, were sent against him, but Wais inflicted crushing defeat on them and made his independence secure' (Ganda Sing 1959: 7).

The conquest of Persia: Mir Wais' family wrangles, the Hotak downfall

Mir Wais ruled Kandahar for six years, not as a king or amir, but 'as one amongst equals'. Instead of being called a king or amir, he wanted to be known as Masher or Spinzhiray, elder or white-beard. In adherence to tribal ways he always sat on the ground with the other elders who represented their tribes and groups. He minted his coins and came to terms with running his newly independent country.

Mir Wais's rule in Kandahar was a transition from gaining the independence of Kandahar and its environs as a city or regional principality, to a state later established by Ahmad Shah. Kandahar under Mir Wais did not have the resources to take on the Safavids or the Moghuls and thus extend the state. So after the initial unsettling wars with the Persians, in order to keep the Afghans united behind him Mir Wais embarked on the process of the reconciliation of the tribes. Though he succeeded in patching up his Ghilzai tribal differences with the rival Abdali/Durrani, his successor son and nephew in their *terborwali* or cousins rivalry brought about the end of Ghilzai rule.

With the Ghilzai coming to power in Kandahar, the Abdali took control of Herat. Kabul and eastern Afghanistan were still under the Moghuls. The Persians, who lost a further 25,000 troops in their initial attacks designed to retake Kandahar, had no choice but to opt for a policy of 'wait and see'. After Mir Wais' death in November 1715 his brother Mir Abdul Aziz, known as Abdullah, was crowned. Abdullah, misjudging the public mood, made overtures to the Persian king, with the view of accepting some sort of Persian influence in Kandahar (Al-Afghani 1938: 24–5). Since Abdullah would not be talked out of his approach with the Persians, Mir Mahmud, with the consent of the influential members of the family and their Hotak tribal elders, accompanied by forty armed men, killed his uncle and took his place. No one apart from Abdullah's immediate family opposed Mahmud's approach.

Mahmud made a fatal error by ignoring Pashtun feuds of revenge killings by not solving the issue of his uncle's murder with his cousins which later cost him his life. Instead he took advantage of the sensitivity of the Afghans towards the Persians and organised a large tribal force, not only to consolidate the Afghan Kingdom in Kandahar but also to take the initiative to overthrow the Safavid dynasty. Mahmud attacked Kerman (1720) and after laying siege to Isfahan, the capital of Persia, took that city in March 1722. He thus overthrew the last Safavid king, Shah Hussian (Wilber 1958: 70). After taking Isfahan, one day the king invited the capital's notables to a party and in revenge for Gorgin's massacre of the Sadozai he put to sword some 124 Persian nobles there and then. Mahmud chose to rule most of Persia and Kandahar from the Persian capital Isfahan.

In line with Pashtunwali, the Pashtun code of honour, his paternal cousin Ashraf, the son of the murdered Abdullah, killed Mahmud. Shah Ashraf continued Mahmud's conquests to other parts of Persia and in 1725, after defeating the forces of Shah Tahmaseb III, he captured Tehran. The Ottoman Turks two years later recognised Shah Ashraf as 'Shah Henshah-e-Fars', King of Kings of Persia.

An Iranian Turkeman, Nader Qoli of the Afshar tribe (son of a leather tailor, later a bandit), known as Nader Afshar, rose in the north and continued attacking and harassing Ashraf's forces. He succeeded in defeating Ashraf in Mimun Shaher and Shiraz in 1730. Following this he attacked Herat which was under Abdali control. After Mahmud's murder the Ghilzai governor of Kandahar turned against Ashraf. The Abdali in Herat also refused to come to his aid to avert the rise of Nader Afshar. The Afghan king while retreating with some of his bodyguards was killed in western Afghanistan.

Nader Shah Afshar, having routed the Afghans from Iran, attacked and captured Herat (1734) and two years later took Kandahar (Ferrier 1858: 25–33; Malleson 1879: 211–66). With this, the Ghilzai rule, which lasted nearly three decades, over Kandahar and Iran, came to an end.[9]

The 1747 *Jirga*: election of Ahmad Shah in Kandahar

Jirga is a Pashto term meaning meeting or assembly. *Jirga* is part of Pashtun social institutions, and has always played a decisive role in forcing adherence to established norms. *Jirgas* are the mechanism through which cohesion and stability are assured. The history of *jirga* is said to go back thousands of years to the original settlers in the area (*Aryana*) now known as Afghanistan, who then had two kinds of *jirgas*, the *Simite/Seymati* and the *Subha*. The first was a village meeting in which everyone concerned took part in order to settle local disputes. The second was a meeting of elders of tribes in times of national and regional emergencies to elect a king or in his absence to take decisions on war and peace (Wajdi 1986: 40).

Some of those Aryan tribes who settled in the Indian subcontinent still use the old terms such as *Luksubha*, the Indian Upper House (Faizad 1989: 15). From those distant times to the present, the *jirgas* of the village, sub-tribe or tribes have been called upon by the Pashtuns to meet the needs and the challenges of the time. Some of these *jirgas* and their roles in times of emergencies will be discussed in the next chapter. Here suffice it to mention three *jirgas* that were formed against Persian hegemony and are associated with the formation of the Afghan state. The 1709 *Loya Jirga* at Maanjah, 30 km north-east of Kandahar, which decided to free the people from Safavid rule; the *jirga* of 1717 which decided to free Herat from the Persians and place it under the Abdali; the 1747 *Loya Jirga* (see below).

The *Loya Jirga* is the Pashtun highest office to decide on national and inter-tribal issues. The following *Loya Jirgas* are landmarks in Afghan history: the *Loya Jirga* of 1709 mentioned above, the *Loya Jirga* of 1747 as explained below, and the *Loya Jirgas* of nineteenth and twentieth centuries regarding responses to the British invaders (1839, 1879 and 1919). The *Loya Jirga* of 1923 adjudicated on Afghanistan's first constitution, and from 1923 onward the *Loya Jirga* became the supreme constitutional body in all the five constitutions that have been passed since. All-important national decisions concerning war and peace were taken or sanctioned by *Loya Jirgas* or Great Assemblies, representing all the people of the country. Since 1956 the *Loya Jirga* has officially been considered as *de dawlat ruken* or the pillar of the state. In the 1963 constitution *jirga* became part of the 'state apparatus' and since then has been an integral part of the Afghan constitution.

The *Loya Jirga* of 1747 was held at the request of Nur Mohammad Khan Alizai, Ahmad Khan's fellow commander in the service of Nader Shah, who proposed it soon after Nader Shah's assassination (Appendix 7). Nur Alizai emphasised to the troops the changing situation and the dangers that lay ahead, before they reached Kandahar. Alizai emphasised the need for unity and the election of a leader to represent them all.

> In this long journey we must have someone under whose orders we should conduct ourselves. Without a supreme chief it is very difficult, nay impossible, to reach Kandahar with the entire body of our troops, followers and dependants in the face of danger from the Qizzelbashes. Let us, therefore, make an effort to appoint a chief to face whatever may happen before we get to our destination'.
> (Ganda Singh 1959: 25, quoting from Abdul-Hasan Gulistani's book, *Majma'ol Tawarikh*)

The troops, Abdali, Ghilzai and a small Uzbek contingent, seeing the danger facing them all, accepted Nur Alizai's proposals and under his leadership left for Kandahar. On the way to Kandahar they invited the elders of tribes and ethnic groups for a *jirga* that was to elect an Afghan king. That *jirga*, a landmark in modern Afghan history, was held 'inside the military garrison of Nader Shah's troops, in Shair-e-Surkh,[10] in October 1747' (Wajdi 1986: 83). In addition to most Pashtun sub-tribes belonging to the Abdali and Ghilzai tribal confederacies, the *jirga* was also attended by other minorities such as Uzbek, Tajik, Baluch, Shi'ah Hazarah and Qizelbash. However, those who spoke with authority and wanted to be considered for the post of the king of Afghanistan were Pashtuns. Every participant tribal elder wanted to become king. They would get up and speak for hours on the importance of their tribe and their personal suitability for the post. 'For a time it appeared that Pushtoon nationalism would be wrecked by tribal jealousies, since each of the chiefs was willing to advance his own candidacy but unwilling to support another' (Fletcher 1965: 42). Ahmad Khan was the only delegate in the meeting who did not speak, but attended every day's *jirga*. It is because of such rivalries and differences that the meeting lasted nine days. The clear favourite appeared to be a Haji Jamal Khan of Mohammadzai, a sub-tribe of Abdali. Then on the ninth day, a holy man brought the *jirga* to an end. Pashtuns believe in holy men and saints. So it was not surprising when a holy man, Sabir Shah-e-Kabuli (from Kabul), who had many followers in Kandahar, rose and said,

> 'Why all this verbose talk? God has created Ahmad Khan, a much greater man than any of you; his is the noblest of all the Afghan families. Maintain, therefore, God's works, for his wrath will sway heavily upon you if you destroy it' no one objected.
> (Ferrier 1858: 68–9; Malleson 1879: 273–4; Ghubar 1944: 82; Ganda Singh 1959: 25–6; Misdaq 1997: 53)

Haji Jamal Khan who knew of the long line of chiefs and rulers of Sadozai, although he had already secured some of the votes, put his weight behind Ahmad Khan Sadozai and was amongst the first to accept him as the leader. All other prominent chiefs followed.

'The selection of Ahmad Khan was undoubtedly due to the relative weakness of his own tribe' (Fletcher 1965: 43). One thing which gave some of the contenders hope was, that since the Sadozai, after Gorgin's massacres and their forcible exile, had been reduced in numbers in Kandahar, they were regarded as no challenge to other numerous and more powerful tribes (Appendix 5). They thought that in time it would be possible to replace Ahmad Khan by one of them. But Ahmad Khan, as an Abdali, came from a long line of chiefs and rulers. The personality and experience of Ahmad Shah more than compensated for the relative numerical weakness of his tribe in the Kandahar region. His forefather, Saddo, was an ambassador of Shah Abbas the Great (1588–1624). Sados' son, Khoja Khizer, a dervish and *sufi* was a national saint of the Pashtuns in Kandahar region. Ahmad Shah's grandfather Dawlat Khan, his father Zaman Khan and even his elder brother Zulfiqar had all left myth-like marks on Afghan national history. Ahmad Khan was imprisoned at the age of ten for six years together with his brother; for nearly a decade he was in the service of the Persian king Nader Shah, taking part in diplomacy and military expeditions. He was felt to be most suited to the job (Appendix 6).

Ahmad Khan as king: final attempt to form the state

After his selection as the king, Ahmad Khan, in the tradition of Pashtun humility, is said to have pleaded his incompetence for the job and stressed the difficulty of forming a state apparatus and an army from nothing. But the holy man, Sabir Shah, seeing that his candidate was acceptable to the *jirga*, is said to have raised an earthen platform saying, 'this is the throne of your kingdom' and platting some wheatsheaf together placed it on his turban saying, 'and may this serve as the aigrette of your crown'. The holy man then said, 'now you are Badshah Durr-i-Durran, king, the pearl of the age (Malleson 1879: 273–5; Ferrier 1858: 68–9). Ahmad Khan, now Ahmad Shah, presumably feeling this to be a rather pompous title, changed it to Ahmad Shah Durrani, thus not long after also altering the name of his Sadozai clan, to Durrani.[11] The term *shah* is king in Farsi. Most Pashtuns including Ahmad Shah took this title with some of its related trappings, though rejecting Persian rule and the aloofness of their kings from the people.

Declaration of independence

Soon after his emergency coronation, Ahmad Shah called a meeting of the tribal leaders and chiefs, and without any voice of dissent, they all agreed to sever relations with Persia and to declare Afghanistan an independent state. After this Ahmad Shah nominated a *meli shora*, a National Council, of the nine most powerful tribal chiefs, who he consulted throughout his twenty-six years' reign on matters of national importance (Singh 1959: 33, 34). This on the one hand kept him in touch with tribal wishes, as had Mir Wais's ad hoc *jirgas* with the tribal elders, and on the other served as an outlet for these chiefs, by bringing them into the decision making. He then selected his cabinet, appointing well known soldiers to high offices and giving them precedence over the wealthy and large jagirs (landholders) some of whom were already in the National Council (Wajdi 1986: 84). He also asked Jahan Khan, his minister of war and *sipah-saular* or commander-in-chief, to enrol those troops who had come with them from Persia into the army. Ahmad Shah then set out to form the rest of the army from amongst the tribes using the existing tribal mechanism of raising lashkar or army, by asking for one fighting man out of ten to join his forces. Ahmad Shah, like other Pashtun rulers before him from Shir Shah Suri to Mir Wais and his descendants, governed as primus inter pares, 'first amongst equals', with the emphasis on equal. While taking part in *jirgas*, all these kings used to come down from their thrones and take their place in the round circle, where the concept of lower and higher position does not come into question.

Back in Kandahar in those days of public holidays and celebrations, a large caravan of camels with goods, and aggregate taxation from the provinces of the Punjab, Peshawar, and Kabul, on its way to Mashhad to the already assassinated Nader Shah, was reported to be arriving. Ahmad Shah took possession of this caravan and suddenly was in a position to pay the troops and also distribute the gifts amongst the guests and elders who were attending the independence celebrations (Ghubar 1944: 189–202).

Ahmad Shah: from king to emperor

During his reign of twenty-six years, Ahmad Shah headed more than fifteen expeditions in all directions from Kandahar, reclaiming back all the lands that the Afghan believed belonged to them (Herawi 1969: 2). He invaded eastern India eight times, conquering the area up to and including Delhi.[12] Ahmad Shah felt that most of western India was part of the previous Afghan Sultanate. He also believed that Afghans, having helped to take Islam to the subcontinent, had millions of supporters there. It was at the invitation of the local Rohilkand Pashtuns and other Muslims, who felt threatened by the majority Hindus, that Ahmad Shah time and again was called on to save them from these idolaters. The Naqshbandi (a Sufi order of Islam) theologian, Shah Waliullah, was one such person of great influence to urge the Durrani King to intervene in Indian affairs for the sake of Islam.

> Ahmad Shah declared a holy war (*jihad*) against the *kuffar* (unbelievers) of Hind, in case the Marathas and Sikhs, who had dared to build their temples even in Delhi in the centre of the *dar ul-Islam*, the house of Islam. Performing his religious duty, the Durrani had, immediately

on his arrival in the Moghul capital, raised these symbols of idolatry to the ground.

(Gomman 1995: 56)

One of Ahmad Shah's most decisive battles in India was the battle of Panipat 1761, fought against the Jats and Mahrattas. These two were a growing power, capturing some Muslim towns and threatening others. The crunch came when the Mahrattas chief Raghunath Rao deposed Ahmad Shah's eleven-year-old son, Timur Mirza, and his advisor, Jehan Khan, from Lahore. After taking that city they turned on Delhi and deposed the Afghan viceroy, Najibu Dullah, the ruler of Rohilkand and the Moghul Nawab (governor) of Oudh. The Mahrattas 'had changed greatly from their ways as simple bandits ... (to then forming) a powerful and aggressive state under the rule of the Peshwas, their King' (Fletcher 1965: 49). As India was ruled on and off for some seven centuries by the Muslims, they were perturbed by the ever increasing strength of the Jats and Mahrattas. Ahmad Shah gathered his forces from Sind and Kandahar and together with local Muslim forces, surrounded the Mahrattas for days in Panipat, cutting their supply lines leading to great losses on both sides.[13]

Ahmad Shah also made a number of expeditions to Persia taking the disputed province of Khorasan, up to Kerman, to which the Afghans had always laid claim, while resisting pressure to launch attacks against the whole of Iran, as had his predecessors the Ghilzais. 'Ahmad Shah knew that the people of Iran were not kindly disposed towards Afghans because of the damages the Afghans had inflicted on them. The difference in religion was another major reason for the distrust. He therefore, considered it unwise to attempt to take on the whole of Iran' (Al-Afghani 1938: 48).

Before all these foreign expeditions, Ahmad Shah captured Ghazni, Kabul and Peshawar, which were still ruled by Nader Shah's appointees. He then sent forces to northern Afghanistan, bringing it under central control. Also in the north the Manchu Chinese, who occupied eastern Turkistan, threatened the Kazakhs who asked for Ahmad Shah's help. In 1763 Ahmad Shah wanted to raise a local army of Muslims to push the Chinese back, but this did not materialise. Five years later Ahmad Shah came with a strong army, liberating eastern Kazakh lands from the Manchu. Ahmad Shah's appointee of Bokhara, the 'Uzbek ruler Shah Murad Bi of Bokhara ... some sources claim ... also presented Ahmad Shah with Khirqa ... the Prophet Mohammad's cloak which was in possession of the Bokharan rulers. This present was generally believed to be an Uzbek acknowledgement of Durrani victory' (Wajdi 1989: 85–6, Gomman 1995: 65). The transfer of Khirqa was believed to have also been the transfer of the prophet's blessing to Kandahar, where it is one of the most important shrines of the city.

Ahmad Shah created a tradition of patrimonial rule not only in Afghanistan, but also over the remains of the old empires of the Safavids, the Moghuls and Chengisid/Shabani Uzbeks. In a detailed letter in 1760 to Mustafa III of the Ottoman Empire, Ahmad Shah accuses Nader Shah of tyranny, oppression and cruelty. He wrote:

> The people of Iran after three centuries of peace and tranquillity under the Safavids became decadent and lustful and that is probably why God sent Nader Shah who occupied Iran, India and Turkistan, overthrowing all their leaders and even extended his hand of oppression and injustice on Afghan tribes.
>
> (Jalali 1967: 8–9)

The same letter also talks about the decadence of the Moghuls and states why infidels everywhere rose to pose a threat to Islam. It was, according to him, due to the lack of strong and committed Muslim rulers in India, Turkistan and Iran that conditions of temporal government had fallen to such a low level. Ahmad Shah wrote that he would much prefer to become a *sufi* and devote himself to God had respected elders of his tribe not called upon him to lead them to safety and honour.

He always appointed a local dignitary back in his office with the understanding that revenue and matters of foreign policy were to be referred to the king himself. In the Punjab in 1753 when the ex-ruler, Muin-ul-Mulk, confirmed in his post by Ahmad Shah, died, one of his widows, Mughlani Begum, was appointed in his place.

On economic grounds, despite Afghanistan's strategic location, the Durranis never took full advantage of developing the ancient trade routes and thus insuring an income for the national treasury. 'The highly decentralised Durrani state was not actively involved in directing this more or less "informal empire", but it was certainly stimulated by it and it benefited from the increased opportunities for credit and taxation' (Gommans 1995: 45). This economic factor was of no great significance when most of the subcontinent and western Iran were paying their taxes to the Afghan treasury. But after Ahmad Shah, when most of these newly acquired lands were lost, the lack of sure income caused the developing political situation to deteriorate.

It was in the name of Islam and the past glories of Afghan and Muslim rulers that Ahmad Shah established the kingdom in Kandahar, turning it during his lifetime into an empire, which lasted for more than half a century. British historian Frazer-Tytler comments:

> Ahmad Shah Durrani has never been given a place among the great conquerors, and while such names as Timur-i-Lang, Mahmud of Ghazni, or Babur are familiar, few people could name the first King of the Afghans or describe his exploits. And yet Ahmad Shah Durrani was not only a great leader but possessed many other attributes of greatness. His arrival on the scene when both the Persian and Indian Empires were largely impotent was opportune, but it required genius

to seize this fortune and to weld so intractable a people as the Afghans into the semblance of a nation.

(1964: 64)

Ahmad Shah's empires stretched from the Oxus River in the north to the Arabian Sea in the south, the Ganges in the east to Khorasan in the west. Starting from almost nothing, when Afghanistan was under the rule of different well-established empires, it is a singular achievement by any standard.

State formation

The struggle that led to the formation of the Afghan state could be interpreted in many different ways. As we are talking about a Pashtun tribal confederacy, sharing the same genealogy, language and culture, the position of the ruler and ruled could be seen as one of patriarchy. Since patriarchy lies at the base of what Weber calls 'patrimonialism' then both Mir Wais's and Ahmad Shah Durrani's rule and authority could be explained as one of 'patrimonial authority'. Since they were both selected by the free choice of tribal elders to head the new states, as an extension of the tribe, no bureaucratic state procedure as Weber points out was present.

> In the pure type of traditional authority, the following features of a bureaucratic administrative staff are absent: (a) a clearly defined sphere of competence subject to impersonal rules, (b) a rational ordering of relations of superiority and inferiority, (c) a regular system of appointment and promotion on the basis of free contract, (d) technical training as a regular requirement, (e) fixed salaries, in the type case paid in money.
>
> (Weber 1947: 343)

These Afghan patrimonial states followed the pattern identified by Weber where 'the prince organises his political power over extrapatrimonial areas and political subjects – which is not discretionary and not enforced by physical coercion – just like the exercise of his patrimonial power' (Weber 1978: 1013).

Patrimonialism in the Afghan case was a relation of balance between the ruler and the ruled, as in a 'consensual community' (Weber 1978: 102). In the case of Ahmad Shah Durrani, this consensual relationship was also one of reciprocity. The tribes provided the troops, through the well-established tribal *lashkar* or army procedure and the king rewarded them with booties of the newly conquered lands in addition to their usual upkeep. The relationship between ruler and ruled was rooted in 'patriarchy', as the king was seen by all his Pashtun subjects like a father in a family. The king himself saw his position as 'first amongst equals'. Mir Wais even refused the title of king or amir. Both these first indigenous

Afghan rulers consulted the tribes through their representatives on all major state issues. This is quite different from the classical image of state and ruler, whether pharaonic Egyptians, imperial Romans or oriental Sultans (Weber 1978: 1013).

Richard Tapper in *Tribe and State*, accepting the monopoly of power and central control as the defining attributes of a state, nonetheless regards Afghanistan to have been a state because of its territorial frontiers, heterogeneity of its population, and central control, however limited (Tapper 1983: 10–11). Ahmad Shah Durrani's government exercised central control over internal and external affairs from its capital, Kandahar. The country included many non-Pashtun heterogeneous social and cultural groups, and although it was operating on a tribal basis, it recognised other ethnic groups as culturally, linguistically, and some even religiously, distinct. When his empire extended into Kerman and Khorasan in the west and the subcontinent in the east, he recognised the autonomy of these conquered people and nearly always appointed one of their own rulers back to his position, but to administer in the name of Durrani.

The reciprocal process between tribes and empires is described by Hager in this way:

> Tribes and empires are structurally complementary, just as the state and tribes are structurally dis-congruous. The career of empire is aggregation of tribal and state units to its imperial order and ideology, while the tribe obtains from empire the means to build up its own internal order and unity against the centrifugal forces that lineage and faction bring to a polity based on personal jurisdiction.
> (Hager 1983: 96)

Similarly, the Afghan state governed an 'empire of tribes' and buttressed tribal order in the localities. Also, in the eighteenth century, the aggregation of different ethnicities was effected by a state that represented a congruence and relative harmony of all the country's ethnic and cultural minorities with the ruling Pashtun majority. This is not to say that they all passively accepted being included within the political borders of the Durrani kingdom or empire. However, the predominance of the Pashtuns and their long struggle and desire for their own state was so overwhelming that they were in a position to dictate the form and content of their administration and presumed that to be good enough for all other social and cultural groups within their frontiers.

Borders demarcated the Afghan state, although borders were expanding. This expansion stopped after Ahmad Shah's reign and during his grandsons' quarrel over power, it began to contract. Within that territorial state lived ethnic communities who shared some cultural and historic congruence. The nation-state on the other hand arrived later in the 1880s as a result of Amir Abdur Rahman's (1880–1901) sixteen years of struggle, known in history as 'the Iron Amir', against rebellious autonomous tribes and other social groups. The drawing together and development of this political/territorial community led to a further consolidation of the Afghan identity, which I shall discuss further in the next chapter.

Conclusion

Present day Afghanistan at the turn of the eighteenth century was occupied by two regional empires, Safavid and Moghul, and the remnants of Chengizid Shabanid. The north of Afghanistan was populated by a number of small ethnic groups such as Uzbeks, Tajiks and Turkmans. These, like the majority of their kinsmen over the Oxus River, were often under the same rule. So we see no Afghan nationalist or Afghan liberation movement starting there against the Uzbek or Turkik rulers. On the other hand the east, the west and the south was predominantly occupied by the Pashtuns. It is amongst these Pashtuns that the struggle for tribal consolidation or statehood against the Moghuls and Safavids led to an initial successful attempt in 1709 and then to an independent state in 1747. Amongst the Pashtuns the first movements against the Moghuls started in the east.[14] The eastern Pashtuns' long familiarity with state and governing, especially in the subcontinent, came as no surprise when they started protracted struggles against the Moghuls. In western Afghanistan the Safavids' and their agents' approaches to the Pashtuns were revengeful, condescending and paternalistic. In tribal Afghanistan, where a man's worth was measured in terms of his honour, this behaviour of the Persians was greatly resented. Furthermore, their Shi'ah brand of Islam was considered extremist and heretical to mainstream Sunni orthodoxy. But Pashtuns had served in the armies of the Persian kings and emperors for over two millennia. Here too, they were used to the art of government, but unlike Persia, which has always been governed from a strong centre, the Pashtun tribes were not prepared to accept such a central monopoly of force. That is why decentralisation is an integral aspect of the Pashtun state. As Hobsbawm noticed, 'the people with the most powerful and lasting sense of what maybe called "tribal" ethnicity, not merely resist the imposition of a modern state, national or otherwise, but very commonly *any* state: as Pushtu speakers in and around Afghanistan [before 1747], the pre 1745 Scottish highlanders, the Atlas Berbers and others' (Hobsbawm 1990: 64). The Pashtun tribal ethnicity, as Hobsbawm put it, has a history of centuries of cohesiveness and consolidation. Everything that did not fit in with their view of tribal structure and social organisation was regarded as alien and resisted. Pashtuns time and again objected to foreign states and resisted being dominated by them. On the other hand they accepted danger in order to reach statehood and once this was achieved under Ahmad Shah, they clung to it, while still preserving a level of tribal autonomy. This in-built autonomy did not lend itself easily to being ruled over from a strong centre. Thus, in the Pashtun tribal belt, the state was a set of reciprocal relations between different tribal groups and the government. This follows Dupree's definition of 'a nation-state in the non-literate sense' as a set of 'special relationships between a central government and collection of tribal, ethnic, or linguistic ... groups within a set of boundaries' (Dupree 1980: 569). The group, or in the Afghan case the tribe, has its own mechanism of how to make itself or individuals within it responsive to the state.

In the following chapter, I take the long period of 1773–1973 to highlight periods of tension and upheavals that have relevance to events since the overthrow of the monarchy in 1973. We shall see that despite the stability of the state under Ahmad Shah, the centre became remarkably unstable and precarious, and yet the state for two and a half centuries, in one form or another, continued to operate.

2 State to nation: 1773–1973

> Every Pashtun imagines he is Alexander the Great and wants the world to admit it. The result is a constant struggle between cousin and cousin, brother and brother and quite often between father and son. This has proved his sole undoing through the ages. They have not succeeded in being a great nation because ... [he] would rather burn his own house than see his brother rule it.
>
> (Ghani Khan 1947)

Introduction

This chapter covers two centuries of Afghanistan's well-documented history, from the start of the reign of Timur Shah in 1773 to the end of the monarchy in 1973. My aim is not to present a detailed historical account, but to look at themes relevant to my argument, although in doing so an account of Afghan history is inevitable. Afghanistan, during its first one and a half centuries fits into the description of a segmentary state. It is only after the 1880s that it begins to turn into a 'unitary state'. Attempts in the 1960s to turn it into a modern constitutional 'nation-state' backfired, leading to the emergence of ethnic nationalists bent on secession (discussed in Chapters 7–8). Three main themes can be identified to account for two centuries of the Afghan monarchy:

1. The fragility of the state (especially in the first century and a half).
2. The attempts at modernisation after the 1880s.
3. The geo-political position of Afghanistan and its vulnerability to external forces.

The fragility of the Afghan state

The fragility of the state can be considered in terms of two historical periods: first, the volatile and unsettling years between the death of Ahmad Shah (1773) and Amir Abdur Rahman's coming to power in 1880;

and second, from the time of Abdur Rahman until the end of the monarchy in 1973. The latter period is also the time when different attempts were made to modernise the state.

The two centuries from 1773 to 1973 can also be characterised as follows: first, in the struggle between the Sadozai and Muhammadzai branches of the Durrani confederacy; and second, from the early 1820s (when the control of the state was transferred from the Sadozai to the Barakzai dynasty) to the end of the monarchy in 1973. During this second period three different Barakzai dynasties attempted to unite the country and to turn it into a nation-state. A major reason for this dynastic turmoil was the destabilising effect of problems connected with modernity.

Rivalry between Abdali (Durrani) confederacies

The rivalry and claim to the throne of Afghanistan by these two branches of the Abdali (the Sadozai-Popalzai and Muhammadzai-Barakzai alliances respectively) goes back to the time of Shah Abas the Great (1588–1624), when Ahmad Shah's great grandfather, Sado (nickname for Asadullah), was appointed as ambassador. Also, at the time of the 1747 *Loya Jirga*, Haji Jamal Khan withdrew his candidature in favour of Ahmad Khan (Singh 1959: 25–6). Most Muhammadzai in later years remarked of that historic *jirga*, with some justification, that in order to achieve national consensus, their great ancestor, Haji Jamal Khan conceded his and his clan's personal claim to power. Thus an unwritten alliance existed since 1747 between these two prominent Abdali (now named Durrani) clans. This alliance was nearly crippled by the murder of Payendah Khan, elder son of Haji Jamal Khan, in 1800, when he tried to replace the Sadozai ruler, Shah Zaman, who killed him for this plot. 'Afghanistan thus entered the nineteenth century a politically disunited, ethnically and religiously heterogeneous, tribal feudal state' (Tapper 1983: 14). After that, the Sadozai kings, partly owing to Muhammadzai manipulation and partly because of their own internal rivalries over the crown, went through a period of rapid turmoil (Mahmud, 1800–03; Shuja, 1803–09; Mahmud again, 1809–18). From 1818 to 1823 although the Popalzai were nominally on the throne, it was the Barakzai who were in control. But it was not until 1826 that internal differences over kingship could be sorted out amongst the Barakzai.[1] 'With the collapse of the dynasty of Ahmad Shah, Afghan nationhood came very nearly to an end ... At this, the nadir of Afghan fortune, a new leader rose to prominence. Surprisingly enough it was Dost Mohammad, the youngest of the Barakzai brothers' (Fletcher 1965: 70, 71). The civil war between 1818 and 1835, during Dost's first term, was threatening to tear the country apart. This continued during Dost's second term (1842–63) and it was only two weeks before his death in 1863, when Herat, the last major province not yet under central control was united with the rest of the country.

The Muhammadzai in the 1820s did not always maintain 'good relations among themselves ... but unlike the Sadozai they [were] able to produce a succession of able rulers to keep the country together' (Fraser-Tytler 1967: 71),[2] partly because the Muhammadzai and Barakzai in the three-quarters of a century of Sadozai rule had played a prominent role as generals, administrators and tribal chiefs.

The three years from 1823–26 were a transitional period from the Sadozai to Barakzai dynasty. The civil war since 1818 had been fought by claimants and counter-claimants for the throne, first between the twenty-three sons of Timur Shah, and second amongst the twenty-two Barakzai sons of Payendah Khan. The role of the Muhammadzai, after the blinding and killing of Wazir Fateh Khan, the eldest of the Barakzai brothers, 'with a cruelty so abominable that men still writhe at the telling of it' (Caroe 1965: 268), by Kamran the son of Mahmud Sadozai in 1818, led to an almost total breakdown of the alliance and the takeover by the Muhammadzai who had previously stood by Sadozai imperial rule. The reason why the Muhammadzai clashed so violently with the Sadozai was over Fateh Khan's own oversight. After seizing the treasure of Herat from Firozuddin Sadozai, the governor of Herat, when he was sent to see to the likely Persian attack, Fateh Khan 'then made an unforgivable mistake, by sending his younger brother Dost Mohammad to the harem of Firozuddin to search the women' (Fletcher 1965: 68–9). This reproach against the Sadozai violated Pashtun honour.

For a period of eight years after 1818, the Sadozai were put on the throne but in name alone. All decisions concerning the running of the state were in the hands of the Muhammadzai. In 1826, Dost Mohammad Khan (1826–39), as the first Muhammadzai ruler, transferred the throne from the Sadozai to his own clan. His first period of rule coincided with the first Anglo-Afghan war (1839–42) when the British brought the Sadozai Shuja from his retirement in India placing him on the throne in Kabul. Dost, in 1839, and to the Afghans' surprise, gave himself up to the British who pensioned him off to India. In the first Anglo-Afghan War when 4,500 officers and troops together with 12,000 camp followers were killed, the British decided to bring back Dost to pick up the pieces. Dost was succeeded by his third son, Sher Ali, who in his two terms of reign (1863–67 and 1869–79) was continuously chased by his father's brothers and their sons, culminating in the second Anglo-Afghan war (1879–81). It was in the 1880s that Abdur Rahman, the 'Iron Amir', effectively stopped these internal squabbles over the throne.

The segmentary state

This first century and a half of fragility and internal squabbles over sovereignty is typical of a segmentary state. In the previous chapter, Ahmad Shah's twenty-six-year rule was discussed in terms of Weber's theory of patrimony. Ralph Grillo, discussing Aiden Southall's account of segmentation in Alur society, points out that 'Southall did not, however, wish to confine application of the term to societies which had segmentary lineage systems. In his view, it was generalizable, and patrimonial states may frequently be described as "segmentary", in a slightly broader sense' (Grillo 1998: 33). The Afghan state is a typical segmentary state that does not easily lend itself to a system of centralised authority. Thus the turmoil and fragility are a reaction to central power wishing to impose rules of succession, administration and uniformity. However, it is through the mutual interest of segments, in this case tribes, clans and lineages, that alliances are frequently made and broken with those in power. So in a strong centre, like the period of Ahmad Shah, power is allowed to be concentrated at the centre, since its acceptance brings political benefits like uniting the tribes, prestige and security from outside attacks or encroachment. On economic grounds the benefits also included such issues as *wolja* (war-booties), grants of land and salaries for the duration of service and stability for trade and commerce. The chiefs, in this case the khans and the maliks under them, also benefit. The khans were given usufruct rights in land, and the maliks, in collecting taxes, benefited personally and also, by excusing some and lowering the rates for others, established their patron-client relationships. However, even when a central power or authority is accepted, it does not mean that its writ is established in the periphery. Only non-Pashtuns were expected to ask for the centre's intervention in disputes, settlements and tax matters. Pashtuns themselves preferred their traditional tribal ways of self-help and self-reliance even in raising an army. To go to the central government's courts for help would indicate weakness and thus make one vulnerable to future attacks and impingement by forces inside and outside the segment.

> The system of interstate relations ... was itself usually grounded in the same principles of patronage and clientage which governed the states internally, and was generally characterised by shifting alliances, changing allegiances, conquests, rebellions, and reconquests, in seemingly endless cycles. Consistent with this general environment, and contributing to it, was the 'segmentary' form that many of these states took.
> (Grillo 1998: 32)

The transition from a segmentary to a unitary state began with the 'Iron Amir', Abdur Rahman (1880–1901). Such a transition, according to Southall, occurs over an extended period. This extended period in the Afghan case was the 133 years between Ahmad Shah's election in 1747 and the Iron Amir's accession to the throne in 1880.

In the Afghan example the unitary state was imposed on a segmentary lineage-based tribal order that hardly worked. Only when steps were taken by a strong ruler, such as Abdur Rahman, to break the power of the tribes, the religious and ethnic sections referred to by the amir as 'those hundreds of petty chiefs, plunderers, robbers, and cut-throats who were the cause of everlasting trouble in Afghanistan...', was the creation of 'one grand community under one law and under one rule' made possible (Munshi vol. ii, 1900: 175ff.). The segmentary state that Abdur Rahman attempted to replace, was one where 'specialised political power [was] exercised within a pyramidal series of segments tied together at any one level by the oppositions between them at a higher level' (Southall 1956: 260).

Attempts at modernisation

Amir Abdur Rahman: the second Anglo–Afghan War (1879–81)

The defeat of the British army at Maiwand near Kandahar in 1879 was a devastating blow to the prestige of the British military. Some 1,130 soldiers lost their lives and all their heavy artillery fell into the hands of the Afghans. Subsequently, British forces occupied Kabul and Kandahar after the legendary twenty-three days' march of General Roberts. However, the defeat of the conqueror of Maiwand (Yaqob Khan) by Roberts left Afghanistan without an amir or leader. As so often in such cases, a religious leader, this time a Mullah Din Muhammad, known as Mullah Mushk Alam, the Fragrance of the Universe, and a tribal leader, Muhammad Jan Khan Wardag, appeared and mounted attacks on the British forces in Kabul. The British, having yet again suffered heavily, wanted to hand over the country to someone and leave. At this time, Abdur Rahman, who had spent twelve years in exile in Russia and had been given 200 fighting men by the Russians, crossed the Amu River, and joined with other Afghan forces in the north, preparing for an attack on Kabul. The Russians, having kept him for so long, naturally wanted their man in power. But as Abdur Rahman later conveyed in his memoirs, he was thankful to the Russians but would not allow his personal feelings to stand in the way of what was good for Afghanistan.

On the other hand, the British saw him as a strong leader and accepted his claim to the throne. Thus a treaty was signed in Shamali, north of Kabul, and the war officially ended on 21 April 1881. The British immediately started aiding Abdur Rahman so that he could bring the anarchical countryside under control.

> In 1880–81 alone he received 3,615,009 Indian rupees. The British also undertook to give him an annual subsidy of 1,200,000 rupees, with which he was to pay his troops and to strengthen the defences of Afghanistan's northwest frontier. By 1889, the Indian government had given him 74 guns, 25,000 breech loading rifles, 11,500 muzzle-loading rifles, and several million rounds of ammunition.
>
> (Gregorian 1969: 131)

After defeating the forces of his paternal cousin, Ayub Khan in Kandahar, Amir Abdur Rahman faced no further challenge from other royal claimants. With Abdur Rahman came a relative break with former practices of paternalism, tribal autonomy and entrenched leaderships. He is regarded as the founder of the Afghan 'nation-state' because he was successfully applying the same laws and regulations to all tribes and ethnic groups. The Amir, aware of the anarchical rule of his predecessors, recorded his consternation in his two-volume autobiography.

> Every priest, mullah and chief of every tribe and village considered himself an independent king, and for about 200 years past, the freedom and independence of many of these priests were never broken by their sovereigns. The Mirs of Turkistan, the Mirs of Hazarah, the chiefs of Ghilzai were all stronger than their Amirs.
> (Munshi vol. i, 1900: 217)

To turn Afghanistan from a tribal state into a unitary central state or nation, the amir passed proclamations, wrote pamphlets and spread his edicts through *jarchis* (town-criers) informing his subjects of their duties, first to the king and then to their country. Thus when faced with disobedience and uprisings he

> invoked the concept of divine right of kings; when threatened by the 'two Infidels (Russia and Britain, he taunted his subjects) ... the name of Afghans should not have been given you...' and if the country complained of high taxes or of his oppression he used a father-son relation to justify his actions, '... the kindness and compassion of the Kings towards his subjects resembles the feeling of a father towards his son...'; when he was faced by a strong tribe like the Ghilzai, he used 'the principle of *divide et impera*, exploiting the traditional rivalry of the Durranis and the Ghilzais to suppress a Ghilzai rebellion'; when faced with the Shi'ah mutiny, 'Abdur Rahman appealed to the orthodoxy and fanaticism of the Sunni Muslims' and when he wanted to subdue the Uzbek and Tajik principalities in the north, he would evoke 'memories of the former greatness of the Durrani empire to muster the support of the Afghan [Pashtun] tribes' and so on.
> (Gregorian 1969: 131–3)

Thus Abdur Rahman mounted campaigns for sixteen of his twenty-one years' reign and succeeded in creating the strong central power necessary for a nation-state or unitary state (see Table 2.1, p. 58 for list of campaigns).

Southall writes, 'the unitary state is a structure in which there is a central monopoly of power, exercised by a specialised administrative staff within defined territorial limits...' (Southall 1970: 260). Though Abdur Rahman ran his administration with the help of 'ten clerks', nevertheless

Table 2.1 Conquests of Abdur Rahman, the 'Iron Amir'

Name of tribal group/opponent or region	Dates
Ayub Khan and followers (Kandahar Pashtuns)	1881
Laghman (eastern Pashtun region)	1881
Taraki Ghilzai (south-western Pashtun region)	1881–82
Kunar (eastern Pashtun region)	1882
Wali of Maimana (northern Uzbek leader)	1882
Mir (Tajik leader) of Sheghnan and Roshan (N-E Badakhshan)	1882
Shinwari (eastern Pashtuns)	1882–92
Mangal of Zurmat (southern Pashtun region)	1883–84
Wali of Maimana (submitted without fighting)	1884
Laghman (eastern Pashtun region)	1885–86
Ghilzai (south-western Pashtuns)	1886–88
Mohammad Ishaq Khan (Pashtun royal claimant in the north)	1888
Safi (Pashtuns of Kunar-eastern region)	1888–96
Badakhshan (Tajik north-eastern region)	1889
Khan of Asmar (eastern Pashtun leader)	1890
Hazarajat (central Shi'ah region)	1891–93
Kafiristan (Nuristan, north-eastern region) converted to Islam	1895–96

he had his own version of a cabinet and parliament that he consulted. However much his subjects disliked the amir, he was the first king who succeeded in breaking the hold on power by tribes, saints and mullahs.

There has been a great deal of adverse publicity, especially in the post-Soviet withdrawal period by secessionist groups such as the Shi'ah Hazarah, the Tajik and the Uzbek, armed groups accusing the amir of taking the side of the Pashtuns at the expense of other ethnic groups. The Shi'ah *Hezb-i-Wahdat* and the small Tajik *Shura-i-Nezar* groups are the most vocal of such propaganda. As can be seen, most of his campaigns were against the Pashtuns and his punishment of the Safi, Shinwari and Ghilzai Pashtuns were severe and legendary. The amir, without any favour or prejudice, used his 147,400 troops and his extensive intelligence network to quell uprisings and to create a strong government and a viable nation-state.

Amir Abdur Rahman, as stated, is regarded as the founder of the Afghan 'nation-state'. A recent observer in a comparative work on the Amir's moral imperatives and the view that the Afghans have of him writes: 'As I began to recognize the distinctiveness of Abdur Rahman's moral station, I also became aware of the way in which his reign appeared to function as something of a divide in the people's minds, and one of the main reasons for this appears to have been his association with the founding of the nation-state' (Edwards 1996: 27). The amir, in creating a nation-state, had to subdue all rebellious Afghan tribal and ethnic groups. Not surprisingly, they hated the king for his uncompromising imposition of central authority. However, as an epitaph to his strong central rule, there was not a single major inter-tribal or ethnic war during his twenty-one-year reign. His drive for modernisation included the completion of the transitional cycle from a segmentary to a unitary state, the founding of a modern army, the employing of Europeans, exploiting the country's mineral resources, and devising plans to implement his internal and external policies.

Internal 'nationalisation' policy

Abdur Rahman, unlike his predecessors, did not appoint his sons or other royal family members as governors to provinces. In the long run this policy was successful, as after his death there was no scramble for the throne. Members of the royal household were kept in Kabul, sometimes to oversee government departments and to advise the king. The king also had two important consultative bodies, the Supreme Council, his equivalent of a modern cabinet, and the *Loya Jirga*, his version of a parliament. The Supreme Council members were religious leaders, heads of the various government bureaux and departments. Members of the *Loya Jirga* were the leaders of tribes, ethnic groups, certain members of the royal lineage and provincial religious leaders. He also established a network of spies as his intelligence service, to serve as his 'eyes and ears'. His European experts mined copper and iron with which he minted his currency. The establishment of his 'single monetary unit, the Kabuli rupee ... replaced a number of regional currencies that had been artificially inflated to equal the Kabuli rupee' (Munshi vol. i, 1900: 203). The Amir in his proclamations emphasised the 'Afghan' identity of his subjects (Gregorian 1969: 130). He abolished the *sar-mardeh* poll tax that was imposed on non-Pashtuns for not being in the army. Abdur Rahman was not going to relax on other taxes, as he needed these to run his government and to pay for his army. He was never satisfied with what he got.

> 'One quarter of the money which is rightly mine, I get without trouble; one quarter I get by fighting for it; one quarter I do not get at all; and those who ought to pay the fourth quarter do not know into whose hands they should place it'.
>
> (Munshi vol. i, 1900: 203)

He also transferred some 18,000 Ghilzai families from south-west to northern Afghanistan. This important move had several implications: first, to break the six-year long Ghilzai resistance to his rule; second, to ensure the safety of the northern border against Turkman raids and Russian incursions; and third, in his attempt to create a modern state, it was his way of encouraging assimilation. Later, the Durrani and other sub-tribes were also re-located in the north (Gregorian 1969: 133; Nancy Tapper 1983: 233–58).

Abdur Rahman's attempt at modernisation could best be described as what the French call 'nationalisation', meaning establishing a framework of national infrastructure, such as an army, roads, mines, intelligence and an administrative network. The amir, from his Russian experience, was interested in material progress and wanted to create the infrastructure to accommodate modernisation and to spur further progress.

The backbone of the amir's success in quelling uprisings and keeping peace and security was the formation of a modern army and intelligence network. He tried to treat all citizens as equal. He removed previous privileges from the royal clan and also from khans and maliks. He made sure all obeyed the same state laws. He gave freedom to his provincial governors to break down territorial claims by local tribes and ethnic groups and to stop tribal systems from operating alongside or in opposition to the state system. 'Any signs of discontent were immediately put down... Land was sold and resold without any regard to the traditional joint ownership of village lands by the clan or lineages. The army was on hand to seal such transactions, if necessary' (Dupree 1980: 420). The Iron Amir thus laid the foundations of the modern Afghan state.

However, the tribal system and its claim to tribal lands were never completely eradicated. People in the tribal areas, especially those near Kabul, faced with a strong ruler, his spies and his army, were pragmatic enough to go along with his wishes. After the amir's death, his son Habibullah adopted a moderate and conciliatory manner, allowing all those who were exiled, accused of rebellion against his father, to return to their villages. The tribes then also re-established their grip over their communal lands.

External policy

The external policies of Abdur Rahman in accordance with the treaty of Gandomak of 1876 were to a large extent in the hands of the British and there was little the Amir could do about it. He was constantly faced with the danger of Russian expansion from the north. According to Gandomak, the British took it upon themselves to speak on behalf of Afghanistan in international conferences and, most importantly, to delineate Afghan borders with all three of its neighbours, Iran, Russia and British India. Apart from the border (north of Sistan) with Iran, which was to the equal dissatisfaction of both countries, the borders with Russia and Britain were to the detriment of Afghanistan. The Russians took thousands of square kilometres of land in Punjdeh (1873) and Wakhan (1891),[3] and with British India came the demarcation of the Durand Line (1893), which split most Pashtun tribes. The Durand Line was at first regarded as 'a line' separating the 'sphere of influences' of the two countries but was later turned into a 'boundary'. Of all the borders, it was the Durand Line that Afghans especially objected to, and questioned its legal validity, as the treaty is considered to have been signed 'under duress' between two unequal partners. The legal invalidity of this treaty was particularly underlined as Afghans argued that a treaty signed between them and the British government (1893 and 1923) could not be transferred to a third country, Pakistan, which came into being in 1947 and was not the inheritor of British India. Of the two newly created states (India and Pakistan), India is in a better position to be the inheritor of imperial Britain, because she took over British assets and accepted that country's legal and international obligations.

The Durand Line has become a bone of contention between Afghanistan and Pakistan regarding the irredentism of Pashtunistan, the land of the Pashtuns. Abdur Rahman in his autobiography repeatedly stated that he never considered any Pashtun areas as permanently ceded to the British. Even Sir Mortimer Durand, the foreign secretary in India who drew the 'line', did not anticipate annexation. 'Durand ... did not propose to move forward the administrative border of India, but merely pushed for political control' (Sykes 1926: 219).[4]

The Iron Amir is rare amongst Afghan kings in that he died a natural death, in bed, after having ruled for twenty-one years. It is also to his credit that after his death, there were no skirmishes between contenders to the throne. His son Habibullah (1901–19) whom he had groomed for succession took over from him. While Abdur Rahman was not successful in encouraging modern education, foreign trade and banking, these were to be achieved to a certain extent by his son and grandson Amanullah. The Iron Amir himself saw some of these shortcomings that he left to his offspring:

> I hope and pray that if I do not succeed in my lifetime in the great desire for making railways, introducing telegraph and steamers, working the mines, opening banks, issuing banknotes, inviting travellers and capitalists from all parts of the world, opening universities and other institutions in Afghanistan, my sons and successors will carry out these desires of my heart and make Afghanistan what I desire it to become.
>
> (Munshi vol. ii, 1900: 173, 212–13)[5]

Habibullah, like his father, continued the drive for modernisation by strengthening central authority in maintaining the efficacy of the army. He founded the country's first military college (Harbiah), and also the first high school (Habibiah), after his name, on the pattern of a French lycée. This was to become the founding of the Afghan public school system developed in the years to come. He started a bi-monthly paper, *Seraj-ul Akhbar*, which also served as an important source of inspiration for Indian nationalists who smuggled and distributed its anti-British articles in India. Furthermore, he established the country's first printing press. Habibullah also employed many Western technicians and built a hydroelectric power station to provide electricity to his palace and some parts of Kabul. He extended roads and built *rabats*, the equivalent of today's motels, to ease communication amongst different peoples of the country. Another of Habibullah's important achievements was the readmission of most of the tribal and ethnic leaders, who in wars with his father had been exiled or had fled the country. Thus, most Hazarah Shi'ah who had taken shelter in Iran or Baluchestan returned home. Also, Mahmud Tarzi, whose family had spent twenty-two years in Syria, came back and became the closest friend of the king. It was he who translated Jules Verne's adventures for the king, who was a fan of Verne, and also it was Tarzi who started the bi-monthly *Seraj-ul Akhbar* paper and ran it for seven years. Tarzi's daughter was married to Amanullah and this pioneer of journalism was to play a decisive role in the reigns of both the son and grandson of the Iron Amir.

Amanullah the Great Reformer: 1919–29

Habibullah, upon embarking on a hunting expedition, left his third son Amanullah in charge of the treasury in Kabul. The amir was murdered on that fatal hunting trip and his murderer was never found.[6] Once again only one of his sons, Amanullah, assumed power and there was no serious attempt within the royal family to challenge him. Although initially Amanullah's elder brother and his father's brother expressed an interest in becoming king, Amanullah's energy and political awareness soon proved too difficult for them to challenge. In a public meeting on 18 February 1919, Amanullah gave a stirring speech in which he vowed to bring the murderers of his father to justice. At this meeting, he also doubled the salaries of the troops, believing in the key role of the army, like his father and grandfather before him. Amanullah had been the leader of the *mashrutah khahan*, reformist movement, at the court since World War One. He was privately educated, well informed about Western culture and married to the half-Syrian daughter of Mahmud Beg Tarzi. The attractive and well-educated queen had much influence over this twenty-nine-year-old king. At his coronation (1 March 1919) the king 'announced three goals: complete Afghan independence, the punishment of his father's murderers, and the abolition of *begeer*, literally "to seize", a kind of forced labour resembling the medieval corvee and much practised by landlords in territories not inhabited by Pashtuns' (Fletcher 1965: 187). Two days later he wrote to the British, who were monitoring his speeches, of his accession and the willingness of the 'independent and free' government of Afghanistan to conclude agreements of a commercial nature with Britain.

Amanullah started by reforming the royal family. Up until his time, most members of the royal family would hold their own *darbars*, or courts, and any person with a complaint could go to them. Worse still, if someone was not successful at one, he might go to another until he obtained the favours he wanted. Amanullah asked Tarzi to reform this system and

Tarzi, using the Ottoman model, created the modern cabinet in which he was the foreign minister and Abdul Qodus the prime minister. The different ministries took over what previously was done in the *darbars* and much more besides.

Three more foreign language colleges were founded: *Isteqlal Lycée*, a French-language high school staffed by French teachers in 1923; Nejat, a German language college mostly staffed by Germans, in 1924; and *Ghazi*, an English language college with English staff in 1928. The king sent many graduates of these colleges as well as some officials in the government abroad for further education.

Amanullah's imposition of a war on the British in 1919 to force them to relinquish responsibility for Afghanistan's foreign affairs and the subsequent British recognition of Afghanistan as an independent state made Amanullah a hero for many Muslims. The Islamic world at this time was looking for a new Caliph, as Mustafa Kemal in Turkey had overthrown the last Ottoman Caliph in March of 1924. In India the Khalifate Party, which wanted to settle Muslims in Islamic states, was also gathering momentum. In 1920 several thousand Indian Muslims were encouraged to sell their property and to go on *hijrat*[7] to Afghanistan. Amanullah, who had seen the collapse of the *khilafat* in Turkey, had the ambition to declare Afghanistan as the land of the caliph or *khilafat* and was at first willing to receive these Muslims. It later dawned on him, however, that a small country like Afghanistan could not house the hundreds of millions of Muslims in the subcontinent. Eventually the *muhajir*, or immigrants, had to return to India at great personal cost.

Amanullah's greatest challenge to conservative Afghan society was the introduction of co-education and the attempt to remove the veil from women and to ask all Afghans in Kabul to wear Western clothes.[8] Amanullah's sister and wife were also active in women's projects, establishing *mo's-esah naswan*, the Women's Institute. The king also instituted the education of the country's two million or so nomads and sent a limited number of teachers to follow the larger groups and to teach them literacy. The king called for a *Loya Jirga* in 1923 to approve his first constitution for Afghanistan, in which the power of the religious establishment was curtailed and women were not required to wear the veil. The *Loya Jirga* of a thousand representatives rejected these as contrary to the injunctions of Islam and Afghan tradition. The king, however, determined to see it through, later asked about one hundred of those representatives who were in favour of the reform to sign the constitution.

Four years later, against the advice of his close associates, the king embarked on a visit to major Muslim and European capitals, Moscow and Delhi. No other Afghan ruler had undertaken such a diplomatic mission before. The tour started in December 1927 and lasted till July 1928. On this tour, diplomatic treaties with Poland, Latvia, Finland, Switzerland, Liberia, Egypt and Japan were signed and the king met with heads of states in Persia, Turkey, India and Egypt, and with government leaders in Rome, Paris, London, Brussels, Bern, Berlin, Warsaw and Moscow.

The king also met with Mustafa Kemal (also known as Attaturk), who was familiar with the radical Muslim ruler's reforms. 'Attaturk warned Amanullah not to start large-scale social and political reforms until he had a strong, well-trained army, and promised to send some of his best officers to train the Afghans' (Dupree 1980: 451). On his return, Mahmud Tarzi, the champion of reform and many other close friends and family members who knew of the adverse propaganda mounted against the royal couple amongst the tribes, asked Amanullah to take Attaturk's advice. Amanullah, full of new ideas and enthusiasm, 'rushed headlong into his disorganised plans to change Afghanistan from a collection of ethnic groups and tribes into the outward appearance of modern nationhood' (Dupree 1980: 452). Thus his efforts to build a modern nation abruptly came to an end. Amanullah regarded the technological progress of the West, but did not appreciate that this advancement was based on long-term economic and social developments, while his reforms of a social and cultural nature needed time, a sound economic and educative basis, and the support of the populace if they were to be realised.

Revolt at home

While the king was on his foreign tour, a revolt broke out in the Khost region of Paktia headed by two *mullahs*, Abdullah (known as Mullah-i-Lang, the limping mullah), and Abdul Rashid. Both were against Amanullah's modernisation plans and when speaking to the public they would hold Amanullah's *nezam-namah* (constitution) in one hand and the Quran in another, asking the audience, 'do you accept the Book of Allah or the *nezam-namah* of Amanullah?' Additionally, the son of the conqueror of Maiwand,[9] Abdul Karim, having sensed the discontent against the king came from India to lay claim to the throne. Karim was unsuccessful, however, in his dynastic assertions, as no tribe would come to his aid. Amanullah's forces also arrested Mullah-i-Lang, and had him executed in Kabul. Successfully averting both these hostile forces, however, did not end opposition to Amanullah. The British, who disliked Amanullah for his fiery anti-British speeches and the war in 1919, spread photographs of Amanullah's queen amongst the tribes, showing her without a veil amongst the *farangis* (foreigners). Rumours were rife that Amanullah had become an infidel or that the couple had been swapped for non-Afghan look-alikes and so forth.

The first major challenge to the king came from the eastern Pashtun tribe of Shinwari. While the king sent his troops to quell them, some defected joining the tribal *lashkar* against him. Meanwhile a bandit with military experience, Habibullah, known as Bachai Saqaw (son of a water carrier) attacked Kabul, forcing the king to flee in his Rolls Royce to Kandahar. From Kandahar the king organised another army that was easily defeated in Ghazni by the Ghilzai. Subsequently, Bachai Saqaw held Kabul for over nine months (January–October 1929).

The Tajik Bachai Saqaw from Kohistan north of Kabul was attracted originally by the high pay for the soldiers and this was the reason he enrolled in the army of Amanullah. He was illiterate, not a dutiful or submissive soldier and was time and again punished for disobedience in the army. He eventually decided to escape to Peshawar 'where he operated a teahouse as a front for smuggling, disposing of stolen property, and a variety of other, equally illegal activities. Returning to Afghanistan in 1928, he gathered a band of followers ... and became the scourge of the caravan routes across the Hindu Kush' before he took control of Kabul (Fletcher 1965: 217). The Pashtuns, who had been in power since 1747, 'especially resented the usurpation of the throne by a non-Afghan [non-Pashtun], a lowly and illiterate Tajik bandit' (Gregorian 1969: 280). With the government treasury depleted and the mines idle, Bachai Saqaw started to print his money on leather, which no one took seriously. The country was going through another civil war, however brief, and its new ruler was finding it difficult to raise money. He therefore:

> reverted to another familiar practice, extortion, forcing the well-to-do merchants and citizens of Kabul to contribute to his treasury ... according to Morrish: 'for months life in Kabul was terrible. None was safe, houses were pillaged indiscriminately, women were ravished, and a reign of terror was established unprecedented in the annals of Bloody Afghan History'. Outside the city Bachai selected members of his clan to act as informers ... to compile reports on the approximate wealth of citizens ... and the income of the prospective victims.
> (Gregorian 1969: 281)

Despite the utter abhorrence of most Pashtuns and inhabitants of the urban areas, there was no national leader to confront Bachai Saqaw and his supporters. When three out of the five Musaheban (lineage name, meaning equerry) brothers, headed by the former General Nadir Khan (who Amanullah had posted as ambassador to Paris) returned to Afghanistan in February 1929, they provided the necessary leadership. Nader Khan, having gathered together his tribal army, had to cancel plans of attacking Kabul twice because of infighting that had developed amongst his tribal forces. His brother Shah Wali, spent seven months in Zazi,[10] and his other brother Shah Mahmud with other tribes in Paktia managed to organise a tribal army from amongst the tribes of Paktia (Zazi,[11] Mangal, Zadran, Ahmadzai, Tota Khel Wazir and Darwish Khel Wazir) and then attacked Kabul, driving Bachai Saqaw and his followers back to Kohistan. Bachai Saqaw was at first given clemency but was later executed along with his seventeen lieutenants.[12] Nader Khan who arrived in Kabul two weeks after its capture (17 October) was selected, by a *jirga* of those tribal representatives who had re-captured Kabul, as the 'King of Afghanistan'.

Nader Shah: 1929–33

Nader Shah's (then known as Nader Khan) first act was to dissociate himself from Amanullah's modernisation plans and, unlike the ex-king, he gave the mullahs, *sufis* and the religious constituency a prominent role in his administration. The British, always wary of chaos on their borders, stepped in to aid Nader Khan in curbing the ongoing civil war just as they had helped the Iron Amir by providing financial and military aid. This consisted of 10,000 rifles, five million cartridges and £170,000 in cash. Many Afghans, who were suspicious of British meddling in their affairs, believed that the Musaheban brothers must have come to power with the blessing of the British and used this aid as a proof. Some people were also disappointed with Nader Khan for not recalling Amanullah to resume power. Most of the tribes who fought for the restoration of the monarchy had been under the impression that the Musaheban brothers, as a prominent family at the court of Habibullah and Amanullah, and with Nader Khan being one of Amanullah's generals and ambassadors, were fighting to restore power to King Amanullah. The Shinwari tribe who revolted against Amanullah and were the main cause of his overthrow, revolted again in May 1930, this time against Nader Khan and in support of Amanullah, saying that their previous revolt was 'not so much anti-Amanullah as against the local tax-collectors at Jelalabad ... the Kohistani Tajik, led by Purdel, revolted in July 1930', but the latter were once again put down by the Pashtuns (Dupree 1980: 460). Nader Khan knew the sentiments of the tribes, and was perturbed by these revolts. He called another *Loya Jirga* in September 1930, which again proclaimed him king (Frazer-Tytler 1967: 227).

Nader Khan followed a laissez-faire political course and wanted to be on good terms with both Britain and the Soviet Union. The Central Asian freedom fighters, that the Russians termed *basmachi*, thieves, lost a supporter when Amanullah was gone. There were close to a million of these rebels who had sought refuge in Afghanistan. The military wing of the *basmachi* was headed by one of their leaders called Ibrahim Beg. Their forces would attack the Russians, and then take refuge in Afghanistan. On one occasion the Russian troops entered Afghanistan for some forty miles in 'hot pursuit' of the *basmachi*. Nader Khan, who was careful not to provoke the Russians, sent his younger brother Shah Mahmud to impress on the foreign fighters that they must not endanger their host country. Shah Mahmud, having failed to disarm or disperse the *basmachis* from near the Russian border, chased Ibrahim Beg over the border into the hands of his enemies who executed him in April 1931 (Frazer-Tytler 1967: 230).

In 1931, Nader Shah wrote another constitution, amending the articles regarding women's emancipation and co-education. This constitution was,

> a hodgepodge of unworkable elements. Extracts from the Turkish, Iranian and French constitutions and the 1923 Constitution of Amanullah ... The 1931 constitution only partly suited the Afghan character ... described as tribal, authoritarian, patrilineal.
>
> (Dupree 1980: 464–9)

In 1933, Nader Khan and his elder brother were killed in revenge for the killing of Ghulam Nabi Charkhi. The Charkhis, like the Musaheban, were a prominent family, serving as generals and ambassadors at the court of Abdur Rahman, Habibullah and Amanullah. The Charkhis regarded the Musaheban as usurpers and it was this difference that sparked the feud between the two. After Nader Khan's assassination, the deceased king's twenty-year-old son, Mohammad Zaher, was put on the throne by his paternal uncle Shah Mahmud. But for the next thirty years the king's two uncles Hashem Khan (1929–46) and Shah Mahmud (1946–53) himself ran the country followed by his paternal cousin and brother-in-law Mohammad Daoud (1953–63) as prime ministers. During these three decades, apart from the *wish zalmian*, the 'awakened youth', an intellectual movement on the pattern of the Young Turks, there were no significant reforms or innovative initiatives on a national level.

Hashem Khan died in office (1946) and his nephew Daoud replaced his brother in a palace intrigue in 1953. Daoud himself was dismissed in 1963 by the king for dragging Afghanistan to the brink of war with Pakistan over the 'Pashtunistan' issue. It was only in 1963 that King Zaher Shah, once all his ambitious elders had died, took control of the country. A new and democratic constitution was passed in 1964, which transformed the traditional absolute and authoritarian monarchy into a constitutional monarchy on the European model, defining and limiting the role of the royal family. The period between 1963 and the end of monarchy in 1973 are known as the 'decade of constitution'. A fuller discussion of this decade will be presented in Chapters 3 and 4.

The geopolitical position of Afghanistan: its vulnerability to external forces

> Ptolemy, and other geographers of the ancient world applied the name 'Aryana' to what is now Afghanistan ... Kabul according to one source figures in history as early as 2000 BC ... and the oldest Iranian chronicles record Turanian (Scythian) races as the inhabitants of west and north [Durrani land] of Helmand River.
>
> (Wilber 1962: 11)

68 A state in the making

The Greek historian Herodotus (b. 490–80 BC) records the provinces of 'Pactuike' Paktia and 'Pactyca' Paktika and its Pashtun inhabitants (Herodotus 1966: 439). Thus Afghanistan's geo-political position can be traced through the centuries. The aim here is not to account for over four millennia of recorded history but to discuss the actions of the two imperial powers, Russia and Britain, in the nineteenth century, as they sandwiched Afghanistan between them. To understand this, we have to briefly review British and Russian policies regarding Afghanistan (see Map 5).

In the nineteenth century, Britain and Russia each regarded the other as a threat to their respective imperial designs. The British, after establishing themselves as the East Indian Trading Company on the coast of Madras (1752), slowly worked their way north and east-wards, occupying Delhi and the Punjab in about a century (see Appendix 8). Russia too, starting from the steppes of the north, rapidly took one Khanate after another approaching the northern borders of Afghanistan by the late nineteenth century. Bolshevik forces occupied the Kingdom of Bokhara in 1920 (see Appendix 9 and Map 5).

The Russians in a circular despatch of 1864, known as the Gortchakow's Circular, had set Sir Darya and Issyk Kul Lake as the limit of their expansion. In later years when Britain pointed to this self imposed limit of the Russians, they would refer to the Memorandum of 5 April 1875, saying that 'the Tsar had never entered into an engagement with any power binding him to a policy of non-aggression' (Ghose 1960: 25). Their argument for new lands and the policy approach as explained continued. Thus Afghanistan and its eastern possessions, as well as Punjdeh and Zulfiqar in the north fell to these Russo-British ambitions. Britain also designed to colonise Afghanistan in order to get even closer to the Russians. However, when they realised that the Afghans were by and large unwilling to comply, they decided to declare it as a 'buffer state', or as stated in the 1907 Convention of St Petersburg, a free and independent country, agreeing not to interfere in its internal affairs. A promise neither was serious to keep. The British went to war with Afghanistan in 1919 and as Russian interest led to the Soviet invasion, the consequences of which forms a major part of this work, a brief review of this contact is pertinent to the later discussion.

In 1885 the Russians occupied the Afghan Punjdeh in northwest Afghanistan. The Afghan king, Amir Abdur Rahman, on an official visit to British India, was in Lahore at the time and requested military help from Britain, but was assured that the Russians did not intend to cross the river, implying that Punjdeh should be considered to have been annexed. In 1896 Britain and Russia signed a treaty making the Amu River the official border between Afghanistan and Tsarist Russia. The 1907 Convention of St Petersburg followed this a few years later, when both Britain and Russia agreed not to occupy or annex any part of Afghanistan, nor to interfere in the internal affairs of that country (Amastutz 1986: 9). The British however, were determined not to relinquish their hold on Afghanistan's foreign policy. On the Afghan side, the twenty-nine-year-old King Amanullah declared Afghanistan free from British diplomatic over-lordship in 1919, sending troops over the border to the North West Frontier Province (NWFP) in the Kurem valley, thus provoking the third Anglo-Afghan war (May–June 1919). After a short war, Amanullah won back control of Afghan foreign affairs. But it was during the ten years of his reign that Afghanistan grew closer to the new Soviet Socialist Republics, which were also the first states to recognise its independence. In November 1919, Lenin wrote to Amanullah:

> The workers and peasants government instructs its embassy in Afghanistan to engage in discussions with the view to the conclusion of trade and other friendly agreements ... is inclined to grant such assistance on the widest scale to the Afghan nation, and to repair the injustice done by the former government of the Czars ... by adjusting the Soviet-Afghan frontier so as to add to the territory of Afghanistan at the expense of Russia.
> (Carr 1953: 238–9, vol. 3; Amastutz 1986: 11)

This was taken to mean the return of Punjdeh and Zulfiqar, as those were the parts of Afghanistan which the Russians had taken by force. However, this promise made by the founder of the Soviet state and brought to the attention of successive Soviet governments, was never honoured. On the other hand, Soviet aid in military and economic developments in the years following this initial contact grew out of all proportions.

In 1921, the Afghan-Soviet Treaty, the first international treaty that country signed after its revolution of 1917, dealt with trade rights and the promise of one million annual gold bars to Afghanistan. Other aid, such as eleven military aeroplanes and Soviet engineers to build roads, telegraph and telephone lines followed. Trade between the two countries steadily grew and the Soviet share of Afghanistan's foreign trade increased from 7 per cent in 1924–25 to 17 per cent in 1933–34; and from 24 per cent in 1938–39 to 79 per cent in the 1980s (Gregorian 1969: 333; Adamec 1967: 214, 245; Rubin 1995: 160–3).

The Afghan authorities in their contact with the Russians never forgot the advice of the Iron Amir, Abdur Rahman, who had spent twelve years in exile in Russian Central Asia because of a family squabble over the throne: 'My advice to you my heirs and descendants is never to trust the Russians'. This explains why Afghanistan in the nineteenth century repeatedly turned to Britain for aid (which rarely materialised) against the Russian encroachment. After the Second World War, when the United States replaced Britain as a world power, the Afghans requested economic and military aid from the Americans against the growing communist influence in the region as well as inside Afghanistan. However, the United States foreign policy-makers lacked the foresight to heed such requests. After the partition of the subcontinent in 1947, the Durand Line dispute continued with Pakistan, turning into the bigger issue of 'Pashtunistan' in the 1950s and 1960s. Thus the Afghans were left with little choice other than asking for assistance from the Soviets. This came extremely rapidly. In 1956, after a high-level Soviet delegation visited Afghanistan, the Russians agreed to a concessionary loan of $32 million for the purchase of Soviet weapons and by 1978 this aid grew in value to $1,265 million still on the low interest rate of 2 per cent. The Afghan historian Sayed Qasem Reshtia values Soviet investment since the 1950s at 'over three billion dollars, primarily to develop – for their own ends – transport and communications systems and to train technical, military, and civilian personnel under Soviet instructors' (Reshtia 1984: 94). At the time of the communist coup in 1978, nearly 96 per cent of the Afghan army's weapons were Soviet made. US aid at this time made up merely 42 per cent of Russian aid, and consisted of loans and grants for training, education, road building, and an agricultural project near Kandahar. Soviet aid was actually greater than the combined aid Afghanistan obtained from the US, the different agencies of the UN, the World Bank and the NATO countries combined. By 1963, Soviet military instructors had replaced the longstanding Turkish military instructors, who had been involved in training the Afghan Army from the time of King Amanullah, a 'blood-brother' to Kemal Attaturk. Having brought Afghanistan into its orbit, the Russian terms were becoming unbearable for the Afghan governments of the 1960s and 1970s. The Soviets, fearful of losing Afghanistan to NATO or the West like its two other southern neighbours, Turkey and Iran, were putting pressure on Afghan governments not to allow personnel and engineers from NATO countries to begin searching for oil, gas and other mineral sources in northern Afghanistan. They considered such actions to be a national security risk. The Afghan president, Mohammad Daoud, who was on an official visit to the Soviet Union in April 1977, stormed out of a meeting with President Podgorny and Prime Minister Brezhnev on this issue. He told his Russian hosts that Afghanistan as an independent country had the right to invite whomsoever it wished to invite. Exactly one year later, pro-Moscow communist elements that had assumed power gunned down Daoud and his entire family.

The Russians, after a century and a half of various attempts and manoeuvres, could not control Afghanistan. Afghan and non-Afghan historians are of the opinion that after the success of the Bolshevik revolution, the Russians devised long-term political, economic and military plans and consistently worked to achieve them. These were to turn Afghanistan into a dependent state, vulnerable and responsive to Soviet pressure, and to separate it from other states in the region such as India, Pakistan, Iran and Turkey who were all pro-West and hostile to the Soviets. The Soviets, turning themselves into Afghanistan's number one economic partner and giving themselves the sole right to explore oil and gas in northern Afghanistan, discovered large reserves of natural gas. Their investment in this prospecting more than paid off, because they piped gas from the gas wells in northern Afghanistan to their own pipelines, also installing the meters for the flow of gas on their side of the border. Taking advantage of the Afghan communists' dependence on them, they fixed a price much lower than that of the world market. In 1978 when I was researching into Zazi youths in the Afghan army, I came across Russian 'engineers' who were connected with the gas wells in the north. When I asked them why they were paying lower than international rates for the Afghan gas their reply was that the gas had a high level of sulphur and that no one else would buy it. They said that the Soviet Union was using it only in factories. When I asked them how they separated this gas from their own gas that also ran through the same pipelines from Uzbekistan to homes in Soviet cities, one of them got agitated and asked for my name and address, which I provided incorrectly. One concludes that they were probably no ordinary Russian engineers, and possibly were connected to the KGB (like so many other Russian personnel in Afghanistan at that time) as these same men were looking for me the next day at the Faculty of Letters, where I had told them I was teaching.

Conclusion

The discussion in this chapter centred on the three themes of the fragility of the state, its modernisation, and the influence exerted on it by external forces. The scramble for the throne and the struggles of kings to maintain their position was partly due to the absence of the rule of primogeniture or some other agreed method. Often dozens of sons from different mothers competed, paying no attention to the will of the king. No importance was attached to consulting the public through *jirgas* or *Loya Jirgas* to legitimise their position and hence wars and uncertainties in the nineteenth century were rife. These competitive forces can be seen as aspects of a segmentary lineage system. However, attempts were made by and after the Iron Amir to change this chaotic situation with some success. But the new centralised approach of 'nationalisation' is caught up in its dilemma of implementing modern reforms. The greatest obstacle in the twentieth century turns out not to have been tribal resistance to being ruled from a strong centre or the tribes losing their privileged position, but the need to reform the attitude of men towards women, especially in the urban centres, by admitting to a public role for women. Women's emancipation in the Western sense is seen as a threat to the fabric of patrilineal Afghan society and contrary to the injunctions of Islam. This issue preoccupies Afghan attitudes to this day. Afghan rulers, in attempting to implement a modern ('Western') conception of female emancipation and by initiating reforms, have either ignored Afghan culture and Islamic edicts or deliberately overlooked them, and this has been one of the main reasons for the issue's continued presence in Afghan politics. Rulers have disregarded the need to reconcile conservative Afghan culture and Islam with modern requirements. Unless these core matters are addressed, the 'women issue' will continue to be regarded as provocative and challenging.

The geo-political position of Afghanistan, like the fragility of the state and the problems with modernisation has hardly changed, after two and a half centuries. If Britain and Russia were the two imperial states of the nineteenth century, the Soviet Union and the United States were the super-powers of the twentieth century, and now the United States is the only super-power around. If Afghanistan fought imperial Russia and Britain because it was encroached on and sandwiched between them, it has since been influenced by, received aid from, and fought against the Soviet Union. If the USA, having replaced Britain as a world power, had helped the Afghans against the Soviet Red Army, she also bombed Afghanistan over its refusal to hand over the alleged terrorist Osama Bin Laden. If Afghanistan was politically important for the imperial states in the nineteenth century, it has become, since the disintegration of the USSR, once again economically important by being the shortest route for the huge gas and oil reserves of Central Asia to the billion inhabitants of the Indian subcontinent and beyond.

In the 1880s the impression was created that the state had advanced from a segmentary to a unitary one and was becoming a nation-state in the process. Afghan governments since the 1880s have tried to strengthen central control and also to involve the people, either through *Loya Jirgas* or parliaments, in the affairs of the country, however limited their powers may have been. Through the expansion of roads, education and mass media, governments have tried to strengthen Afghan culture and identity. To this end, excavations of historic relics and conferences celebrating Afghan historic figures under the auspices of different UN bodies were aimed at cementing the fabric of Afghan ethnic and tribal links. But the decades of war and uncertainty since the overthrow of the monarchy in 1973, have brought into focus the importance of tribal and ethnic networks and the desire amongst some ethnic activists to exploit these and break away from the centre. The case of Afghanistan also demonstrates that statehood and nationhood is not something, once achieved, which can automatically be built on. Much depends on internal developments and also on what happens outside, in this case in neighbouring countries that share ethnic, racial and religious links with the people of Afghanistan. In other words, deep divisions within Afghan society exist. Since the late nineteenth century there have come rulers who wanted to modernise the state but were faced with internal blocks that needed to be overcome. Colonial powers, the British and the Tsarists, used these divisions to their own advantage knowing well that they could not buy or conquer the Afghans and so they agreed to turn Afghanistan into a vassal or buffer state. The Soviet Union broke this stand-off by its military and ideological invasion in 1979.

Part II
Sowing the seeds of turmoil

3 Daoud's republic: 1973–78

Introduction

The previous chapter dealt with the development of the state over a period of 200 years. One of the problems Afghan rulers began to face was modernisation. After Amanullah another important figure that addressed the modernisation issue was Mohammad Daoud, a key figure in Zaher Shah's government since 1933. Paternal cousin, brother-in-law and also two years older than the king, graduating with him from the same Kabul *Harbi Showanzai* or military school, Zaher Shah always listened to his advice. But Daoud's five years as President, internally marred by coup d'etats, political arrests and murders and externally by the ever growing Soviet grip over Afghanistan was a time of uncertainties, intrigue and upheaval with disastrous consequences for himself and the country.

Daoud had held the premiership, the ministries of defence and the interior and was commander of *qawa-i-markaz* the central forces in Kabul when he replaced his uncle, Shah Mahmud in September 1953. His uncle had embarked on a short phase of 'democracy' after the 'Liberal Parliament' of 1949. About half of the 120 parliamentarians in session were reform-minded *wakils* or MPs, who questioned cabinet ministers on budgets and other irregularities in their ministries and pressed for freedom of the press. Ministers used articles (43, 73–8) of the 1931 constitution giving them unlimited power, not to be answerable to any one outside government. Only article 76 made ministers 'responsible to the National Assembly as regards the policy of the government in general and of the ministry under their charge in particular'.

The 'Liberal Parliament' did pass laws permitting freedom of the press and almost overnight many newspapers sprang up. The papers became very critical of the government and the religious sector and were banned after only two years (1951–52). Students at Kabul University, who had formed their own union, organised debates and discussions, as part of the newfound freedom. Their union too was closed down in 1951. Preceding all this was the *Wish Zalmyan* or the Awakened Youth Movement, founded in 1947, some of whose members were publishers and supporters of the press. With the rise of the Awakened Youth, demands for reforms and the fragility of the state once again came to the surface. The state did not take these demands on board by incorporating their leaders and so the movement was declared illegal and went underground, waiting to surface again with much vigour later. It was against this background that in a royal family coup, instead of addressing the real issues of discontent, uncertainty and demands for an open society, the king agreed in 1953 for Daoud to replace his uncle who had been Prime Minister since 1946. The Prime Minister Shah Mahmud later told elders who went to see him. 'I could have predicted my death but not this coup by Daoud and Zaher against me'.

In a US Kabul Embassy secret report to Washington (27 June 1951) it is said that Shah Mahmud knew of Daoud's opposition and while in US for treatment he also wanted to go to Italy to meet the former exiled King Amanullah. The two eventually met in Switzerland and Shah Mahmud wanted to get his consent for his policies and thus present it to Daoud and Zaher Shah's followers. This report states that the meeting between the two was not very friendly (State Deprt. Document No. 789.11/6-2751).

Unlike the Afghanistan of the nineteenth century there was no blood spilt and the change-over was a smooth one. As minister of defence and the interior, Daoud had built up the reputation of *Liwanay Daoud*, the mad Daoud, as one who stood for no nonsense and got things done. So there was a great deal of expectation, but as Prime Minister he moved slowly wanting to achieve steady social and economic progress. In ten years (1953–63) as Prime Minister he used Afghanistan's position as a neutral country to attract development aid from the USA and the USSR as well as from West Germany, Japan and other countries. But dependence for arms and aid on the Russians was historically a sensitive issue for Afghanistan. To balance this Daoud strengthened Afghanistan's non-aligned status by turning it into an active member of the non-aligned countries, a Third World Movement, playing a prominent role in the Bandung and Belgrade meetings alongside Sukarno and Tito.

Daoud as a youthful energetic leader managed to dampen religious objections to his modernisation programme. His introduction of regional development plans alongside national projects such as roads, the expansion of trade and hydroelectric dams were noticeable steps towards modernity. He removed the veil through voluntary means by first lifting the veil from women in his own family to view a public parade in 1959. But the single issue that he could not resolve was the issue of 'Pashtunistan', the legacy of the 1893 Durand Line agreement, separating the Pashtuns in present-day Pakistan from those in Afghanistan. It was this issue which at the end led to his resignation in 1963.

Daoud's return to power in 1973, as President of the Republic of Afghanistan was fatal in more than one way. First, he alienated the rest of the population through his dependence on the communists without whose help he might not have succeeded. Second, he failed to achieve his aim of modernisation. He did not win the trust of the religious and traditional elements or manage to dampen demands for freedom of speech. Third, he could not reconcile his nationalist feelings with the ideology of his communist supporters. Fourth, his overthrow was a personal tragedy leading also to the murder of his entire family. Fifth, his death ended 230 years of Durrani rule.

This chapter is a discussion of Daoud's shortcomings and the general level of fragmentation that existed among the small groups of political activists. More precisely it is an appraisal of Afghans coming to terms with the requirements of a plural society. I want to start with an evaluation of his Pashtunistan policy.

Pashtunistan

The Pashtunistan issue is the product of the Durand Agreement of 1893 between British India and Afghanistan. This agreement, that was subsequently recognised as a border treaty by King Amanullah in 1919, remained a contentious issue after the division of the sub-continent between India and Pakistan. (For a further discussion of this issue see Appendix 10). The Pashtunistan issue preoccupied Daoud's administrations both as Prime Minister 1953–63, and President 1973–78. Other Afghan governments also questioned the legality of the Durand Line, in that the agreement was signed between Afghanistan and British India. That agreement in international law could not be passed on or inherited by a third country (Pakistan) born out of the 1947 Partition of the Indian Subcontinent.

The dispute with Pakistan took a regional dimension, bringing Afghanistan closer to Pakistan's rival India and also pushing Afghanistan into the arms of Soviet Russia and its ideological influences. Daoud like Amanullah was committed to technical and economic modernity. While Amanullah relied on the new Soviet State, Daoud exploited the global rivalry of the USA and USSR as super powers and received aid and investments for Afghanistan's economic infrastructure from both. The bases for these investments were the two five-year Soviet model development plans (modelled on Soviet experience) starting in 1956 and 1967, in which the Soviet Union outstripped investments by the USA and other Western countries.

Following Stalin's rapid development programmes in the USSR, Daoud too embarked on such development plans. He counted on foreign aid and personnel to fund and carry these through. The US government, for example, altogether provided some $532.87 million in aid for the Helmand Valley project, a major US agricultural project near Kandahar, started in 1946 and the two five-year plans. American aid stopped in 1979, when its ambassador, Adolph Dubs, 'was killed in a shoot-out . . . by a Tajik anti-Pushtun separatist group, the *Setam-i-Meli'* (Cordovez/Harrison 1995: 34). The budget for the first five-year plan (1956–61) was 38.5 billion Afghanis and the second (1962–67) 31.3 billion Afghanis. These two five-year plans, in which the Soviet foreign aid share was much higher than that of any other country, played a crucial role in the modernisation process of Afghanistan. Some 1,700 km of dirt roads were improved and paved, three times more schools were opened, agriculture and hydro-electric power was boosted, light industry introduced and generally the infrastructure for foreign and private enterprise and investment was laid.[1] These plans, owing to lack of funds, unscientific estimates as to the costs, unsure funding sources and the government's inexperience in implementing plans of this scale, were not 100 per cent successful. But the fact that the country had plans, with a specific budget and a time limit to achieve it, worked wonders for Afghanistan. That is why, long after Daoud was gone, his second five-year plan was nevertheless undertaken. In 1967 the leader of the Progressive Democratic Party, Mohammad Hashem Maiwandwal as prime minister even started a third five-year plan. However, his arrest and the changing political situation in the country prevented the implementation of the plan.

However, the deterioration of relations with Pakistan (the border was closed three times) badly affected the Afghan economy. Karachi served as an important seaport for Afghanistan's imports and exports as a landlocked country. The closures of the border with Pakistan in 1961 also brought to a stop some two hundred truckloads of import and export overland trade with India; and this led to Daoud's removal from office in 1963.

Daoud's credibility suffered because of this last closure of the border (1961–63). The king and other forces within and outside the royal family were discontented with Daoud's reliance on the airlift and the re-routing of some trade to Russia. So the king's first important political act, since he first ascended the throne in 1933 was the removal of Daoud from office with the latter's consent. For the first time a commoner was appointed in Daoud's place. According to many close to the royal family, Daoud was getting too powerful and was not easily amenable to suggestions. Daoud was of the opinion that he would be brought back to the government sometime in the future.[2] However, family and other influential well-wishers persuaded the king that he should make a fresh start. The king till this time was just a figurehead. First it was his uncles and then Daoud who ruled the country in his name. In 1963, he took the advice of family and advisors to heart and decided to take control himself. On a national level people in the urban cities more than in rural areas had changed along with developments taking place in the region and in the world and were demanding more say in the running of the country. It was because of such considerations that the king decided to pass a new constitution in which the country would be turned into a constitutional monarchy. The unprecedented freedom agreed to in accordance with the constitution was what urban Afghans had been clamouring for since the 1940s. Thus the ten years prior to Daoud's coup, between 1963 and 1973 retrospectively became known as the decade of constitution.

The decade of constitution

The aim of the 1964 constitution was to turn Afghanistan into a constitutional monarchy as in Western Europe. The constitution put an end to other members of the royal family holding high political, military and administrative positions. Article 24 defined the 'Royal Family', as comprising the king and his sons and daughters and their siblings. This article also forbids any member of the royal lineage from holding high offices. Daoud and his brother Mohammad Naim (foreign minister and advisor) considered this article to have been specially drafted to exclude them from any future office.

The constitution also provided for political parties. Though the king never signed the bill to make political parties legal, these like scores of newspapers mushroomed in a few months after the promulgation of the new constitution. Strikes and demonstrations in Kabul and other parts of the country become an everyday affair.[3] Debates in parliament were broadcast live. Freshly elected left-wing radical and communist MPs, dominated these discussions. As proceedings were nationally broadcast, they used the opportunity to incite the public against the government. As a result, government after government fell not being able to gain a vote of confidence from parliament (Kushkaki 1993: 60–97). The king, Mohammad Zaher not known for decisiveness 'would ask any minister to resign and appoint another in his place, simply because they were criticised in parliament' (Akram 2001: 177).

Daoud was resentful of being stopped from holding office again. After all he was married to the king's sister and was his first cousin. Afghan royal prefer endogamous marriages. Although exogamous political marriages have a long tradition, most royal family marriages are between cousins. Marriages are alliances, if they are to flourish they need to be maintained from the moment they are contracted (Goode 1964: 40). 'Marriage alliance always involves a choice between those with whom one is allied and on whom henceforth one relies for friendship and help, and those with whom an alliance is declined or ignored, and with whom ties are severed' (Levi-Strauss 1969: 435). The Afghan royal families, throughout the period of this study seem to enter into such alliances in the hope of maintaining and nourishing them, but often give in to other political considerations. For Daoud to assume power, his links with communists and others were more important to this end than a marriage alliance with Zaher Shah or his other cousins. That is why like the communists and other dissidents, during the decade of constitution, he made use of the country's new-found freedom of speech and press to build up a number of new young followers.

Experiment in democracy

In 1963 after replacing Daoud as prime minister and appointing a commoner, Dr Mohammad Yosuf[4] in his place, King Mohammad Zaher promulgated a new constitution. This constitution and the ten years of unchecked press and media freedom that followed it opened a 'Pandora's box' of many parties and groups, from Afghan nationalists and Islamists, to social democrats and many different shades of leftist movements, all making their debut on political stage (see Table 3.1). This is despite the fact that the section of the constitution dealing with the formation of political parties was never ratified by the king (Kushkaki 1986: 29–114). The appointment of a new prime minister also normalised relations with Pakistan. The three years that disrupted trade were also over because the Port of Karachi was once again open to Afghan trade.

The 'experiment in democracy', ran into major problems. Government after government fell because they could not win the approval of parliament. Ministers would be summoned by MPs and asked questions about the monarchy or the prime minister that they could not answer satisfactorily. Even the king came to the conclusion that things had gone too far and there was no way of meeting the demands of the communists or of the Islamists for that matter. The king as a last resort appointed his sixth

Table 3.1 Parties and ideologies from 1966

Party	Publication and date	Ideology
1. Khalq (PDPA)	*Khalq*, Masses 1966	Pro-Moscow, militant, anti-establishment
2. Parcham (PDPA)	*Parcham*, Flag or Banner 1968	Pro-Moscow, moderate
3. New Democratic Party	*Shola Jawed*, Eternal Flame 1968	Pro-Peking, extreme left
4. Setam-e-Mili	*Piam-e-Wejdan*, Voice of Conscience 1968	Rights for non-Pashtun minorities
5. Afghan Social Democrats	*Afghan millat*, Afghan Nation 1966	Nationalist Pashtun, Pro-Pashtunistan
6. Millat, Nation	*Millat 1971*	Leftist (breakaway from no. 5 above)
7. Islamic Party	*Gahiz*, Morning 1968	Islamic, anti-leftists, conservative
8. Progressive Democratic Party	*Masawat*, Equality 1966	Evolutionary Socialism, Parliamentary Democracy

Note
There were over thirty newspapers and periodicals reflecting parties and pressure group views. Some were anti-one and pro another: (*Mardum*, masses or people was published to oppose Khalq No. 1 above; *Hadaf* or Goal was anti-Masawat No. 8 above).

prime minister in ten years, Musa Shafiq (Dupree 1980: 666). Shafiq had studied at the Islamic world's most respected university, Al-Azhar, in Egypt as well as at Columbia University in New York. His first act was to pacify the radical religious elements, the Islamists, by including them in his government. In this way Shafiq wanted to draw Afghanistan closer to Islamic nations and dampen its relation with the Soviet Union. By appealing to Muslim countries as a source of aid, Shafiq wanted to check the spread of communism in Afghanistan. He reassured Pakistan by not making any demands on the issue of Pashtunistan, a product of the 1893 Durand Line Agreement that was itself the subsequent result of the treaty of Gandomak (26 May 1879).[5] Shafiq's government also signed a treaty with Iran papering over disagreement that existed since the 1860s about the water of the Helmand River.

Assessing the decade of constitution

The decade of 'democratic experiment' had many positive and negative outcomes. On the positive side, the free press and media, the freedom of travel and associations probably raised the Afghan consciousness to an unparalleled extent. Afghans learned more about their rights as individuals, groups, parties and democracy as a whole in those ten years, than in the previous one hundred years. On the negative side, there was the fact that the king did not ratify the part of the constitution dealing with political parties, their formation and obligations, and hampered successive governments from building a parliamentary base embedded in party affiliations, so that they could be held accountable through legal and parliamentary process. In all six governments it was the king who appointed the prime minister, with the cabinet ministers also coming from outside parliament, which meant that winning the support of the MPs was on *ad hoc* and patronage basis. The MPs would only promise to vote for the government if the government would do something for their constituencies. Since the list of the demands of every MP was long, these demands could not possibly be met. This obviously was one reason why successive governments failed to secure majority votes in parliament and, therefore, fell with such rapidity in those ten years.

The experiment with democracy also brought to the surface the ethnic, linguistic and religious cleavages that had been dormant in Afghan society. As a result ethnic minorities began to express their resentment of the Pashtun majority. Within the minorities, the urban Tajiks in particular who had practically monopolised the bureaucracy since the founding of Afghanistan in 1747, were resented by the Pashtuns, Shi'ah Hazarahs, Uzbeks, Turkmen, Nuristanis and others who had also to learn their Dari language. Some had to learn Pashto as well, as both were national and formal languages of the country. All these ethnic groups in turn resented the Pashtuns for providing the country's leadership for over two and a half centuries. Although as pointed out earlier, these leaders and rulers were originally Durrani Pashtun most spoke Dari as their first language and felt more like urban Kabulis than elite Pashtuns. For example Daoud's brother Mohammad Naim, who was his foreign minister in the 1950s on a visit to Pakistan found himself highly embarrassed when the then President of Pakistan, Yaqob Khan, spoke with him in Pashto and he could not reply. Yaqob Khan then told him, 'how come you want Pashtunistan but, do not speak their language!'.[6]

The discontent of Afghanistan's 9 per cent Shi'ah population came to the fore when their region of central Afghanistan was hit by drought in 1971–72, also affecting southern Afghanistan. Some Hazarahs were forced to give their children away to other Afghans in the hope of escaping the famine. The Qizelbash Shi'ah until then, in order to avoid discrimination used to pass themselves off as Sunni or/and Tajiks. These Shi'ah groups could not pray openly like their Sunni counterparts and had to observe their religious ceremonies in the old quarter of Kabul, *Chendawel*, which was practically closed to the Sunni. The decade of democracy provided the opportunity for them to air these grievances. They also built a large mosque in western Kabul and went about their religious practices openly.

Daoud's comeback

Asem Akram in his biography of Daoud divides his ten years of retirement into three phases: '1. from retirement (1963) to the promulgation of the new constitution (1964); 2. the seven year long period of "dissatisfaction" and 3. The last phase of "preparation" to come back to power' (Akram 2001: 182–3). While in retirement Daoud was holding frequent seminars at his home with dissidents and elements from the army trying to analyse why his term as prime minister was not successful; what was wrong with the decade of constitutional democracy; and what could be learnt from both,[7] (Arney 1990: 69; Arnold 1985: 56). 'For more than a year the subject [of a coup] was being considered by some friends, and various plans discussed. Only when anarchy and the anti-national attitude of the regime had reached its peak was the decision for taking action taken' (Hyman 1984: 64). On 17 July 1973 when the king was in Italy, at dawn that day, Daoud put his coup plan into action and by 7:00 am almost all strategic places in Kabul were taken. By 7:20 am he went to the radio station to announce the toppling of the monarchy and its replacement by a republic. This was a bloodless coup and its casualties were a handful of soldiers all killed by accidents.[8] One reason why this was a textbook coup was because of Daoud's long experience and familiarity with the government and the army. He had been defence and interior minister in the 1940s, commander of Kabul Central Forces in the early 1950s and subsequently prime minister, 1953–63. In his inaugural speech, which seems to have been written by his communist colleagues, Daoud declared the monarchy, 'utterly corrupt and that is why we sacrificed our family and class interests for the sake of national interest and the interests of the deprived classes. Corruption reached a point that no nationalist Afghan's conscience would allow him to remain silent' (Daoud 1973: 2–3).

After the coup, Daoud formed his cabinet and also announced his 'Central Committee'. The 'central committee', a hallmark of communist administration, though announced, was rarely publicised in his five years as president. To the surprise of us Afghan students in the UK, the public did not know most of his cabinet ministers and as time went by they were found to be the least qualified for their jobs. These were mostly the young and those left-wingers who had lost hope in the monarchy and had also kept in touch with Daoud in the ten years that he was in retirement. Of the two pro-Moscow communist parties, Khalq and Parcham, and the two pro-Peking, Shola Jawed and *Setam-i-Meli*, it was the Parcham faction that he favoured.

> Half a dozen closet communists were included in his cabinet. Amongst them Hassan Sharq[9] (who was to make a dramatic reappearance fifteen years later when he was drafted in as Prime Minister at the tail end of the Soviet occupation), the army's major Faiz Mohammad, allotted the powerful post of Interior Minister. Other left-wing officers like Abdul Qader and Zia Mohammad Zia were rewarded with senior military appointments. Parcham top civilian leaders including Babrak Karmal himself, Anahita Ratebzad and Noor Ahmad Noor – became members of the Central Committee and of Daoud's inner circle.
>
> (Arney 1990: 71)

Daoud was no communist but he was not correct in saying that he and others close to him had no knowledge or attachment to communists.

> ...no fewer than eight out of fourteen were known – then or later – as PDPA [Peoples Democratic Party of Afghanistan] members, former members, or strong sympathisers ... six of the eight leftists were to hold important positions in government under Babrak Karmal in 1980: two were to be ministers; three, ambassadors, and one advisor to the Prime Ministry...
>
> (Arnold 1985: 56–7)

Around 160 other Parcham members were appointed to the provinces in positions from governors to the post of chief of education, army and judiciary. These were expected to build a rank and file communist movement in the countryside assuring the founding of a socialist Afghanistan. The Parchamis had no specific tribal or ethnic base. While Daoud shared their enthusiasm for progress and modernisation, he considered them as of no challenge to his authority. Meanwhile the Parchamis, in co-operating with

Daoud, wanted to slight the Pashtun ethnically dominated Khalq. But most of these urban communists, some of whom had never been to the Afghan countryside and knew little of the multiplicity of rural cultures and the aspirations of ethnically dominated regions, soon found out that instead of winning supporters, they were turning the public against them. They had little regard for religion, or appreciation of the rough and arduous rural ways of life. They simply wanted people to change and accept progressive ideas instantly.

Daoud's Soviet connection

The communists and leftists elements in Daoud's republican government through their manipulation of western media soon made him known as 'the Red Prince'. The Soviet Union who had dealt with Daoud while he was prime minister knew that he was the architect of closer Afghan-Soviet relations, and was someone they could do business with. His coup was therefore assessed positively in Moscow. Soviets became the first to recognise the new republic diplomatically. The Soviets by then were also disappointed with the king. King Mohammad Zaher tried to distance Afghanistan from the Soviet sphere of influence through his short-lived but energetic prime minister Musa Shafiq (Dec. 1972–July 73). He signed treaties with Afghanistan's pro-Western neighbours, Iran and Pakistan, assuring them of Afghanistan's friendship and cooperation.[10] The Soviets had always wanted to draw Afghanistan closer to them. Through the two pro-Moscow Khalq and Parcham parties the Soviet Union 'was pressing Kabul to take an implicitly anti-Chinese stand of adhering to Brezhnev's 1969 concept of an Asian Collective Security Agreement, thus trying to draw Afghanistan closer to it' (Bradsher 1985: 55). The Soviets knew that on their southern borders, they had three unfriendly Muslim states: Turkey as a member of NATO, Iran with its anti-communist and pro-US and the West stance, and Pakistan which was pro-China and the West. The Soviet Union was not prepared to let Afghanistan turn into yet another southern Muslim state opposed to the interests of the USSR.

Daoud's relations with the Soviets were close. He was the one who, in 1955, for the first time invited Soviet party and government chiefs, Khruschev and Bulganin to Kabul, where they made the largest ever loan to Afghanistan of $100 million on very favourable terms. On the other hand the Americans, from President Eisenhower to Richard Nixon, all turned down Afghanistan's requests for the purchase of arms and noticeable development aid. America wanted Afghanistan to take up membership of CETO and CENTO [regional pacts aimed at hardening the southern flank of the USSR], like its neighbours. Afghanistan on the other hand insisted on its neutrality and non-aligned status and did not want to provoke the Soviets (Wakman 1985: 60–3).

During the decade of Daoud's premiership (1953–63), four political organisations sprang up and some of the leaders of the communists who came to power in 1978 were originally members of these radical groups. These organisations were: *Wish Zalmyan*, the Awakened Youth, Nur Mohammad Taraki and Babrak Karmal, the first and second communist presidents after the 1978 coup were amongst its members; *Neday-e-Khalq*, Voice of the Masses, led by a Maoist, Dr Abdur Rahman Mahmudi; *Cloob-e-Meli*, National Club. Daoud himself headed this group, which wanted sweeping internal reforms. Most importantly he also worked and encouraged the *Itehad-e-Pashtunistan*, the Pashtunistan Alliance. Overtly Daoud wanted the Pashtuns in Pakistan to decide on their own future, in a plebiscite under international supervision. But covertly, as a nationalist he wanted these Pashtuns to join Afghanistan so that Afghanistan as a modern and developing state could also have access to the sea.

Why Daoud came to power

In his decade of forced retirement, Daoud gauged accurately the government's vulnerability, and planned and waited for the day so that once again he could take centre stage. It is also true that the population as a whole grew tired and disappointed with the king who had been on the throne since 1933. There were also two years of drought (1969–71), causing the death of some 40 per cent of animals in the drought-hit regions and leading to widespread malnutrition and death. The ten years of experiment with democracy had not impressed the ordinary man in the street. 'In the 1965 elections, nine out of ten voters stayed at home. The Assembly that was elected aroused so little interest that even its members stayed away, meetings were often inquorate' (Urban 1990: 5). Bribery and nepotism, as ever, were rife. Though the free press could occasionally highlight instances of these and write about them, it in effect led to the unleashing of other forces and pointed to the in-built weaknesses of the judiciary and the police who were unable to follow such issues to a successful conclusion.

In July 1973 the king had gone to Italy for his annual holiday and health checks, accompanied by General Abdul Wali, his son-in-law and cousin, commander of the Kabul Central Forces and a number of other royal family members. On receiving information about Daoud's coup plan, the king sent General Abdul Wali to Kabul to keep things under control. It is said that General Wali, on receiving the list of the names of the conspirators, was misled by the Chief of Staff, General Abdul Karim Mustaghni and the Minister of the Interior, Ne'matullah Pazhwak. Both of these were secretly Parcham members-cum-sympathisers and said that the coup was set for a date several months later. 'As minister of interior, with security responsibilities, Pazhwak was in good position both to warn Daoud that his conspirators' identities and plans had been compromised and to mislead Abdul Wali as to the date of the probable coup' (Arnold 1985: 58). In addition to these two highly placed communist sympathisers, other key military Parcham communists and leftists featured prominently in the 17 July coup. From the air force: Colonel Abdul Qader, Brigadier Pacha Gul Wafadar; from the army: Major Abdul Qadir Nurestani, Colonel Ghulam Sarwar, Faiz Mohammad, Abdul Hamid Mohtat, Captain Mohammad Aslam Watnjar, Sher Jan Mazdoryar and a non-commissioned officer, Sayed Mohammad Gulabzoy. The last four were enthusiastic pro-Soviet communists and played a key role five years later, in the April 1978 communist coup, by killing Daoud and his family in a bloody coup, and in the subsequent takeover by communists. What is not quite clear is whether or not the Soviets were involved in this coup. As a result of the level of Soviet economic investment and through their contact with the Afghan communists, they certainly were in the picture. Judging by the events that followed over the next two decades, it is not unlikely that they might even have encouraged it. Russia and the Soviet Union did not fear Afghan monarchs. They were no challenge to Imperial Russia nor did they pose any threat to subsequent Soviet interests. Though, judging by Eastern European standards and communist regimes elsewhere, the Soviets were much more at home when dealing with a regime that would mirror them.

Daoud in his retirement made up his mind that in the short-run democracy in a country like Afghanistan was not practical. His Parcham communist supporters and other dissidents also convinced him that in Afghanistan, where tribal and regional loyalties take precedence over national issues, democracy needs time and requires an all-round dedication for it to succeed. The overwhelming rate of illiteracy, the lack of modern communications and the general economic underdevelopment made it difficult for people to appreciate the ideals of democracy.

> Government failure to get on with passing a political parties law is in part to blame for this situation, but it is doubtful that even legal sanction would have permitted a rapid enough development of various party organisations and loyalties to have forestalled the 1973 coup.
> (Arnold 1985: 56)

As a result of the interplay between internal and external forces in the Cold War with America and the West having their supporters and the Russians theirs, there was less room for an Afghan consensus to develop. These outside ideologies fought their rivals with their Afghan support. Thus Daoud compared the decade of constitution to 'the law of the jungle, despotism and anarchy ... The only way left was to overthrow the monarchy' (Daoud 1973: 7). He was of course not totally justified in lashing out at the monarchy of which he was an influential member, having moulded and changed that system over some thirty years. Further his republican administration failed to correct these shortcomings. The machinery of the government continued, more or less, in the same corrupt way as before. Daoud could not leave behind his royal appendages and despite declaring himself as the 'President and Prime Minster of the

Republic of Afghanistan', he acted as if he were a king and soon earned the title of the 'Royal President'.

Daoud in office

Soon after Daoud's July coup, the Khalq leader, Nur Mohammad Taraki, sent a letter to Daoud offering dedicated and patriotic personalities to serve in his government instead of the present corrupt officials, Daoud declined to reply.[11] Five years later when Taraki replaced Daoud in a bloody coup as the first communist president, Taraki bitterly complained.

> We supported Daoud, hopeful and confident that he would allow us to participate in the government ... We thought that Daoud would indeed carry out actions in the interest of the subjugated class. Daoud deceived not only himself but also the whole nation.
>
> (Bradsher 1985: 58)

Taraki elsewhere, criticised his rival Karmal, saying that the Parcham leader, unable to recognise Daoud's real intentions, wanted the Peoples Democratic Party of Afghanistan (PDPA) dissolved, arguing that now Daoud was committed to doing what the party wanted to achieve. Babrak Karmal was the most trusted Soviet agent. According to Vladimir Kuzichin, a KGB official in charge of Afghan affairs in Moscow, who defected to the West, Karmal had been 'a long time KGB agent, long before he became president', and always had been an active member of Soviet intelligence (*Kuzichin Times Magazine*, July 1982).

Daoud was careful to distance himself publicly from these leftists and other political parties and groups saying:

> We have no connection with any group and linking us to any group or movement is a sin. We only serve our nation with the spirit of serving our country, with complete faith and all our power. If in spite of this there are people found who create discord, and disturb our national interest, then we also know what to do with them.[12]
>
> (Daoud 1974: 2–3)

Meanwhile the Parchamis, in their contacts with other Afghans, despite what Daoud said were making it known that Daoud was 'their man'. They would confirm this by saying that had it not been for Daoud's support, their leader Karmal might not have been so brave and overtly critical of the monarchy inside and outside parliament during the decade of constitution. These young communists were forgetting that it was Daoud, a skilled politician, who was using them as an organised political movement. As an Afghan nationalist and member of the ruling family, Daoud was no communist. He was dedicated to Afghanistan's technical and social progress. With this in mind, he wanted to use the resources of the Soviet Union and that is why he came closer to its Parcham communist minions. But as he was to find out at the cost of his life, the Soviets too had their long drawn out plans and were not going to let him become an obstacle.

Prince Turki who was Saudi's head of intelligence for some twenty years in a detailed interview with the Arab TV Middle East Broadcasting Corporation (MBC) (3 June 2003) said,

> Saudi officials warned President Daoud, who took power by overthrowing his cousin, King Zahir Shah in 1973, against relying on the Communists to consolidate his rule. President Daoud however brushed aside the suggestion and told the Saudis during a visit to the Kingdom in 1977 that he would move on the Communists first by 'having them for lunch before they had him for dinner'. What happened was that the Communists moved fast and had him for breakfast.

Prince Turki added that the Russians had plans since the days of the Czars to establish for themselves a foot in warm waters. 'It was obvious that the invasion of Afghanistan was one step towards reaching other countries, specially Pakistan and then moving on to the Gulf and the Arabian Peninsula'.

One of the first things Daoud did after coming to power, in July 1973, was to abolish the thirty or so private newspapers, journals and magazines that had sprang up in the decade of constitution.[13] Only the government controlled press was to continue as the mouthpiece of the regime. On 19 January 1974, the president summoned provincial directors of information and culture telling them:

> The difficulties faced by the developing nations, including Afghanistan, are grave and of a continuing nature. The country would be fortunate if these problems could be tackled in one or two generations. You and we are the sons of the nation, and are well aware of the conditions in our country. [Referring to the embryonic free press he said:] The person who claims that he can change the prevailing conditions by a few words, I think that neither he should entertain such thoughts, nor deceive others.
>
> (Daoud 19 January 1973)

Daoud justified his action in an address to the nation, a month after his coup, on 23 August 1973, on the occasion of the 55th anniversary of Afghanistan's independence:

> We shall strive, step by step to bring about fundamental changes in the economic social and political life of the society, in conformity with the plans ... I and my colleagues will adhere honestly and loyally to this ideal ... Anti-national policy followed by the monarchy during the

past decade ... rapid changes in the region and the World in favour of freedom and progress ... did not permit any conscious and patriotic Afghan to remain silent ... It was [with] ... this sense of patriotic responsibility that we ... hoisted the banner.

(Daoud speeches, pp. 2–3 and 7)

Also in the same speech he made promises that his republican regime was going to undertake, 'universal compulsory primary education; land reforms and agricultural co-operatives...' Needless to say, none of these promises were fulfilled in the five years that he was in power. He was too experienced in government not to know that promises such as these were not easy to carry through. On the one hand Afghanistan lacked economic resources, technical expertise and educated cadres, on the other hand with the fragmented nature of the state still lurking, the population were suspicious of governments and any central authority which meant that they were unlikely to co-operate across the country. Added to these socio-economic problems were the government's badly paid civil servants who, out of necessity if not greed, would always put themselves before any national ideal. Such a bureaucracy could hardly be counted on to carry out the new reforms of a 'revolutionary' regime. The number of dedicated communists and leftists were not enough to replace the former corrupt officials. Despite all this, his communist supporters urged him to say:

The Republican state ... will strengthen the country's defence forces ... will reform the administration from the view point of efficiency and management ... will expand democratic rights and liberties ... The State amongst its first steps will fix minimum wages ... will formulate ... progressive and democratic labour laws ... will establish social security insurance for workers ... It will make vigorous efforts to fix rents for houses organisation and shops.

(ibid., pp. 9–13)

Daoud understood the power of tradition and also his limitations in implementing these promises. He was simply playing politics and mentioning these reforms merely as a way of establishing his new power base, hoping that if left in control he might one day fulfil some of these undertakings. But for the time being he felt very insecure. His family members, also sensing this, unsuccessfully tried to arrange for his assassination by using a family confidante.[14] At one time Daoud held four other ministries in addition to his presidential and premiership post. Daoud used to announce coups against him thus imprisoning those he disliked and/or feared. On 20 September 1973,

the ex-Prime Minister Maiwandwal was implicated along with forty-four generals, colonels, ex-MPs and merchants.... Maiwandwal returned from a foreign trip in July hailing the declaration of the republic. His imprisonment came as a shock, but his death in prison on 20 October was a disaster for the image of the republic and the prospect for a democratic transfer of power'.

(Hyman 1984: 65)

The Kabul magazine *Pashtun Zhagh*, Voice of Pashtun, convinced no one by carrying the forged signature of Maiwandwal, confessing to 'crimes and committing suicide by hanging himself by his tie' (November issue, 1973). An Afghan exile publication, *Mujahed Woles*, in 1994–95 ran a series of articles by eyewitnesses confirming previous stories that his interrogators, headed by Samad Azher, who subsequently sought refuge in Germany, had viciously killed him.

Others arrested and killed included a well-known Ghilzai general, Shapur Ahmadzai, some former MPs and various professionals. Most well informed Afghans concluded that these were all 'fabricated coups', engineered by Parcham communists so that all their opponents could be eliminated without any question of them being involved. Most of the men who were killed or imprisoned were either strong nationalists or religious leaders.

Daoud's u-turn on the communists

Daoud also faced two major internal problems: one regarding the Islamists and the other regarding communists. First, he had to face growing opposition from religious elements, against the ever-growing power of the communists and leftists within his administration. The *Jawanon-e-Musulman or* Muslim Youth, whose guiding force was a lecturer of theology, Professor Niazi, spearheaded this opposition group. He soon attracted other 'Islamist' scholars, such as Abdur Rasul Sayaf, Burhanuddin Rabbani, Mawlawi Mohammad Yonus Khales and some student activists, such as Gulbodin Hekmatyar, Din Mohammad, Ahmad Shah Masoud, all of whom became leaders and important commanders after the Soviet occupation in 1979.

As this was a movement violently opposing the communists, they found themselves at the receiving end of being arrested and imprisoned by Daoud's administration. Every one of the above 'Islamists' had to escape to Pakistan to avoid arrest and imprisonment. This was also a God-sent opportunity for Pakistan, who did not lose time but trained, armed and sent them back to Afghanistan to make trouble for Daoud, in order to pay him back for his insistence on the Pashtunistan issue. These men laid the foundation of a movement that became the centre of resistance against the Soviet Red Army in the 1980s, which will be discussed in Chapter 6. The second issue that threatened Daoud from inside was the presence of communists themselves, at all levels, within the government. It became gradually apparent to Daoud, a fervent nationalist, that these communists owed more allegiance to the Soviet Union and to the ideals of communism than to Afghanistan or its traditions. After his speech to the polytechnic graduates on 27 February 1974 in which he said, 'we have no connection with any group, and linking us to any group or movement is a sin', Daoud started shedding Parchamis and other leftists in his cabinet, replacing them with some old technocrats and some fresh faces he had got to know while in retirement. These included the former finance minister, Mohammad Khan Jalaler,[15] Qadir Nurestani, Sayed Abdullelah, Wahid Abdullah and others. Shedding communists, replacing them with former traditionalists in Kabul and in the provinces also meant the deterioration of relations with the Soviet Union. As Afghanistan was dependent on Soviet military and economic assistance, Daoud had to find alternative sources to replace it.

Daoud was invited to Moscow from 4–7 June 1974. In his speech Daoud thanked the Russians for their aid in connection with road building, the construction of the Salang tunnel (the world's highest tunnel), the agricultural sector, the citrus fruit farms in Jelalabad and the prospecting for oil and gas. His planning minister, Ahmad Ali Khoram, on returning to Kabul announced that, 'the Soviet Union promised economic and technical co-operation for the implementation of 21 projects' at a further cost of $428 million (Daoud Speeches 1974: 23). This was in addition to granting an interest-free ten years' moratorium on the $100 million debt Afghanistan already owed to them. At this stage, in return for all this, his host, President Nikolai Podgorny, expected Daoud to keep to his original commitment of bringing PDPA members into his government. Afghanistan's 'great and complex tasks renovating political, economic and cultural life ... can be solved successfully ... when broad popular masses are drawn into the work of building a new life, and when the forces which are sincerely interested in strengthening the new system act vigorously and in close unity' (Bradsher 1985: 61–2). Podgorny and Brezhnev were simply following in the footsteps of Khruschev and Bulganin, the General Secretary and the Premier of the USSR, who had visited Afghanistan in December 1955 and offered $100 million in a long term development loan for projects agreed on by both sides (Dupree 1980: 506). Podgorny in December, by way of returning Daoud's visit, came to Kabul. This visit was also planned by the Russians to impress on Daoud that it was the Soviet Union and not Iran or the Gulf States that had helped Afghanistan in the past and was prepared to continue to do so. The Russians also assured Daoud in the language of the Cold War, that their friendship with Afghanistan was a:

> 'model of peaceful coexistence of countries with different social systems'. Daoud by then counted too much on Iran and these other Muslim states and this coolness was sensed by the visiting Soviets, which amongst others also included a deputy defence minister, army general Ivan Pavlovskiy [more on him in Chapter 5] who was to return

to Afghanistan for two months in an unannounced visit in 1979, studying the possibility of Russian invasion in December that year.

(Bradsher 1985: 311)

Having purged all the leftists by 1975 and severed his dependence on them, Daoud made a U-turn as far as local communists and the Soviet Union were concerned. He undertook new foreign policy approaches aimed at reducing his military and economic dependence on the Soviet Union. For this he turned to India and Egypt, who also had Soviet military hardware, to train Afghan military personnel without exposing the Afghans to communist dogma. He also turned to Saudi Arabia, then a staunch anti-communist state and to Iran and the Gulf States for economic aid. Iran, in return for ratifying the Helmand River Water Treaty, which was signed by the king's last government in 1973, promised $2 billion dollars in aid and the building of a railway to Kabul, joining it to Bander Abbas on the Persian Gulf, as an alternative route for Afghanistan's import and export. Previously, Russia, together with Pakistan, was one of the two land routes available to Afghan businessmen. These Gulf and Middle Eastern countries also offered to help economically, thus reducing Afghanistan's dependence on Soviet Russia. Although there were no detailed plans worked out [and the substantial Iranian offer never materialised] the Russians saw it[16] as an attempt to prise Afghanistan away from the Soviet Union. The USSR, having invested in Afghanistan since the early 1920s and having increased these financial investments during Daoud's two terms in office, was not going to stand by and see Afghanistan drift into its Western enemy's camp. So the Soviets' nervousness about Afghanistan's increasing independence starts from this turn around in Daoud's policy.

In order to maintain their grip, the Soviets pursued a two-pronged approach to Afghanistan. First, the USSR and its East European Bloc continued to provide more aid for Afghanistan than the USA and the newly-found regional states of Iran and the Middle Eastern countries put together. Second, secretly working through the Communist Party of India (CPI), especially through its secretary general, N.K. Krishnan and another CPI central executive member, M. Farooqi, they tried to unite the two Khalq and Parcham wings of the PDPA. This unity, though very precarious and fragile, was achieved in March 1977. In July of that year, when the PDPA held its secret conference to iron out its differences, one of the issues that they agreed on was 'the removal of the dictatorial regime of M. Daoud' (Bradsher 1985: 69–70).

Daoud, in order to legitimise his coup, though belatedly, called a *Loya Jirga* for January 1977 to ratify the constitution and to elect a president, in this case Daoud himself, as there was no other candidate. That very evening Daoud went to the hospital bed of one of his cousins, an ex-Minister of Defence, informing him 'I won' as if there were other challengers for the post.[17] After his re-election, Daoud ousted all leftists from his government and gave no role to any members of the Parcham faction in his new administration.

On Daoud's second visit to Moscow as President, 12–15 April 1977, Brezhnev, who was then Head of State and the Party, spoke on the second day, as protocol requires. Brezhnev's countenance at some point during his speech, according to Afghan eyewitnesses changed, and with it soon the look on the translator's face too. Brezhnev said that 'some NATO personnel in Northern Afghanistan who are spies and are a security risk to the USSR should be removed'. These were some American and European satellite and seismological specialists, the French Total Oil Company prospecting for oil and gas, some development experts in Kunduz and Mazar. The Afghan president trying to remain composed, spoke loudly after Brezhnev finished his speech saying: 'Afghanistan is a free and independent country and we will not tolerate anyone telling us who to allow and who not to allow to work for us'. After this utterance, Daoud got up and without saying goodbye made for the door. The Soviet Foreign Minister, Gromyko at this moment said, 'let us have a break of a few minutes'. The Afghan Deputy Foreign Minister, Wahid Abdullah, caught up with Daoud and informed him, 'protocol requires that you should bid farewell to your host', Brezhnev. Daoud heeded this advice and went back to shake hands with Brezhnev, whereupon Brezhnev said, 'you wanted us to have a tête-à-tête meeting, I am ready now'. Daoud seeing that the situation had deteriorated said to Brezhnev, loudly so that everyone else could hear, 'There will be no need for that meeting now' and left the Kremlin.[18]

While this state visit was in the preparatory stage, the Afghans wanted such a meeting between the two heads of states. Daoud knew that the communist Khalq and Parcham were controlled from Moscow and wanted to have a private discussion with Brezhnev to emphasise on him the need to stop agitating against the government policies (Akram 2001: 225). The Russians never gave them a concrete answer before the trip, saying, let us play it by ear and if it was possible such a meeting could be arranged.

This was the most dramatic rift between the leaders of the USSR and the Republic of Afghanistan, and one that the Russians never forgot. They did not want to face a repetition of it from another Afghan leader in the future. The only other Afghan who stood up to them was Hafizullah Amin, whom the Russians murdered on 27 December 1979, and invaded Afghanistan.

Murders, assassinations and Daoud's overthrow

Daoud did not announce any coup d'etats after his fourth year in power. That year is marked by three important murders. In August 1977, Aryana Afghan Airline's chief pilot, Mohammad In'am Gran, was shot by armed men who stepped out of a white Mercedes outside his apartment in the

Microrayon housing complex. It was never clear why Captain Gran was killed or who killed him, as he was neither a politician nor active in any group or party. Some said that Daoud's anti-communists ministers who wanted to kill Karmal might have killed him by mistake, as he in someway resembled the Parcham communist leader. Others said that such a mistake was not possible and that he had been killed in a family or tribal dispute, which again has never been explained.

The second murder was that of Ahmad Ali Khoram, the American-educated planning minister and an influential force behind Daoud's modernisation programme. He was 'assassinated in Kabul's Pashtunistan Square by a teacher. A big treason trial of twenty-five Afghans implicated in the plot began in February 1978, with the 'Ikhwani (Islamists based in Pakistan) officially blamed' (Hyman 1980: 71). It is not clear to this day whether the Islamists killed him for his Westernised ideas or whether the communists did it to threaten and intimidate Daoud.

The third and the most significant murder occurred on 17 April 1978 and this time it was the Parcham ideologist, Mir Akbar Khyber, who had introduced Karmal to Marxism in prison. 'Khyber's murder was not only the most significant but also the most mysterious. Generally known as the ideologue of the Parcham group, he was also its organisational brains, thus playing for Karmal the role that Amin did for Taraki' (Bradsher 1985: 73). The murder was mysterious because despite both the Khalq and the Parcham being in power, no one mounted an enquiry to find out who was behind Khyber's killing. However, most people watching the inter-party rivalry between the Khalq and the Parcham concluded that he must have been killed by the Khalq and probably by Amin. But if this were the case, Karmal, in his six years in power, would have investigated the murder officially. Others thought that Daoud's ministers must have done the killing, as he was the most important Marxist around. His funeral became the place for a large crowd to show their displeasure with Daoud's government as some 10,000 to 15,000 people turned up, both Karmal and Taraki delivering fiery anti-government speeches at his graveside. That so many people should attend the funeral surprised Daoud's government and in the fourteen days that followed this murder, the government for the first time saw the looming communist danger. Even then it took Daoud six days to order the arrests of the PDPA leaders. He wanted to put them on trial for anti-government and anti-national offences and other trumped up charges.

The relationship between Daoud and the communists came to a head when in April 1978 Daoud got wind of serious activities against him by the communists. It was time for him to prove his threat of 'what [he would] do with' those who acted against the national interest. After hearing of communist involvement in the plan to overthrow him, he ordered the arrests of their leaders. Taraki and Karmal were taken in; other key members of the Parcham and the Khalq were put under house arrest.

Daoud held a cabinet meeting to decide their fate. The opinion in the cabinet was split on life imprisonment or execution. But the communists, who had rehearsed many times for such a day, had planned that the arrest of Taraki should be the signal for an uprising. And so while Daoud was taking his time over the fate of the communists, tanks surrounded his palace and on 27 April 1978 Daoud was removed. The next chapter is a discussion of the communists and how they in turn paved the way for Soviet intervention.

Conclusion

Daoud (b. 1912) was two years older than the king. The king instead of calling him by name, always addressed him as '*agha lalah*', a term of respect for one's sister's husband. Daoud was also the eldest son (of Mohammad Aziz Khan), the eldest of the four Musaheban brothers, who in the previous generation had left the comfort of France and gone to fight the brigand, *Bachai Saqaw*, for the capture of Kabul in 1929. Such seniority, coupled with his seriousness and steadfastness, gave him the edge not over the king, but over all other of his cousins.[19] Unlike most of the other members of the royal family he was also dedicated to his family and was a devout and practising Muslim. His experience of long years in the government was unrivalled by any other member of the royal family. However, he did not read books or long reports. These, he would give to others to read and brief him. His other main shortcomings were his stubbornness, his fiery temper and his conviction that due to his superior wisdom he did not need to listen or to allow the press to write about issues, which made his position as an autocrat difficult. This attitude made it difficult for anyone to tell him correctly what was happening on a national level. His two most trusted friends, Mohammad Hassan Sharq and Mohammad Khan Jalaler, are said to have been KGB plants; others such as Dost Mohammad Dost, foreign minister during the Soviet occupation, alongside many people in other ministries were secretly communists and pro-Soviets. These men continued to keep the Russians informed about every detail of his actions. It was they who had drawn him into the Soviet orbit in the first place, a position from which he could not easily retract. It was also these men who had encouraged him to overthrow the king, as they knew the nation would not tolerate anyone else bringing the two and a half century-old Durrani monarchy to an end. It was they who kept the Russians informed about his approach to Islamic countries and his u-turn on the communists. As a result of his including young inexperienced communists and other activists in his cabinet and high government posts, the public lost hope in his claims of 'progress and development'. The only qualifications these men had for the posts they occupied were their participation in Daoud's 17 July coup or their membership of the Parcham faction.

Daoud's presidency ended the steady build-up of central power, painfully achieved since the 1880s by all rulers. In those decades the state had struggled to establish and strengthen the nation and its central control. Daoud in his zeal, stubbornness and naivety unleashed forces within the elite and intellectuals that led to his demise and the eroding of the power base of the state. This new and modern force, as opposed to the traditional segmentary force, though spearheaded by a small number of political activists, led Afghanistan to a civil war and a level of destruction never experienced before.

Daoud looks like the ideal of an Afghan leader, fatalistic, proud, strong, pious and generous, but impatient and hot-tempered. Even at the eleventh hour, when all was lost, his presidential palace taken, when an officer from one of the coup leaders, General Qader from the air force came and asked Daoud *taslim shoa*, Submit or give in, the President asked 'submit to who', the officer said 'to General Qader'. *Qader*, meaning 'capable', is also one of 99 names of Allah. Daoud is reported having said to the officer, 'I only know of one *Qader* and that is my Allah' and produced his pistol to shoot the officer. The officer and two accompanying soldiers then machine-gunned Daoud and the whole of his eighteen-member family. This is what his brother Mohammad Naim and his eldest son Mustafa had feared and they had wanted Pacha Gul Wafadar to oblige them by assassinating Daoud, which he refused (see note 14). A journalist colleague summarises the Afghan President in these words: 'Daoud ... had the temperament to be an Afghan ruler. He was a military man and an autocrat, with a violent temper and an unshakeable belief in his own destiny' (Arney 1990: 36).

Daoud's regime was a period of uncertainty: coups, murders and the gradual destruction of over a century of enforcing and strengthening of central power. Those who were most used by outside interests were the communists and the Islamists. However, writers, intellectuals and the public at large did not make a stand against these groups, who also disliked one another. Thus the resulting suspicion and disunity eroded the power and authority of the centre. In addition to these internal factors there was the Soviet Union, which was committed to prising Afghanistan from any Western grip, while at the same time neither the West nor the Muslim countries of the Middle East were prepared to extend effective aid to Daoud's regime as an alternative to that supplied by the Soviet Union.

4 Afghan communist parties and personalities

Introduction

In the previous chapter we saw how Daoud worked with the communists to overthrow the monarchy and was later destroyed by them, eliminating him and his entire family. This chapter will trace the origin of these communists, their parties, leaders and the followers they attracted from amongst the Afghan ethnic and linguistic groups. In line with the general argument of this book it would appear that the individualism of the Afghans as a cultural motif is not just confined to the domain of the tribe and the jealousy and rivalry that occurs among agnates, but also occurs among intellectual activists. People do have choices, but these choices are limited by other factors.

> ... self-interest and group advantage tend to coincide, since it is only through his own group [ethnic or tribal] that any individual can protect or improve his position ... Group commitments may be assumed and shed at will ... individuals are able to plan and make choices in terms of private advantages and a personal political career.
> (Barth 1965: 2)

Any tribal and ethnic Afghan, depending on the situation, can choose between group advantages and personal interests. Family, tribal and ethnic links are far more important than an ideology like communism or Wahhabism. As it will be seen in this and following chapters, communist ideology, despite the communist takeover of Afghanistan and the full force of Soviet might, did not succeed in uniting even members of the communist Peoples Democratic Party of Afghanistan (PDPA). When in the segmentary conscious Afghan society group interest is chosen, as it is alleged that members of minority ethnic and linguistic groups wanted to use the utopian ideology of communism to improve their own and their groups' standing, that choice too led to suspicion, disunity and war. The individual and group distrust that is created permeates all levels of Afghan society, from the monarchs down to enlightened intellectuals and party demagogues. Thus modernist intellectuals are as much prisoners of their upbringing as are the rural tribesmen and peasants. As we shall see in this book, at the base of it all lay the cultural, linguistic and ethnic issues.

Leftists and nationalists come of age

The history of liberal progressive and communist-like radical thinking in Afghanistan can be traced back to the 1920s, the *Jawanon-e-Afghan* the Young Afghans, and then to the *Wish Zalmyan* the Awakened Youth movement established in 1947 in Kandahar (Dupree 1980: 496; Sharq 1991: 50). The Young Afghan movement was modelled on the Young Turk movement and the philosophy of Sayed Jamaludin Al-Afghani,[1] with a Pan-Islamic agenda. For the Young Afghan to serve as a bastion of Islam alongside Turkey and Iran, 'Afghanistan had to be modernised so that it might become a stronghold for the defence of Islam' (Gregorian 1969: 214). However, the collapse of the Ottoman Empire and the overthrow of the last Caliph by Mustafa Kemal gave way to a nationalist agenda viewed as parochial by Pan-Islamists. The *Wish Zalmyan* movement in Afghanistan activated just such a nationalist, modernist agenda. The *Wish Zalmyan* soon attracted a broad cross-section of Kabul's newly emerged intelligentsia too who had one aim in common and that was radical internal political and social reforms. The Soviet historian Akhramovich, brought up in a Marxist milieu describes this movement in these terms.

> Not possessing a distinct organisational structure and noted for its mixed membership, the movement at first was more like a trend made up of the most diverse social views and sentiments, and often the only thing that was common to all of them was the desire to find a way to get rid of the confusion ... in the country. This movement became the centre of social ideas around which began the consolidation or polarisation of forces on a class basis.
>
> (Quoted in Male 1982: 25)

The *Wish Zalmyan* movement became known through several of the movement's newspapers, which served as its platform. These were *Watan*, the Homeland, edited by the historian Mir Gholam Mohammad Ghobar; *Angar*, the Burning Ember, named after and edited by the Kandahari nationalist, Faiz Mohammad Angar; *Woles*, Public or Masses, edited by the poet and writer Gul Pacha Ulfat and *Neda-i-Khalq*, the Voice of the People, edited by the leftist and later pro-Peking Maoist, Abdul Rahman Mahmudi. The movement and its press then were concerned not so much with Marxism and communism, but with basic rights. The nationalists, *Watan*, *Woles*, *Angar* and the communist *Neda-i-Khalq* for example, equally stressed similar reforms and rights:

> ...to defend the common interests of civil servants and peasants, workers and pensioners, to work for the passing of democratic legisla-

tion to cover all civil matters, equal rights for all, freedom of choosing an occupation, freedom of movement, the inviolability of the person and property and observance of the law by the court. [*Neda-i-Khalq* too aimed at] ... achieving a secure social life, political rights, free speech and press ... Fair conditions for the employed and universal education ... accepting the necessity of the monarchy at least for the time and supporting the government's foreign policy.

(Male 1982: 25–6)

Afghanistan's first and second communist presidents after the 1978 communist coup, Nur Mohammad Taraki and Babrak Karmal, were members of *Wish Zalmyan*. In the 1960s the two pro-Moscow and the two pro-Peking movements took over the radical programme of the *Wish Zalmyan* with better organisation. In the same way *Afghan Millat* (1966) and *Millat* (1971) took over the nationalist mantle of *Angar*, *Woles* and *Watan*. The two pro-Moscow groups started publishing their own individual papers: *Khalq* (1966), *Parcham* (1968), *Shola and Setam* (1968) and also see Chapter 3, Table 3.1.

Although there was no organised communist party till the mid 1960s, some members of both of these groups had been privately teaching Marxism and communism since the 1950s in the hope of forming a party, modelled on the Soviet or Chinese example. It was the two pro-Moscow parties of *Khalq* the Masses and *Parcham* the Flag that prepared the ground for the communist takeover in overthrowing the government of President Daoud in 1978. Of these pro-Moscow groups, it was *Khalq* with its connections within the army and air force that mounted the coup and toppled the government. This chapter therefore is a discussion of the two pro-Moscow communist parties and their role in inviting the Soviet intervention in December 1979, which lasted till February 1989. The implications of this communist action have been of colossal socio-political significance for Afghanistan. Tribal, ethnic, linguistic and the interference of neighbouring and regional powers in what has happened in Afghanistan will be discussed in Part III of this book. My concern in this chapter is to describe and analyse the national picture and to show the role the elite and certain key communist personalities played in fashioning these events.

The entry of the communists

Communists and leftists of all shades and opinion, like other political activists, took advantage of the democratic atmosphere provided by the king. More than a dozen of the leftist-cum-communist parties and groups regularly held demonstrations, published their own papers and magazines and, through their MPs in parliament, made a flood of demands on the governments of the day. Two well-known leftist figures, Nur Mohammad Taraki, a Ghilzai Pashtun and Babrak Karmal, a Dari speaker, headed the

Table 4.1 Khalq and Parcham recruitment and political leanings

Khalq or 'Masses'	Parcham or 'Flag'
Leaders: Taraki 1978–79 Amin 1979	Leaders: Karmal 1980–86 Najibullah 1986–92
Mainly Pashtun, forming majority of PDPA members Mostly urban intellectuals, peasants and farmers, traditionalists More radical and purist, pro-Moscow and anti-establishment Afghan nationalists at heart, overthrown from power by Soviets in December 1979.	Mainly non-Pashtuns forming minority of PDPA members Mostly urban civil servants, military leaders, educated Dari-speaking More moderate, broad-front, pro-Moscow, accepted reformist monarch for time being Committed communist installed in power by Soviets in January 1980

Note
Diagram showing at a glance at the PDPA's two factions – its stand and its supporting constituencies.

communist factions (see Table 4.1). The followers of Taraki were mostly a rural elite belonging to the Pashtuns, the largest ethnic group in the country. The followers of Karmal were mainly Tajik, the second largest ethnic group, urban city dwellers, especially the sons and daughters of high-ranking civil servants and military officers. Both groups' leaders were KGB agents since the early 1950s and remained loyal to the Russians and their communist system throughout their active political life, while Moscow always kept them under close observation.

> The Center [KGB Moscow] set out its opinion of the work with Taraki and Babrak in an operational letter to Kabul on 25 October 1974. 'In the course of regular meetings and conversation with 'Murid' [Babrak] and 'Nur' [Taraki] you must carefully, in the form of friendly advice and without referring to instructions from Moscow, tell them not take any steps without prior agreement by us which could be used by their enemies . . . compromising them. Murid and Nur should also be warned again that they must desist from attacking each other . . . as this plays into the hands of the reactionary forces and will lead to the collapse of the democratic movement in Afghanistan. We request that you inform us by telegram of your meetings and conversation with 'Murid' and 'Nur'.
>
> (Metrokhin 2002: 26)

Recruitment to both Khalq and Parcham was through personal contacts. The leaders recruited their close lieutenants and each of them in turn recruited others and so on. Membership was small, numbering in the hundreds. Even when the Peoples Democratic Party of Afghanistan (PDPA) came to power in 1978 it boasted a membership of 20,000, which by then was believed to be half that. At the height of their power in the 1980s, the PDPA is believed to have had a membership of no more than 165,000. Neither these two communist parties nor other political groups ever disclosed their sources of income. Khalq and Parcham claimed their party expenses were paid out of members' subscriptions.

The leaders of both Khalq and Parcham, at least since 1963, held group discussions and seminars on Marxism-Leninism, without any fear from the authorities. But it was on 1 January 1965 that Nur Mohammad Taraki secretly held the first communist congress at his home in Kabul. Twenty-seven activists participated, who were later to become known as the founder members. Both factions joined together forming the Peoples Democratic Party of Afghanistan (PDPA), appointing Taraki as the PDPA Secretary General and Karmal as his deputy. The party chose a five-member central committee and approved their programme of work. At this stage the party took care to avoid any mention of Marxist/Leninist terms and also advocated a broad front of democratic, progressive and patriotic forces. Anthony Arnold, himself a former CIA operative in Afghanistan, says that a member of the Western embassy (probably another intelligence source) in 1978 came across the 'secret' constitution of the PDPA approved at this meeting, which was full of communist phraseology and called the PDPA the 'Party of the Working Class of Afghanistan' (Arnold 1983: 242).

A bureaucratic elite had run Afghanistan at least since the 1880s. This old elite, who for a century represented the monarchy, continued to work in the recently overthrown republic too. The communists for the first time were part of a different formation of the elite. They emerged through party affiliation and had no previous experience of bureaucracy. With the communists coming to power, some of the old and nearly all of the new elite prepared themselves in a new political and economic spirit. Those in Parcham, despite their slogans, were not from the working class, though those in Khalq were mainly from peasant families. A good sprinkling of both had received a modern education in the West and in the Soviet Union. For effective political purposes both groups organised themselves on cultural and linguistic lines. 'The more culturally homogenous the group, the more effective can it organise for political action' (Cohen 1969: 3).

Most PDPA members in the years since have admitted that the Soviet Union, through its embassy, the largest of all foreign missions in Kabul, and especially through their experienced ambassador, Alexander Puzanov, stationed in Kabul for over ten years, was encouraging them to organise themselves as political parties and to attract supporters. The Soviet aim at this early stage was probably not so much to turn these communists into the government of the land, but more to counteract through them other groups, such as the militant Islamists, the Maoists and the nationalists, who were all opposed to the Soviet Union and its influence in

Afghanistan. But the ethno-linguistic schism and the rural/urban differences that existed amongst both of these pro-Moscow parties hampered Soviet attempts at uniting them and as we shall see in this and the following chapter, remained a headache for Moscow to the end.

Elections under the new constitution for *Wolesey Jirga* or the Lower House were held in September 1965, but Khalq's strongman Taraki was defeated. Vasily Metrokhin, who worked in the KGB's Moscow archive, explains PDPA and Taraki's source of income.

> Despite the fact that 'the PDPA was financed by the CPSU Central Committee. Its newspaper was also financed in this way. In 1965 Taraki was given 50,000 Afghani for the election campaign ... he [Taraki] was also given a personal allowance of 180 hard currency rubels, the equivalent of 4000 Afghani, and food supplies'.
>
> (Metrokhin 2002: 22)

Khalq's other strong man Hafizullah Amin (see below) was in the USA at the time and was elected four years later in the 1969 elections. The Parcham leader Karmal and his female colleague, Anahita Ratebzad, and two other Parchamis were elected in this very first free and democratic election in the history of Afghanistan. Karmal's 'connection with his reputed mistress Anahita Ratebzad had been an open scandal since at least the early 1960s' (Klass 1987: 410).[2] With Parcham now in parliament and debates in the Lower House broadcast live on national radio (there was no television in the 1960s) the communists took advantage of the situation by interrupting other speakers, making long and involved speeches and provoking their supporters and the general public to come out against the government. Students from Kabul University and some students and pupils of the capital's colleges and schools often responded by coming out in demonstrations. In one such incident known as *Say Aqrab* (Afghan month) 25 October 1965, students clashed near the prime minister Dr Yosuf's house and in the ensuing shoot out three people were killed. The communists seized on this by commemorating this date every year.[3] Most MPs after a year of the communists filibustering and other delaying and interrupting tactics became frustrated. In an infamous attack on the communist MPs they broke the chairs within the debating chamber to use to beat the communist MPs. Karmal was beaten most severely of all, and spent some time in hospital. Had it not been for Anahita Ratebzad throwing herself on him, and the Afghan custom of not beating a woman in public or touching her, he may well have been killed by the angry MPs. One of the men, who did most of the beating, was Mohammad Nabi Mohammadi, who during the Soviet occupation formed his moderate resistance party, the *Harakat-i-Inqilab-Islami*, Movement of Islamic Revolution whose members were mainly Taleban and religious leaders. (See Chapter 6 on resistance parties and their leaders).

Strife among the communists

The disunity and rivalry that characterises Afghan tribes went all the way in the eighteenth and nineteenth centuries to the monarchs and were important reasons for installing or overthrowing rulers. Similar disunity and distrust had also filtered through to the intellectual elite and among the communists. The communist party that came out of the secret congress at Taraki's house in Kabul in 1965 was riddled with disunity and internal strife. The two pro-Moscow wings of the PDPA hardly agreed beyond the general goal of establishing a socialist order in Afghanistan. There were many reasons for this: the paternalistic approach of the Parchamis who, because of their high family positions and city sophistication, considered themselves to be better qualified in dealing with the Russians and other 'fraternal parties' and always attempted to bulldoze their way on every party issue. The Russian approach to both leaders was overtly even handed but they were much closer to Parcham leadership than Khalq.

> Taraki and Babrak were totally unable to do their party work together ... The Residency [Soviet KGB agents in Kabul] defended Taraki as it has ... Babrak. It viewed him [Taraki] positively and considered him a true and sincere friend of the USSR who cooperated conscientiously [and] observed the rule of secrecy and carried out an assignment in the American embassy. Babrak, as an educated man, tried to follow more flexible tactics in practical work of the PDPA.
> (Metrokhin 2002: 24)

Karmal and others, without much foundation, wanted to be the intellectual light that guided the party. The Parchamis because of their urban background were more Westernised and often their party meetings were said to end in disco dancing (Shahrani and Canfield 1984: 306–40). Their language Dari (a dialect of Farsi), the *lingua franca* in Afghanistan, gave them the advantage of easily attracting other ethnic minorities.

Much of the bitterness in the two communist parties flowed from personal rivalries among the upper echelons of both factions and inter-party rivalry.[4] On the other hand, the Khalq group was much more in touch with rural areas. Their support base, unlike that of the Parcham, was not confined just to Kabul. They had much wider support among the Pashtun urban elite and Pashtun peasants and farmers. The Khalq faction because of their Pashtun origins claimed to represent the majority of the population in Afghanistan and, therefore, were not going to give in to sons of 'generals' (like Karmal) and other technocrats, most of whom had never travelled in the Afghan countryside, nor knew of the real day-to-day problems of rural Afghanistan. Their leader, Taraki, unlike Karmal, was brought up in poverty and knew what dispossession and oppression meant. At the heart of this divide was the question of linguistic, regional, rural and urban cultural difference. The urban Parchamis, who were mostly Dari speakers, never got on with the rural Khalq Pashtuns and vice versa. There was also a doctrinal difference between the two factions' approaches.

> Parcham was ready to pursue a 'common front' approach, i.e., outward and temporary collaboration with non-Marxists, pending seizure of power. Khalq on the other hand rejected such collaborations and demanded loyalty to 'pure', uncompromising revolutionary socialism. But the origin of bitter conflict between them actually lay less in doctrine than in traditional cultural sources: ethnic differences, social differences, the enduring mutual contempt between Kabuli and provincials . . .
>
> (Klass 1987: 141)

After eighteen months, this internal strife led to the breakdown of the PDPA in 1967 into two factions. However, neither side ever officially admitted the breakdown at the time. Within the party apparatus, Karmal tried to remove Taraki as secretary general of the party and when this could not be achieved, he offered his resignation. To his surprise Taraki and the majority of the central committee accepted it. 'The Karmalites' then took their supporters with them and started their own party with Karmal as its secretary general and his close colleagues as members of its central committee. In March 1968, they started their weekly, *Parcham*, the Banner or Flag, and were subsequently known as Parchamis. This paper, unlike *Khalq* (see below) was much more moderate and was soon dubbed by the Khalqis as the paper of 'the royal communist party' because of its accommodation of the monarchy. In one article in the paper, Karmal called the king 'the most progressive king in Asia', for introducing the democratic constitution and for giving so much freedom to the people. This aroused a great deal of sarcasm and opprobrium from Khalq and other opponents. It was because of this solicitous approach on the part of Parcham that their paper lasted till July 1969, only to be closed on the eve of that year's general elections in which Amin and Karmal alone were elected from the PDPA to *Wolesy jirga*, the Lower House.

The Pashtun faction, under Taraki and Amin, despite Arnold's claim about the 'real' PDPA constitution, never minced their words and vigorously campaigned to win support and change the regime. Kabul intelligentsia read their weekly *Khalq* with great interest. *Khalq* or The Masses, also lent its name to this faction, the Khalqis. Its very first issue sold 20,000 copies and later editions settled at around 10,000. In a country where some 90 per cent of the population was illiterate and in Kabul where more than forty daily, weekly and monthly publications had sprung up since 1964, this circulation was enormous. The *Khalq* was outspoken and openly wrote about class struggle and 'the boundless agonies of the oppressed peoples of Afghanistan'. Additionally it stated, that 'the main issue of contemporary times and the centre of class struggle on the world-wide basis, which began with the Great October Socialist Revolution, is the struggle between international socialism and international capitalism' (Nyrop and Seekins 1986: 221). The last straw for the paper was an article by a PDPA founder, Mohammad Rafi, who wrote a *durood*, or religious blessing for Lenin.[5] Mullahs and many MPs were furious, saying that a *durood* can only be sent to the Prophet and to send a *durood* to an atheist and communist was blasphemy.

Only six editions of the paper came out between April and May 1966. The *Khalq* was eventually censured on the basis of being 'anti-Islamic, anti-constitutional and anti-monarchical' (Dupree 1973: 608).

The positive impact of the decade of 'democratic experiment' was the freedom of press, of speech and association and the freedom to travel abroad. Until then a passport to travel abroad was largely reserved for the members of government and the royal family. Afghans learned more about democracy and their rights in those ten years than in the previous decades of the twentieth century combined. Its negative impact was of the king's making, by not ratifying laws dealing with political parties, thus hampering accountability through the legal and parliamentary process. The king, contrary to the ideals of his 1964 constitution declaring him as constitutional monarch and a symbol of unity, continued to appoint prime ministers who in turn chose their cabinet ministers from outside parliament. Thus instead of creating an atmosphere of trust and accountability, the gulf between parliament and government widened.

Another negative effect of the experiment with democracy was the surfacing of ethnic, linguistic and religious cleavages that were quiescent. Ethnic minorities began to express their resentment of the Pashtun majority and the urban Tajiks' monopoly of bureaucracy. The Shi'ah, who until then hid the fact that they were Shi'ah and observed their religious ceremonies only in the old quarter of Kabul's *Chendawel*, off limits to the Sunni, came into the open airing their grievances. They built a large mosque in western Kabul and went about their religious practices openly.

The Maoist *Shola*, the Flame, and the other pro-Peking movement the *Setam-i-Meli*, National Oppression, were both the products of the decade of the constitution. *Shola*, which had an international agenda of anti-imperialism, was also internally against Pashtun rule and wanted Maoist-like reforms in Afghanistan. Setam on the other hand had an entirely internal programme of provoking minorities to armed resurrection to stand up to Pashtuns. Their leader Taher Badakhshi was an Isma'ilia Shi'ah and one time member of the Parcham faction. The leader of *Shola*, Dr Abdur Rahman Mahmudi, though a Dari-speaker like Karmal, criticised the latter's pro-Moscow stand as revisionist. 'While Karmal was known as *chap* or left, Mahmudi was *chap-e-chap* left of left' (Hyman 1983: 59). Their anti-Pashtun stance was more of a Shi'ah versus Sunni *Afghan*,

Dari speaking intellectuals versus Pashtun rulers and majority versus minority rather than based on actual exploitation or misrule by the Pashtun kings. The Afghan Durrani leaders were no doubt Pashtun by origin. But most rulers and urban Durrani, during the period of 130 years of Persian Safavid control over them in western Afghanistan, and their subsequent adoption of the Farsi[6] language, culture and their assimilation to it, made them over the years, much closer culturally to Dari speakers and other non-Pashtuns (like Hazarah, Uzbek, Nuristani and so on) than to the Pashtuns. Nearly all of the Musaheban family for example, who had ruled for forty-eight years, had forgotten their language, Pashto. These ruling families through such a voluntary assimilation had developed a distance between themselves and the rest of the Pashtun tribes. That is why no government in Afghanistan since its foundation in 1747 has ever used Pashto as the language of bureaucracy or has been dominated by Pashtuns (Rubins 1991: 73–100, WAKFA 1999: 55).

However, the two non-Pashtun parties by being pro-China were caught up in regional politics. As China had good relations with Pakistan, and Pakistan was opposed to the Pashtunistan issue, these two movements (more so for political reasons internal to Setam's) became pro-China and Pakistan, and by implication anti the Soviet influence in Afghanistan. While *Shola* was hounded by pro-Moscow sympathisers and went underground after the communist takeover in 1978, the position of *Setam-i-Meli* changed after 1982 when they saw that Soviet military campaigns were primarily aimed against the Pashtuns. The Setamis, to which factions within Jam'iat Islami and *Shura-i-Nezar* belonged, joined the Parcham government and the Soviet invaders to aid them fight the mainly Pashtun Hezb of Hekmatyar and to evict and brutalise Pashtuns, especially those from the northern provinces, where they had settled since the 1880s. Thus Pashtun homes and villages were the only ones bombed and mined to force them to flee. In the rest of Afghanistan too, the Ten Years War was mainly fought in Pashtun areas. Over 90 per cent of the ten million plus mines in Afghanistan have been planted in Pashtun areas. Most of the 1.5 million killed in the war were Pashtuns and the majority of the refugees, some still abroad, especially in Pakistan are Pashtuns. Almost a quarter of a century after the Soviet occupation, Pashtuns are still not allowed by Tajik Setami, Hazarah Shi'ah and Uzbeks warlords to return to areas under the latters' control.

After this preliminary observation of ethno-linguistic and rural/urban rifts that surfaced amongst the communists in the decade of democracy, I now want to highlight the leaders of the two pro-Moscow communist parties, and in the following chapter show how they came to power and why they were so disunited.

Key communist leaders

Three men, Nur Mohammad Taraki, Babrak Karmal and Hafizullah Amin are the key figures in the two communist factions. Each man, in his own particular way, reached the rank of the general secretary of the PDPA and the president of Afghanistan. Each one served as a central figure in precipitating, opposing or accommodating the Soviet invasion. A fuller discussion of their political involvement with the Russians will be presented in the next chapter. Here I want to give brief biographic information about each of these three men in order to assess fully their role in what has become Afghanistan's greatest tragedy.

Nur Mohammad Taraki

Taraki, as he became known, was the oldest of the three. He was born in 1917 to a peasant family in the village of *Sowr Kalay* (ironically Red Village in Pashto) near Ghazni. Despite his poor background, he attended school in Kandahar and after leaving school at the age of 15 he went to work in 1932 in the port city of Bombay for a Kandahari merchant family in their firm 'The Pashtun Company'. He learned of this merchant family when at school. Three important events seem to have made a lasting impression on him. First, while still in school, he witnessed the fall of the progressive King Amanullah, who stayed in Kandahar on his way to Bombay (1928), from where he took the boat to exile in Italy. Second, while taking night school classes in Bombay to complete his matriculation and to learn English and Urdu, he came across some members of the Communist Party of India (CPI). Although he never became a member of the CPI, he was impressed by their arguments about social justice and how that could be achieved through communism. Third, while in India he met with the Pashtun nationalist leader, Khan Abdul Ghafar Khan, leader of the Pashtun Red Shirt Movement in British India and after the partition of 1947, the leader of Pashtunistan, also a passionate admirer of Lenin's achievements.

Taraki returned to Kabul in 1937 and started work under Abdul Majid Zabuli (the founder of modern banking in Afghanistan) then Minister of Economics. Zabuli had met personally with Lenin and is said to have introduced Taraki to the Russians. Taraki later became deputy head of Afghanistan's national news agency, Bakhter, and made a name for himself as a writer and poet. One of his books is called *De Bang Mosaferi* the Journeys of Bang (1960). 'Bang' in Pashto has many meanings: fuzzy headed, unaware, disillusioned etc. This work is presumably an autobiography, in which Taraki highlights the socio-economic difficulties Bang faces and the dreams he has for himself and other similarly deprived people. This and a number of other works describing the social conditions of the peasants and poor were, in the early 1960s, translated into Russian, prefacing these works as 'scientific socialist themes' and raising Taraki to the status of 'Afghanistan's Maxim Gorky'. On a visit to Moscow 'he was received by Boris Panamarev, the head of International Department [CPSU] and other members [of the Communist Party]' (Metrokhin 2002: 20). After he became president, the Soviet press reported that Taraki 'wrote many stories on acute social issues which have been translated into various languages, including Russian ... These stories relate to the formation of the proletariat in Afghanistan and the transformation of rural peasants into city inhabitants and workers' (Bradsher 1985: 37).

When, in 1952, the new government of Prime Minister Mohammad Daoud clamped down on radicals, Taraki, because of his skill as a writer (also at that date not a prominent anti-establishment figure), was sent to Washington as press and cultural attaché in the Afghan embassy. But after a few months there he denounced the government in Kabul as autocratic and dictatorial. Taraki, as a member of his country's mission in Washington, publicly criticising it, received wide publicity in the USA and not surprisingly he was recalled to Kabul. When he arrived in Kabul, it is said that he telephoned Prime Minister Daoud from the airport saying 'Shall I go to prison or home?' However, either because of the wide publicity he received in the USA or because Daoud did not consider him a threat he was ignored and was not offered another job with the government and was for some time unemployed. In 1956 Taraki found a job as a translator at the United States Overseas Mission in Kabul. The Americans appreciated him as a capable translator. However in 1958 he left this job and opened his own, 'Noor Translation Agency'. Four years later in 1962, he returned to his job as translator, this time with the American Embassy in Kabul only to quit it again a year later. From 1963, he devoted all his time to laying the foundations of the PDPA.

Taraki's encounter with the Communist Party of India and also with the most prominent Pashtun, Khan Abdul Ghafar Khan, convinced him that Marxism and communism was a way out of Afghanistan's underdevelopment and social injustice. 'Taraki had a genuine concern with social justice that comes out strongly in his novels and short stories' (Bradsher 1985: 36–7). His memories of the uprising against King Amanullah gave him the hope that the current monarchy could also be replaced through a well-organised proletariat revolution.

There is no doubt that he was a Marxist by the early 1940s, and was among the few Marxists who secretly taught Marxism-Leninism to groups of enthusiasts. Arnold holds that Taraki was a KGB agent (Klass 1987: 414). Metrokhin provides the proof.

> Some of the KGB agents adherents of Marxism-Leninism and a few became active in International Communist and Worker's Movement with the help of the organs. One such agent was Nur Muhammad Taraki, code name 'Nur'. He became an agent in 1951 and was in

contact with following operatives in Kabul: Sagadiev, Kozlov, Fedoseev, Spiridonov, Kostromin, Kozyrev and A.V. Petrov.

(Metrokhin 2002: 19–20)

But, when this was the case, why did the Soviet intelligence not keep him in Washington or as translator with the Americans in Kabul? In both places he was privy to many confidential documents and other information, much valued by the Russians. Why did they let him open up his own translation agency, which mainly involved filling in forms and writing telegrams in English for Kabul businessmen?

Those who knew Taraki say that he was a softly spoken and kind man. After becoming president of the Democratic Republic of Afghanistan (DRA), he, in a patriarchal gesture like monarchs before, invited shop-keepers and all his friends and acquaintances in the *Kart-e-Char* area of Kabul where he lived, to the palace. After a sumptuous meal he told them 'I am going to be busy from now on, but you should not think that I would ever forget you for the long years we spent together'.[7]

In 1979, when resistance to communism was building up in the country, Taraki is said to have asked the Russians for military intervention under the 1978 treaty, which says that in the event of danger to one country, the other will intervene. But when the Russians intervened in December 1979, they killed President Amin and some of his cabinet colleagues thus making a mockery of the treaty's provision by killing the leaders of the government, who had asked them to help repel the 'imperialist' threat, a charge the Soviet never answered satisfactorily.

Hafizullah Amin

The second key figure in communist circles was Hafizullah Amin, another prominent Pashtun nationalist and intellectual who turned Khalqi. Amin like Taraki belonged to the Ghilzai tribal confederation. While Taraki belonged to the Taraki tribe of the Ghilzai Andar branch, Amin, like the resistance leader Hekmatyar (Chapter 6) belonged to the Kharuti tribe of the Ghilzai. Amin was born in 1921 and lived in the holiday resort town of Paghman, ten kilometres to the west of Kabul. His father was a minor civil servant and later the governor of Kabul's main prison, Dehmazang. He studied physics and mathematics at Kabul University and after graduation taught these subjects at Ibn Sina (Avicenna) School in Kabul where he himself was a former pupil. He won a scholarship in 1957 to study at the Teacher Training College at Columbia University in New York. After completion of his MA in Education, he returned and was appointed head of his old school, Ibn Sina, and later of the Kabul's *Darul Mo'alemin* Teacher Training College. At this time he also taught part time at one of the capital's only two Pashto-language schools, where I met him. He taught us physics and mathematics from grade eight to ten.

At this time Amin's preoccupation was the Pashtun cause and he felt deeply about the injustice of the Pashtuns in NWFP being separated from Afghanistan by the machinations of the British colonial powers in India. He returned to Columbia in 1962 to read for his doctoral degree in education and this time became an active member of the Associated Students of Afghanistan (ASA) becoming its president in 1963. He regularly wrote for the ASA's and other Muslim student unions' newsletters. He became very critical of the monarchy and especially the dictatorial attitude of Prime Minister Mohammad Daoud (1953–63). As a result of these activities, his scholarship was discontinued and he was recalled home. He wanted to complete his PhD, claiming that 'three quarters of the thesis was already at hand'.[8] It was because of this determination that he came to London in 1965, thinking that because there was an exchange agreement between Colombia and London Universities, he would be able to complete his PhD here. But as he could not get a work permit from the Home Office to teach in order to support himself he had to leave the UK.

I was studying for my GCEs then and had the opportunity for nearly two weeks to get to know Amin, not as a teacher/pupil, but as a friend. I called on his hotel in Gower Street nearly every day to find out about the progress of his application. One day Amin told me why he had been 'forced' to leave the US. He showed me a letter, one and a half lines long, signed by the then Minister of Education Dr Mohammad Anas, saying, 'please return to Afghanistan without delay as we need you here'. Amin told me 'The FBI several times called on me in New York telling me to return to Afghanistan otherwise we would force you on to the plane'.

He left London for West Germany where his friend, Dr Ali Ahmad Popal, was Afghan ambassador, and when he could not help him, he went to the American University in Beirut. He was unable to get admission there either and wrote me a letter from Beirut, saying that there was no possibility of him 'studying here either and so even if Kabul is hell, I have no choice but to return'.

There is no justification in the claim that he 'returned to Kabul via Moscow' or 'because his politicking left him little time for study and he flunked out' (Klass 1987: 411). The circumstances of his expulsion from the US were not even fully known to Amin himself. Years later, when Foreign Minister, he said in a radio interview: 'I did not know whether I was ousted or summoned. The American authorities said that the Government of Afghanistan had summoned me, and in Kabul they told me that the American authorities had ousted me. I demanded to continue my study at my own expense but my demand was turned down' (SWB, part iii, Sep. 1979).

That he became interested in Marxism while studying in the US there is no doubt. 'During the summer of 1958, while still working for his Master's degree, he took courses in political science and economics at the University of Wisconsin. He also joined the Socialist Progressive Club. This seems to have been a turning point' (Male 1982: 28).

I myself saw several books in his London hotel room on Marxist ideas with the margins full of notes and translation of words written in pencil. Amin thought he could cut across ethnic and linguistic barriers through socialism and unite the whole country to implement his dream. When I asked him why he was interested in communism now he answered like a typical modernist of the time, 'America and the West is rich and much advanced, we can never become like them and it takes a long time. So communism is the only way for our development and advancement as a country'. The toppling of the monarchy was for him just an afternoon's picnic. He confided in me, 'I told the Americans that I need only $20,000 to overthrow the regime'.[9]

Amin was very resentful about a regime that could not tolerate criticism and so when he went to Kabul, though missing the PDPA congress on 1 January 1965, he joined the party and made regular contributions from his salary to the party funds. Amin by joining the Party invigorated it. Taraki could not believe his luck in the addition of an intellectual of such a calibre to his Khalq ranks. 'His expulsion from the United States ... was a blessing in disguise' (Male 1982: 39). Although Taraki and his supporters particularly welcomed him, his ambitions and energy frightened Karmal and his followers, who also knew him as a Pashtun nationalist. After his death Karmal stamped him as a 'CIA' agent, a claim Karmal did not prove even after six years in power. A Russian journalist on Amin's 'CIA' accusation has this to add:

'I interviewed Karmal, who now lives in Moscow, in April 1989: "Did you really believe Amin was a CIA agent?" I asked him. "I could only judge him on the basis of his actions," Karmal replied. "Even if the American had spent a hundred billion dollars on the destabilisation of Afghanistan, they couldn't have harmed it as much as Amin did." "But if you follow that logic," I said, "Brezhnev, who really made a mess out of the USSR, must've been an agent of every Western intelligence agency at once". As he had before, Karmal responded with a quotation from Lenin. "Tell me," he then asked with a cunning smile, "has it yet been made illegal to mention Lenin's name in the USSR?" His own loud laughter was the answer'.[10]

(Brorovik 1990: 5–6)

Amin was not a committed communist like Taraki or Karmal. He was more in the mould of other Third World nationalist leaders such as Gandhi and Nehru in the 1930s or Ho Chi Minh, Kenyatta and Nkrumah in the 1960s, all of whom came to London and Paris to study and became revolutionaries leading India, Vietnam, Kenya and Ghana to independence. Amin in his turn wanted to use communism as a way of obtaining power quickly and after getting the initial funding for a socialist infrastructure from the Russians, he wanted to take Afghanistan on its separate road to development and democracy. In a speech broadcast on the national radio during his 100 days as head of state he said, 'we are criticised by becoming a Soviet Satellite ... which other country is prepared to aid us to the extent that the Soviet Union has done?' (SWB, Part iii, Oct. 1979).

Amin despite his overt pleading for a Soviet-like system, underneath it all remained a patriot and a nationalist. Amongst many reasons why the Russians killed him on 27 December 1979, one was his refusal to give them sole landing rights at Shindand airbase in western Afghanistan. This airbase was important for the Russians who thought that if in response to the Iranians taking the American embassy hostages in Tehran, American and NATO forces were to take southern Iran, as in the Second World War, the Russians would be best placed to make a rush for northern Iran, through Azerbaijan and westward from Afghanistan. Amin was reported as telling his colleagues, that the 'nation will not tolerate' handing over a part of Afghanistan such as an airbase to the Soviets for their sole use. A Russian conspiracy in September 1979 for Taraki to kill Amin, ended up in Amin killing the latter and then insisting that Soviet ambassador Alexander M. Puzanov, who had led him into the trap, was expelled from Kabul. This was another well-known attempt by Amin to tell the Russians to mind their business. However, he never understood that the Russians were not going to tolerate such impudence from someone so overwhelmingly dependent on them.

While Taraki and Karmal could not find themselves respectable jobs, Amin with his teaching background had no difficulty. After returning from the US he was appointed as principal of *Ibn Sina* college and the *Darul Mo'alemin* Teacher Training College; an official of the Teacher Training Institute at the Ministry of Education; lecturer in education at Kabul University and before that he taught at different boys' and girls' schools in the capital. It was in these schools and educational establishments where Amin recruited some of his impressionable students to serve with him later in the PDPA.

Amin was a disciplinarian and would not stand for nonsense from anyone. At our school examination time, he would wear his dark glasses and stand in the corner of the examination hall, probably with his eyes shut relaxing but giving everyone the impression of being watched. When in the PDPA he also started watching everyone, including Taraki, and soon became the undisputed leader, despite Taraki being at the head of the party. When the party formed the government after the April coup of 1978 he was appointed as Deputy Prime Minister and Foreign Minister, working an eighteen-hour schedule. He had notices posted on the Foreign Ministry's gates giving his timetable to see the public and 'party comrades'. Amin, despite being impatient with Daoud's dictatorial regime, was himself dictatorial, authoritarian and ruthless against his opponents. However, this view of Amin is disputed by his biographer, Beverly Male who writes that Karmal's government and the Soviet Union have played a not inconsiderable part in perpetuating the image of Amin as mass murderer, although Babrak Karmal has ... been completely unsuccessful in discovering even a single mass grave, despite his early exhortations to the Afghan people to search for the many he claimed existed. And yet the myth of Amin as a mass murderer persists, perpetuated by refugees who fled an Afghanistan no longer being run in their class interest; by Babrak Karmal's regime, which depends heavily on it in order to legitimise its own seizure of power; by the U.S. which uses Amin's 'appalling human rights record' to excuse its failure to heed his appeals; and by a group of leftist intellectuals outside Afghanistan for whom the alternative is too embarrassing to contemplate.

(Male 1982: 17)

He was, however, ruthless and uncompromising particularly against his party opponents and resistance foes. In a radio interview, in October 1979, he said about the latter 'if the *Ekhwanul Shiatin*' Devil's Brothers, his derogatory way of referring to *Ekhwanul Muslemin* the Muslim Brotherhood, 'continues to attack us we cannot tie our hands behind our backs', thus justifying the torturing and killing of resistance members. He was similarly ruthless in his dealings with Parcham opponents. But at the same time, while Taraki and Karmal were prepared to offer Afghanistan 'on a plate' to the Russians, Amin was vehemently opposed to Afghanistan losing its independence and national sovereignty. Russian hostility was apparent from the time when on 17 June 1978, at a meeting of the Revolutionary Council he was the leading exponent of the government's refusal to work with the Parchamis. It was decided at that meeting that Karmal and half a dozen of his close colleagues should be exiled to embassy posts abroad. The Parchamis tried in an unsuccessful coup to come back and take over the government but they were caught. Amin was prepared to go along with the Russians provided that this tactic did not compromise his power or damage Afghanistan's independent status. The Russians could not tolerate Amin's headstrong attitude and thus, when the opportunity arose on the night of 27 December 1979 a Russian special force which was placed around his palace went into action, killing Amin, his entire presidential guard and his family, except for his wife and a daughter (now in Germany) who could not be located at the time.

Babrak Karmal

Karmal, the third of the key leaders, was born in Kabul in 1926. Although he invariably claimed to have been a Pashtun of Kakar and again of the Babeker Khail tribe, in fact his forefathers had come from India and lived in Kamari village near Kabul.[11] His father Mohammad Hussain, a military officer (reaching the rank of general before retirement) was once governor of Paktia. Probably because of contacts in this Pashtun province the young Babrak later claimed affinity with them and even chose his surname as '*Karmal*', meaning in Pashto, 'friend of work or labour'. However, his past, like his origins and academic background, is a chequered one. According to Klass he was an 'Afghan communist *par excellence* and, according to the KGB defector Vladimir Kuzichin, a paid agent of the KGB for many years before the 1978 coup. 'Karmal' is a *nom de plume* adopted earlier on, possibly for its double meaning: 'friend of labor' but it can also be interpreted as 'Kremlin' (Klass 1987: 408). He was, she notes 'a mediocre student', failing his entrance examination to the faculty of law in Kabul. Finally in 1951 he was admitted but, as a result of the government clampdown on radicals, he was imprisoned for four years, although he was well-treated by the prison authorities because of his father's contacts. 'While in prison he met Mir Akbar Khyber (a prominent Afghan communist), whose Marxist views had a formative influence on him' (Nyrop and Seekins 1986: 210). He completed his degree in 1960 and also his compulsory army conscription. He used to be seen going to the Soviet embassy in Kabul, just across Kabul River from the law faculty. That he worked for the Russians was an open secret. It was because of this contact and the adverse reputation that it entailed, together with his anti-government and anti-establishment rhetoric, that his father publicly disowned him and his mother, taking another wife and living in a separate part of Kabul. However, his father made it up with him after he came to power in 1980 by trying to persuade, often unsuccessfully, some of his retired army officers to work for his son's government.[12]

While Karmal was not studious, he was a good orator and a 'gifted demagogue'. Rosanne Klass of the Freedom House in New York, who interviewed him during the 1965 elections found out that, 'a few questions elicited the fact that he had never heard of the French or any other revolution other than the Bolshevik Revolution' (Klass 1987: 409). Karmal was not very successful in keeping jobs and held a number of minor posts between 1960–64. After 1964, he devoted himself fully to laying down the foundations of a communist party in Kabul. 'Babrak's morals were not beyond reproach, and had an affair with Politburo member Anahita Ratebzad' (Metrokhin 2002: 137). He was also totally unfamiliar with the Afghan countryside and, unlike Taraki and Amin, apart from a brief visit to India on party matters had never travelled abroad till he came to power in January 1980. Neither did he speak any foreign language, learning a smattering of Russian after he came to power. That is why he acquired his knowledge of Marxism and communism from books translated into Farsi. Karmal's recorded speech on coming to power was broadcast on the same wavelength as Radio Afghanistan from Tashkent radio in Uzbekistan and he himself arrived three days after Amin's death in a Soviet military plane to Bagram Airport, 20 km north of Kabul.

The KGB and the Soviet leadership, seeing the deteriorating security situation in the country, also lost faith in their trusted 'Murid' Karmal.

> The Residency considered that Babrak was not up to the task of leading the party ... He was limited by his narrow Parcham view, failed to differentiate between the supporter of Taraki [Nur later Dedov] and the supporters of Amin ... wanted Taraki and Amin and the Khalqi faction to be completely discredited ... He often complained: 'it was not my idea that I should sit at the same table with the Khalqis'.
>
> (Metrokhin 2002: 132)

After six years of the Soviet Union's relentless efforts to pacify the country, they failed and had no choice but to remove their trusted Karmal in stages from May 1986, replacing him by Dr Najibullah as the PDPA Secretary General. Since Karmal still had supporters amongst the Parcham and the government he provoked them into making life difficult for Najibullah. In 1987, he was sent for 'medical treatment to the Soviet Union' where he died (1996). His body was secretly brought to Hairatan, in northern Afghanistan, where his former communist militia general, Abdul Rashid Dostum buried him, next to a scrap yard. When the Taleban took Balkh in May 1996, one of the things they did was to exhume his remains saying, 'communists should not be buried in marked graves' and threw his bones into the Amu River.

Conclusion

The history of the leftist activists was traced to the *Jawanon-e-Afghan*, the Afghan Youth movement, in the 1920s, although this movement in a milder form was around in the late nineteenth century. Their aim was to secure a place for Afghanistan within their pan-Islamic beliefs. The second, more radical group, was the *Wish Zalmyan* the Awakened Youth, in the 1940s, whose papers served as a platform to vent their views about Afghanistan's progress and modernisation and how the rights of individuals and groups within it could be advanced. The third group of leftist activists were the two pro-China parties *Shola* (Flame); *Setam-i-Meli* (National Oppression), and the two most vociferous pro-Russia groups were the Khalq (Masses) and the Parcham (Banner). These latter two groups wanted to grab power and take Afghanistan forward as a modern socialist state according to their ideology. All these groups in their ways were at the forefront of modernisation and globalisation. For them to be modern was to ensure their power base and from there to progress and transform Afghan society into an environment which could cut through ethnic, linguistic and religious boundaries. They forgot that modernity 'pours us all into a maelstrom of perpetual disintegration and renewal, of struggle and contradiction, of ambiguity and anguish' (Berman 1988: 15). The sources of the maelstrom of modernity are continuous changes in science, technology, communications, development 'binding together the most diverse people and societies; increasingly powerful national states ...

striving to expand their powers' (ibid., p. 16). For the communists the Soviet Super State was such an example.

The modernist aspects of some of these groups were in tune with the aspirations of some of the rulers from the 1880s onwards, although the leftists' communist activities of 1960s were considered to be out of step with the expectation of the governments, the tradition of Afghan society and its Islamic heritage and pronouncements. All these movements and groups at best formed a small fraction of Afghan society. However, despite their small numerical number, their influence was far beyond their size. Despite their progressive and modernist slogan ('anti-imperialist', in the case of the first two groups and 'internationalist' in the case of the communists), none of these groups and parties was able to shake off the constraints of their ethnic and linguistic upbringing. That is why social fragmentation of an unprecedented type happened even at the level of these comparatively enlightened, better educated, right-wing, left-wing and centre groups.

The communist influence on Afghan society has been of a massively negative nature. The next chapter will discuss how Russians were physically brought in to save the embryonic Afghan communist movement and its government.

5 Events leading to the Soviet invasion

Introduction

With the coming to power of the communists, the uncertainty and fragmentation that was already present became exacerbated. The inter-party rivalry between the pro-China and pro-Soviet communists on the one hand and the intra-party rivalry between the two pro-Moscow factions on the other exacerbated the ethnic, tribal and religious fragmentation already prevalent. The main reason for this was the communists' underestimating of the public reaction to their plans for modernisation such as internal reforms and external dependence on the Soviets. The Soviet leaders made the mistake of ignoring both their own scholars' ethnographic and politico-historic studies of Afghan society and their own past imperial contacts with the Afghans. They rushed into an agreement with the Afghan communists who were a tiny proportion of the country's population not representing the majority and thus entering into Afghanistan's affairs in an unprecedented way.

The Russians had been interested, for imperial reasons, in Afghanistan for over 140 years (see Appendix 14) and had invested in the country on a relatively large scale since the early 1950s. For ideological and economic reasons they had committed themselves to maintaining these investments. It was because of such commitments, rather than recognising how Afghans or the world community would react, that they accepted great risks and occupied Afghanistan. In this chapter, the events that paved the way for the intervention of the Red Army in December 1979 will be analysed, underlining how the USSR guarded its investments and worked methodically to keep Afghanistan within its orbit.

Soviet annoyance with Afghan leaders and their fear of losing power within Afghanistan started with Mohammad Daoud, especially after his Kremlin walkout, as explained in Chapter 3. Having rid themselves of Daoud, they did not want to face another headstrong Afghan nationalist leader again. It is also important to highlight how the Soviets, who thought they had secured Afghanistan from the West (after the *Saur*, April 1978 coup/revolution) became impatient with the People's Democratic

Party of Afghanistan's (PDPA) inter and intra-party squabbles. They continued to hold on to Afghanistan by replacing one group of communist leaders and their party with others as and when necessary, like proverbial pawns in a game of chess. In analysing this, I shall give a fuller picture on the one hand of Khalq-Parcham inter-party rivalry and on the other hand of Taraki-Amin intra-party distrust and personality clashes. Lastly, I shall give details of Soviet preparation during Amin's 104 days in office to topple him and his Khalq faction; how they invaded the country and then put in place the Khalq's rivals, the Parchamis, with whom the Russians closely identified. (For chronology of initial months of communists in power, see Appendix 11).

PDPA internal tensions play into Soviet hands

Khalq vs. Parcham

Immediately after the coup the PDPA created, using Soviet communist terminology, the *Shura-i-Inqlabi* (Revolutionary Council) and made important announcements in its name. Like every other communist party they announced through their *Komita Merkazi* (central committee), but this was not used because Daoud also had such a body (although he never used it in practice either) and the public might suspect that the same people who had worked under Daoud were now working with the communists.

> Officers who had brought about the Revolution had joined the government as a third force and none of them was a member of the Central Committee... Another reason why the name of Central Committee was not used at the time was the army officers were not taken on to [this body]. [After they joined] the Revolutionary Council gradually disappeared from view.
>
> (Anwar 1988: 112–13)

It was Amin who raised the question of the army officers' membership of the central committee, though Karmal and Taraki wanted to keep them as a third force. But neither of these two senior leaders could oppose Amin because of his link with the army and air force.

The PDPA also had a *Buro-e-siasi* (Politburo) whose job it was to control the central committee. Amin was not a member of this body but thanks to him, the inclusion of the army officers as members of the central committee was the first item on its agenda when the Politburo met on 24 May 1978. Amin, through the armed forces department, produced a pamphlet about *De Saur Inqlab* (the April Revolution) two days before this meeting. The pamphlet glorified the role of the Khalqis and by implication denigrated the Parcham faction for not playing a prominent role and also accused some of its members of actually siding with or fighting for Daoud.

Amin knew that as soon as Karmal objected to the pamphlet, it would be evident to Taraki and the Khalq group that he was not willing to accept Taraki as 'the great leader' ... Amin used flattery to win over Taraki, referring to him in Party and Cabinet meetings by such sycophantic titles as 'the star of the east', 'the great thinker', 'the great leader' etc. etc.

(Anwar 1988: 114)

The communists now in power were more dangerous to one another than ever before. Amin's pamphlet and membership of the central committee comprised the first instance of a clash between Khalq and Parcham since the PDPA came to power. The Khalq faction emerged as the victors. The second clash occurred on 12 June in another central committee meeting again on two contentious issues, first the changing of the national flag from the tricolour black, red and green[1] to all-red, and second the stripping of Afghan citizenship from members of the royal family and confiscation of their property. Just as Karmal feared the elevation of junior army staff to positions of responsibility in the party, he also feared a backlash from the general public and considered the issue of changing the flag as adventuresome and therefore inappropriate. However, the Kabul daily *Anis* 'on 18 October 1978 heralded the introduction of the new flag of the DRA and the new emblem which replaced the ferocious eagle of the Daoud regime' (*Anis*, 27 Mizan, 1357, 18 Oct. 1978). On the question of the royal family Karmal also suggested that they should be released from prison provided they undertake never to take part in politics again. Despite the objections by Karmal's Parcham faction, the resolutions were passed on both issues. However, when Karmal came to power sixteen months later, in January 1980, one of the first things he did was to bring back the traditional tri-colour flag and to allow members of the royal family to leave prison for abroad. Regardless, the already fragile relationship between the two groups was further damaged by this enactment.

For the first three months both factions equally shared cabinet posts, as they had shared other jobs in the rest of the communist power hierarchies. However, during a four and half hour central committee meeting on 17 June 1979 in which the growing rebellious resistance in Pakistan and Iran as well as inside Afghanistan, and also the reaction of most of the Free World towards their government were discussed, the Khalqis are said to have come to the conclusion that they could not work with the Parcham faction. Karmal's followers at this meeting too had lost the debate by two votes.[2] In a Politburo meeting on 24 June, two prominent members of Parcham, Suliman La'q and Bareq Shafi, sided with the Khalq faction and agreed that in order to maintain the unity of the party, Karmal and his close associates should be sent abroad as ambassadors.[3] Thus within a week all top members of the Parcham faction were posted as ambassadors abroad. Having exiled the Parchamis abroad, Taraki announced on a radio broadcast on 19 July 1978, 'there was no such thing as a Parcham party in Afghanistan, and there is no such thing now'. On 27 September 1979, Amin, also speaking on Radio Kabul, also denied the existence of Parcham as a party.[4] Thus the fragmentation of central power within the PDPA began and soon uncertainties were to engulf not just the political hierarchy of the PDPA but also the rest of the population, who until this time had not been affected by these intra-party squabbles.

In retrospect, on the part of Khalq, this move was not very insightful, since their opponents in the various world capitals could do them untold damage. However, since Amin's Khalq took over the secret police (AKSA), he was of the view that he could control their activities, even abroad. Before Karmal left for his ambassadorial post in Prague on 10 July, he put in place a coup plan that subsequently became known as the *Eid* Conspiracy (One of two annual *Eid* religious festivals, this *Eid* being the one after the holy month of *Ramadan*). Karmal, for four weeks before leaving the country, finalised a plan for the coup. The planning minister, Sultan Ali Keshtmand, who was caught by Amin's intelligence network, confessed that he was one of those entrusted with this job.[5] According to the plan the uprising would occur on *Eid* day. Karmal told him that 'since the present government was deviating from the path of socialism', they were to establish a general united front under the leadership of Abdul Qadir of the air force and that all those leaders exiled like himself would return in time to take part and lead the uprising. This supposed uprising on 4 September did not materialise because Qadir, who was to head the new 'Peoples' Democratic Republic of Afghanistan', admitted that he was unable to organise his men in a coup because 'all of them were either Khalqi or their sympathisers'. The failure was not Qadir's alone. 'Despite the fact that Babrak Karmal is frequently presented as the most popular of the PDPA leaders, he was unable to attract enough support either in the PDPA or the armed forces to mount a successful challenge to Taraki or Amin' (Male 1982: 130).

The KGB was not going to stand by while Amin arrested and killed some of these men who were all in KGB pay.

> Amin was told [by KGB] that these people were doing useful work for Soviet intelligence and thereby contributing to the people's democratic revolution in Afghanistan and strengthening the friendship between Afghan and the Soviet people. People mentioned [to Amin] included former Deputy Prime Minister under Daud, H. Sharq, the former head of police and gendarmerie Samad Azher ... the former Minister of Public Works Mohammad Rafi, the former Deputy Minister of Trade, Abdul Salam, the Defence Minister Qadir [Keshtmand] and many others.
>
> (Metrokhin 2002: 42)

To please their Russian supporters, Amin commuted Keshtmand, Qadir and these others; sentences of execution to life imprisonment. Raja Anwar (a youth leader in Lahore for Pakistan's prime minister in the 1970s, Zulfiqar Ali Bhutto) who was serving a three-year prison sentence in Kabul's Pul-i-Charkhi prison at the time, writes that 'between 400–500 Parcham workers and leaders were in jail after the exposure of the "Eid Plan". Nearly 250 Parchamis and *Setam-i-Meli* workers were executed' (Anwar 1988: 123).

On 6 September after the conspirators were named, nine were expelled from the central committee. The chief of army staff, General Shapur Ahmadzai, was executed and all Parcham ambassadors were recalled. These ambassadors were not naïve enough to return and face Khalq's wrath. Every one of them took the budgets of their embassies with them and for the time being disappeared, going underground in Eastern Europe and Moscow, biding their time.[6] As a gesture of disapproval, Taraki 'deprived him [Karmal] of Afghan citizenship' (Kakar 1995: 37).

The Parchami leaders now in exile were appealing to their Soviet comrades to intervene and save them. Karmal's half-brother Mahmud Baryali (his KGB name 'Shir') who was coached in diplomatic manners while Afghan ambassador to Pakistan by his Soviet colleague, Ambassador B.N. Batrayev, after meeting Karmal in Prague went to Moscow, reaching his contact Nekrasov, saying

> The Parchamists were in critical situation, the situation was critical and they all faced death. He begged for urgent measures to be taken to save Babrak and his supporters. 'In the name of humanism save us! In the name of humanism save us!' he repeated this phrase several times and sobbed as he did so. 'I do not know what to do. I have no means to support myself. All our hopes are in our Soviet comrades. I have a letter from Babrak but I do not know to whom to give it'.
> (Mitrokhin 2002: 37)

Karmal and Parcham did not play a crucial role in the April coup. They also faced defeat after losing on crucial issues in central committee and Politburo meetings. Therefore, they reverted to coups and conspiracies, again unsuccessfully. Having failed again and again, they were delighted when the Soviet forces handed power to them, as it were, 'on a plate' on 27 December 1979 by killing President Amin and removing his Khalq party from power.

Tension within the Khalq leadership

The tension within the Khalq faction can be attributed to its top two men, Taraki and Amin. People who knew Taraki said that he was a gentle and fatherly figure. He was simple enough to take to heart all the titles like 'brilliant revolutionary leader', 'genius of the East', 'an original thinker', that Amin bestowed on him. So with the revolution accomplished, and the

Parcham gone, true to what the Russian novelist Dostoevsky said that revolutionaries in the last analysis turn on one another, these two Khalqis did exactly that. Amin was against unification with Parcham back in 1977. A plan was devised by the Soviets and put into practice on their behalf by the Indian Communist Party and Awami League Party of Pakistan to bring back the Parcham. Taraki gave in to these foreign pressures and went against Amin's advice. On two crucial occasions in 1978, once in March (by trying to cut Amin's link with the army) and again in September (in attempting to actually gun him down) Taraki, in collaboration with other pro-Soviet elements, set out to eliminate Amin.

In the first few months of the revolution, the two men were very close to one another. 'Amin and I are like nail and flesh, not separable', claimed Taraki in a television speech in July 1978. In such close relationships, Taraki was always the 'great teacher or leader' and Amin 'the true disciple and student'. Amin (according to Anwar 1988; Bradsher 1985; Kakar 1995) having built Taraki as Afghanistan's Kim Il Sung, primarily to take the leadership of the PDPA from his rival Babrak Karmal and keep it, now realised that he had created a monster. Taraki, thinking that he really was 'brilliant', refused to take any suggestions made by Amin. Since Amin had all the contacts within the army, and it was the support of the army that made the April coup possible, Taraki at an army officers' gathering in December 1978 tried to put Amin in his place by saying that,

> 'Our Comrade Amin is one of the most brilliant students of our school who had taken part in every regard. There is no doubt that other friends have also taken part. Comparatively I should say that whatever plan I have given Comrade Hafizullah Amin he has put it into action very well.' Taraki was telling the officers that 'whatever Amin had done, had been done on his, Taraki's, instructions and however important Amin role may have appeared he was merely one among many'.
>
> (Male 1982: 157)

Amin's daughter was heard by her schoolmate saying, 'we gave Taraki his *kish-i-shakhsiat* (personality cult)'.[7] As far as Amin was concerned, he was using Taraki to win arguments and have his way in places where otherwise he could not be effective. For instance, in making the Khalq party Afghanistan's foremost communist party and defining its leadership as the true representative of the aspirations and the inspiration of the Afghan people. He knew that Taraki was more effective and acceptable in the party's foreign relations and in its standing within leftist movements in Afghanistan. It was to this end that Amin had built up a personality cult for Taraki, an oversight he soon began to resent.

Again in August, when Taraki wanted to assert his authority over Amin in the government, both men clashed. Amin had appointed his brother as military chief of Afghanistan's northern zone, comprising several provinces. Amin's brother-in-law was the army chief of staff. His nephew (now also son-in-law) was head of the secret police and his eighteen-year-old son the deputy of the youth movement. When Amin also appointed the same son-in-law as a deputy within the foreign ministry without formally announcing it, Taraki is said to have accused him of nepotism. Amin having lost his temper is said to have shouted at Taraki saying, 'Should I kill my family?'.[8]

Young and ambitious army officers who had played crucial roles in the April coup also sided with Taraki. The most prominent of these young officers were Aslam Watanjar, Sayed Muhammad Gulabzoy, Sherjan Mazdoryar and Asadullah Sarwari. Their relatives and friends claim that none of them knew much about Marxism,[9] but rather had joined the PDPA purely out of political ambition. Every one of them stood up to Amin, counting on Taraki's support. The Russians, who were annoyed with Amin for sending Parcham leaders abroad, also tried to drive a wedge between Amin and Taraki whenever possible. These four officers, the oldest of whom was only thirty-three years of age, had a close relationship with the Soviet ambassador in Kabul. 'These [four], impatient, ambitious and naive, were easy prey for the wily Soviet Ambassador, Alexander Puzanov, anxious to find a means of striking at Amin' (Male 1982: 163). When Amin took over after foiling Taraki's plan to have him killed, Mazdoryar was captured and imprisoned. Asadullah Sarwari, Aslam Watanjar and Sayed Muhammad Gulabzoy were given refuge in the Soviet Embassy and some say later shipped in metal boxes to the Soviet Union for the whole three and a half months that Amin was in power.[10]

After an uprising on 17 March 1979 in the city of Herat, where some Russians as well as Afghan soldiers and officers were killed, the Politburo and the Revolutionary Council established the Homeland Higher Defence Council (HHDC) with Taraki as its chairman and Amin as its deputy. Amin, who until then was defence minister, was also appointed to the prestigious office of *Lomray Wazir*[11] or prime minister. The defence ministry went to Watanjar and, at the HHDC, defence decisions rested with Taraki. The prime minister could appoint his cabinet, but here too all appointments and dismissals had to be approved by the president. Amin seems to have only realised later that Taraki, through such a manoeuvre, was distancing him from the army, his closest and most reliable constituency.

The next clash between the two men was their last. On 4 September 1979, Taraki left for the non-aligned conference in Havana. With Taraki abroad, Amin had the opportunity to eliminate the so-called 'gang of four' (Watanjar, Gulabzoy, Mazdoryar and Sarwari) but decided not to do so. However, through some possible error in his intelligence network, Sarwari telephoned Taraki in Havana on 7 September, telling him: 'Amin is planning to either arrest us or have us all killed, so that he can take over the government before your return' (Anwar 1988: 167). Acting as the leader of the gang of four, Sarwari devised a plan to have Amin killed on the day he drove to the airport to receive Taraki. He entrusted his nephew Aziz Akbari (also his deputy) to execute the plan, instructing him to pick ten men from his department and train them in shooting a fast moving car, without disclosing any more detail. Aziz Akbari was also an informant for the Russian officer assigned to the secret service (AKSA), and so without his uncle knowing he informed the Russians. The Russians, who did not want Amin removed in such a dramatic way, told Akbari to inform Amin of the plan and to tell him to change his route on that day. They also told another of Sarwari's deputies, Nawab Ali, to keep a close eye on Amin so that Sarwari would not harm him. Amin, who knew then that the Russians were also involved in this, wrongly concluded that in the intra-faction wrangling the Soviets were on his side (Anwar 1988: 167–8).[12]

On 10 September, after his participation in the sixth non-aligned summit at Havana, Taraki stayed in Moscow for a few days, meeting Brezhnev, Gromyko and other high-ranking Soviet officials. The meeting on 10 September with Soviet government officials was attended by all of the Afghan entourage (Wakman 1985: 105). Taraki only attended the meeting on 12 September. Although Foreign Minister Shah Wali, Minister of Culture and Information Kheyal Muhammad Katawazi and Police Chief Major Sayed Daoud Tarun were with him, Taraki went to meet Gromyko on his own. It is said that the Russians had also brought Karmal to this meeting and wanted to reconcile the two and thus move Amin and his supporters to diplomatic posts, so that both factions could once again be brought together. At Havana Taraki met with the president of Pakistan, General Zia-ul-Haq, who was supporting the anti-communist Mujahideen. Taraki's entourage, according to commonly held opinion, became suspicious as to whether 'the great leader' Taraki was plotting against Amin or whether he was privately asking the Russians for advice on his meeting with the Pakistani president. By then Pakistan was beginning to receive Afghan refugees by the tens of thousands and was also active in training Afghan guerrillas. But 'it is reportedly believed by some senior officials of the neighbouring Asian countries that Amin was tipped off to the "made in Moscow" plot by Shah Wali when he returned home with Taraki' (Bradsher 1985: 112). Others maintain that Tarun and Katawazi, both also Amin's men, could have passed on this information to him.

Taraki's plane from Moscow was to land at 2:30 in Kabul Airport. While thousands of supporters were waiting for the arrival of the 'great leader', Akbari had deployed armed men in front of the radio and television buildings on the main road to the airport. Sarwari was impatiently pacing up and down inside the building. Meanwhile on Amin's order Taraki's plane was not given clearance to land for another full hour. After Amin arrived through a different route in a white Volkswagen at 3:30, the plane was allowed to land. Amin wanted to make it clear to Taraki and the gang of four that he was effectively in control of the government.

Amin walked up to the president's aircraft and as Taraki came down, he received him quite normally. 'Where are those four?' was the first thing Taraki said. 'I did not eat them up. They must be somewhere around', Amin answered dryly. The poor workers, quite unaware of what was going on, began shouting [Orwellian!] slogans of 'Long live the great leader', 'Long live his disciple'.

(Anwar 1988: 169)

On his arrival at the presidential palace Taraki had informed the four conspirators of his plan to propose an ambassadorship to Amin. That evening, Amin visited Taraki and gave him his report about the state of the country; also on a separate piece of paper he asked for the dismissal of the gang of four. Taraki read Amin's letter and in his gentle manner smiled, telling him, 'Amin, to me you are the most important, but things being what they are in the country and the party, I think you should go out briefly as an ambassador. As soon as the situation improves I will call you back'. Amin did not let Taraki continue. Raising his voice angrily, he shouted, 'you are the one who should quit. Because of drink and old age you have taken leave of your senses'. He then rose abruptly and left the room.[13] Amin was the power in the country and Taraki was naïve enough to think that he would go for a mere ambassadorship.

On the following day, Taraki invited Amin for lunch together with the gang of four but Amin declined, saying he preferred their resignation to having lunch with them. A day later, Taraki invited the Soviet ambassador who is said to have 'persuaded Amin by a promise of safe conduct to visit Taraki, from whom he had become estranged' (Amstutz 1986: 43). This time Amin accepted and as he was entering Taraki's room with Police Chief Sayed Daoud Tarun and Intelligence Officer Nawab Ali, the guards opened fire, killing Tarun and injuring Ali. Amin escaped to his waiting car and put the army on alert. He 'returned with a contingent of soldiers and arrested Taraki' (Nyrop and Seekins 1986: 239). The gang of four 'disappeared' into Soviet hands for the duration of Amin's 104 days in power.

According to Amin's nephew Mirwais, Amin sent a message to Brezhnev saying, 'Taraki is still around. What should I do with him? If you wish, I can send him to Moscow'. On 6 October 1979, Brezhnev's answer was received. 'There is no need to send Taraki to Moscow. This is your problem. You solve it in the manner you consider best' (Anwar 1988: 180). Amin must have concluded from this that his hunch that the Soviets preferred him to Taraki was right and this accounted for why they were not concerned with what might happen to Taraki. He was mistaken. The Soviets wanted the situation in the Khalq party to deteriorate so that they could bring their trusted ally Karmal and his Parcham faction back to power. Amin had Taraki smothered with pillows and 'on 9 October a brief announcement on radio and TV said that the "ailing Taraki" had died' (Anwar 1988: 181).

Soviets prepare the grounds for invasion

The Soviet Union had developed a tradition from the 1920s onwards of signing friendship treaties with countries of the Third World in order to shore up the image of the leaders of such client states. 'The Soviet Union [uses] the tactics of such treaties as a tool of its foreign policy to enhance its sphere of influence. The Soviet Union has ... signed friendship treaties with twelve countries ... of these, Egypt and Somalia have unilaterally abrogated their treaties sensing ulterior Soviet designs in these treaties' (Wakman 1985: 75). One such treaty was signed with Afghanistan on 5 December 1978, when Afghanistan for all intents and purposes was completely dominated by the Soviet Union.[14] In Afghanistan's case, since she was the first country recognised by the Union of Soviet Socialist Republics (USSR) in 1919, the warm relationships then created led to the 'Soviet-Afghan Treaties of 1921 and 1933 which laid the basis for friendship and good neighbor relations between the Soviet and Afghan peoples' (Tabibi 1985: 184). Article four of the 5 December 1978 treaty, laying the foundation for future Soviet intervention, says:

> The High Contracting parties, acting in the spirit of the tradition of friendship and good neighbourliness, as well as the U.N. Charter, shall consult each other and take by agreement appropriate measures to ensure the security, independence, and territorial integrity of the two countries.

In order to keep Afghanistan as a Soviet satellite, Article six confirms that each country 'solemnly declare that it shall not join any military or other alliances or take part in any groupings of states, as well as in actions or measures directed against the other'.[15] The Soviet Union as a world power was already in the Warsaw Pact and had many other alliances with its client states. This article was obviously aimed at Afghanistan as a neutral country, that it should not join any military or economic alliances within the region or elsewhere, thus remaining in the Soviet bloc.

On 3 December, the Soviets sent Brezhnev's own shiny silvery plane to Kabul, taking all high-ranking party and government officials to Moscow for the signing ceremony.[16] The treaty seems to have been imposed on Taraki and his pro-Moscow faction. When the rumour of such a treaty was circulating in Kabul, Amin was asked some three weeks earlier if such a treaty was to be signed. He 'replied by referring to the Treaty signed in 1921 which he said had been renewed several times, implying that nothing more was contemplated' (Male 1982: 146).

Soviets taking stock of uprisings and discontent

I now want to present details of a crucial uprising that highlighted the inadequacies of the regime and the disillusionment of the Soviet officials who came to investigate it. These officials' reports were for the information of the inner circles of the Soviet hierarchy and could have helped to pave the way for the Red Army's intervention. The event in question was the uprising of Herat City on 5 March 1979. The regime and subsequently the Russians were to experience many other uprisings in other parts of the country. Since this was the first major insurrection, it shook the regime and its Russian backers. There was an angry mob of ex-workers in Herat, some of them trained in Iran by the Shah's infamous secret police force SAVAK 'to act as a restraining force in case [an] Oman-like situation arose in Afghanistan threatening Iranian security' (Anwar 1988: 156). The mob attacked the office of the governor of the province and also ransacked ammunition depots, setting vehicles and other government property on fire. The situation continued to deteriorate till 16 March. The government was forced to bring in new forces from Kandahar and also to use planes from the nearby Shindand airbase to bomb the rebels' quarters. By 27 March when the situation was brought under control, some 3,000 to 5,000 Heratis, out of a population of 150,000 were dead and also some Russians and local communists had been killed, their bodies badly mutilated. The hatred of the local people towards the Afghan communists and the ineffectiveness of the Afghan army in taking such a long time to quell this uprising astonished the Russians. To rectify the situation the Russians sent in 'General Alexia A. Yepishev chief of the main political directorate of the Soviet Army, to ... assess the military and political situation and the possible consequences of deeper Soviet involvement ... Within weeks of Yepishev's visit, further Soviet aid of every kind began to pour into Afghanistan' (Schofield 1993: 52–3).

In 1968, before the Warsaw Pact invasion of Czechoslovakia, Yepishev was sent 'to assess the situation there and had returned to Moscow favouring the Warsaw Pact military intervention to prevent the loss of Soviet-style political control' (Bradsher 1985: 102). Six other generals now accompanied Yepishev on this visit to Afghanistan. In their week-long mission they found that the 'low level of political training, the extreme religiousness and downtrodden nature of the masses of soldiers, and the social heterogeneity of the servicemen' was making it possible for the Afghan resistance to penetrate into the armed forces and to demoralise them (ibid., p. 102). Their report also said 'the Afghan armed forces [are] weakened by defections, divided by Khalq-Parcham infighting, damaged by purging of non-communist officers, and therefore in need of greater Soviet involvement' (ibid., p. 151). The aid they suggested for delivery to the Afghan army included MI-24 Hind helicopters, firing rockets, machine guns and MI-6 troop carrier helicopters. They also supplied tanks, Armoured Personnel Carriers (APCs) and additional MiG-21 fighter-bombers. All of this equipment was new and so Russian technicians had to be sent with them to train Afghan personnel to use them. The provision of technical know-how and modern war machines proved successful later in the war in carrying out Russian plans.

Yepishev's report also brought to Afghanistan another high level Soviet official. This was Vasily S. Safronchuk, a career diplomat who had been Soviet ambassador to Ghana and also deputy permanent secretary of his country's mission at the UN for five years up to 1976. He, however, had no particular expertise on Afghanistan or even the Muslim world. Why he was chosen to advise the Khalqis on how to run the party and the government is not immediately apparent. 'Perhaps the Soviet experts on Afghanistan were already discredited either in Moscow or with the Kabul regime' (Bradsher 1985: 104).

Safronchuk had two offices, one in the Afghan foreign ministry and another in Taraki's palace. 'Safronchuk worked as if he were the minister of foreign affairs in Kabul' (Kakar 1995: 187). Next to the Soviet ambassador Puzanov, he was the second highest Soviet official resident in Kabul.

Both had been in close contact with Taraki. Amin, who wanted to know all the details of government 'reportedly manoeuvred to keep Safronchuk or Puzanov from seeing Taraki, as they tried to do almost daily, thus ensuring that he became the main contact man with the Soviets' (Schofield 1993: 104). Safronchuk's main goal was to make the regime tolerable to the Afghan public, as the number of those who were daily taking arms against it was increasing. It was because of Safronchuk's advice that Taraki and Amin both started going to mosques for the Friday congregations and then publicising their prayers, in the hope of convincing Afghans that their leaders were not atheists, but practising Muslims. However, most communists would speak openly about their atheist beliefs and so their publicised prayers did not fool the public. Safronchuk also insisted that the base of the government should be broadened to include non-party members and non-communists. Another of Safronchuk's ideas was to make the people defend the revolution and to this end, the government was asked to organise the *Meli Mutahadah Jabha,* or United National Front. This materialised two years later when the Karmal government changed the title to *Jabha Meli Padarwatan,* the National Fatherland Front (NFF), and appointed Salih Muhammad Zairay as its head. The movement achieved limited success, but the Khalq still refused to bring back the Parcham members from abroad or even release those put in prison in order that they could join the government.

The NFF did not succeed in recruiting non-communist Afghans. This body, like many other organisations such as those for youth, women, workers, writers, peasants and so forth, never achieved noticeable success. To their dismay, the regime and their Soviet backers always found that only those committed to the ideals of communism came forward to serve in these organisations. Even the few who were based in Kabul and had to enrol for work to earn their families keep, either did not work wholeheartedly or served as informers and sympathisers for the Mujahideen resistance or both. The Soviet officials were aware of this and knew that the Khalq would refuse to accept Parcham officials in order to broaden the base of the government. Thus they presumably thought if they were to replace Khalq leadership with Parcham, the latter would heed their advice and make the regime more popular and acceptable to the general public.

Yepishev's 'visit was followed by a survey of the situation by a group of middle-ranking KGB officials. In addition to its foreign espionage duties, the KGB was also responsible for suppressing dissent in the Soviet Union. In Afghanistan the group presumably found missing the kind of political and police controls needed to do the thorough job that was done at home' (Schofield 1993: 151). Russian eyewitness Vasily Kolesnik (see p. 133) and Afghan writers are of the opinion that some of these KGB officers were amongst those who directed and entered Amin's palace on the night of 27 December 1979, killing Amin, his family members and his guards.

The seventy-one-year-old general Ivan G. Pavlovskiy, who had retired in 1978, followed these visits in mid-August. 'Unlike that of general Yepishev, general Pavlovskiy's visit was given no publicity and it is not clear on whose initiative he came or if in fact he was an uninvited guest' (Male 1982: 184). Pavlovskiy headed a large team of generals representing the KGB, the Soviet defence ministry, and civilian officials. They spread themselves out to all parts of Afghanistan to assess the situation and found that most areas were in the hands of the resistance and those organisations such as the 'Revolutionary Defence Committee', the 'National Fatherland Front' and others existed primarily on paper alone. Pavlovskiy stayed on till mid-October and 'what he reported to the [Soviet] Defence Minister Demitri F. Ustinov is not known yet, but it soon became apparent that the Soviet Union feared that the guerrillas in co-operation with disaffected Afghan army units might overturn the Amin government' (Bradsher 1988: 124). Pavlovskiy's report is said to have confirmed the Soviet decision to remove Amin. From October onwards, military preparations were taken in the Soviet Union, rather than depending on sending advisors and technicians abroad, as they had done thus far. The Soviets had to decide how to bolster the flagging communist government and to weigh their decisions as to what was possible militarily and how that would be tolerated diplomatically and explained to the world community.

There were some 650 Soviet experts and technicians working on different Soviet-backed projects during President Daoud's government (1973–78). However, within three months after the April 1978 coup, the number of military advisors alone reached 700. Some 650 other civilians, some already in the country, started working in government ministries and departments. Every ministry and government department had its own advisors. Initially, because of the language problems, the Soviets brought trained personnel from the central Asian states, whose Tajik, Uzbek and Turkmen languages were understood by some Afghans. Later the Russians abandoned this approach, fearing that Afghan devotion to religion and independence might influence their Muslim subjects. These were qualities the Russians did not want to confront on their own soil. These advisors now turned out to be the administrative and executive powers in the land. Nothing could be done without their consent and approval. Most Afghans, even PDPA members, came to resent them. Their influence on the Afghan military, judiciary, education, press and their techniques of brainwashing in the ten years that they were in Afghanistan resulted in that period being known as the 'decade of Sovietisation'. The Sovietisation process, far from being successful, had disastrous consequences for the regime. Through desertion, the army was reduced from over 100,000 to just 30,000. These losses were, however, more than compensated for by the presence of the Red Army.

Of about 1,000 lecturers in Kabul University, over 700 of them left for abroad or were imprisoned or killed. Soviet and unqualified Afghan communist teachers soon filled their places. Kabul University's student population 'of 14,000 in 1977 was reduced to just 6,000 by 1984. The majority of those left were girl students, since the boys were sent to war against the Mujahideen' (Elmi 1988: 10). Men between the ages of fifteen to fifty years were forcibly recruited to the army. Most families were forced either to send their young men abroad or have them join the resistance. The number of Soviet advisors, which had reached about 1,500 in the first three months after the coup, accelerated steadily. 'The number of non-military Soviet advisors (including college and university teachers) was around 10,000 in 1984 (in every department of the University of Kabul, there were Soviet teachers who used to lecture their classes with the help of Tajik Farsi-speaking interpreters)' (Anwar 1988: 223).

All of the above Soviet reports pointed to the unpopularity of the communists and the inefficiency of Afghan administrative bureaucracy to deal with a revolutionary situation. Each one of these prominent Soviet delegations reached the conclusion that in order to stop the new state from collapsing, it was necessary that the Soviet Union should play a much more active political, economic and military role.

Amin's 104 days in office

Amin took over on 14 September 1979. He appointed Akbari to head the intelligence department, which in Pashto was now called, *Kargari Atla'ti Mo'sesah* (KAM), or the Worker's Information Bureau. Amin later sent Akbari as ambassador to Iraq, thinking that he had his loyalty. In fact, Afghans who know Akbari say that he was one of many KGB agents, and it was probably because of this link that he continued in office long after Amin and the Khalqis were gone. In January 1980 when Karmal was placed in power, instead of sending Akbari to prison, he made him first secretary in the Afghan embassy in Mongolia, where his 'hot-headed uncle' Sarwari was in effect exiled to serve as ambassador. This time he was to keep Karmal informed about his uncle's activities.

Amin, from the time he killed Taraki (9 October 1979), was a marked man living on borrowed time. Unfortunately for him, he did not realise this till the last moment of his life. The Russians were determined to discard him at the earliest opportunity. Amin did his best to keep on the right side of the Russians and he incorrectly thought that he was successful in this. For some three weeks after his attempted assassination, Amin tried to control his anger with the Soviet ambassador, Puzanov, who had driven him into that trap. On 6 October his foreign minister, 'Shah Wali, invited all the communist ambassadors in Kabul except the Chinese, who were helping the resistance with arms, to a meeting ... At the meeting Wali accused Puzanov of complicity in the abortive attempt to remove Amin ... Wali as Foreign Minister, formally asked the Soviet Union to replace its ambassadors' (Bradsher 1982: 117). He also tried to repair differences with Pakistan, but the military ruler Zia-ul-Haq was in no hurry to accede to his requests. President Hag's hanging of the former prime minister, Zulfiqar Ali Bhutto, had made him a pariah and thoroughly unpopular around the world. Now that the Russians were next door in Afghanistan, the United States and the West considered Pakistan as 'a front-line state', and were prepared to overlook the hanging of Bhutto.

Zia-ul-Haq was not going to jeopardise this valuable opportunity by offending the West, in making overtures to Amin. 'General Zia ul-Haq later revealed that from early December Amin sent him frantic messages seeking an immediate meeting, (Male 1988: 204). On 22 December, Pakistan's foreign minister Agha Shahi was to visit Kabul but this was cancelled because of the snow on the ground and his plane instead of landing in Kabul went on to Tehran. The next day Soviet planes were landing in Kabul airport. '... The choice of 22 December suggests that Pakistan still did not share Amin's sense of urgency. Pakistani officials have indicated that the main stumbling block was US refusal to take the situation seriously. Until the US made a move there was little Pakistan could do on its own' (ibid., p. 204). Amin also tried to approach the Americans. 'In an interview with the *Washington Post* and *Los Angeles Times* correspondents at the end of October, Amin said, "we want that in a realistic manner the United States should study the situation in this region and provide us with more assistance"' (Anwar 1988: 184). Through low-level contacts the Americans told Amin that they did not want to compete with Russia in aid.[17] In mid-December Amin was telling the world, 'No Soviet military base will be allowed in Afghanistan because we don't need them' (ibid.) As a former lecturer at the faculty of science, Amin invited some of his Kabul University colleagues to dine with him and confided in them, 'You professors may or may not be with us, but as long as I am alive I will never allow any foreign power to dominate our fatherland' (Kakar 1995: 42).

After the American embassy hostage crisis in Tehran in November, the Russians were apprehensive in case the United States invaded southern Iran, as they had done during the Second World War. The Soviets asked the Amin government to give them sole use of the Shindand airbase in western Afghanistan. Amin is said to have refused this request, saying that the Afghan people would not tolerate it. 'Amin's refusal to give the Russians a base in Shindand, while no doubt annoying for Moscow, is not the stuff of which invasions are made' (Male 1982: 207). But no doubt this refusal was yet another instance of Russian distrust and annoyance with the inflexible Amin.

From the Russian point of view the situation was worsening by the day. Resistance to the communist government in Kabul was growing bolder, making regular attacks in Paktia in the south, Kunar in the east and also the central provinces. Most of the Parcham leaders were either in exile, in hiding or in prison in Kabul.

> At different times Karmal said publicly 'tens of thousands of Afghan patriots became the victims of Amin's executions ... Amin ... mercilessly destroyed more than one million' ... After discounting such political language, it is still possible to believe that Amin was responsible-both as Taraki's strongman and on his own – for well over 6,000 executions.
>
> (Bradsher 1985: 121)

Beverly Male in a chapter, 'In Search of Hafizullah Amin', discounts stories of Amin being a bloodthirsty and ruthless megalomaniac as myth. She asserts that Karmal in his six years in office, with all the support he was receiving from the Soviet presence was not able to unearth one single mass grave or name all these 'hundreds and thousands' who were supposed to have been executed by Amin. She writes, 'Amin was certainly a powerful figure, both in the party before the revolution and in the government afterwards, though his power has usually been exaggerated, was always under challenge, and was nowhere near decisive until he became president in September 1979' (Male 1982: 17).

Russian sources indicated that the Soviet Union, even before sending its top generals to investigate the situation first hand, had in May 1979 decided on intervention in Afghanistan.

> That is why as early as May 1979, intelligence reports reaching the United States government 'suggest [ed.] that the Soviets are already moving forward with plans to engineer replacement of the present Khalqi leadership of the DRA, perhaps with the exiled Parchamis leaders including former Deputy Prime Minister Babrak Karmal, now believed [to be] hiding in Europe'.
>
> (Bradsher 1985: 104)

The Soviets thought they could replace Amin and his Khalq party with their trusted and reliable Parcham faction and that once they had organised the

Afghan army, they would be able to withdraw, leaving the Afghans to run Afghanistan along Soviet lines. But little did they know that Afghanistan was no Hungary, invaded in 1956, or Czechoslovakia, overrun by the Warsaw Pact armies in 1968. Afghanistan was to become the main factor in them losing their empire and the ending of their Soviet-style communism.

> On the 2nd May 1979 Colonel Vasily Kolesnik of the Spetsnaz (Russia's SAS or Green Berets) staff in Moscow was summoned to his boss's office. Peter Ivashutin the Chief of the GRU (Soviet Military Police) tasked the colonel to fly to Tashkent, the same day, to start forming a special purpose battalion. The personnel were to be selected from the Turkistan and Central Asian Military Districts.
> (Schofield, 1993: 51)

Kolesnik narrating the story says,

> Neither the men nor I knew what they were being trained for, but it was obviously something important. For the first time in the history of our country we were told not to count ammunition or bother about fuel. We trained intensively for combat in mountain and desert conditions ... In mid-October [1979] we were ordered to Tashkent. We knew by this time that we were to go to Afghanistan and we knew roughly what we were to do there. On 18th–20th November we flew straight to Bagram [air base, 40 km north of Kabul] ... taking ammunition, food and parachutes, as well as personnel. The combat equipment was flown from Tashkent to Bagram'. In Moscow, General Staff planning for a major operation in Afghanistan intensified. Motorised rifle units in Tashkent and Central Asian Military Districts had been ordered to a higher level of combat readiness early in the summer and in the middle of August they began to mobilise. Ivan Raybchenko then commander of 103 Guards Airborne Division says ... 'In October my regimental commanders, the commanders of the separate units of the division and I were sent to Kabul and Bagram as 'tourists', in civilian clothes, to assess the situation for our selves and get to look at the lie of the land.
> (Schofield 1993: 51–3)

Apart from preparation of these crack troops who were to overthrow Amin's government, On 21 December US officials revealed that in the previous two weeks more than 30,000 Soviet troops had been placed on alert near the Afghan border and that three battalions of armoured and airborne troops had been flown to an airbase near Kabul [Bagram]. US officials drew an analogy with Soviet preparations for the invasion of Czechoslovakia in 1968 (Male 1982: 204).[18]

After 20 December, people in Kabul said they lost sleep as some 300

Soviet military transport planes started landing in Kabul airport throughout the day and night.

> Between 23 and 26 December, 10,000 Soviet troops landed in Kabul and were accommodated in the city's major cantonments ... the dispersal of the Red Army was considered necessary so as to rule out the chances of any Afghan troops [from these cantonments] coming to Amin's aid. The 4th Armoured Corps had a majority of Khalqite officers. On the 26 December Soviet engineers, on the pretext of inspecting its tanks, divested all the mounted guns of their firing pins. That the Afghan cantonments remained quiet on 27 December is therefore no surprise. The arrival of the Soviet army was justified to the Afghan troops by telling them that China and Pakistan were about to launch a joint invasion of the country and this had forced the government to invite the 'friendly' Soviet army to defend Afghanistan.
>
> (Anwar 1988: 191)[19]

On 15 March, after an uprising in Herat, Taraki asked the Soviets to send a small force for his protection as well as a contingent of central Asians to fight against the rebels. In a telephone conversation on the subject of Herat Soviet prime minister Alexei Kosygin asked Taraki, 'what are your suggestion regarding this situation?' Taraki replied, 'We ask you to render practical and technical assistance with men and armament'. Kosygin pointed out, 'But the whole world will learn about this immediately. The rebels have radio sets [stations] and they will inform the world right away'. Taraki then suggested to him that central Asian troops dressed in Afghan army uniform and in planes painted in Afghan colours would not be suspicious to anyone. But Kosygin, while prepared to aid Afghanistan both with equipment and economically, would not commit the Soviet Union by sending large-scale troops (*Journal of South Asia*, 1994).[20] Amin seems to have been unaware of Taraki's requests. In September and October of 1979, Amin is on record as saying that he did not want Soviet troops in Afghanistan. On 9 September Amin said, 'We are proud that we have not asked any foreign country to fight for us or to provide our country with security and safety ... so far we have never thought of utilising foreign forces to defend and protect our revolution' (Bradsher 1985: 108). Again in a radio speech early in October, Amin said, 'the Soviet Union was providing "whatever we can use" to defend Afghanistan, but "we will ourselves defend our country ... [and will] never give this trouble to our international brothers [Russians] to fight for us"' (Bradsher 1985: 117). So why did he not do something to stop the Soviet troop build-up?

> Why, with the party and the armed forces behind him did Amin not make some attempt to resist the Soviet attack? He may not have been able to prevent the USSR achieving its goal, but he could have made

> victory much more costly for them. He could also have escaped from Kabul and continued to provide leadership for Khalq opposition to the occupation forces.
>
> (Male 1982: 206)

In fact Amin was not thinking anything of the sort. He had, as explained below, wrongly put all his trust in the Soviets and their pledges to aid Afghanistan in its hour of need by bringing thousands of troops and military equipment to Kabul. Amin also moved his residence on 20 December from the centre of Kabul to *Tapa-e-Tajbeg* palace, some five kilometres away on the southern outskirts of Kabul. The reason why the Afghan monarch's residence, the old bastion, renamed by the communists as the *People's House* had been good enough for the Afghan kings for decades and even for Taraki for over a year, but were now not good enough for him, was as follows. Russian advisors had explained to him that he would be safer and more easily defendable if he were outside the centre of Kabul. As it turned out he was eventually persuaded to move out by the Russians so that they could avoid any collateral damage in the event of a full-scale attack. Salih Muhammad Zairay, his cabinet minister, told this author that when he went to visit Amin 'on the last night [26 December and asked him] why have you moved to this secluded area? It is like being in a *dasht*,' [desert]. Amin replied, 'I moved here on their [Soviet advisor's] recommendation. They said there would be less danger to me here. Staying at the People's House, they said was dangerous'. Zairay said, 'Because of the situation in Iran, the Russians were telling us that there was the possibility of an air attack by the US. We had preparations at hand of how to switch the city's lights off and had informed the people to draw their curtains in the event of such an attack. We were receiving intelligence reports repeatedly about the possibility of such an attack'.[21] So the Russians had convinced the Afghan administration that the thousands of landing troops were to protect Afghanistan and Amin's government, in accordance with the 1978 Friendship Treaty. Russian advisors deceived Amin and those around him while Soviet preparation for Amin's doom was continuing.

> There were to be three lines of defence altogether. The first line was to guard the palace itself, which was built on a hill. This first line was to consist of Amin's personal bodyguard company, made up of one hundred and fifty officers who were personally devoted to him, many of them relations ... The second line of defence was the battalion [Soviet 103 Guards] which was to guard the palace at a distance of 500 meters from the sentry groups. The third line of defence consisted of battalions from Amin's personal Guard brigades [infantry, air and machine-gun companies] all in all, the third line of defence of the palace consisted of 1200 men.
>
> (Schofield: 1993: 55)

The Russians had done their research and trained their men for most of the latter half of 1979 and now that their plan to replace Amin was in place, they prepared to execute it. Their initial plan was to go about it quietly, as Amin had two Russian cooks and a Russian governess, they decided to poison him. The cooks put the poison in the food. That day Mrs Amin was playing host to Mrs Zairay and Mrs Shah Wali. Amin also was there for lunch, but as he had a bad stomach from the previous day, he did not eat except for a few morsels. Mrs Amin was waiting for her eldest son, Abdul Rahman Amin, also did not eat.[22] The Russian plan was to incapacitate Amin and then kidnap him. That is why his Soviet physician wanted to send the unconscious Amin to the Soviet embassy for treatment but Amin's wife, Patmanah, instead asked for Afghan doctors (Arnold 1983: 186).

> As soon as they had finished, they all fell unconscious, including Amin. Mrs. Amin immediately sent for the commander of the presidential guard, Mohammad Iqbal [who sent for doctors]. The Afghan doctors gave the unconscious men, women and children a stomach wash and injected them with antidotes. At about 2 p.m. Amin opened his eyes.... The first thing that Amin said to his wife was 'believe it or not, this is the Taraki's group doing' ... According to the Amin family, the first tank shell hit ... *Darul Aman* at exactly six o'clock in the evening ... GHQ was also under heavy fire, but what was strange was that not a single Afghan soldier had moved from the cantonments. 'Where then is the fire coming from?' Amin said. Then he told his ADC, 'get in touch with those asses at the GHQ again and asked them to recheck which particular cantonment the troops have been moved from' ... the HGQ was right. No Afghan unit had moved from its base, nor were there any reports of unrest or mutiny elsewhere ... At 6:30 p.m. guard commander Iqbal said to Amin: 'we are under attack by the "friendly army"' ... 'That is impossible' Amin rasped back. 'It is our mutinying troops, let me speak to the GHQ', Amin instructed that immediate contact should be established with the Soviet army headquarters and assistance requested.... At 6:45 the invading force was in front of Amin's residence. The resistance being offered by his guards was petering out. Amin ordered his ADC to extinguish all lights, then he turned to his wife and said 'don't worry, the Soviet army should be coming to our rescue any minute'.... Suddenly there were men outside the house shouting: 'Amin where are you? We have come to your help' ... these were Soviet Tajik soldiers speaking Persian with a Tajik accent. Abdul Rahman ran down the stairs screaming, 'this way, come this way. This is where Amin is' ... He was shot dead on the lower veranda.
>
> (Anwar 1988: 189–90)

Amin was shot in the temple with his head resting on the table. 'At 20:00 on the 28th, Colonel Kolesnik reported.... 1,500 Afghan Army personnel, including the survivors of the Guard Brigade, had been taken prisoner ... Vasily Kolesnik acknowledged the role by the KGB in the planning and execution of the operation to take the palace in Kabul' (Schofield 1993: 59–60). Afghan sources and Vasily Mitrokhin a former KGB archivist who defected to Britain in 1992 and was in charge of Afghan Archives at the KGB in Moscow between 1978–83 say that 'over one hundred of the KGB were killed in the attack on the palace' (Mitrokhin 2002: 101). For details of the December coup against Amin see Mitrokhin 2002: 84–168. Only Amin's Soviet-trained physician, who spoke with the invading troops in Azeri and was hiding behind the Russian nanny, was spared.

Those others who were still unconscious from the poison, woke up twenty-four hours later and found themselves in Pul-e-Charkhi prison. Amin, his two sons and his ADC were shot on the spot. One of his daughters was shot in the foot and spent years in prison with Mrs Amin and others of the Amin family.

With the killing of Amin, any pretence of an Afghan revolution also died with him. The Soviet Union sent in its 40th army, which in a matter of weeks reached the strength of 40,000 and then of 80,000 and by the end numbered about 155,000 troops. The Russians replaced Amin by the long-established and well-known agent Babrak Karmal, but they did not ultimately succeed in subjugating the Afghans nor were they able to export Soviet-style communism to Afghanistan.

The Russian case against Amin seems to have been based on grudges; for expelling their ambassador; for not giving them the sole right to the *Shindand* airbase; for sending Parcham leaders into exile; for killing Taraki; for not being Moscow's man. True, the political situation in the country was worsening and the Russians were also apprehensive as to what the Americans might do, because of their hostages in Tehran. Neither of these could be justification for sending in troops and killing the president of an independent country. The Soviets had been using the 5 December 1978 treaty as a justification to intervene; however Article One of the treaty says,

> The High Contracting Parties solemnly declare their determination to strengthen and deepen the inviolable friendship between the two countries and to develop all-round cooperation on the basis of equality, respect for national sovereignty, territorial integrity and non-interference in each other's internal affairs.

Even if faced with danger, the Treaty requires the consent of the other party before rendering any such assistance. The danger was there because of mounting resistance in the country, but Amin seems to have said again and again that he did not want external forces to fight for Afghanistan's territorial integrity nor to defend its revolution. So why did the Soviet Union gamble in killing Amin and thus becoming immersed in a quagmire from which they could not extract themselves intact? I shall return to this discussion in later chapters.

Conclusion

The Soviets in many ways were repeating the mistakes of the local communists. They thought that they could rectify a political situation by administrative reorganisations. They thought that if only they could replace Amin by Taraki or the Khalq faction by Parcham, this would solve the problem and that Afghanistan would become similar to a docile east European satellite-state. Their diagnosis of the problems of the Afghan communists was that they did not know how to implement progressive socialist ideas or to build a communist society. The massive numbers of advisors who they had placed from the office of president down to the smallest department were expected to rectify the cultural traits of the Afghans; namely mistrust in central authority, jealousy and resentment amongst the ethnic groups and local and cultural divisions on linguistic, ethnic and religious bases. They never appreciated that the Afghan state, though it might seem to the Russians as corrupt and inefficient, nonetheless somehow worked for a developing country like Afghanistan. The old monarchical system that had been around for some 230 years did not challenge the country's dominant tribal regions. The bureaucracy that had evolved had an element of tribal patronage built into it. Tribal representatives served as advisors to rulers in the eighteenth century or as permanent members of the national council for most of the nineteenth century or members of the *Loya Jirgas* throughout and had a great deal of influence over bureaucracy. The system, therefore, was not totally unfamiliar even to those who lived in rural areas. This system did not need thousands of advisors or armies of soldiers to make it function. A deeply Islamic and traditional society like Afghanistan needed time and resources to bring about changes in stages. These changes had been happening since the 1920s and the Russians were part of the process of change through their development projects and political acts such as the 1921 and 1933 Treaties of Friendship with Afghanistan and their development aid since the 1950s. Instead of following that route and turning Afghanistan into a friendly and a possible client state, the local communists and the Russians were both in a great hurry to transform Afghan society almost overnight to a socialist state. They had forgotten the saying that 'Afghanistan least ruled, best governed'. Had the Russians spent a fraction of the Ten Year War expenses of some '60 billion roubles'[23] (Borovek 1990: 14) on economic infrastructure, education and literacy and had continued to work through Afghans rather than to take over the state machinery and attempt to run it, as if they were operating within the Soviet centralised bureaucracy, the Afghan public if not converted to communism would not have become their enemies either and the Soviet Empire might still exist. In fact, the advisory system like the direct intervention of sending thousands of troops did exactly the opposite. The Afghans became more and more suspicious and hostile and their hatred intensified both against the Soviets and their Afghan allies.

The Soviets underestimated Afghan resolve against foreign invaders, and essentially they relied too much on assurances by the communists. The West also in the first three years could not believe that a poor, small country could reverse the brutal Soviet war machine. They made statements to the effect that Russians could have Afghanistan provided they did not go further nor endanger Middle East oil reserves. Afghanistan has always been an attractive place for invaders, but all previous intruders learnt at their cost that taking Afghanistan is one thing, keeping it is quite another. It took the Soviets ten years to realise this.

Part III
Battleground of superpowers

6   Afghan resistance: 1975–92

Introduction

Pashtun/Afghan life is governed by a code of honour and shame epitomised in the institutions of '*pashtunwali*', namely *nang/izat* (honour), *badal* (revenge), *milmastia* (hospitality) and *nanawatai* (refuge). (For a brief account of these institutions see Appendix 2). A Pashtun's honour extends from the individual to the family, the clan, the tribe, the nation and even to religion. 'The communist take over in 1978 threatened all of these. Resistance therefore became a matter of honour, incorporating the requirement of revenge' (Klass 1987: 205). The Afghan mujahideen, or 'holy warriors', especially in the initial years of the Soviet invasion, came from nearly all ethnic groups and tribes in the country. 'What united them was the will to resist the godless Soviets and their "servants" in Kabul. The strength of this patriotic fervour was such that the resistance showed remarkable resilience in confronting a highly organised enemy army' (Urban 1990: 293). While united against Soviet invasion, the resistance never managed to form a national leadership. Pakistan, the USA and the Arabs tried forming governments in exile and giving them platforms in the Organisation of Islamic Conference (OIC), the UN and regional conferences, but Afghan resistance groups failed to agree to produce an overall national leadership (for a brief history of mujahideen resistance parties see Appendix 12). The situation was no better in Kabul under direct Soviet occupation. There too the communist factions fought it out to the last, refusing to accept one or the other as their sole party or leader. As for the mujahideen resistance, the West took solace in the fact that because of its fractured nature, it could not be wholly bought by the Soviets.

This *muqawomat* (resistance) which later played a decisive role against the Soviet forces (1979–89) started as an embryonic movement in the 1960s and was turned into a small fighting force by Pakistan against Daoud, because of his demand of autonomy for 'Pashtunistan'. This formative period I shall refer to as Phase One of the resistance, and resistance to the communists' initial twenty months in office (April 1978–December 1979) as Phase Two. Although hard-line religiously motivated students and academics from Kabul had dominated the resistance up to this point, the invasion of the Soviet forces provided the impetus for this small, initially unpopular uprising to eventually become a nation-wide insurrection, which could be termed as Phase Three. After nearly ten years, the Soviets failed to smother the resistance or make it safe for their installed governments in Kabul and so with their departure in February 1989, the resistance, though on a reduced scale, continued its struggle against the communist surrogate government they left behind. I shall call this period Phase Four. With the fall of the communists and the departure of Soviet forces, the Islamist groups, despite Islam's emphasis on unity and brotherhood, turned against one another, which I shall discuss in Chapter 7. Before all this, an explanation of the institutions of the resistance and their organisation is warranted.

Manning, finance and the organisation of resistance

Given Afghanistan's position, in Arnold Fletcher's words, as 'the highway of conquests', it is not surprising that over the centuries Afghans have developed local ways and means of raising and funding armies to confront such invaders. However, in the last thirty years a modern Islamist way of organising resistance also became popular and this proved quite effective against the Soviet troops.

Traditionally, organised resistance is an old and well-tested system, in which resistance to an encroachment or invasion is debated within the *qawm* (tribe) and an appropriate force or *lashkar* (army) is raised. Amongst the Pashtuns, it is the *jirga* that initiates proceedings for the war. The *jirga* is open to all male, sane and mature members of the community. Everyone taking part in the discussion, regardless of his social position and wealth, is considered equal to everyone else. This is demonstrated in the circular seating of the members of the *jirga* to indicate that there is no upper or higher place in the debating area. The *jirga* then selects *meshran* (elders or leaders) of the *arbakai*[1] (tribal soldiers or police). The *arbakee* (plural) representing their lineages, clans and even tribes, then decides on raising an army. Depending on the severity of the encroachment, the *arbakai* could ask for one out of five or one out of ten fighting men in each lineage. Their kinsmen subsequently are responsible for the provision of arms and food for them for the duration of the conflict.

Before the 1970s, all wars (including religious ones), such as the Roshani movement against the Moghuls in the seventeenth century, or religiously led wars since, as against the British in the nineteenth century, were organised upon tribal principles. Religiously motivated wars are organised on a larger scale involving intertribal co-operation and are the closest the tribes could mount in matching the regular armies of an invading state. In such wars, although the tribesmen supply their own arms, they depend for their food and shelter on the people in whose areas they are mounting the attacks. The *ulama* (religious scholars) often aid or lead the *lashkar* fighting side by side with the *qawm* (tribal) leaders in accordance with the principles of *qawmi arbakai* or *lashkar*. Famous *ulama* who fought the British in the last century included Mullah Mushk'alem, Shami Mullah, Haday Mullah, Ipi Faqir and others.

The Islamist resistance differs in that they are trained in government religious centres unlike the traditional *ulama*, who receive their training in private seminaries or *madrassas*. The term 'Islamists' is used by the French sociologist Olivier Roy to indicate those religiously motivated individuals and groups who 'are almost all products of the government education system, either of scientific schools, or of the state *madrassas*' (Roy 1986: 69). The term 'fundamentalist' on the other hand is a loose term used by the Western media to cover different radical Islamic movements. 'In the general debate, the term "fundamentalist" is loosely applied to a wide-ranging spectrum of religious-political movements in the Muslim world' (Olesen 1995: 236). The usage of the term 'fundamentalist' could, therefore, be misleading. For example, all Muslims are expected to believe in the *Quran*, the *hadith* (the tradition of what the Prophet said or did, or his tacit approval of something said or done in his presence), and the *sunnah* (the tradition of the Prophet; the normative legal custom or precedent). Thus they would not object to the application of the tenets of Islam, as these are *fundamental* to Islamic ideology. According to such a misleading definition, all Muslims qualify as *fundamentalists*.

The Islamists are yet another school of thought that has come to prominence since the 1920s. Most of those on the Afghan scene are the followers of the Muslim Brotherhood, founded by Hassan al-Bana in Egypt in 1928. The Afghan Islamists were also influenced by the writings of Muhammad ibn abdal-Wahab (1699–1792) of Arabia, Pakistani thinker Abul 'Ala Mawdud, of the 1940s and 1950s, and Ali Shariati of Iran of the 1970s, whose reformist philosophies they followed. On the other hand, the *ulama*, trained in privately funded smaller *Madrassas* (seminaries) provide the traditional Muslim leadership. Their training of up to sixteen years at one of these *madrassas*[2] equips them to handle fourteen centuries of development in Islamic jurisprudence and the application of the sacred laws, *Shari'ah* (the law of God), *Sunnah* and *Hadith*. Up to the 1940s it was the *ulama* that ran the judiciary, the many thousands of mosques in the country and the *madrassas*. It was only in 1951 that a *fakolteh Shari'ah* (theology faculty), was founded at Kabul University so that the state *madrassa* graduates could further their studies. On completing university courses some might proceed to further Islamic studies in Egypt's famed Al-Azhar University or similar institutions in Saudi Arabia, Syria and Iraq.[3]

While the *ulama* were not totally dependent on state jobs, the Islamists, having been through the state system, expected a job with the government upon graduation.[4] The Islamists used their own gatherings, the *shura* (religious assembly) which is a concept taken from the *shura* that sat to appoint the first *khalifa* (caliph) after the death of the Prophet in 632. The *shura*, unlike the *jirga*, is often open to those who have some kind of religious qualification and is not solely confined to tribe or locality. The Islamists were not entirely dependent for arms or money on the local people. They received these through their *tanzims* (parties or groups) and also through countries that had personal interests in the conflict. They held their own meetings to decide on the day-to-day course of the war and on recruitment. Every local group was headed by one or more members of the Islamist parties and after establishing themselves in an area they then went about recruiting both locals and non-locals by either paying for their fighters or absorbing them into their *tanzims*. Another difference between the *ulama* and Islamist resistance organisations was that while the first normally fought in the area of which they were the *mullahs* of mosques or teachers of *madrassas*, the Islamists who had less tribal allegiance often fought in areas away from their homes and villages. With arms and money at the Islamists' disposal, their attitude towards the *ulama* changed from one of ambivalence to open hostility during the ten-year Soviet invasion. The clashes between the Taleban *ulama* and the various Islamist groups after 1994 are a good example of these differences.

The Islamist movement in Afghanistan[5]

The opening of the theology faculty in Kabul University (1951) provided an opportunity for some of its graduates to travel to other Muslim universities. The single most important university for the Afghan graduates was the famous Al-Azhar University in Cairo, which also helped in establishing and staffing the faculty and later continued to have exchange relations with it. The former King Zahir Shah's last prime minister, Musa Shafiq, as well as several later leaders of the resistance, Sebghatullah Mujadedi, Burhanuddin Rabbani and Abdul Rasool Sayyaf, all referred to as *ustaz* (teachers), are all graduates of this university. However, the person who started the Islamist movement in Afghanistan in 1958 was another graduate of Al-Azhar, Professor Ghulam Muhammad Niazi, who later became the Dean of the Faculty of Theology. Except for Shafiq, all others were members of the then little-known, *Tahrik* or *Nuhzat Islami*, Islamic movement, which was no more than cells of interested intellectuals. In the late 1960s, the *ustaz* formed a *shura* that was headed by Professor Niazi until his arrest in 1972. 'In 1973 the *ustaz*, in a secret meeting, founded *Jam'iat Islami*, Islamic Society' (Rubin 1995: 83) with Burhanuddin Rabbani as its head and Abdul Rasool Sayyaf as its deputy. Another important figure in this movement was Minhajudin Gahiz, who in 1968 founded a newspaper named after him, *Gahiz* or Morning. This paper became the organ of Kabul-based Islamists, who also contributed articles and some of the printing expenses. Gahiz was murdered by unknown men in 1972. Mawlawi (highest *ulama* rank) Muhammad Yonus Khalis (later a prominent resistance leader) was another member and deputy editor of an Islamic journal printed by the ministry of justice. Below these *mawlawi* and *ustaz* there were the Islamist students, who were recruited from Kabul University and high schools throughout the country. Some of these recruits who later became well known in the resistance included Gulbodin Hekmatyar, Ahmad Shah Masoud, Nurullah Emad and Abdul Haq.[6]

Initially, contact with the Islamic world was individually through those who had studied in Muslim countries. However, by the late 1960s many students from the campus of Kabul University were absorbed into the movement. By 1965 when the PDPA was formed, the small number of Islamist students also established their own *Sazman-i-Jawanon Musselman* (Organisation of Muslim Youth). By the early 1970s their numbers grew and they started winning elections within the student body at Kabul University.

From the very beginning, the Islamist students, like the communist youth, were opposed to Western and regional hegemony and imperialism. They demonstrated against Daoud's hegemonic policy over Pashtunistan and were also opposed to the division of Pakistan in 1972 from which Bangladesh was created, as well as to Zionism because of the Palestinian issue and to the United States because of American involvement in Vietnam. Their bitterest enemies, however, were the communists with whom they had open clashes, even killing one, Sayyedal, for which Hekmatyar was sent to prison.

The Islamist ideologues outside the Al-Azhar graduate circle included Minhajudin Gahiz, Mawlawi Muhammad Yonus Khalis who in 1960 was the first to have translated a work of a well-known Egyptian member of Muslim Brotherhood, Sayed Qutb.[7] The *hazrat* of Shorbazar, Muhammad Ibrahim Mujadedi helped the Islamist publication *Neda-i-Haq* (The Voice of Truth) and there was also Mawlawi Ataullah Faizani with his own *Khaddam al-Furqan* publication. Faizani, an *alem* (scholar) and *pir* (saint), established his *Madrassa-e-Quran* near the newly opened library at the famous Pul-i-Kheshti mosque in central Kabul. Except for Muhammad Ibrahim Mujadedi 'the *Hazrat* of Shorbazar',[8] all others worked very closely with the Al-Azhar circle. Faizani was arrested for organising an army coup. The authorities discovered the plan; Daoud executed Faizani and other leaders in 1975.[9] Several others, including the Shi'ah Sayyed Ismail Balkhi, were imprisoned.

According to the Islamists the *ulama* have been in the service of hereditary Amirs and kings, knowing full well that Islamic leadership should be on merit. Islam only approves of an Amir, a ruler, chosen from amongst the *ulama* to serve the *ummah* (Islamic community) and he should be replaced if he becomes tyrannical or incompetent. Thus in the view of the Islamists, all the previous monarchs, including even those of twentieth century and their constitutions, reigned unlawfully. Thus the first Afghan constitution of Amanullah (1923) followed by that of Nader Shah (1933) and that of Zaher Shah (1964) were not Islamic in that they legitimised control over the *ummah* through hereditary monarchy. In other words the

Islamists set themselves the goal of establishing an Islamic society that had not been in existence since the *khilafat* era. To realise this, they had to achieve political power, hence,

> For many of them, the return to religion has been brought about through their experience in politics and not as a result of their religious belief. The *ulama* define politics on the basis of relations within society as established by law: The state is the means by which justice is able to operate within Muslim society; it is the Muslims or rather the community of Muslims [*umma*] who provide the basis for political thought; politics is an extension of law ... For an Islamist ... 'the objective must be the setting up, not of a national Muslim state, but an Islamic state'.
>
> (Roy 1986: 80)

The Islamists, like their counterpart the communists, have failed to realise their dream. An important reason in the case of both is their disregard for the realities of the prevailing customs and traditions that have developed since the period of the *khilafat*. Such Islamists as the *Wahhabis* in Saudi Arabia, those in the Libya of colonel Mu'ammar Qadhafi and the Iran of Ruhollah Khomeini, although emphasising the Quran as the Word of God and Shari'ah as the divine law, interpret generalities in the Quran to suit themselves. As for Afghan Islamists, despite their claim of upholding the correct version of Islam and their criticism of the *ulama*, they continuously quarrelled and fought one another along ethnic, regional, linguistic and religious grounds.

Over the centuries, in addition to the Quran, the Hadith and the Sunnah, the *ulama* have developed *qiyas* (precedence), *ijma* (consensus) and *ijtihad* (deduction or reasoning) as valid methods of jurisprudence. These deductions and interpretations in the light of the Quran have been developed by the *ulama* into *Usul ul-Fiqh*, the Foundation of Jurisprudence. A major wish of the Islamists is to escape from these restrictions and to create a society they could justify through Islam. Thus in the second of a series of articles on 'who are the true inheritors of Islamic Revolution', Hekmatyar's *Hezb-i-Islami* paper *Shahadat* wrote '...those whose lives have been spent in perfidy, corruption and wickedness, as the Quran says, have no right of inheritance and ruling in the land of Islam' (*Shahadat* 28 March 1988). How can 'perfidy, corruption and wickedness' be proven? Why for example, despite Hezb's charges, could the *ulama* not recall the ex-king or one of the many former bureaucrats, technocrats, to rule as an Amir, which is what the majority of Afghans demanded? The stance of the other three Islamist parties was no different from the Hezb. Rasul Sayyaf's official party line was 'the war in Afghanistan is between Islam and Kufer [unbelievers]. There is no one who cannot be either Muslim or Kaffer. 'Neutrals' and 'good Muslims'[10] do not exist' (*Rays of Jihad*, p. 14, 16 Jan. 1988).

Islam provides for the needs of the individual and the community through the Divine Law, *Shari'ah*. This has been provided in Quranic injunctions, supplemented and exemplified by the Prophet's tradition (*Sunnah*) and later by *fuqaha*, jurists. However, even if one chooses to obey Allah and the sources of Islamic law, one may not be able to do so fully. Although the primary purpose of the *Shari'ah* is concerned with man's righteousness as an individual, it is obvious that the effectiveness of the law requires the co-ordinated efforts of the *ummah*, or community. When the application of *Shari'ah* is missing, as in Turkey and the countries of North Africa, however dedicated an individual may be, he/she cannot totally fulfil his/her religious obligations.

> From this it follows that an individual however well-intentioned he may be, cannot possibly mould his private existence in accordance with the demands of Islam unless and until the society around him agrees to subject its practical affairs to the pattern visualized by Islam.
> (Asad 1985: 3–4)

After this short discussion of *ulama*, Islamists and Islamic law, I now want to turn to the various phases of resistance in which all the above factors were key issues.

Phase 1: resistance against Daoud

Daoud came to power with the help of the Parcham faction of the PDPA on 17 July 1973. His interior minister, Faiz Muhammad, a Parchami like other communists in the government, knew most Islamists from their time as students at university. But apart from the imprisoning of Faizani and his 'co-conspirators', the government was content to be left alone to establish the new republican order and did not pursue the Islamists.[11] However, the inclusion of communists in the government and the arrest of Faizani and some Shi'ah leaders created fears amongst the Islamists. Gulbodin Hekmatyar, the Islamist student leader in charge of political affairs, was in prison for two years till 1974 for the alleged murder of a Maoist student. With Professors Niazi and Sayyaf also in prison since 1972, the remaining theology *ustaz* and student activists fled to Pakistan in order to avoid being arrested. In Pakistan they were more than welcomed by President Bhutto who decided to use them against Daoud to pay back the latter for his revived demands about Pashtunistan. The Pakistani Military Inter Service Intelligence (ISI) was instructed to train these disaffected young Islamists and to attract more opponents of Daoud in order to send them back to Afghanistan to make trouble for Daoud's government. Thus, Burhanuddin Rabbani, Gulbodin Hekmatyar, Muhammad Yonus Khalis, Ahmad Shah Masoud, the brothers Din Muhammad, Abdul Qadir, Abdul Haq and many more were given monthly allowances by Pakistan, plus arms, ammunition and training in sabotage and explosives.

> Tahir Amin from the Department of International Relations, Quaid-I-Azam University, Islamabad writes that the Pakistani government, worried about president Daoud's revived Pashtunistan policy, welcomed the Islamist exiles from Afghanistan and clandestinely trained a military force of close to 5,000 Afghans at secret camps in Peshawar.
> (Amin 1984: 378 in Olesen 1995: 254)

The then Minister of the Interior of Pakistan, General Nasirullah Baber, himself a Pashtun, is on record naming all those Islamists who later became important in the resistance against the Soviets as having been settled in Pakistan with a stipend from his ministry. They were trained for guerrilla warfare in order to dampen the demands of Daoud for Pashtun autonomy in Pakistan. The strategy employed by Pakistan's ISI was to send these men back to their own villages so that they could incite uprisings against the central government. By July 1975 and after eighteen months of training, the ISI wanted to test the result of their work and so Masoud was sent to his native Panjsher, Mawlawi Habibur Rahman to Laghman, Hekmatyar to Paktia, Abdul Haq to Kabul, Nasratyar to Herat and so on. Since the public 'did not see the Islamic movement as being a bulwark of Islam, any more than they considered the Daoud regime to be pro-communist' (Roy 1986: 76) the attempts of these young Islamists to entice uprisings in their areas completely failed. However, Rabbani when in office (1992–96) claimed that in his native Badakhshan there was an 'uprising'. This is unlikely since this north-eastern province, one of the least populated, most poor and isolated, would have been no challenge for the government and its zealot communists. Hekmatyar is remembered in Paktia as a *mullah* in a local mosque with a single shot rifle (indicating his poor status). A Maoist group, headed by a man known as Pahlawan, chased Masoud back from Panjsher. (When Masoud obtained the upper hand later in the war, one of the first things he did was to kill Pahlawan and over sixty of his supporters). Nasratyar and Abdur Rahman were arrested with their colleagues on reaching Herat and Laghman respectively. All the rest had to make their way back to Pakistan. The ISI 'plan failed miserably as no popular support was forthcoming and a couple of hundred Islamist activists were imprisoned – later to be executed in June 1979 after the PDPA takeover' (Olesen 1995: 244; Roy 1886: 75). This failure sent shock waves through the movement and the Jam'iat Islami, headed by Rabbani, split with Hekmatyar seceding to form his own *Hezb-i-Islami*, Islamic Party. A 'rift had been evident at least since the early 1970s ... after the 1978 coup, another group, led by Mawlawi Yonus Khalis, broke with Hekmatyar and formed a second Hezb-i-Islami' (Rubin 1995: 83). The two subsequently became known as Hezb Hekmatyar and Hezb Khalis (see Table 5.1). However, the French writer Gerard Chaliand, who was travelling with the resistance explained to The New Statesman,

Table 5.1 Afghan Sunni parties based in Peshawar

Party	Leader	Ethnic origin	Ideology	Share of foreign funding
1. Hezb-i-Islami Hekmatyar	G. Hekmatyar	Ghilzai Pashtun	Islamist	Received largest share
2. Jam'iat Islami (JI)	B. Rabanni	Tajik	Islamist	Received second largest share
3. Itehad Islami Afghanistan	A.R. Sayyaf	Half Ghilzai Pashtun	Islamist	Received third largest share
4. Hezb-i-Islami Khalis	M.Y. Khalis	Ghilzai Pashtun	Islamist	Received small share
5. Mahaz Meli Islami (NIFA)	S.A. Gailani	(Qaderia)	Sufi (moderate)	Received larger share of moderates
6. Harakat Inqlab Islami	Muhammadi	Ghilzai Pashtun	*Ulama* (moderate)	Received smaller share of moderates
7. Jabhe Nejat Meli (NLF)	S. Mujadedi	(Naqshbandi)	Sufi (moderate)	Received smallest share of funds

Note
One to four Islamist parties; five to seven moderate parties; of the two, moderates got less of the funds.

Table 5.2 Afghan Shi'ah parties

Hezb-i-Wahdat (HW)	K. Khalili	Shi'ah Hazarah	Islamist	Islamist, comprise of eight small Iran-backed groups
Harakat Islami (HI)	A. Muhsseni	Shi'ah Qizelbash	Moderate	Moderate, Based in Iran, later in Pakistan.

after the execution of the eminent theologian, Professor Niazi, who was the undisputed leader of the Islamists, none of the second-in-command who then took over – Hekmatyar, Rabbani and Yunus Khalis – had a charismatic enough personality to hold the movement together, so the Party split.

(New Statesman 12.12: 1980)

Phase 2: resistance against the communists

The coming to power of the communists intensified the struggle between them and the Islamists. While the communists had the support and resources of the Soviet Union behind them, the Islamists at this stage could only receive limited Saudi and Pakistani support. By 1978 only three Islamist parties, Jam'iat and the two Hezbs, were in existence. Also, while the PDPA was recognised as the government and was receiving aid from Russia and other Soviet bloc countries, the three Islamist parties could only count on the support of Mawdudi's Jamaat Islami Party of Pakistan and some unofficial circles of the Muslim Brotherhood in the Middle East. It is worth noting that the communist, Khalq and Parcham, like the Islamists, suffered from the general malaise of Afghan society, namely distrust and disunity in their ranks. Such disunity was more detrimental to the Islamists than to the communists. With smaller funds and fewer followers, the Islamists were no match for the communists, who had all state facilities at their disposal. So for the Islamists, success, however small, was dependent on the skill of their leadership to arrange their resources in such a way as to make maximum impact on the ground. This meant obtaining weapons and finding financial sources; recruiting more followers; training them and making sure of keeping their loyalties; serving as a link between the people of Afghanistan and the international community; mounting media campaigns and recruiting writers and public speakers to explain their cause; grounding the movement in its ideology of Islamism as its bastion. All of these were also the priority of the communists in Kabul. The major part of the Islamists' resistance was operated from Pakistan. To a limited extent, the minority Shi'ah parties of Shura-i-Inqlab-i-Islami, Harakat-i-Islami Afghanistan and Sazman-i-Nasr-i-Islami operated from Iran, with the last two being founded, trained and supported by Iran.

These Islamists parties, supported, organised and trained by the governments of Pakistan and Iran, remained at all times a small fraction of the resistance. Afghan nationalism and traditional Islam, as expounded by the *ulama*, had existed for a long time. It was the tradition of autonomy and accepted Islamic ways that formed the basis of Afghan resistance. However, in the face of the Russian onslaught new techniques of warfare had to be learnt. A distinguished resistance ideologist, Professor Baha'udeen Majrooh (murdered in 1986) admitted, 'we are training our fighters in new guerrilla methods. We want to change our techniques of hiding and plan for a new offensive. We have to plan new routes because the Soviets have blocked the old ones' (*Newsweek* 12.12: 1980).

The resistance to the communists stemmed from different sources. To the communists, those with more than an average land holding were disapprovingly known as 'feudal', and those who took more than one wife or demanded the traditional bride price for their daughters as 'backward'. So apart from the Islamists, their other enemies were the landowners, *ulama* and other political opponents. The landowners, known in various parts of the country as *Khan* (among Pashtuns), *Mir* (among Dari speakers), *Baay* and *Arbab* (among Turkic speakers) and *Sayed* (among Hazarahs) were amongst the first to suffer. Although small in number and holding less than 1 per cent of arable land, they were considered as the bourgeoisie and the 'exploiting class'. As men of power and influence amongst their people, they were regarded as a source of threat to the new regime. Most landowners throughout the country who opposed land reform or spoke out against the government were either killed or imprisoned.[12] The *ulama*, totalling some 320,000 (Bradsher 1985: 91) as the *mullahs* or *imams* of the country's mosques and the *pir*[13] (saints) of the established three Sufi Orders (*Naqshbandi, Qaderi* and *Chishti*), were another category of influential men who received harsh treatment at the hands of the communists. Other *roshanfikir* (intellectuals), whether former government officials, nationalists or university lecturers who spoke out or demanded a platform for their views, by starting a newspaper or reviving their banned publications of the pre-Daoud period, were one by one arrested or killed (Majrooh and Elmi 1986: 73–141).[14]

In a speech on Kabul Radio (25 May 1978) President Taraki said that those who engage against the authorities in 'sabotage, anti-revolutionary actions, corruption, infamy, bribery, cruelty, oppression and administrative inefficiencies' could expect to be arrested. So it was the combination of supporters of these categories of influential men and their family members, who suffered greatly by their loss, together with the general uneasiness about the communists (regarded as a threat to Islam) that led to the swelling in the ranks of the resistance. However, the government also continued to count on the *ulama* as under its sway in areas under its control. Babrak Karmal in a speech to *ulama* and *mullahs* on 30 June 1980 said,

> You *ulama* and *mullahs* [clergy] are the heirs of great prophets and messengers. On the one hand, it is the duty of the people and government to show you sincere and cordial respect. On the other, you have duties to the people in view of your sacred task – guiding the people towards peace, happiness, good deeds, fraternity, piety and virtue.
> (SWB, FE/6461/C/1, 3 July 1980)

By 1978, people in most of the south, south-east, west and central Afghanistan had started attacking government posts. At first they fought with whatever they had. The south and south-east Pashtun region, having a tradition of arms, used their most prized possessions, the British First World War Lee Enfield, known as *melkhai* (locust-like) which fired eleven shots without having to change the magazine, and a Second World War Italian rifle, called *ghwaigawar* (with ears), which held five bullets in the magazine. It was because of the availability of the arms and the familiarity with their use that the first attacks on the government posts started in the provinces of Paktia in the south and Kunar in the east. Other attacks in Panjsher or Herat were led by either Islamists trained by Pakistan's ISI such as Ahmad Shah Masoud, or by defecting army colonels, such as Ismail Khan and Ala'udin Khan in Herat. 'The first stage of resistance, against the Khalqis before the Soviet invasion, consisted of largely spontaneous uprisings under local leaders. Using local weapons and local resources, insurgents often succeeded in driving the government from their areas' (Rubin 1995: 170–80). However, in central, western and northern Afghanistan, except for those who had spent their two years of compulsory conscription service under the previous regimes, the rest of the population were completely unfamiliar with guns and rifles, nor could they obtain them easily. But with the attacks intensifying on government military centres, small amounts of arms and even smaller quantities of ammunition were captured here and there. One reason why the fighters from these areas in the years to come proved to be more disciplined was their respect for those army officers or conscripts or even those Islamists trained by the ISI or Iran for their knowledge of handling guns and explosives. On the contrary, in Pashtun tribal lands everyone considered himself to be as good as the other. Together with inter-tribal rivalries, discipline there became a rare attribute.

With the attacks on the army cantonments came the reprisals from the government, which were severe. Such retaliation forced many in the border areas to cross over to Pakistan for safety. Once it was found that the refugees were welcomed in Pakistan, the trickle soon turned into a torrent. 'The number of Afghan refugees in Pakistan, which was about 40,000 a year ago [1979] soon swelled to over one million. This has caused further problems for the guerrillas, as it is hard for them to find food in the depopulated areas' (*New Statesman* 12 December 1980). Yet Amin in a speech in June 1979 refused to admit that they were refugees running from war. He claimed that these were nomads who had been crossing to neighbouring countries from time immemorial. Even by late 1980 when the number passed the million mark, the government was still officially refusing to call them refugees. For the resistance they became a reliable source of recruitment. The organ of the PDPA, *Haqiqat-i-Inqlab-i-Saur* (the Truth of the April Revolution), acknowledged the flight of Afghans to Pakistan adding that the DRA 'resolutely condemns the support given by the military regime of Zia-ul Haq to the Afghan separatists and bandits who have become entrenched in the territory of Pakistan' (SWB, FE/6489/C/1, 5 August 1980).

By December 1979, major uprisings had taken place in Paktia, Paktika, Herat, Kunar and Kapisa provinces. The Soviets, through their various military and intelligence reports, had come to the conclusion that resistance was gaining the upper hand. Most of the provinces were not under government control. The army was deserting in large numbers. Their recommendation to their superiors in Moscow was that if the tide of revolt against the embryonic socialist state was to be averted, they had no choice but to intervene.

Phase 3: resistance against the Soviets

With the invasion of Soviet forces, the situation in Afghanistan was no longer an internal matter of some disaffected Afghans not coming to terms with socialist progress. The invasion was seen by the West as a threat to Middle East oil reserves; the fulfilment of the Russian dream to find an outlet to warm waters, and thus a threat to the status quo in the region and beyond; an encroachment by a superpower to add by force another republic to its vast land mass. It was considered as an opportunity for the West and especially the Americans to repay the Russians for their support of North Vietnam in the Vietnam War, a chance to dent the might of communism by making the occupation of Afghanistan politically and economically as expensive as possible.

As for the Afghans, the impact of the invasion was totally unexpected and therefore stunning. The majority of Afghans could not believe that an alien communist power had come to 'force on them' a small communist intelligentsia, who knew little of the views of the majority in the country.

The invasion was not unforeseen by NATO countries. Back in May 1979 they knew of the build-up of the Soviet forces near the border of Afghanistan. They knew that the Soviets would enter if the communists in Kabul seemed to be losing control. So after the invasion, nearly everyone thought that Afghanistan had been lost to the Soviets, arguing that Russians usually stay put once they go into a country.[15] Afghanistan, they said, was not going to be an exception. Apart from the British, no one else had read Afghanistan's history carefully enough to know that it is one thing to invade Afghanistan and quite another to keep it. The BBC's eastern service administrator, James Norris (28 December 1979), who had written a book on *The First Anglo Afghan War: 1838–1842*, was the first to say on the World Service that if the British in three attempts could not hold Afghanistan, the Russians would never succeed either. This theme was later picked up by the British Foreign Secretary, Lord Carrington, who in January 1980 on behalf of the European Community visited Moscow to deliver a similar warning and got, according to *The Times* of London, 'a frosty reception'.

However, the West at this early stage was even prepared to let the Soviets have Afghanistan provided they promised not to go any further.

Few outside Afghanistan, as well as the Parcham communist faction inside the country, believed that resistance could be sustained in the face of such an overwhelmingly powerful military machine. Anahita Ratebzad, the alleged mistress of Soviet-installed president Babrak Karmal, said on Radio Kabul, 'Now we have such a friend and ally [Soviet Union] that our enemies by merely looking at him will be blinded' (January 1980). Despite such rhetoric, resistance as a spontaneous movement was growing daily. Eight months into the invasion, Kabul's chief of the political department of the Afghan army, Major General Gul Aqa, admitted to reporters 'that no more than 30,000 bandits, trained primarily in Pakistan, are still operating in small units, largely along the Afghan-Pakistan border' (SWB, FE/6509/C/1, 29 August 1980). Meanwhile, once the Afghans were assured of world condemnation of the invasion, the ranks of the resistance grew and grew.

World reaction

The reaction of the world to the occupation was swift. On 7 January 1980 the non-aligned group deplored the intervention, calling for 'the immediate and unconditional withdrawal of foreign troops' sponsored the United Nations Security Council Resolution. (The expression 'foreign troops' instead of naming the Soviets was diplomatic jargon aimed at avoiding humiliating the Soviet Union and was used by the UN throughout the occupation).

On 14 January the UN General Assembly[16] adopted by 104 votes to eighteen [communist bloc], with eighteen abstentions [India, Iraq, Syria, Yemen, Ethiopia and others countries with close economic and military links with the Soviet Union], a resolution sponsored by seventeen non-aligned states calling for the 'immediate, unconditional and total withdrawal of foreign troops'. In November the UN General Assembly approved a second resolution calling for the withdrawal of 'foreign troops' by a majority vote of 111 to twenty-two with twelve abstentions.

During 27–29 January at an emergency session of the OIC (the Organisation of Islamic Conference, a Saudi-based organisation to which fifty-four Muslim states belong) was held in Islamabad and attended by the Foreign Ministers of thirty-four countries, which concluded to condemn the Soviet invasion as a 'flagrant violation of international law'. The conference suspended Afghanistan's membership of the OIC, giving the seat to the Mujahideen resistance and called on member states to withhold recognition of the 'illegal regime' in Kabul.

It is often forgotten that the Soviet people were far from pleased with what their government had done in their name.

> 'Operational reports from the Ukrain for example, noted the negative reaction of the intelligentsia to sending of Soviet troops to Afghanistan.' The Soviet Union really strives for World domination,

but why has it picked on Afghanistan? Even some members of the KGB overcame their fear of being denounced and confided their dismay at the action of the Kremlin chiefs to their friends. 'I am ashamed to be Russian. We are serfs and beggars ourselves and make others captive and poor'.

(Metrokhin 2002: 111)

Afghan reaction[17]

The Afghan permanent deputy representative at the UN, Dr Abdul Hakim Tabibi, almost immediately resigned, 'as a protest against the violation of my country's independence and sovereignty by ... the Soviet Union' (1985: 4). On 8 January, *shabnamahs* (night-letters), were clandestinely distributed in Kabul by the resistance calling on Afghans to rise up against the Soviets and President Babrak Karmal, who was seen for the first time in Kabul on 1 January. On 19 January two moderate resistance groups, NIFA and NLF, belonging to two Sufi orders announced their forming into a 'United Islamic Front of Afghanistan'.

On 27 January six Afghan nationalist groups based in Pakistan announced the formation of an Islamic alliance for the liberation of Afghanistan with the stated aim of setting up a 'truly Islamic' state in place of the 'alien and atheist' regime. 'In Peshawar there is an Islamic alliance for the liberation of Afghanistan. There are some weaknesses in the alliance, but new plans are underway to make it a substantial alliance...' (Majrooh in *Newsweek* Dec. 12: 1980). This was one of many alliances and later governments in exile that did not live up to expectations.

By August the number of refugees in Pakistan had passed the one million mark. Additionally, 'the Afghan army, which was 80,000 strong in 1978, has shrunk to half the size through desertion. Many of the deserters have joined the resistance, taking with them their arms and equipment' (*New Statesman*, 12 Dec.: 1980). The communists could only count on about 10,000–15,000 troops for combat. Meanwhile, even by February, the number of Soviet troops inside Afghanistan had increased to 75,000.

By September, 250 employees of the Afghan national airline Ariana had defected to the West from its offices abroad. In October, at the UN world communication conference in Belgrade, Afghanistan's chief delegate, Akhtar Muhammad Paktiawal, in an emotional speech denounced the Soviet occupation and was given rousing applause by the participants and granted asylum in West Germany by the West German delegation.

The Soviet occupation was condemned on scores of international platforms over the next ten years. Internally, the Afghan resistance went through many 'enforced alliances', imposed on it by its paymasters, the USA, Saudi Arabia and Pakistan. However, no genuine unity was ever achieved amongst the ranks of the resistance, who were divided among themselves, first into the two broad categories of 'fundamentalist',

Islamists and 'moderates', and then on ethnic, religious, linguistic, tribal and provincial bases. As a result of such fragmentation, the resistance groups that had been formed in Pakistan since the coming to power of the communists in Kabul in April 1979 had mushroomed to over thirty, representing all shades of Afghan opinion. However, it was clear right from the beginning that Pakistan was not going to allow a united Afghan resistance front on its soil, because of its past experience of Afghan nationalism and the question of Pashtunistan. That is why soon after the Red Army invasion, Pakistan formally recognised the three Islamist parties, the two Hezbs and Jam'iat, whose leaders they themselves picked and trained. To these they added the three moderate parties of the two Sufi orders: the *Jabh-i-Nejat Meli* the National Liberation Front (NLF) of Sebghatullah Mujadedi; *Mahaz-i-Meli Islami* the National Islamic Front of Afghanistan (NIFA) of Sayed Ahmad Gailani and an *ulama* party, *Harakat-i-Inqilab-i-Islami* the Movement of Islamic Revolution, headed by an *alem* and a former member of parliament, Muhammad Nabi Muhammadi. Late in January 1980 the Soviet-installed Babrak Karmal, in an attempt to win the support of the people, opened the gates of the notorious Pul-e-Charkhi jail. Another former leader of the Islamists, Abdul Rasul Sayyaf,[18] who, due to his maternal relationship with Hafizullah Amin, unlike Professor Niazi, had not been executed and was subsequently freed along with thousands of other prisoners. Sayyaf made his way straight to Peshawar and soon, because of his command of Arabic and connections with the Saudis, he was allowed by Pakistan to establish his own party, *Itihad-i-Islami Afghanistan*, the Islamic Unity of Afghanistan (IUA). This brought the number of Islamist groups to four and of moderates to three. These were the only seven parties recognised by Pakistan and through Pakistan introduced to the Americans, Arabs and the Free World as the resistance parties of Afghanistan. (Iran in competition with Pakistan set up eight small Shi'ah parties, some having no more than a couple of hundred members).

The Americans and the West soon came to the conclusion that if the Afghans were to resist the Soviet military might, they would need substantial military aid. All military and financial aid that came from abroad was channelled by Pakistan's ISI to the seven parties based in that country. They also decided to help the refugees who were pouring over the border to Pakistan and Iran. The humanitarian aid was also being extended to those internally displaced, whose numbers were even higher. Once the West was convinced that Afghans were not going to stand for the invasion of their country, aid from the United States and Saudi Arabia commenced. The Saudis, who had no diplomatic relations with Moscow and regarded communism as a threat to Islam and ultimately to their own dynasty, made it known that they 'would match United States aid dollar for dollar'. The Gulf States, Kuwait, the United Arab Emirates, Iraq[19] and Libya, together with private Arab sources all contributed towards the war. The aid that started arriving was massive by any standards.

> The Carter administration allocated $30 million for the programme in 1980 and about $50 in 1981. Under the Reagan administration this amount increased to $120 million by fiscal 1984 ... In the fall of 1984 Congress took the initiative of nearly tripling the administration's 1985 request, to $250 million. Saudi Arabia approximately matched U.S. aid ... The U.S. budget for aid to the Mujahideen, reportedly still matched by Saudi Arabia contributions, climbed to $470 million in 1986 and $630 million in 1987 ... By mid 1989, however, the United States and Saudi Arabia had agreed to supply $600 million each to the Mujahideen by the end of the year; an additional $100 from the United States brought the total to $1.3 billion.
>
> (Rubin 1995: 180–2)

With this money supply lines were set up between the countries that produced Russian arms, such as China and Egypt, and were paid for by the CIA and its Saudi equivalent, the *Istikhbaria*, with money to these countries' Swiss and other Western bank accounts. The main reasons why the West decided on supplying Russian arms to the resistance were twofold. First, they wanted to be in the position of being able to deny helping the mujahideen resistance and in this way would avoid direct confrontation with the Soviet Union. Second, since the resistance were capturing some Russian weapons both from Afghan communists and Russian soldiers, it would be simpler for them to complement these with what they procured from Western channels. Thus the resistance instead of fighting with outdated weapons or the small amount of arms they captured from government forces, now had available to it a whole arsenal of Russian weapons such as AK 47 Kaleshnikovs, Kalekoves, rocket launchers, anti-tank grenades, Dhshka, Zekuyak (tripod mounted heavy machine guns), hand grenades, mines and so on. For the resistance to handle such modern arms they had to be trained and so, from 1981 onwards, the ISI set up hundreds of training camps in the border region and literally thousands of fighters passed through them in order to gain confidence in handling the new weapons. But the main fear of the resistance was gunship-helicopters, which were immune to small arms fire. So, with the money coming from America and Saudi Arabia in 1982–83 some Russian Surface to Air Missiles (SAM) were purchased. These had low hit records because of faulty manufacture. In 1984–85 these were complemented with the British blowpipe anti-aircraft missiles. These were too heavy and their hit record was no better than the SAMs. In September 1986 the US Congress approved supplying Stinger laser-guided missiles to the Mujahideen. This was the first time that the US military had agreed to supply a force outside NATO with these shoulder-held, highly secret missiles. The large increase in the amount of military aid to the resistance after

1986 was largely due to the $250,000 price of each of these missiles, plus training and transportation to the war front.[20] Altogether the US supplied about 500 Stinger missiles between 1986 and 1989, some of which are still in the hands of the former resistance and the Taleban.

After 1989, the eight small Shi'ah parties[21] that Iran had nurtured, in competition with the seven Sunni Pakistan-based parties, became more active. Though the population of Shi'ah in Afghanistan amounts to no more than 9 per cent[22] of the total population, Iran asked for 25 per cent representation for their parties in any future government. The seven party leaders, with the exception of the small moderate NLF, all opposed such demands on two grounds. First, they represented no more than 9 per cent of the total population and second, these parties or the mountainous region of Hazarajat to which the majority of Shi'ah belong, had taken no part in the fighting against the Soviets. The Hazarah inelegancies who were in the Soviet installed government made sure of that. That is the main reason why, while the south, south-east and western parts of Afghanistan are still infested with millions of Russian mines, no such mines were thrown from the air or planted on roads, foot paths agricultural land or abandoned homes in Hazarajat.

Wahhabist Saudi Arabia, which was staunchly opposed to Shi'ah Iran, was alarmed that Iran might gain the upper hand[23] and so in 1989 was prepared to sharply increase its share of $1.3 billion for Afghan resistance. 'By November 1989, the United States and Saudi Arabia came up with another $715 million for fiscal 1990. The US share of the aid was only $280 million ... Saudi and Kuwaiti princes also contributed $100 millions of their private funds' (Rubin ibid., p. 182). The major share of this and previous money and arms that was sent to the Mujahideen, went to the four Islamists parties, all opposed to militant Shi'ism.

However, after the Soviet troop withdrawal in February 1989, the United States contribution was reduced for the first time in the belief that the resistance was more than a match for the communist government that the Soviets had left behind. Thus the US budget in 1990 was reduced to $30 million and in 1991 to a contribution of Iraqi Russian manufactured tanks and arms, captured in Kuwait and passed on to the Mujahideen by the Bush senior administration.

The impression that the resistance always conveyed was that their war was with a super-power. Once that was out of the way the 'Kabul regime could be toppled even by school girls in Afghanistan'.[24] Not all Afghans agreed with such an under-estimation of Kabul's power. 'Should Mujahideen decide to launch an attack on Jelalabad, they will face a difficult task. Regime positions are strong. Resistance sources estimate that the regime has 10,000 soldiers and militias defending the city' (AIC, No. 95, p. 20). However, the overconfidence amongst the rank and file of the Islamist resistance encouraged the ISI to capture a place near the Pakistan border so that the Mujahideen government in waiting could be transferred there and, with the fall of the communist regime, they could move to Kabul. The place that they decided on was Jelalabad, a city in eastern Afghanistan within fifty miles of the Pakistan border. In February 1990 a major attack by the hard core of the Peshawar parties was mounted and after considerable damage to the city and much loss of life on both sides, the resistance failed to take the city. Some local Shinwari, Mohmand and Khogiani tribes in the hope of *woljah* (war booty) casually joined in, but were unable to tilt the balance in favour of the resistance.

However, Sayyaf, then prime minister of the interim government, said that 'the fall of Jelalabad is expected soon' and the foreign minister, Hekmatyar was making arrangements for 'amnesty to all those who are surrendering or defecting from the regime forces' (*The Afghan Mujahid*, March and April 1989, pp. 8, 10). The failure of this major attack emboldened the communists, who raised the stakes for a peace deal and instead of completely handing over to the resistance, they wanted a 50/50 or at least 40/50 share in the future government.

The failure to capture Jelalabad was mainly due to the lack of support by the general public. The public, while putting aside all their religious, ethnic and linguistic differences during the occupation no longer saw the urgency to continue fighting the regime in Kabul whose officials were repenting and speaking of 'national reconciliation' even changing the name of their PDPA to Fatherland Front. On the resistance side most people had already become disillusioned with the 'new Islam' of the Islamists and the corruption of the resistance parties. They were not prepared to die for one or the other to come to power.

The Kabul government's counter resistance

The Kabul authorities and the Soviets, in their response to the military, financial and humanitarian assistance to the resistance, intensified their military and ideological campaign within Afghanistan. They concentrated on internal PDPA organisations by founding the Democratic Youth Organisation of Afghanistan (DYOA), the Democratic Women's Organisation of Afghanistan (DWOA), *Khedamat-i-Dawlati* (KhAD otherwise known as National Security), the' equivalent of the KGB and other Peasants' Workers' and Writers' organisations. Every one of these organisations sent 'volunteers' to the National Guard and joined the *Sarandoy*, the police of the ministry of interior. Others served as regular army officers in the armed forces. Thus, 'Kabul University law students training for work in the armed forces' (SWB, FE/6497/C/3, 14 August 1980); 'Second PDPA volunteer contingent leaves for front line' SWB, FE/6495/C/2, 16 August 1980; starting on 16 August, 'action against counter-revolutionary criminals' (SWB, FE/6502/C/1, 20 August 1980) were headline announcements made daily by the regime on Kabul Radio. Of all these, the National Guard, which was built up to some 20,000 strong, were the best trained and well-pampered, receiving double the normal salary and many other perks. They were directly under the control of the President Najibullah (May 1986–April 1992) and were key in foiling Defence Minister Tani's coup against Najibullah in 1990. Of the others, the *Khedamat-i-Amniyat-i-Dawlati* (*KhAD*) which in January 1986 was transformed into the *Wezarat-i-Amniyat-i-Dawlati* (*WAD*), the Ministry of National Security, which like the National Guard comprised ideologically committed troops, who were well trained and paid.

The other forces that the Soviets paid for and organised were the extended militia forces of the *Jowzjani* (named after their province) the Uzbeks, headed by Abdul Rashid Dostum; the Kayan Isma'ilia Shi'ah in central Afghanistan headed by Mansur Naderi; the Andarabi militia in the Hindu Kush, headed by Jummah Khan; the Achekzai militia in the south-west, headed by the one-time resistance commander, General Asmat Muslim. All these were *qawmi* (tribal forces) that the regime referred to both as *oparatifi* (operative) and *watanparast* (patriotic) forces. The tribal militias received training in handling arms and most importantly in monitoring Mujahideen movement in their areas. Their numbers were between 40,000 and 60,000 paid and registered men. Their main job was to keep the roads open. The road between the Soviet Union and Kabul was of vital importance. The Soviets placed the militias led by Dostum, Naderi and Jummah Khan in charge of guarding the vital road to the north of the Salang Tunnel. In addition to these, Ahmad Shah Masoud, the Tajik commander who was presented as the 'Tito of Afghanistan' by MI6 to certain journalists in the UK, was also a fifth columnist amongst the resistance, guarding the road for the regime to the south of the Salang Tunnel. Masoud twice signed a truce with the Soviet forces in 1982 and 1984 and never mounted an attack to block the Salang Highway passing next to his Panjsher district. Nor did he even once blow up the oil pipeline that ran along this highway to the Bagram airfield 20 km north of Kabul to demonstrate his opposition to the invading army. The Russians paid him $350,000 for signing the 1982 truce and later donated one fifth of all food products that passed through the Salang. These Masoud would produce to foreign journalists, saying his forces had 'captured them from the Soviets'.[25]

The Soviet aim when organising these militia forces was at first to keep the roads open. Soon they demanded that these militias stop resistance movement and any other such activity in their areas. The third aim was to airlift militias, especially the Uzbek Jowzjani, to other parts of the country to fight the Mujahideen alongside Soviet and Afghan government troops. These Uzbeks soon gained the name of *gilamjam* because they looted everything that came to hand, including *gilems*, rugs.

The militias came under the Ministry of Tribal Affairs headed by a Sulaiman La'q an ex-student of the theology faculty turned communist. The other committed forces consisted of the DYOA, and DWOA, both trained in handling arms. Their leader, Farid Mazdak,[26] was providing fighting troops to the National Guard, closely connected to WAD, the *Sarandoy* police and certain officer ranks within the armed forces. Another important force was that of the old KhAD and later WAD, who had trained men and women all over the country for intelligence purposes and whose numbers were estimated at about half a million. However, those who were trained in armed combat and sent to face enemy forces numbered upward of 40,000 fighters and came under the minister of WAD, headed by Ya'qubi.[27]

Thus, in addition to the depleted Afghan army and the presence of over 110,000 Soviet troops, the government in Kabul with Soviet support and backing was able to count on *maleshah qawmi* (tribal militias), WAD, *Sarandoy* and youth forces. These made up for the thousands of mainly illiterate, non-committed conscript soldiers who had no motivation to fight their own countrymen.

All these paramilitary forces for the Kabul government did not come cheap. The Soviets and East European countries picked up the bill. Similarly for the West the war in Afghanistan was one of the largest covert operations mounted against the Soviet Union. The war cost the West a fraction of what the Soviets had to divert to keep it going. Not all aid that was approved for the war went into Afghanistan. The level of corruption in the aid destined for the Afghan war from both the Soviets and the West was immense. The main reason for this was that it passed through too many hands before reaching its destination. The covert world of intelligence also made it hard to check. Of the two, the Soviet aid, which was mainly in arms, was directly handed to Soviet and Kabul sources in a better way, while that of the West was sent through many channels before it reached the ISI, then Afghan resistance leaders, then commanders and down the line before it reached the fighting Mujahideen.

The Kabul government and the Soviet expenses of war

The United States, Saudi Arabia and other Middle Eastern and Free World contributions to the resistance during the ten-year occupation mounted from $5.5 to $6 billion. The long, secret supply line from Washington to Saudi Arabia and then through Pakistan to Afghanistan was at all times very 'leaky' and difficult to manage and supervise. One Congress enquiry team in 1987 wrote that out of over $700 million joint contribution by the US and Saudi Arabia, only a fraction of that was sent inside Afghanistan and the rest was lost along the 'leaky pipeline'. The CIA, the Pakistani ISI and other government officials, the leadership of the resistance and even the commanders inside Afghanistan siphoned off aid at every point. It was an open secret that the two Sufi moderate groups, of Mujadedi and the Gailani, were selling truckloads of A.K.47s to the arms markets in Pakistan. Their excuse was they had to pay for their offices, personnel and other expenses. In fact it is rumoured that every one of the seven resistance leaders in Pakistan accumulated $200 to $500 million, deposited in their private bank accounts. This became apparent when the four Islamist Sunni, and the Shi'ah Hezb-i-Wahdat group used some of this capital and most of the interests of these deposits, to foot the bill for the four years and seven months of their destructive war amongst themselves. After the 1990 Gulf War, which was opposed by the Islamists on the grounds that American forces had entered the sacred soil of Saudi Arabia, all Saudi and American contribution to these groups stopped.[28]

The Soviet Union, in addition to arms, soldiers and military expenses, had also to pay for food and even fuel for the urban centres. The Soviet bloc also provided training, technical skills, food and clothing. One source of Kabul income was, in part, from the sale of natural gas in northern Afghanistan, which the Soviets completely controlled. Even the meters were on the Soviet side of the border. The Soviets paid for this in arms and machinery that was needed for the war, buying the gas at a price lower than on the world market because, they reasoned, of its 'high sulphur content'.[29] The regime had some limited income from custom and excise duties and charges at the ports. With these revenues and the money the regime received from the Soviet Union and communist bloc, they paid for 50–60 per cent of the national expenditure. Taxes from land and other income disappeared because of the war. However, the expansion of the government's counter-operative forces increased government expenditure far more than the combined sources at its disposal. As the Soviet Union was the major source continuing to foot the bill, it drove itself bankrupt in the process. This was immediately apparent after its collapse in 1991.

Phase 4: resistance against the Soviet surrogate government

When the Soviets changed the leadership from Karmal to Dr Najibullah in May 1986, the new leader was told that the Red Army could not stay indefinitely in Afghanistan and would have to withdraw. The Soviet leaders received the green light regarding withdrawal in February of that year when the Soviet Communist Party in its 27th Congress asked for the withdrawal of its forces from Afghanistan. The cost of the war was mounting for the Soviets. They were taking consolation in the fact that the PDPA with its new leadership and its new policy of 'national reconciliation' and the training of its cadres was strong enough to fight its own war.

Pressure was mounting on the Soviet Union internationally, economically and from within its borders, especially when their casualty figures began to be uncovered and revealed to the public through several well-publicised examples of investigative journalism. The USSR was embarrassed every year at the United Nations General Assembly, by a consistent majority of the Free World asking them to withdraw from independent and non-aligned Afghanistan. The vote of non-aligned and Third World countries was particularly embarrassing for them. Even China, with her dispute over the border with the Soviets, made the normalisation of the two giant communist countries dependent on Soviet withdrawal from Afghanistan.

In 1984, a year before the build-up of all these pressures, the Soviets had appointed a new leader, Mikhail Gorbachev, whose comparatively liberal views of *Glasnost* and *Perestroika*, restructuring and openness, were making headline news. Gorbachev in his Alma Ata (Kazakhstan) speech promised to withdraw from Afghanistan and in his 1986 famous Vladivostok speech he called the war in Afghanistan 'a bleeding wound'.

For the resistance the Stinger missiles were the turning point in the war. Before the arrival of the Stingers, the Mujahideen gave the impression that they were fighting a local war, in their own tribal and ethnic regions and that there was no overall national scheme. This, to a certain extent, was actually the case. The local people whose lives had been disrupted by the communist decrees wanted to remove these obstacles and to continue with their lives as before. As always in the history of decentralised Afghanistan, a national leader sitting in Kabul is far removed from their imagination and is of little consideration to most people in the provinces. But the arrival of the Stingers, for whose training and distribution the CIA and the ISI were responsible, at least for the time being turned the war strategy into a nationally planned and executed project. The Stingers were spread to most parts south of the Hindu Kush, where the war was at its heaviest. Although accurate figures are difficult to obtain, it is said that the hit rate was high, probably five out of ten. Fighters like Mullah Yar Muhammad in Kandahar, and Mullah Abdul Salaam, nicknamed 'Mullah Rocketi' became nationally known as highly skilled in firing these missiles. The Soviets were forced to fly high, which reduced the accuracy of their bombing and constantly used flares to fool the missiles.

The war in the first two years of Gorbachev's rule (1985–86) intensified. Most observers concluded that he was giving the Soviet generals their last chance of proving themselves against the Afghan resistance. But the continuing Red Army atrocities further hardened Afghan resolve. After his promises of withdrawal it took three more years before the Soviets started pulling out 50,000 of their 155,000 troops between May and August 1988, quitting Afghanistan completely by February 1989.

On the political front, however, Kabul was emboldened by the Jelalabad debacle. It is worth noting that a former senior advisor to the Kremlin on Afghanistan, Major General Kim Tsagolov, writing in the liberal Moscow *Ogonyok* magazine, pointed out 'that "in not a single" province had eight and a half years of war permitted the government in Kabul to impose its will beyond question' (*The Independent*, 25 July 1988). But the official policy of the Soviets, despite admitting to the loss of 13,833 dead and 330 missing,[30] was to provide Kabul with all kinds of aid including military hardware. Thus in October 1988 they provided the devastating Scud missiles and also supplied '30 Mig-27 fighter bombers which arrived in Shindand [air base] at the same time' (AIC Monthly Bulletin, p. 9, No. 93, 1988). The Soviets also supplied other needs of Kabul during the rest of 1989 and 1990. This seemingly endless supply line dried up after the break up of the Soviet Union in 1991. A year later the Kabul government, while announcing to hand over power to a group of neutral technocrats in accordance with the Geneva Agreement, disintegrated.

Conclusion

Afghanistan's geographical position has been both a curse and a blessing. It has been a curse for lying on the main east-west division and since the Russian's interest in a warm water, north-south route connecting the Middle East and Europe with the Indian subcontinent, and the Central Asian mass with the Indian Ocean and the Arabian Gulf. As a result, throughout history the area known as Afghanistan has been traversed and occupied by foreign forces. Its location is a blessing, because of its mountainous features and the resilient character of its people. Many ambitious rulers and their armies from Alexander the Great to Chengis (Genghis) Khan, and after that a spate of Muslim hegemonists, including Tamerlane, the Moghuls, the Safavids, then the British, the Soviets (now the Americans and their coalition) have been dealt defeat at the hands of those within the country. All these powers in their own times discovered the impossibility of ruling over Afghanistan. Thus despite the historic fragmentation of Afghan society, Afghan and especially Pashtun society, has been able to use its established tribal mechanism in raising armies to deal with any external intervention. Uncertainty and fragmentation are built into the tribal and ethnic fabric of Afghan decentralised society. The underlying reason for such disparity in Afghan society is the lack of the 'ideological, moral and cultural cements, which bond a society together' (Forgacs – A Gramsci Reader (1988: 190). Even common language, religion and culture at times have been unable to bring unity into the ranks of the same tribe or ethnic group. That is why resistance against the Soviets and communists and also among the resistance groups themselves, was fragmented on the lines of tradition/modernity; *ulama*/Islamists; moderates/'fundamentalists'. The next chapter will delve into more detail of these differences and discuss how this uncontrolled rivalry with the availability of lethal weapons has lead to the destruction of most of the country and untold miseries for its people.

7 From common cause to internal war and the rise of the Taleban

Introduction

After the fall of the communist government in April 1992, the resistance entered a new stage of struggle, this time attempting to seize power on a national level. Up to this point all resistance parties, despite not having a common leadership, shared the common cause of overthrowing the communists and driving the Soviets out of Afghanistan. From this time on a new stage of vicious accountability based on ethnic and religious 'indebtedness' began. This chapter is also the continuation of the discussion of the resistance's last two phases, the internecine war amongst the Islamists and then between the remnants of the Islamists and the Taleban. The vested interests of Pakistan and Iran, with money and arms from America, Saudi Arabia and the Soviets for the two opposing sides helped the resistance from its embryonic stage to its later development. It was during those years that the resistance acquired the training, experience and resources for the destructive war that was to follow amongst them.

The Islamists were the major groups who organised resistance against Daoud (1973–78), against the communists (1974–79), against the Soviet invasion (1979–89), against one another for power (1992–96), and finally against the Taleban (1994–2001). With the fall of the communist government the war continued unabated for nearly five years amongst the Islamists, the Shi'ah and the former communist militias who formed and dissolved alliances frequently. The ostensible reason for this protracted war was the refusal of Jami'at leader Burhanuddin Rabbani and his first man Ahmad Shah Masoud to hand over power according to an arrangement reached between the resistance parties in Pakistan, back in April 1992. Rabbani renewed his term of office unilaterally four times. All the major parties, the two *Hezb Islamis*, the Hazarah *Wahdat*, the Uzbek *Jumbish* and the three moderates, rejected Rabbani. During 1992–96 with Rabbani/Masoud in power, the fighting between these groups who had occupied separate parts of the capital took a heavy toll on Kabul citizens, inflicting immense damage to life, property, honour and the Afghan tradition.

Once the communists and the Soviets as a common enemy had gone, Afghanistan was left in the hands of a multiplicity of factions led by warlords who had networks of support based on ethnicity, language, religion, political ideology, kinship, regional loyalty and so on. They also had access to arms, money and external resources. Hence they turned public property into private killing fields. The same external powers that waged a proxy war against each other at the expense of Afghan lives replaced Afghanistan's central power with their favoured bands of armed groups. This situation provided the grounds for the fractured nature of the Afghan society to reach boiling point, playing havoc with the lives of thousands for almost five years. This chaos culminated in the rise of the Taleban, a turning point, which accounted for the defeat and disarming of many warlords as discussed in the second half of this chapter.

The West, despite Rabbani/Masoud's usurpation of power and the violent opposition to them by all ethnic and religious groups, continued to recognise Rabbani as the legitimate government. The UN, under pressure from Russia, the USA, Britain and France, continued to deal solely with Rabbani, a leader with no fixed address, no cabinet, or any semblance of government. But after the fall of Taleban, through US air bombings in October 2001, they picked Hamed Karzai, a long time US favourite, and then unceremoniously dumped Rabbani. No one, including the UN, raised an eyebrow over such a change.

The struggle for power

United Nations mediation started soon after the Soviet invasion and was concluded by the signing of the Geneva Accord of 15 May 1988. This agreement paved the way for the withdrawal of the Red Army's 155,000 troops by February 1989 (for details of Geneva Talks, see Appendix 13). Although the Soviets physically had left, they continued to support the government in Kabul with arms, food and cash for the next two years. However, after the disintegration of the Soviet Union in 1991, the already dwindling amount of aid from Moscow stopped and the communist government saw its days numbered. Meanwhile, UN chief negotiator Diego Cordovez continued UN efforts to find a negotiated solution to the 'Afghan Problem' between Afghanistan and Pakistan. The resistance refused to negotiate with Kabul, fearing that would legitimise the regime. Therefore, Pakistan, 'representing' the Afghan resistance, entered into talks with Kabul and signed the Accord after nearly six years of negotiations. Geneva also provided for international guarantees,

> The Government of the Union of Soviet Socialist Republics and of the United States of America, expressing support that the Republic of Afghanistan and the Islamic Republic of Pakistan have concluded a negotiated political settlement designed to normalize relations and

promote good-neighbourliness between the two countries as well as to strengthen international peace and security in the region (Article V).

The Kabul communists, the *Loya Jirga* and the king

After achieving the Geneva Accord, the UN was empowered by the General Assembly to work for a representative government in Afghanistan. Its special representative Diego Cordovez then embarked on the second phase of his assignment. In May 1988 he travelled to Tehran, Islamabad and Kabul to sound out these countries on the formation of such a government. The Iranians introduced him to the leaders of the eight minority Shi'ah parties that they had formed in competition with the seven majority Sunni parties that operated from Pakistan. Pakistan was willing to accept any government provided that Dr Najibullah, who was associated with the Soviet invasion, was prepared to leave. But Najibullah and the Soviets for some time had been working on a government of national reconciliation that the resistance and the Americans rejected outright. The American Secretary of State George Shultz said that in such a government the communists would continue to have the upper hand by holding on to important ministries. The Afghan resistance did not want to share any future arrangements with Kabul and regarded the officials of the Kabul government as instruments of the Soviet invasion, responsible for the atrocities of the occupation. The UN, however, wanted 'good Muslims' from both sides to form a transitional government. These comprised nationally known administrators and bureaucrats who had kept their distance from both the communists and the resistance parties. Some resistance groups were prepared to admit such people, even from Kabul, if that meant the dismantling of the communist system. The UN also thought that if the Kabul government agreed to be dissolved, half the battle for forming the next government would have been won. It was with this view that Cordovez went to Kabul and outlined his proposal to Najibullah, who replied,

> I sure know what you mean ... I am prepared, I am ready, to step down if you provide adequate assurances that the Pakistanis and their friends will also act in conformity with your proposal. I will not step down unless I am absolutely sure that they will not flout the agreement and kill my compatriots. I will step down if adequate assurances are given to us that a *Loya Jirga* will be properly held, and that our participation is guaranteed.
>
> (Cordovez and Harrison 1995: 373)

After this, Cordovez met the Russian ambassador in Kabul who told him, 'it was an insult to ask a head of state to step down', but nevertheless was very keen to 'know Najibullah's reaction to my proposal'. This *Loya Jirga* would have required the summoning of traditional elders as well as the representatives of political parties. The gathering would have been expected as in the past to produce a national government. However, it seemed unlikely that such a national government, in which the resistance and the communists would proportionally have minimal parts, would be acceptable to the Islamists or to their patron Pakistan. Pakistan and the Islamists, back in 1982 and again in 1984, objected to the formation of *Loya Jirgas*, in Baluchestan and in NWFP respectively, lest they produce a national government which might revive the Pashtunistan issue and also minimise Pakistan's influence. The Islamists were against it, as this would deny them a leading role in the government. The Kabul communists, however, were of the opinion that through the *Loya Jirga* they would be in a better situation. They were satisfied that as long as the Islamists were denied majority rule through the *Loya Jirga*, this would fit with their long-term objective of rehabilitation as a party. Another aspect of the *Loya Jirga* that did not appeal to Pakistan and the Islamists was the role of the former King Muhammad Zahir, who most probably would have been called upon to serve for an interim period.[1]

The former king's forty-year reign (1933–73), in view of the chaos created by Daoud, the communists, the Mujahideen and later the invasion, was remembered by most Afghans as a golden age. This explains why the king is seen as a father figure and a symbol of unity to most Afghans. The ex-king's return has been a real possibility for most Afghans. When Professor Baha'udeen Majrooh, in a survey in 1987 in Pakistan refugee camps asked who they would like as the future ruler of Afghanistan, 73 per cent mentioned the king's name, 1.5 per cent named various commanders and only 0.5 per cent named some of the leaders of the resistance.[2]

Cordovez, who had spent a good deal of time talking to Afghan exiles and also those in refugee camps and in Kabul, came to the conclusion that the institution of *Loya Jirga* and the 'options' of the king were possibilities he must explore. But Cordovez said that when he put this to the Soviet ambassador at the UN, the latter 'smiled and said "so you want to be a king-maker", I then realised that the idea was not entirely unacceptable to the Soviets' (Cordovez and Harrison 1995: 296). On 20 May, during a visit to Italy, the Soviet leader Gorbachev had already given an interview to the *L'Unita* of Rome in which he said, 'he would not oppose a move by the Kabul government to "seek partners among emigrants, and perhaps in your own country"' (ibid., p. 269). In mid-June during a central committee meeting, Najibullah made more specific references to the king, which were seen by *The Times* of London as being said 'both with the approval and encouragement of his backers in the Kremlin'. The paper speculated that this Soviet-inspired scheme might be aimed at dividing the resistance even further (*The Times*, 16 June 1987).

On 29 July, Cordovez met in total secrecy with the king in Rome and emphasised that he should go to Peshawar to meet the refugees and thus, like Prince Norodom Sihonauk of Cambodia, make a comeback. As there was much good will and support for him amongst the majority of Afghans, no Islamist group could have done much about it. But the king, notorious for procrastination, did not give a definite answer although he was prepared to 'help his people to bring about a "just and balanced" solution and to reinstate Afghanistan's "independence and peace"' (Cordovez and Harrison 1995: 298).

A new anti-Pashtun alliance

The Afghan Rulers from 1747–1978 have always been Durrani Pashtuns. Even after the communist takeover, Pashtuns dominated three out of four communist rulers in Kabul and six out of seven Mujahideen resistance groups in Pakistan. This time, however, after nearly two and a half centuries, once again Ghilzai Pashtuns came to prominence forming both sides of the warring parties. While the war on both sides maintained its ideological dimensions, most Afghans remained loyal to their grassroots tribal and ethnic affiliations. Throughout the period of fighting against the communists and the Soviets, all groups maintained and utilised these horizontal networks which became crucial after the fall of the communist regime.

Benon Sevan, who replaced Cordovez as UN representative,[3] asked Najibullah to announce his intention of stepping down, which he did on 18 March 1992. Weeks before that (February 1992), an anti-Pashtun alliance was formed in Mazar, the northern stronghold of the Uzbek communist militia. For the first time, two Mujahideen groups, the *Jami'at Islami* of Rabbani and *Shura-i-Nezar* of Ahmad Shah Masoud joined with the communist Uzbek and Isma'ilia militias and the Shi'ah *Hezb-i-Wahdat*. Until that point, with the exception of the Shi'ahs and *Shura-i-Nezar*, all the Mujahideen groups had been fighting against the Soviet/Afghan government militias. It is claimed that an important object of this new alliance was the formation of a government from amongst these groups, waiting for the right moment to announce it to the world. Their aims were first to overthrow the communist government in Kabul and then to end 'Pashtun domination', with either full autonomy for their ethnic groups or secession.[4]

The swelling ranks of the Uzbek, Tajik and Isma'ilia militias north of the Hindu Kush began to ask for extra payment from the government, at a time when Kabul was least able to pay, and were already making their disappointment clear with the Najibullah government. In order to exert his authority, Najibullah replaced the Tajik commander, General Abdul Mu'min of the north, with the Pashtun general Jumu'ah Achak, not knowing that this would be the flash point for which the warlords were waiting.[5] Dr Najibullah sent one of his generals, Nabi Azimi, to explain the government's viewpoint that 'we are not prepared to fight our comrades'. On arrival, Azimi too joined the conspirators. The parties, headed by

Rabbani, Masoud, and the Hazarah *Hezb-i-Wahdat* (hurriedly put together by Iranians from the eight minority Shi'ah parties in Tehran)[6] joined the communist militia groups. This new formation became known as the Northern Alliance. The first thing this alliance did was to disarm all government forces in the north. It later committed itself to self-autonomy within a federated state and if that was not possible, they would secede from Afghanistan, either by joining their ethnic neighbours across the border or by working for the independence of their regions. Given the distribution of population however, the idea of autonomy or secession along ethnic, linguistic or religious grounds would have been difficult to achieve, short of drastic ethnic cleansing. Since there was little support for such an ethnically nationalist agenda, the Northern Alliance withered away and nearly all its centres later fell to the Taleban.

The struggle for political power

When the communist government of Dr Najibullah fell in April 1992 and the president was not allowed to board the UN plane with Benon Sevan at Kabul airport, Najibullah was forced to take protection with the UN in central Kabul. 'There had been great hopes when the Soviet-backed government fell ... [that] a broad–based Islamic government would be established and that there would at last be peace after 14 years of conflict' (Marsden 1998: 61). But with the Mujahideen unable to agree on power sharing, such hopes were dashed. The two Islamist resistance parties, one headed by *Jami'at* now with the support of the northern communist militias, and the other *Hezb* of Hekmatyar, with some Pashtun *Khalqis* joining it, took positions to the north and south of Kabul. Both knew that the other would not tolerate its occupation of Kabul. Both asked the leadership in Peshawar to come up with a solution for a Mujahideen government in Kabul to replace the fallen communist government. In Peshawar they hammered out a temporary arrangement in stages. Accordingly, Sebghatullah Mujadedi, the moderate head of *Jabh-i-Nejat Meli,* the National Liberation Front, was to take over immediately for two months as interim president. He was to be followed for four months by the *Jami'at-i-Islami* head, Burhanuddin Rabbani, with Ahmad Shah Masoud as the defence minister and Hekmatyar as the prime minister.[7] Mujadedi's term ended in June 1992 and although he tried to lengthen it he was pressured by Sayyaf, Masoud and Hekmatyar to quit immediately, to which Mujadedi reluctantly complied. Rabbani's term was to end in October and during this time he was expected to arrange for a representative Shura to agree on some form of interim administration, before putting in place some permanent governing body. But street-to-street fighting took place between the two Islamist parties, *Jami'at* and *Hezb Hekmatyar.* Rabbani, at the end of his four months did not step down, using the fighting as an excuse for not being able to work for a representative Shura. The leadership of the Peshawar Seven, who were by July also joined by the Hazarah *Hezb-i-Wahdat*, gave him another ninety days. When that expired, Rabbani hand-picked 1,335 members, mostly from his own *Jami'at*, Masoud's *Shura-i-Nizar* and some smaller groups,[8] reviving an archaic Arab gathering the *Shura-i-Hal wa'qud*, never convened in Afghanistan before.

The *Shura-i-Hal wa'qud*, the 'council of those who can solve and make decisions', appointed him to continue for a further two years. The council was rejected by the majority of the resistance parties and also by the former king who said that such a gathering did not represent the will of the people, as most of the delegates had been hand picked or bribed.[9] Since the public had made their preference for a *Loya Jirga* apparent to the UN, these rivals *Shuras* of the Islamists and of Rabbani were not acceptable to them.

The urban guerrilla war

With Rabbani defying the rest, fighting broke out between *Hezb Hekmatyar* and the 'government' and soon the Uzbeks and the Hazarahs who had broken with the Northern Alliance also joined Hekmatyar.[10] Hekmatyar's men killed and injured large numbers of civilians in the city by firing hundreds of rockets on Kabul. With Uzbeks and Hazaras turning against the government, the Rabbani/Masoud forces were confined to a small part of the city. Kabul was thus divided between these warring factions. All those Afghans who had fought against the Soviets and the local communists in the hope that a national or Islamic government would be formed to heal their years of suffering were soon to find that much more destruction and killing were to come.

The war against the communists and then the Soviets was fought on nationalist and religious grounds, aimed at freeing Afghanistan and averting any threat to the Islamic culture of Afghanistan. This common cause turned into an internal war, sparking sectarian, ethnic and linguistic differences that had played no role in the war beforehand. The ideological differences between the powerful and well organised foreign-supported Islamists and the moderates were compounded by the differences that became apparent amongst the Islamists. The Islamists, throughout the one and a half decade of struggle (1978–92), always united against the *tariqat* (Sufi Orders) the *qawmwali* (tribal based nationalists) and the *ulama* (scholars). Another fact about the common cause worth noting is that because of the lack of national leadership or the existence of a strong national centre, this one and a half decades that had brought people of all regions of Afghanistan much closer was not utilised to work for a government of national unity. Nor was this period used to emphasise modern statehood in which all Afghans, regardless of their status and qualifications would play their role. The ongoing war dismantled the state and its infrastructure. For thousands with their source of income gone, the only employment on offer was to fight for these groups in return for payment.[11]

After nearly a year of infighting, the parties under pressure from Pakistan agreed to a meeting. This meeting was held between Rabbani and his opponents on 7 March 1993 in Islamabad. The term of Rabbani's rule was reduced at this meeting from two years to eighteen months. It was also decided that a constituent assembly was to be formed and this assembly was to draw up an interim constitution so that a new government could be in place by 28 June 1994. This would have also coincided with the expiry of Rabbani's and Hekmatyar's terms of office. Again, the deadline came and went with Rabbani not fulfilling the terms of the agreement. Apart from Rabbani's stubbornness, the Islamabad meeting had many shortcomings; *Hezb-i-Khalis* boycotted it; Dostum was not invited because of his past record; Hekmatyar opposed Masoud as defence minister but could not remove him either and so forth. For example, a sixteen-member defence council (two from each of the eight parties) was to work to raise a regular army. Masoud, Hekmatyar's main rival as defence minister, was viewed to exercise more control over the defence council. There was also to be an economic affairs council that was never formed. The Islamabad meeting therefore was a non-starter. If anything it led to the intensification of party rivalries between the five groups who divided Kabul amongst them, Rabbani/Masoud's *Jami'at/Shura-i-Nizar*; Hekmatyar's *Hezb*; Mazari's *Hezb-i-Wahdat*; Dostum's *Jumbish* and Sayyaf's *Itihad-i-Islami*.[12]

Fighting continued between the Islamist forces of the Hekmatyar, Mazari and Dostum militias on the one hand, and the Masoud/Rabbani and Parcham forces on the other. Nearly all of Kabul's treasures such as the national museum, the national archives, the libraries and anything worth turning into cash were looted by the forces of Masoud/Rabbani, the Hazarahs, Uzbeks and the small groups of Mohseni and General Mu'min. Hekmatyar's men continued their barrage of rockets on Masoud's area, and Masoud in return indiscriminately bombed the Pashtun residential areas of south and east Kabul. Also to the south of Kabul the fertile valley of Logar was totally destroyed by Rabbani/Masoud's day and night aerial bombings. According to the Red Cross some 60,000 citizens were killed in these urban internecine wars with some half a million fleeing the city in all directions.[13]

Rabbani continued in office for the full term of two years, despite protests from all quarters, saying that because of the war he was not able to fulfil his commitments. At the end of that period, Rabbani asked his chief justice to renew his term for another four years. It was obvious to all that Rabbani was not going to relinquish his position as head of the nominal government, whatever the cost. He could only be removed by force. Such force arrived in the shape of the newly formed Taleban movement, who in one afternoon, on 26 September 1996, swept Rabbani/Masoud, Sayyaf, Mohseni, Hekmatyar and the Shi'ah leaders out of Kabul. Hekmatyar, after being thrown out of his strongholds in the south and south-west of Kabul by the Taleban prior to their capture of the capital, had joined the 'government' as prime minister for the second time and wanted to bury his differences with Masoud/Rabbani. However, too much water had gone under the bridge and the rift never healed. That is why he was operating from the south of Kabul, fearing reprisals from Masoud/Rabbani, rather than moving to the prime ministry in the centre of Kabul.

The Taleban

The Taleban emergence in the summer of 1994 and their occupation of nearly all of the warlord centres in less than four years 'marked the most dramatic shift of forces in Afghanistan's recent history. Their rise to power spoke volumes for the bankruptcy of their Mujahideen foes and the exhaustion of the population eager for peace' (Davis 1998: 43). A single person, Mullah Muhammad Omar, the leader of the Taleban, started the movement.[14] 'By now there is an entire factory of myths to explain how Omar mobilized a small group of Taleban against the rapacious Kandahar warlords' (Rashid 2000: 25). The same myth-like story of their origins that was narrated to me by several Taleban in 1997 goes as follows.

> Mullah Muhammad Omar was walking in the area of one warlord, Mansur, when a woman in distress and panic came to him and said, 'I was abducted by Commander Mansur[15] and have been made *"bay'zat"*, dishonoured. Now he has abducted my young son, please will you help I have no one else to turn to'. Mullah Muhammad Omar went to the nearest mosque and after the prayer he explained to the thirteen men who had come for prayer, some of them graduates of madrassas, if they would join him to rid Kandahar of the likes of Mansur and his commanders. Only three out of the thirteen joined him. They were Mullah Rabbani, Mullah Berader and Mullah Abdullah. Others said they could not confront these warlords who were armed to the teeth. Mullah Muhammad Omar went to another mosque and this time some thirty people who heard the helpless woman's story, all pledged to stand by him. The story of this woman was one of hundreds of such examples known to local people. Mullah Muhammad Omar then went to Amir Lalai,[16] a moderate warlord and also an opponent of Mansur, and asked for arms to take on Mansur. Lalai provided them with AK47s and plenty of ammunition. All thirty-four rushed on Mansur's residence, firing in all directions. After killing a number of Mansur's men they captured the culprit himself and immediately freed the abducted boy. They held an Islamic court and passed the death sentence on Mansur, hanging him from the turret of his own tank. The news of this dramatic gesture went through the province of Kandahar

and neighbouring provinces like wildfire. People heard that a religious group called 'Taliban' had risen against the warlords. Mullah Omar and his men then went to the refugee camps in Pakistan to recruit more men.

The rise of the Taleban

Overwhelming numbers of the Taleban are former Mujahideen, belonging to various Islamist parties such as the two *Hezbs* and Sayyaf's Islamic Unity Party. The majority of the leadership, however, belonged to the moderate Muhammad Nabi Muhammadi's 'Movement for Islamic Revolution'. Muhammadi is a well-known '*alim* (singular of *ulama*). In the beginning of the 1980s, his party was at its most numerous. Its fighters were either village mullahs, graduates of *madrassas, ulama*, or tribal men mainly belonging to his Ghilzai tribe, loosely held together by Muhammadi.

There are two important facts about the Taleban, which are not often emphasised. First, as they were part of the resistance and had fought against the Russians and communists, they were well informed about all the groups that fought during the occupation. This familiarity with other resistance groups paid off in their initial success, when they gave the impression that they were siding with Rabbani's *Jami'at* in Kandahar, thus securing his party's support (see note 16). They then turned against the other four main groups in that city, who were disunited and more unpopular with the public. Second, unlike most Pashtuns, who one way or another end up learning Dari, the mostly Pashtun Taleban moved to Pakistani refugee camps at young ages and later went to study in some of the madrassas there. So their second language is Urdu and not Dari and they also know a great deal more about the state infrastructure and bureaucracy of Pakistan than any other Afghan group.

> The Taliban's unprecedented depth of contacts and support in Pakistan enabled them at times to defy the ISI, by enlisting the help of government ministers or the transport Mafia. At other times the Taliban could defy the federal governments in Baluchestan and the North West Frontier Province. Thus the Taliban's main advantage was that they never depended upon an exclusive relationship with just one Pakistani lobby. They had access to more influential lobbies and groups in the border regions than most Pakistanis. The Taliban's linkages with these groups are what constitute the nature of their 'support' from Pakistan.
>
> (Rashid 1998: 71)

After the Soviet withdrawal in 1989 and the fall of the communist government in 1992, many resistance commanders were not prepared to be part of the internecine wars. They left their parties to study in one of the nearly

2000 *madrassas* in NWFP, Baluchestan, Sind and some inside Afghanistan that were still functioning. The word *Talib* (singular) or *Talib-ul 'Ilm*, 'seeker of knowledge', refers to one who studies theology.

In the absence of proper schooling for the displaced Afghans, the *madrassas*, traditionally private centres of learning, received a boost in the war years from Saudi Arabian, Pakistani and even Western money, so that Afghan refugees could study there. The party whose name and philosophy is connected with the *madrassa* training and education system in Pakistan is the *Jama'at Ulama Islami*, the Society of Islamic *ulama*, whose two wings are headed by Mawlana Sami'ul Haq and Mawlana Fazlur Rahman. The latter's father, Mufti Mahmud, founded this party. These *madrassas* are free and residential like seminaries in the Christian world, where students study long hours, live a frugal life, and have plenty of time for debating and camaraderie. The *madrassas* are basically for the sons of 'akhunds', those mullahs and *ulama* who have been through the *madrassa* system. But since their doors are open to all, a large number of laymen's sons are also attracted each year. All those who have graduated from *madrassas* call themselves *alims* and end up teaching in government schools, serving as mullahs in mosques, and working for the authorities in areas where their religious knowledge is needed, as in courts, the Ministry of Justice or for religious publications.

Now that the Taleban had entered the scene, they needed men and arms and could not depend solely on well-wishers' contributions of arms. An extremist Islamist party, which throughout the Soviet occupation had fought with nearly every other resistance group, was Hekmatyar's Hezb. Taleban leaders feared Hekmatyar's Hezb more than any other resistance party or group and knew that in order to establish themselves they would have to remove Hezb from the scene. It so happened that Hezb had one of the largest arms dumps, in Pasha, just on the border with Baluchestan in Spin Boldak. The Taleban, after raising fighters from some 200 refugee camps and seminaries from across the border, divided themselves into three groups, attacking the Pasha arms depot on 12 October 1994. In two hours, seven Hezb men were dead with the loss of only one Talib and they were in occupation of the depot that contained 18,000 AK 47, artillery rounds, rocket launchers, ammunitions and vehicles. (Davis 1998: 45; Rashid, 2000: 26–7). This was, according to an anonymous Pakistani intelligence source,

> an extremely large ammunition dump that had been moved across the border from Pakistan in 1991 ... [this] was a huge dump, a central dump with rockets, artillery ammunition, tank ammunition, and small arms-both captured from the (pre-1992) Afghan government and western supplied ammo. I believe they have sufficient stocks to run their affairs for quite some time. For years even.
>
> (Davis 1998: 46)

Davis and also Hekmatyar in his book, *Hidden Conspiracies and Known Faces*, speak of the support given to the Taleban by the Pakistani border militia, which the Taleban denied publicly. I interviewed Taleban spokesman Mullah Khairullah Khairkhwah on 13 October 1994 and asked if Pakistani forces assisted them, which he denied. There remains a lack of evidence regarding the direct involvement of Pakistani troops, although because of the nature of the arms flow through Pakistan to Afghanistan, long since established, it is difficult to speculate on the exact amount of arms received by the Taleban and their diverse range of supporters.

After the capture of the Pasha arms dump and Kandahar, the name and fame of the Taleban gathered momentum and they reached 12,000 volunteers by December 1994. 'In the next three months the Taleban were to take control of twelve of Afghanistan's thirty-one provinces, opening the roads to traffic and disarming the population. As the Taleban marched north to Kabul, local warlords either fled or were waving the white flags in surrender. Mullah Omar and his army of students were on the march across Afghanistan' (Rashid 2000: 29–30).

Before the rise of the Taleban, the sole means by which to combat aggression perpetrated by the warlords was through other warlords. Such inter-group wars created more mayhem for ordinary citizens, as loyalties constantly switched and bad blood between parties increased correspondingly. The Taleban appeared at a time when the public had reached the point of desperation from the excessive aggression of the warlords and were also exhausted from the long war against the communists, Soviets and then amongst their own leaders. These conditions account not only for the rise to prominence of the group themselves, but also the early widespread support they enjoyed from amongst the common Afghans, especially in rural Pashtun areas. Mullah Omar, in a relatively early interview, gave a simple explanation of their uprising, 'We took up arms to achieve the aims of the Afghan *jihad* and save our people from further suffering at the hands of the so-called Mujahideen. We had complete faith in God Almighty. We never forgot that. He can bless us with victory or plunge us into defeat' (Yosufzai, *The News*, 2 February 1995). A year later when a *New York Times* correspondent toured Kandahar attempting to construct a picture of the rise of the Taleban, he was told that 'we were fighting against Muslims who had gone wrong. How could we remain quiet when we could see crimes being committed against women and the poor?' (11 December 1996).

The Taleban leader's tactic of voluntary recruitment and mobilisation was their strength. Only those who were committed joined them. Initially this was largely because of the overwhelmingly simple appeal and charisma of Mullah Muhammad Omar and other founding leaders, who were very much viewed as a return to the ideal tenets of a good Muslim leader, that is, noble, chivalrous and above all, devoted to God, which was a far cry from the corruption and power-hunger evident in the former Mujahideen leaders. Later on, once they had occupied 90 per cent of land within Afghanistan, their recruitment methods adopted army-like organisation, and conscription was prevalent, obviously to their detriment in some areas. But unlike an organised army, there was no set length on service. Pakistan's Foreign Secretary Najmuddin Sheikh on 18 November 1994, speaking at the United Nations, spelt out Pakistan's analysis of the Taleban phenomenon,

> As a reaction to the state of anarchy in Afghanistan. It was neither the ideology the Taliban propounded, nor the religious fervour of the people that accounted for their subsequent success. Rather it was the war weariness of the populace which stood ready to welcome any force that promised the disarming of the local brigands, the restoration of peace, the semblance of an honest administration, no matter how rough and ready its system of justice.
>
> (Rashid 1998: 72)

For the ordinary people who had suffered from the excesses of the communist Khalqis and Parchamis and the Islamists, the Taleban were quite different in that they were from amongst the poor, uneducated and unprivileged masses and were therefore closer to ordinary people. From the very beginning they told people that their aim was to rid the country of the warlords, to inaugurate an Islamic system and to hand over power to qualified technocrats and those dedicated to an Islamic system of government. The warlords on the other hand, in their ever-pettier squabbles, were destroying entire cities and adding to the miseries of the previous long years of war for ordinary people. For example, on a sixty-mile stretch of road from Kandahar to the border of Baluchestan in Pakistan, in November 1997 I counted no less then seventeen *potaks*, or checkpoints, manned by the armed men of various Mujahideen and warlord groups collecting road tax from vehicles, goods and passengers. Because of the excesses of the road toll, most truck drivers would rather go through the dangerous mine-infested sandy deserts, thus risking being blown up, looted by robbers and damaging their vehicles, than go through this main thoroughfare. The ordinary people saw the warlords' actions, such as compulsory road taxes, seizing of property, abducting of women and enlisting fighters by blackmail and threats, as contrary to Pashtunwali and Islam. Such disaffection of the public benefited the Taleban in their attempts to establish themselves as an effective fighting force in the post-communist phase.

Taleban conquests

Kandahar and the eastern provinces

In October 1994 two important episodes were said to connect the Taleban to Pakistan. The first was Pakistani Prime Minster Benazir Bhutto's meeting at Ashgabat, with the governor of Herat, Isma'il Khan, and the Uzbek militia leader General Dostum, both agreeing to give safe passage to a convoy of Pakistani goods (which would be guarded by the Taleban) through their territory up to Central Asia. Then there was a well-publicised visit to Kandahar and Herat by the Pakistani Minister of Interior, retired Major General Nasirullah Babur, a family friend of the Bhuttos, a Pashtun from NWFP and an old hand in the Afghan resistance. Babur took six ambassadors[17] with him on this trip, attempting to raise $300 million for the repair of the road between the Pakistani border at Chaman (in Baluchestan) and the Turkmen border. He also estimated $800 million for a railway line next to the highway.[18] On 29 October, a fifty-truck food and medicine convoy from Pakistan was escorted by two NWFP Pashtun ISI agents, Colonel Imam (the pseudonym of Sultan Amir), and another agent by pseudonym Gul, accompanied by two Taleban commanders – Mullah Burjon (killed September 1996 in Sarobi) and Nuruddeen Turabi, later Minister of Justice. They had negotiated their way through most of the *potaks*, but were stopped in Takht-i-Pul by the local warlord commander Mansur Achekzai, who told them that a permit for this kind of convoy could only be issued by his and the other three party representatives in Kandahar.

A tribal *Jirga* sent to Takht-i-Pul, some 13 kilometres from Kandahar City, proved unable to resolve the issue. With Taleban reinforcements arriving from the border area, war broke out between the Taleban and four of the local warlords. In two days of fighting, the Taleban routed Hezb Hekmatyar, Sayyaf, Mansur and Amir Lalai, killing forty-three of their fighters with the loss of only seven of their own men. Having routed these warlords they went on to take Kandahar airport, thus for the first time capturing aeroplanes including six MIG-21 fighters and four Mi-17 transport helicopters. They proceeded to Kandahar City and were received by thousands in jubilation. They also took control of twenty tanks belonging to the Hezb Hekmatyar strongman, Sarkateb and two Mi-17s.[19] From Lalai and Mansur, they captured huge amounts of arms, multi-barrel rocket launchers and BMP armoured vehicles. The Jami'at Islam party, which had over 2,000 fighting men, remained neutral in accordance with Rabbani's instructions.[20] Meanwhile, the convoy on its return loaded with raw cotton paid the Taleban $5,000 in tax.

The Pakistan Interior Minister, Nasirullah Babur, 'took credit for the Taleban's success, telling journalists privately that the Taleban were "our boys". Yet the Taleban demonstrated their independence from Pakistan, indicating that they were nobody's puppet' (Rashid 2000: 29). Rabbani too in asking his powerful Kandahar commander to give in to the Taleban had said that the Taleban are 'our soldiers'. When I put this question to Taleban leader Mullah Muhammad Omar in 1997 in Kandahar, he said 'many people have claimed us as "theirs". Now they say we are working for the Americans. We never said anything about these claims, but our objective is our country and Islam, we are in nobody's pay. I am the leader of this movement and I have not met with any Pakistani or American officials'.

After the capture of Kandahar, the Taleban movement continued to grow. In December, taking advantage of the local resentment against the three Akhundzadah drug/warlord brothers, they told the surviving Ghafar and his supporters to withdraw to their native district, Kajaki. Two weeks later Ghafar was asked to submit his arms, as the Taleban did not allow anyone to carry arms. His Alizai tribesmen, fearing the worst from all those with whom they fought over poppy fields, rose against the Taleban. But the combined forces of the Taleban and the local opponents of the Akhundzadah family proved too strong hence the Akhundzadah and his Alizai supporters took to the mountains of Ghor. The Alizai soon pledged their support to Taleban's opponent, Isma'il Khan, the governor of Herat and through him to the Kabul government. Thus after this first taste of resistance outside Kandahar, the Taleban took control of Helmand province and soon would subdue the provinces of Uruzgan to the north and Zabul to the east. In Zabul an important commander of Sayyaf, Mulla Abdul Salam, known as Mullah Rocketi for his skill in firing Stinger missiles, joined them. After Zabul they crossed to Ghazni province where the Taleban told Muhammadi's most prominent commander, Qari Taj Muhammad, popularly known as Qari Baba (father), that he could continue as governor provided he agreed to be disarmed. The Qari had little choice but to comply. He too, like Mullah Naqib of Kandahar, was depreciated after a while.

On 5 February 1995 the forces of Hekmatyar in Maidan Shah, ten kilometres to the southwest of Kabul, confronted the Taleban. In the four days of fighting, over 200 fighters were killed from both sides and on 7 February the Taleban were repulsed from Maidan Shah. But then on the night of 10 February the Taleban, taking advantage of the dark, which later became one of their operational hallmarks, attacked and before daybreak Hekmatyar's men were seen abandoning everything and running for their lives over the hills. The defeated Hekmatyar withdrew to Char Asyab to the south of Kabul in Logar province. The Taleban, without taking stock or re-organising, continued eastward and by 13 February they took from Hezb the districts of Chak and Barakibarak in Logar province, entering the strategic town of Pul-i-Alam.

These blitzkrieg operations sent clear signals to all other warlords that their days were numbered. The Taleban's night operations, their speed, mobility, discipline, skills at repairs and the maintenance of tanks, arms and communication skills were at variance with any known resistance group. This deadly efficiency of the young movement is pointed to by its supporters as proof of Divine Help, while critics claim proof of external military involvement.

Soon after capturing Logar province, Ahmad Shah Masoud, Rabbani's strongman, met for the first time with the Taleban in Maidan Shah. A Taleban leader Mullah Masher, 'told him we are coming to disarm your and Rabbani's men too. Masoud told the Taleban leader, "How could I give my arms to the Taleban when two aggressive forces like Hekmatyar and Hezb-i-Wahdat are laying siege to Kabul?"'.[21] After Masoud heard of the Taleban's plan, he and Sayyaf, without bidding farewell, quietly sneaked out and drove at speed back to Kabul.[22] The Taleban who had not confronted Masoud/Rabbani forces thus far, gave the impression that they had taken Masoud's words at their face value and immediately set out to chase Hezb Hekmatyr from Wardak and Logar provinces. Masoud had radio contact with Hekmatyar. When the Taleban entered Logar province, Hekmatyar made several frantic telephone calls to Masoud asking him for help against the Taleban. When that did not materialise he made a hasty retreat to his last stronghold of Sarobi, to the east of Kabul.[23] Meanwhile, the Pashtun provinces of Paktia and Paktika, where the local populace were tired of Hezb Hekmatyar and Sayyaf's men's attitude towards them, hoisted the Taleban flag, inviting them to come and assume responsibility for these provinces which they wasted no time in doing.

The drive to the west

By August 1995 the Taleban force had grown to some 15,000 men. After the January defeat of Ghafar, the Taleban focused on their westward advance and by March 1995 they took Neemroz and most of the province of Farah. Isma'il Khan, the self-appointed 'governor of Herat and Amir of south-western Afghanistan', had marched from his centre in Herat to confront the Taleban. Isma'il and Masoud were the strongmen of Jami'at, both jealous and hateful of one another. When Isma'il lost some ground to the Taleban in Farah, Masoud airlifted 2,000 of his fighters[24] and high officials of Jami'at to replace Isma'il with his deputy, Colonel Ala'udin Khan, and to bring the Herat front under the tighter control of the Kabul-based Jam'iat and Masoud's Shura-i-Nizar. These forces and their generals met in Shindand airbase (Farah province) and made provocative and inflammatory speeches about the Taleban. Several of the speakers took the oath 'to bring back not just the Taleban's wives but those of all the Kandahari as well'. When the Taleban obtained the tape of these speeches they played it over Kandahar Radio. Disrespect to one's wife is the worst kind of shame one can inflict on a Pashtun man. It was not surprising that in two days, some 40,000 Kandahari men volunteered to fight against Masoud and Isma'il Khan's combined forces.

Meanwhile, the opposition forces had come to within twenty kilometres of Kandahar City (at Gerishk). After the Taleban had armed these volunteers, they attacked and inflicted some '2,000 casualties', according to Isma'il Khan's own interview with an exile paper, on the joint Masoud/Isma'il Khan forces. The remainder of their troops were either forced to flee or surrender.²⁵ The Taleban, with the help of local residents who had all turned against Isma'il Khan first took the airbase of Shindand with some seventeen fighter planes and then continued to Herat. Isma'il Khan and his men loaded their belongings, the cash from Herat Bank and valuables belonging to the various NGOs onto some forty trucks and escaped to Iran. When the people of Herat woke in the morning, they saw the Taleban patrolling the streets. This was in September 1995. The war in western Afghanistan was the first time Masoud showed the Taleban that he was not going to simply surrender to them as easily as all the others had.

Taleban venture to Kabul

After the Taleban takeover of the Hezb Hekmatyar positions at Char Asyab, Masoud and the Hazarahs started another of their many deadly urban skirmishes. The Taleban, who had counted on the support of ordinary people against the warlords, thought that if they could play a role in stopping the fighting in Kabul, they might win the support of the Kabulis and thus their job of disarming Masoud and Hazarah fighters might become easier. When the Taleban were asked by Masoud and the Hazarahs to mediate between them, they agreed. A force headed by Mullah Abbas (later minister of health), was sent via Dar-ul Amman to the south of Kabul. This force was received by 'the Hazarahs who tricked us by telling us to continue on the Dar-ul Amman Avenue and that "we shall be following you". After a short distance we were fired on by Jami'at and Masoud men and when we told them who we were they stopped. We walked to their post and started talking to them but their attitude towards us was uncivilised'.²⁶ Having entered Kabul, the Taleban soon started disarming the Hezb-i-Wahdat beyond their frontline with Rabbani/Masoud in west Kabul. The Hazarahs gave in their small arms but when the Taleban came to replace them at the front line with their own men and asked them to hand in their heavy weapons, they resisted. Fighting broke out between the Hazarahs and the Taleban. Meanwhile their leader, Abdul Ali Mazari wearing a Burqa (all-enveloping woman's veil), sitting between two women in the back of a Russian taxi in a large convoy of cars, arrived in Char Asyab on his way to central Afghanistan. The Taleban commander Mullah Nekmal, when searching the convoy, discovered Mazari and arrested him together with another infamous Hazarah from Jaghori, together with Mazari's son and his son-in-law. Mazari was put on a helicopter for Kandahar but tried to commandeer the chopper in mid-air. In the ensuing shoot-out, Mazari and his bodyguards were killed. Meanwhile, when on Friday 8 March Masoud saw skirmishes between Taleban and Hezb-i-Wahdat, he ordered his planes, helicopters and troops in a large attack on both. In one afternoon the Taleban and the Hazarah Hezb-i-Wahdat were flushed out of Kabul and after nearly four and a half years, Masoud suddenly became the only power left in Kabul. The Hezb-i-

Wahdat and the Taleban, after suffering hundreds of casualties ran for their centres in Central Hazarajat and Maidan Shah respectively while Masoud's men started looting Shi'ah houses and killing anyone who stood in their way.[27]

After seizing Logar province, the Taleban were invited by the people of Paktia to established themselves in their province as well, which they did by flushing out Hekmatyar's and Sayaf's men. From there they attacked Hekmatyar's base at *Spina Shaga* and, after taking it in October 1996 they crossed into the neighbouring provinces of Nangarhar, Laghman and Kunar capturing all three without much fighting.

A Shura dominated by Hezb Khalis's men ruled Nangarhar. In Nangarhar they provoked one tribe against the other and there was much infighting amongst the groups that sat on the Shura. In other words, the people of these three provinces like other Afghan civilians were thoroughly fed up with the strongman tactics of the members of the Nangarhar Shura and especially of its governor, Haji Qadir. So when the Taleban moved to these eastern provinces they were more than welcomed by the local people. The Taleban now surrounded Kabul Province from three directions, with the exception of the north. To get closer to Kabul, they went eastward to Sarobi for a final attack on Hezb Hekmatyar. Hekmatyar, now weakened and no danger to Masoud, joined forces with him, mining the road to Kabul that passed through the tortuous gorge of Mahipar in the hope of stopping the Taleban advance to Kabul. On 25 September, despite the mines, the Taleban overran the Hezb Hekmatyar and Masoud posts.

> Early this morning they captured Sarobi, about 50 miles east of Kabul, sending waves of tanks and militiamen crossed heavily mined fields. Hours later, they took the Kabul suburb of Pul-i-Charkhi before passing on to the capital itself. Hoping to stem the Taliban drive, governments jets screamed in low over Pul-i-Charkhi, dropping bombs on insurgent positions before returning to Bagram military airfield, 20 miles north of Kabul.
>
> (*Washington Post*, 26 September 1996)

The Taleban, in their zeal to chase their enemies, opted to charge straight over the mines, whereupon some 200 of their fighters, according to their account, were lost. Their commander and the conqueror of Jelalabad, Mullah Burjon, was also killed in Sarobi.[28] When Masoud's men saw that the Taleban were willing to sacrifice themselves to gain martyrdom and would not be stopped even by mines, they started retreating towards Kabul, and after packing their bags, they left for their Panjsher valley at the southern foothills of the Hindu Kush. The Taleban, still in hot pursuit, on arriving in the Panjsher valley saw that Masoud had dynamited a mountain to block the Salang Tunnel, the sole entrance to the valley. Within days, Masoud made a comeback from the safety of Panjsher by sending small guerrilla groups to join his armed 'civilian' co-linguists of Shamali, who were asked to stay put. In the fighting that took place, some 300–400 Taleban were killed and Masoud's forces came within thirty kilometres of Kabul. In less than a month Masoud was again forced to flee to Panjsher, where he remained till September 1997. At that date he once again came to his previous position in Shamali, laying siege to it from the north. In 1999 the Taleban for the third time chased Masoud from Shamali, relocating some of the population in Kabul to deprive him of their support, cutting down vineyards and destroying canals so that Masoud's men could not take shelter.

In Kabul one of the first things the Taleban did was to capture the former communist president Najibullah, who had been in shelter in the UN building since April 1992, together with his younger brother, and to execute them, hanging their bodies for two days from lamp posts. In Kabul, the deputy foreign minister, Mr Sher Muhammad Stanekzai, assured journalists that the leadership of the Taleban had had no hand in Najibullah's killing. He said, 'under his leadership our country was destroyed. It was the anger of our people that killed him' (*Guardian*, 2 October 1997).[29] Stanekzai said that lynching was no part of Taleban policy.

After September 1995 the capture of Herat and in September 1996 the capture of Kabul, it became clear to everyone that the Taleban were now a permanent factor. Meanwhile other forces still on the ground such as the Uzbek and Isma'ilia militias, Hezb-i-Wahdat and Masoud groups were shaken by the rapid success of the Taleban, who at this stage seemed almost unstoppable.

The drive to the north

After capturing Herat, the Taleban moved northeast to the province of Badghis. Familiar with Uzbek fighting skills, training and their abundance of arms, the Taleban offered Dostum a share in the government, provided that the Uzbeks allowed themselves to be disarmed. While the militias were slow in giving a clear answer, the Taleban forces proceeded and reached the Uzbek militia's front line in Badghis. Torghundi, the border post with Turkmenistan, fell to the Taleban, but the Uzbek forces did not retaliate.

This stand off was altered in a dramatic way after the middle of May 1997. The forces that lay immediately in front of the Taleban in Faryab province were those of General Abdul Malik, spokesman on foreign affairs within the Uzbek Jumbish Movement. In 1996 Malik's brother, Rasul Pahlawan, who like Dostum had been trained by the Soviets as a militia leader, was machine-gunned by one of his bodyguards for fear of his own life. It was later alleged that the bodyguard was also in the pay of Dostum, who feared Rasul as a possible challenge to his leadership position.

As Malik could not challenge Dostum, he remained silent. In May he contacted the Taleban in Badghis, with the view of joining them so that the whole of the north and especially the city of Mazar-i-Sharif, the only major city not yet in Taleban control, could be captured. By this time the Taleban were already in control of three-quarters of Afghanistan, including the cities of Jelalabad, Kandahar, Herat and the capital Kabul. Malik informed the Taleban of his dislike and disapproval of Dostum as a 'whisky-lover' and of all the non-Islamic and illicit nightclubs and prostitution rackets that were rife in Mazar. These are issues regarding which the Taleban had made a name for themselves in standing against. In order to prove his good intentions he also agreed to hand over Isma'il Khan of Herat who was sent by forces loyal to Iran to join Malik's forces at the frontline and recapture Herat. The handing over of Isma'il Khan and some of his supporters was a great gift for the Taleban.[30] The Taleban then joined Malik's forces by sending some four thousand of their fighters to expel Dostum from the northern provinces of Jozjan, Balkh and Samangan and to disarm his men and take control of Mazar.

The Taleban explained that to stop the fighting in the north, as they had done in other areas under their control, they would disarm people along the way. Malik suggested that it should not be done until they had taken Mazar, after which they could do as they pleased. The Taleban accepted Malik's proposal, reasoning that to disarm people along the way would slow their process and give time to Dostum to organise and counter-attack.[31] So on 19 May 1997 a report emerged of a coalition between Malik and the Taleban and on 20 May both forces with some 10,000 fighters set out to take Mazar. They routed Dostum from his stronghold of Qalizal in Sheberghan (Jozjan province), and triumphantly entered Mazar on 25 May. On 26 May the Taleban started disarming people within the city. A BBC film crew then in Mazar recorded this. While Malik's men knew this would happen, the Hazarah Shi'ah took exception to being disarmed. On the night of 28 May, Malik was locked in a long dialogue with the Hazarah and Uzbek leaders inside the city from where the Taleban had been turned back. The Uzbek General Fawzi, the Hazarah leader Mohaqeq, and members of Iranian Consul General who had been very active after the fall of Herat, all wished to ensure that the Taleban did not succeed in taking northern Afghanistan. Malik was made to change his mind that night, although earlier in the evening when he spoke to Mullah Muhammad Omar on the phone, he was still firm in his backing of the Taleban. On 28 May, fighting started from all directions in the city of Mazar. At first the Taleban were unaware who was fighting whom but they soon realised they were the only objects of the attacks. On that day several hundred Taleban were killed in the surprise attack, their bodies littering the streets for days afterward. After mounting resistance for some eighteen hours, Taleban forces withdrew to the west, trying to retrace their steps back over three provinces to Badghis. Some of them took shelter with local Pashtuns in Balkh City and the Chamtal district,[32] others were captured and held prisoner by the forces of Malik, the Hazarahs and Dostum.

In October, Malik objected to the Hazarahs taking control of Mazar, a traditionally Uzbek city. Headed by Muhaqeq, the Hezb-i-Wahdat breakaway faction in Mazar invited Dostum, who had fled to Turkey to join his family in Ankara, to return. On arrival, Dostum soon established himself again as the leader of Jumbish and fought Malik, forcing the latter to flee in his helicopter to Turkmenistan and then to Iran.

In November, Dostum announced the discovery of the mass graves of Taleban prisoners and local Pashtuns in the desert of Laili in Sheberghan. The UN inspected these mass graves and a report to the General Assembly was presented. It is said that the Hazarah and Malik's men killed not only all Taleban prisoners of war and also all the women and children of those Pashtuns who supported them. The total figure for these killings is estimated at about 10,000 to 14,000, the single most horrific event of all the twenty-plus years of war in Afghanistan. The Taleban knew who were responsible for the killings, but when in power they only mentioned the name of Malik, 'because we still have to deal with these other armed gangs'.

After a month of American aerial bombing of Kundoz and other Taleban frontlines in the north in October 2001, the Taleban delegation, after meeting with Dostum and his Junbish leaders, were promised to be handed over to the UN, gave themselves up to these Uzbek forces. The prisoners were then put in sealed containers for the long journey to Sheberghan Dostum jail and according to the Irish film maker Jamie Durran, some 3,000 Taleban prisoners of war were killed by lack of air and water. Mr Durran's film which was first shown in the European Parliament and then in Britain, Italy, Australia and only by one channel, 'Democracy Now' in May 2003 in the USA, has documented these killings and says that American Special Forces and the CIA agents were present and ordered the trucks to Laili desert for burial before they could be seen by satellites.

Back on 25 May 1997, after their joint force entered Mazar, the Taleban government announced the appointment of Malik as their deputy foreign minister and also on that day Pakistan recognised the Taleban officially as the legitimate government of Afghanistan followed by Saudi Arabia and the United Arab Emirates. These remained the only three countries recognising the Taleban administration till just before the American bombing of the Taleban in 2001. American pressure since the 9/11 WTC and Pentagon attacks was mounting on these countries to withdraw their recognition.

As soon as the joint Taleban and Malik forces from the West reached Mazar, another expeditionary force of 2,000 Taleban fighters crossed the Salang highway, headed for Pul-i-Khumry in central Afghanistan. At Salang, a Masoud commander, Bashir Salangi, announced that he had joined the Taleban.[33] The Taleban expeditionary force leader, Mullah

Amir Khan Muttaqi, told the BBC from Pul-e Khomry that he left 'Salang in the hands of Bashir sahib'.

People in Pul-i-Khumry, Baghlan, Taloqan and even in Faizabad, then the stronghold of Rabbani, hoisted the white flag of the Taleban. Many of those interviewed by the BBC TV team in Mazar were relieved that at last Afghanistan would be united and these wars would come to an end. But after the news of the massacre of Taleban in the streets of Mazar, fighting broke out between the Isma'ilia Shi'ah and the Taleban in Pul-i-Khomry. Bashir Salangi announced on the BBC that his alliance with the Taleban was 'a political compliance', and the flags of support for the Taleban that had gone up three days ago in the cities of central and northern Afghanistan were brought down one by one. The expeditionary force withdrew to Baghlan joining another Bashir, this time the Hezb Hekmatyar Pashtun commander, Bashir Baghlani. This Bashir too, thinking that the Taleban were his prisoners actually 'sold them' to Masoud without the Taleban even knowing it. When the Taleban and the local Pashtuns heard of the deal, the local leaders came to verify the situation for themselves.

At this meeting the Taleban told them, by reciting some Pashto poems, that they had come at the cost of their lives to safeguard their honour. The local Pashtuns, in accordance with Pashtunwali, turned on commander Bashir for misinforming them about Taleban forces. From there 'Taleban bounced back to capture Konduz province, situated on the border with Tajikistan, to set up the stage for further inroads into opposition strongholds in northern Afghanistan' (*The News*, 3 October 1997).[34] Three weeks after their defeat in Mazar, the Taleban laid siege to that city once again. The expeditionary force did this from Konduz, also taking the river port of Hairatan on the border of Uzbekistan. But within a month Iran and associated interested parties bribed the local Pashtun commanders in Balkh, Chamtal and Hezb Hekmatyar into stopping support for the Taleban and to open up their regions to the Hazarah and Uzbek forces.[35] When this was achieved, the Taleban withdrew from Hairatan to their frontline in Konduz, confessing that 'they could only take a place with the co-operation of the local people. They are not in a position to station Taleban soldiers in every village in the country'.

Mazar fell into the hands of the Hazarahs and Dostum's forces. Soon the leader of the Hazarahs, Mohaqeq, quarrelled with Dostum again regarding control of Mazar City. The Iranians invited both of them to Tehran for four days up to 17 May 1998 but 'failed to resolve their differences' (*The Nation*, 17 May 1998). Further to the east the Taleban took the strategic Ishkamish district from Masoud in the third week of May 1998, cutting his supply line to Tajikistan. The Taleban announced they had taken the Burka district south of Ishkamish and then the Nahreen district so that in this way they could join the local pro-Taleban fighters in Baghlan. In this sweep they captured an area the size of about half of Konduz province.

In June 1998 Pashtuns in the Chamtal and Balkh districts, who had known of the massacre of Taleban POWs and their own people the previous year, joined with the Taleban. In a rapid sweep they recaptured Mazar, Balkh and Hairatan, inflicting heavy losses on those who resisted them. These consisted mainly of Hazarah and Uzbek forces, and their allegedly armed supporters from amongst the people of the area.

Meanwhile Masoud's main forces, returning to the Shomali area in July 1997 remained there for nearly two years. Masoud's men, like the Hazarahs and Uzbeks, had made a name for themselves as a force that would engage in banditry, with scant regard for ordinary people.

> One reason the Taliban swept through two-thirds of Afghanistan so quickly is that they did not pillage. Refugees from areas seized by Masoud's forces have confirmed their reputation as robbers and looters. An old man who fled his home in the city of Charikar spat in disgust. 'They did not even leave one needle in our homes. If the Taliban comes again, I will even obey their donkey'.... The prospect of liberation by Ahmed Shah Masoud has not filled the people of Kabul with joy. A significant number would rather remain under the yoke of the Taliban, simply because, as the single strongest force in the country they represent the best chance of peace.
>
> (*Daily Telegraph*, July 31, 1997)

In the two years that they were stationed in the Shomali plains, Masoud's forces fired rockets on Kabul airport and surrounding residential areas. In a large attack on 21 May 1998, witnessed by the Red Cross and other non governmental organisations, dozens of civilians were killed. On 17 June 2000 in a rocket confrontation, both sides lost dozens of fighters. Such attacks and confrontations became an every day affair.

A closer look at the Taleban movement

The Taleban consistently stated that they themselves did not want power, lest they gave the impression that they, like all the previous Mujahideen groups, were there solely for personal interests. The movement emphasised that as long as the next government continued to be Islamic and applied Islamic laws and regulations, they would hand over power to them. Ultimately the end of the war would be the time to test their real intentions. In several rounds of talks with the opposition, the Taleban accepted any change in the government provided that their leader, Mullah Muhammad Omar (the Amir ul-Mu'mineen or 'commander of the faithful') remains as head of state, ensuring the Islamic continuity of the government.

Taleban ruled through two Shuras (Islamic assemblies), one in Kandahar headed by their leader, and one in Kabul led by his number two, Mullah Muhammad Rabbani (no relation to the former 'president').

The Kandahar Shura consisted of his core advisors and the one in Kabul was comprised of religious leaders, cabinet ministers and deputy ministers. Although the majority were Pashtun, other ethnic groups such as Tajik, Uzbek and Hazarahs were also represented in these Shuras and in their government as ministers and governors, but on the whole, at much lower frequency than that of the Pashtun Taleban.

Of the twenty-four Taleban leaders in the government, fourteen had been physically disabled in the war against the Soviets and communists. Mullah Muhammad Omar lost his right eye and thirteen ministers have lost legs, arms and eyes. Ahmed Rashid, referring to the paraplegic conditions of the Taleban leadership writes that 'one does not know whether to laugh or be sorry'. In any case this level of personal sacrifice is a record no previous Mujahideen resistance leadership can match.

The Taleban had made themselves unpopular regarding their stance on the seclusion of women and limits placed on female education, their insistence on men growing long beards, forbidding music, TV, photographs and so on. On the issue of women's rights and education they repeatedly stated that co-education is forbidden in the Quran and that they will provide single-sex schools and universities, like in Saudi Arabia, once the war was over. They said they were prepared to make a start on universal education, provided that the UN or other organisations come forward to establish the infrastructure, which has been severely damaged by Mujahideen infighting. Nine out of ten schools in the country have been totally demolished in the four and half years of fighting amongst the Islamist groups. The Taleban said they would decide the syllabus and would insist that any education system must reflect Afghan and Islamic culture and history and should not be an attempt to copy the Western education model, as has happened in the past.

Taleban representatives in 1997 and 2000 told me that many countries criticise them, but that no one has come forward to help rebuild schools, pay for the training of teachers and to try to bring back Afghan teachers and lecturers from abroad, reflecting their inability to deal with these issues themselves. While this is true and some high-ranking Western officials when confronted with such arguments had promised to help, none have fulfilled their promise. A group of MPs from Holland, the foreign minister of Norway and a number of UN organisations are some such examples that they mentioned to me. However, this is not by any means the whole story. While there remain thousands of girls attending schools, these are all at primary level. After the age of twelve, girls are not encouraged to attend schools and that is why they have closed existing secondary schools in Kabul, Herat, Kandahar and other cities. Their arguments about lack of security, lack of funds, lack of teachers or the corrupting influence of women over their own troops were never satisfactory answers as to why girls could not continue with their studies, especially where there existed teaching facilities. I can only put it down to fiercely traditional Pashtun culture, and thus the Taleban possibly regard educated, empowered women as a challenge to the patrilineal Pashtun society, and a phenomenon completely unfamiliar to their rural upbringing and traditions.

On the other hand, however, the Taleban have made many statements in favour of women's rights and proudly argue that women's rights in Islam are extensive and go back fourteen centuries. This was not the case, they point out, elsewhere either then, or for many centuries afterwards. According to the laws of Islam, women can initiate divorce, cannot be married against their will, can own property and are equal in the sight of Allah. '...And they [women] have rights similar to those [of men] over them in kindness...' (Quran 2: 228). The Quran in numerous verses speaks of the equality of men and women. Here is one such verse,

> For Muslim men and women, for believing men and women, for devout men and women, for true men and women, for men and women who give to charity, for men and women who fast, for men and women who guard their chastity, for men and women who engage in Allah's praise, for them has Allah prepared forgiveness and a great reward.
>
> (Quran 33: 35)

Islam continues to be deeply misunderstood in the West. Often cultural attributes, like the issue of the Taleban and women's education, are confused with traditional Islamic teaching's. 'Within the Western psyche there appears to be an almost paranoid fear of Islam as something wild, mindless and potentially overwhelming. As attitudes towards women have changed within Western society, particularly during the 20th century, there has also been a perception of Islam as a religion that is oppressive towards women' (Marsden 1998: 57).

Following Islamic edicts, the Taleban argued that women's dress should be loose-fitting and thus not show their bodyline. The all-enveloping *burqa* that Afghan women wear has nothing to do with Islam, but is actually an Indian costume that came to urban Afghanistan some four centuries ago. The Taleban opened thirteen girls' schools in Kabul as of January 2000 according to the Swedish Committee (an NGO) which also stated that some 1,500 schools, most of them co-educational at primary level, are open in different parts of the country under Taleban control. It must be mentioned, however, that where education to female students was available, it consisted mainly of religious instruction and ceased beyond the age of around twelve. The Taleban 'will provide higher education to our sisters when the war ends and they can move in honour and dignity and the government can provide transport and educational facilities' (Mullah Muhammad Omar, *The News*, 15 July 2000). I visited the first Taleban girl's *madrassa*, attached to a main mosque in Kabul in September 2000 where girls up to the age of fourteen are attending religious education six days a week from 5–7 am. and from 2–4:30 pm.

Their insistence on the growing of a full beard stems from their belief that all the Prophets grew beards. Prophet Muhammad 'did not trim his beard all his life' and so all Muslim men are urged to grow beards, a natural attribute of masculinity in Islam. Especially in the more traditional rural areas, shaving one's beard off would be considered effeminate and shameful and the Taleban had forcefully imposed this view onto the more modern societies of the urban cities, drawing criticism from Islamic scholars around the world who cite the Quranic verse '*La Ekra Fi Deen,* Let there be no compulsion in matters of religion'. Concerning music, they argue that since the day is punctuated by five daily prayers, music has a seductive effect and can distance people mentally from prayer and repentance. Besides which, musical instruments are, and have always been, shunned in orthodox Islam.

According to an orthodox Islamic viewpoint, photographs and TV create living images without souls. According to them, they are challenging Allah's creation and yet unable to put souls into them. However, on this matter the Taleban told me they were thinking of calling for a meeting of *ulama* to decide whether they should permit TV, filming and photography. They admit that even in the Islamic world there is a huge gulf between what they do and what is ordained by Islam, that an attempt these days to return to pure and undiluted Islamic values sounds primitive and archaic. Privately they admit that reforms and improvements in all these areas could be introduced once the war comes to an end. A *shura* of *ulama* in the country would then be given the job of deciding through *Ijma* or consensus what shape these reforms should take, while not in any way compromising Islam. The Taleban by themselves do not consider it within their authority to take responsibility for deciding for the whole of the Afghan Muslim community. They brought together 1,200 *ulama* from all parts of the country on 20 March 1996 who declared Mullah Omar as *Amir ul-Mu'mineen,* 'the Commander of the Faithful'. Again in November 1998 they gathered a *shura* of 2,000 *ulama* in order to decide what to do in the face of Iranian threats and the stationing of some 200,000 troops on the Afghan border, threatening to invade Afghanistan in revenge for the killing of their consulate officials in Mazar-i-Sharif. That meeting through *Ijma,* advised the Taleban not to be aggressive and agreed that if Iran attacked, a *jihad* should be declared. It would have been this kind of external gathering of Islamic scholars that would have decided on future political, economic and foreign relation issues once the war ended, and not the Taleban leadership themselves.

The Taleban 'have demonstrated enormous single-mindedness in focusing on the military campaign, on the eradication of corruption and on the achievement of law and order' (Marsden 1998: 45). However, despite managing to restore security, they have not been able to bring peace, as Masoud, the last of the warlords, continued to elude the Taleban. An important factor in the success of the Taleban was their commitment to Islam in comparison to previous Mujahideen groups, most of whom abused the name of Islam by turning themselves into warlords, raping, stealing and murdering people, often within their area of control.

In the 95 per cent area under Taleban control, the general public complained of the lack of education, especially secondary schooling and above for girls. They also complained of economic problems and unemployment, but they were not naïve enough to point the finger at the Taleban's abuse of Islamic edicts or accuse them of lavish living and corruption, which was what the Mujahideen leadership were accused of. As for the country's two decades of an increasingly fractured economy and lack of employment opportunities or secondary and tertiary education, the Taleban Minister of Education, Amir Khan Muttaqi told me, 'we can not do much about these till we restore peace to the whole of the country'. Mutaqi claimed that 'once the war is over, the rebuilding of the country through foreign and Afghan investment would start generating jobs and through that we will be able to train teachers, build and open schools and colleges for all'.

The Taleban's stance regarding their Islamic principals and their achievements in contrast to the previous groups are salutary. Women in Pashtun culture are synonymous with 'honour'. After nearly five years of raping, abductions and the proliferation of brothels in the cities, the Taleban were credited by most Afghans as having restored honour to women and putting an end to all anti-Islamic and anti-Afghan practices. In the chaos and anarchy of the Mujahideen years, there was no authority to which one could complain. The Taleban set up courts and, through the application of Shari'ah law, everybody knew that swift justice, brutal as that may have been, was applicable to all, whether well-connected or not.

Some ethnic groups were previously determined to secede from Afghanistan or to have full autonomy. The Taleban had insisted on one strong central authority and, since regional autonomy is regarded as a first step in splitting the country, they rejected that option. The Taleban had defeated most of the warlords and collected millions of arms dispersed throughout the country, an accomplishment that no one has ever achieved. [After their down fall, the Karzai government has devised a $200 million scheme on a voluntary basis to buy arms from the warlords and their militias starting in July 2003. It would be optimistic that those whose power lay in their possession of arms would voluntarily give up this personal instrument of power.] Some neighbours of Afghanistan, who for political reasons wished to see Afghanistan split through the armed groups they were supporting, had been made to realise by the Taleban that, a) they will resist any such attempts and b) they themselves will not remain immune from such a disruption. For example, the Turkmen, Azeris, Baluch and Kurds would ask Iran for their secession. The Pashtuns in Afghanistan would join with those in Pakistan and these forty million would demand their independence and this might lead to the disintegration of

Pakistan itself. The Afghan Uzbeks and Tajiks with their experience of war, instead of strengthening Uzbekistan and Tajikistan, would plunge those countries into chaos and disorder by demanding changes and a larger share for themselves. Due to such considerations even countries that actively wanted to see a disintegrated Afghanistan in the early 1990s have come to the conclusion that a united Afghanistan is in their interests too.

Despite their rapid rise and control of over 90 per cent of the country, the UN did not recognise the legitimacy of the Taleban movement and considered their government as a non-entity. The UN insisted that Afghanistan was one of its earliest members, has stood by UN decisions in the past and that the Taleban should continue to honour that. The UN also said that the Taleban had brought peace to most of Afghanistan but no security, as fighting was still going on in some remote and mountainous valleys to the north-east and also near Kabul itself. According to the UN, they can't therefore, claim to be the government of the whole country. As to Afghanistan's territorial integrity, the UN pointed out that its northern neighbours and Iran do not accept the Taleban rule in north and western Afghanistan, by saying that people in these provinces may not have voluntarily accepted Taleban rule. Another reason that the UN sometimes put forward was that the will of the people of Afghanistan was not tested in an election or referendum, and so it was not clear whether they would have voted for the movement of their own free will.

These were some of the reasons given by the UN accreditation committee, whose responsibility it is to forward the accreditation of a country to the Security Council and the General Assembly. Since one or more of the five countries connected with the power of veto was always included in this nine member committee, they had always been the first to reject the Taleban's request for membership of the UN and thus their recognition. Predictably, the Taleban viewed the UN as part 'of the West's dislike of an Islamic State', and claimed that their partiality towards a 'true' Islamic state was clear.

Conclusion

In the aftermath of the Soviet withdrawal, the fractured nature of Afghan society came to the fore, falling apart into ethno-linguistic and religious segments led by warlords and often fed by weapons and money from outside powers each with their own forces within the country. Reflection on this leads us then to think about the nature of ethnicity in Afghanistan, both recently and in the long term. This will be discussed in the final chapter.

The communist Khalq and Parcham rivalry, which went back to the mid 1960s, is accused of the initial exacerbation of ethnic hatred. That rivalry for power between the two soon took on linguistic, religious and ethnic dimensions. The Russians, during their occupation, turned this rivalry into hatred amongst political and ethnic factions by favouring the Parcham over the Khalq and by setting up the 'Ministry of Nationalities', in which 'unions' of Hazarah, Uzbek and other minorities were established to 'safeguard' their rights against the country's majority. The Soviets, fearing their own minorities in the USSR, had ample experience in persecuting and exiling them to the far corners of that country. In Afghanistan too, they bombed the Pashtuns out of their villages and laid millions of mines to stop them from returning. Meanwhile, they appointed a Hazarah as prime minister for almost the whole duration of their occupation. They trained minorities in the rival military organisations to the army, at first in order to blunt the army's leaning towards the Pashtuns and later to rival Amin's army supporters. These were the Sarandoy police of the ministry of the interior, the KhAD forces in the ministry of national security and the various *qawmi*, tribal or ethnic militias.

The idea of a 'ministry of nationality' was an anathema to Afghans. They see themselves as belonging to different tribes and ethnic groups, but within one unified *milat*, or nation. 'All Afghans vehemently believe in a unitary state structure and this sense of Afghan nationalism, rather then Islamism, has prevented ideals of separatism taking root despite 22 years of war' (*The Nation*, 19 July 2000). The question of language became so acute that even the Pashtun-born and bred President Najibullah would refuse to give interviews in Pashto saying, 'this is a sensitive issue for us'.[36] He even opened his *Loya Jirga*, a Pashtun institution *par excellence*, in 1988, speaking in Dari.

With the fall of the communist government in Kabul, the extremist elements amongst the minorities joined with members of the armed institutions including dozens of well-known Parcham generals and party activists to form the 'Northern Alliance'. However the war did not go according to the Russian's, the disgraced communists' or the ethnic extremists' plans of splitting Afghanistan. Four and a half years of internecine war fought along political, linguistic and sectarian differences greatly exacerbated ethnic issues.

The Taleban's appearance on the scene in 1994 and their spectacular successes in taking over 90 per cent of the country in four years are mainly due to the state of anarchy and lawlessness that had prevailed in the country. People were exhausted of war and the uncertainties of everyday life. The Taleban pledged to restore law and order by removing the warlords 'who soiled the name of *Jihad*' and had inflicted wounds on the people. True to their promise, they defeated warlord after warlord and collected millions of arms, making it an offence for individuals to carry or to own arms. In applying the rules of Shari'ah law, they chopped off thieves' hands, highwaymen's legs and flogged sexual offenders. All this had a positive effect on the lives of ordinary people, in the sense that theft, murder and other crimes were drastically reduced, though at the cost of several restrictions that changed life drastically for many Afghans, especially those in more progressive, urban dwellings.

Afghans inside Afghanistan saw the Taleban's Islamic agenda as a brutal but necessary way out of the ongoing morass. Since Afghanistan is nearly 100 per cent Muslim, it would have been unheard of to reject the Taleban's agenda. They applied the restrictions without any regard to tribe, ethnicity or linguistic affiliation, although it must be said that their edicts were much more amenable to rural Pashtuns than any other group. They still had to defeat the last of the warlords, Ahmad Shah Masoud, who was supported by the West, Russia, India and Iran. It is in none of these countries' interests to see a strong, stable Islamic government in the region that could risk their trade and investment in oil, gas and minerals in Central Asia.

The USA, a former friend of Afghanistan, has incurred the enmity of almost the entire nation by abandoning its promises to help rebuild and ensure peace after the Soviet withdrawal. [Washington is accused of similar negligence once again, after embroiling itself in Iraq.] The Saudi national, Osama bin Laden, whom the CIA helped bring to Afghanistan to use his wealth and influence in fighting the Russians in the 1980s, is now wanted by the USA on charges of terrorism. The Taleban continued to refuse to hand him over. In view of his role against the Soviet occupation, the Pashtunwali's *nanawatai*, shelter or refuge code, the fact that there was no extradition treaty between Afghanistan and the US and, according to the Taleban, the fact that no proof of his involvement in terrorism had ever been handed to the Taleban government all constituted reasons for the Taleban's refusal to comply with the US demand. Hence the US stopped the building of an oil and gas pipeline from Turkmenistan to Pakistan via Afghanistan with lucrative tax and employment implications for Afghanistan; it had imposed its own sanctions and also through the Security Council further aviation and investment sanctions on Afghanistan.

Such measures, apart from increasing ill feeling towards the US in the region and the damage caused to the war-ravaged Afghan people, were unlikely to make the Taleban change their mind. One thing that was certain of the Taleban was that economic and other types of sanctions would have had no positive effect. They were a people well-used to seeing suffering and dealing with hardships. They seemed to be particularly disappointed in the UN Security Council. It failed to condemn US cruise missile attacks on Afghanistan or even on a pharmaceutical factory in Sudan in 1998 and yet is used, they said, by America to further its new policy of global order. The international community, in the eyes of the Taleban, had changed its focus from the problems of Afghanistan, which is the result of the USA and the USSR superpower proxy war, to the problems that they alleged the Taleban were creating for others. The fact is that the problems of Afghanistan deepened when American, Soviet/Russian and neighbouring countries' interests (especially those of

Pakistan and Iran) took over. The Taleban complained that problems of life and death such as millions of landmines, drought, disease and outside support for warlords had just become seminar topics, never seriously dealt with in reality. Afghans must be allowed to plan their own future and make their own mistakes. 'They need a chance to balance their own interests with the world's – and not have the world do it for them' (*Los Angeles Times*, 30 August 2000).

8 Post-communist ethnicity

Introduction

In the previous chapter we discussed the fact that when the common enemy, the Soviet invaders and the Afghan communists had gone, the uncertainty within the fractured Afghan state came to the fore. This chapter is a discussion of the politicisation of such uncertainty, in the post communist period, manifesting itself in terms of ethnicity. Ethnicity in Afghanistan, as in most other parts of the world, has been changing, but instead of congruence and coextensiveness with its territory, culture and ethnic population as in some other nation-states, the opposite has happened. The ethnic activists thought of themselves as 'nations', who were incorporated by Pashtuns in the middle of the eighteenth century within a territorial state. However, they did not want to or did not understand that incorporation, often by conquest, was the rule almost everywhere in the past. 'This was the way, the original ethnic states expanded from a much smaller area and began to incorporate through [further wars and] bureaucratic means the outlying population' (Anthony Smith 1986: 139).

In discussing the politicisation of Afghan ethnicity I want to pose the following questions:

1. What is the reason for ethnic politicisation in the post-Soviet period?
2. What factors are responsible for such intense abhorrence amongst Afghan ethnic groups towards one another and towards Pashtuns?
3. Is this aversion common in all ethnic groups to one another, or is it confined to their politically motivated 'leaders'?
4. Does what has been happening since the 1980s have any precedent in the previous 250 years of Afghan history?

I would argue that post-communist ethnicisation could be traced to three main factors: a) the Khalq and Parcham communists' rivalry for power, exacerbating linguistic, religious and ethnic issues, b) the Soviet invasion and the military and political opportunities it provided for minorities at the expense of the Pashtun majority and, c) financial and international support from neighbouring countries for their co-religionists and ethnic kith and kin through their warlords and militarist forces.

An appreciation of the how and why of post-communist ethnicisation requires, (i) an account of ethnicity in the pre-state era, (ii) information about ethnicity during the period of the Afghan kingdom and (iii) the contrast of the above two with post-communist ethnicity. In other words, a comparative study of the discussion of the above periodicisation into three phases, with exceptional focus on ethnicity in the last twenty years, because of military, economic and political factors.

Ethnicity in the pre-state era

Prior to the formation of the Afghan state, the area now known as Afghanistan formed part of the domain of two empires and in the case of the north, part of the remnants of the Shabanid Uzbeks. The conquering commanders of Tamerlane (1336–1404) settled amongst the Uzbek, Turkmen and Tajik ethnic groups in the north. Tamerlane or *gwad Timoor*, the Limping Timor, as he is known to Afghan history, was a 'Muslim' ruler who massacred Afghans by the thousand in each city, only sparing skilled artisans, whom he took with him to put to work in his capital Samarkand. Such despotism was only comparable to that of Genghis Khan in the thirteenth century.

Western Afghanistan was for some 130 years under the Safavids; eastern Afghanistan was in the hands of the Moghuls. We see no movement for independence or autonomy against the Central Asian rulers or the Safavids. The ethnic groups in these areas, sharing common language and culture with the ruling dynasties, regarded themselves as an extension of those states, while the Pashtuns in the east and south-west since the sixteenth century never accepted the Moghuls and later also rose against Safavid rule. Thus the Pashtun harassment of the Moghuls, according to some historians, led to the Moghul dynasty's weakening and its eventual replacement by the British East India Company. Meanwhile, the Pashtuns uprising in Kandahar against the Safavids lead to the physical overthrow of the Persian colonial power and the declaration of Kandahar Independence in 1709. The Pashtuns subsequently in 1747 formed the Afghan state and became the dominant ruling group.

Ethnicity in the Afghan kingdom

Historically, despite Moghul and Safavid domination, the Pashtuns emphasised their cultural and ethnic distinction and valued their autonomy. There were examples of Pashtun principalities on the sub-continent and in the Suri and Lodi dynasties that governed India as the *Delhi Sultanate*, as well as their own autonomous kingdoms in Ghore, central Afghanistan.[1] Pashtuns also had centuries of trading experience in the region and served in the armies of the Persian, Uzbek and Indians, thus learning the art of statehood and the importance of being their own masters. This phase starts from the time of the founding of Afghanistan by the Pashtun Darrani tribal confederacy in 1747 ending in 1978. During these 231 years, Pashtun ethnic distinction led to the creation, unification and preservation of the Afghan state. Pashtun nationalism demonstrates that political boundaries (with some changes) have been generally coterminous with their cultural boundaries.

All governments from the beginning of the nineteenth century to the reign of the 'Iron Amir' (1880–1901) and the Musaheban brothers (1929–78), used Pashtun ethnic political organisation and distinctiveness to fight foreign invaders, be they the imperial British, Tsarist Russians or Soviets. Pashtuns were sent in the 1880s, often against their will and sometimes by force, to northern Afghanistan to put an end to the endemic raids by the Turkmen tribes from across the border. This policy's concomitant approach was the safeguarding of the country's vulnerable borders from the southward drive of Tsarist Russia and also the weakening of Pashtun power in their tribal land of the south-west and later south-east, thus reducing any threat to central government.

In the nineteenth and most of the twentieth century, Pashtun nationalism and ethnic distinction advanced unchecked. Other groups in central and western Afghanistan, speaking dialects of Dari, or the Altaic Turks in the north, having lost their former patron rulers, adjusted to Pashtun rule by adapting some of their customs. 'Pashtun culture has exerted powerful influence on all of them giving them in one degree or another the characteristics one can call "Afghan"' (Barth 1987: 190). Pashtuns have centuries of trading and business background, in Central Asia, the Iranian plateau and, most important, in the Indian sub-continent. Having discovered the empty lands and under-populated regions in northern Afghanistan, they used their initiatives and entrepreneurial experience to settle, irrigate the unclaimed land and use its pastures for their flocks (N. Tapper 1991: 28; R. Tapper 1984: 235–6).[2]

Thus, during the Afghan kingdom, we see Pashtuns as the major ethnic group who have gone to war time and again in order to maintain and preserve Afghanistan's independence. Other major groups are Turkic and Tajik/Farsiwan (Persian speakers). Smaller groups such as Arabs, Pasha'i, Gojars, Jats, Mongols, Karakulpak, within the areas of these three culturally predominant groups, primarily adapted to the dominant culture of one or more of these group(s). The Pashtuns as an ethnic group, in the two and a half centuries of their supremacy have rarely gone to war against another ethnic group. There have of course been local differences over grazing with Hazarahs or trading with others. But such regional difference has never drawn in the whole of the Pashtuns. Even under the much-despised Taleban, atrocities were mainly confined to the ethnic armed activists. Taleban told me they could not even punish those responsible for massacring their own Taleban when they were their prisoners of war, lest it inflames the situation and prolongs the war. Nor have Pashtuns as an ethnic group rallied around the Taleban to fight other groups. In fact the Taleban are nowhere on record saying they 'represent the Pashtuns'. That is why, apart from their own madrassa graduates not even a handful of educated Pashtun have gone to join the Taleban government. Similarly, no other group as a whole, despite their ethnic activists' advocacy, has risen against the Pashtuns or any other group. In short there is no history of ethnic wars in Afghanistan. What has happened since the Soviet invasion is unique and has no historic parallel.

Pashtuns in northern Afghanistan have done their utmost to coexist with other ethnic groups. Some 7 per cent in their attempt to integrate have even forgotten their language, Pashto, adopting the Dari and Uzbeki of the local population. Uzbek, Turkmen and other smaller groups have made similar sacrifices at the expanse of their mother tongues learning Dari and some Pashto.

All Afghan rulers, despite their Pashtun ancestry, had adopted the Dari/Farsi language as the *lingua franca*, employed Dari speakers in the government and entrusted non-Pashtuns, whom they considered no challenge to themselves, with major diplomatic, military and administrative posts. In contrast the two Pashtun provinces, Paktia and Paktika, with 100 per cent Pashtun population are amongst the most under-developed provinces in the country. It is even more ironic that the Musaheban dynasty, brought to power by the people of Paktia at the end of the 1929 civil war, has not done much for these Pashtuns. No one from amongst them was appointed in the forty-three-year rule of King Nader Shah and his son Zaher Shah as minister, ambassador or even deputy to any ministry. Government investments in roads, education and health infrastructure was minimal in these provinces. The only noticeable concession was to agree to the demand of the *Loya Jirga* of 1929 by not enlisting them for conscription. Conscription brought men from remote villages and provinces to the capital and other urban centres, and was seen as one of the best 'education' available in rural illiterate Afghan society. Some educated Pashtuns from these provinces later came to resent being deprived from this only process of modernisation that was freely available to all other groups.

Post-communist ethnicity

This last phase of ethnic development starts with the communist coup of April 1978. The short period of communist rule (April 1978–December 1979) and the ten years of Soviet occupation and the subsequent years, have been seized upon by Afghanistan's neighbours, to ensure their influence in the future political set-up in the country. For this purpose, at huge financial and political cost to themselves, they armed and trained groups with whom they could identify.[3] The process of ethnic awareness, started by the neighbouring countries, Pakistan, Iran and since 1991 Uzbekistan, Tajikistan and Russia, aimed at putting a government of their choice in Kabul. With such newly found foreign support and the practical military training and psychological boost provided by the Soviets during their invasion, related ethnic groups embarked on a process of exaggerating their cultural identity and exclusiveness, expressing resentment towards the Pashtuns and one another.

The communists, whose campaigns and recruitment were on linguistic and ethnic lines, were the first to arouse ethnic emotions. The Russians nurtured this passion during their ten years of occupation, in providing practical opportunities for minorities, as I have shown elsewhere. The neighbouring countries provided financial, international and moral support based on ethnic and religious grounds. The local ethnic activists, in order to realise the dream of cessation, embarked on ethnic atrocities.

Briefly, over the past three centuries, the broad processes of ethnicity in Afghanistan has gone through three stages: 1) preserving ethnic identity as in the case of Pashtuns; 2) adapting to the culture of the dominant Pashtun, Turkik and Tajik groups and; 3) exaggerating and emphasising ethnic distinction, as has been the case since communist takeover in the late 1970s.

The ethnic divide

In order to highlight the unprecedented ethnic awareness of the last two decades, I want to pose and tackle the following questions outlined in the introduction. The reasons for the unprecedented ethnic awareness; the hatred of these groups towards one another; whether this aversion is common to all or confined to ethnic activists and whether there is any resemblance to ethnicisation in the two and a half centuries of Afghan statehood.

The reason for the rise of ethnic awareness in the post-Soviet period is the key question to my enquiry. There are several aspects to ethnicity in Afghanistan: origin, language, culture, creed and locality. Of these language and locality were the first ethnic factors exploited by communists in the late 1960s. This is the reason why the Khalq followers were rural Pashtuns and the Parcham mainly urban non-Pashtuns. This ethnic division became more prominent when the two factions broke from the PDPA in 1977, which had been created in 1965. By the time they came to power in 1978, their linguistic, rural/urban and ideological differences had already created such a gulf that the two could not run the government together. Thus after three months in power, the Parcham leaders were exiled to embassies abroad (Chapter 4) only to come back 'on Soviet tanks' in January 1979. From that date on, the Parcham faction not only imprisoned, killed and forced its political rivals out of the country; it also embarked on a campaign of denigrating anything Pashtun. Pashto language coverage in newspapers and magazines was reduced and then stopped. Pashto's over 50 per cent share of the media was reduced to a nominal 10 per cent of news, announcements and the occasional article. What is more, Pashtuns who came to apply for the compulsory *Tazkerah*, identity card, were registered as 'Tajik'. Sultan Ali Keshtmand, the communist Hazarah Prime Minister during almost the whole period of Soviet occupation, is on record as saying he was committed to turn Pashtuns from a majority into a minority.[4] When some protested that they were not 'Tajik', the ministry of the interior would only correct their ethnic origin on the *Tazkerah*, making no such changes to the main population census books. It was because of such ethnically hostile policies that more Pashtuns than any other group were forced out of their homes and villages, turning them into internally displaced and external refugees. The trickle of initial displacement intensified during the Soviet occupation and remained steady in the years following Soviet withdrawal. The refugees to the two neighbouring countries numbered an estimated three million in Pakistan and two million in Iran, with a similar number becoming internally displaced. The Pashtun refugees in Pakistan, who had travelled for weeks over hazardous mountain passes, did not just come from the provinces bordering these countries, but also from the northern and north-eastern provinces of Mazar, Kunduz, Takhar, Badakhshan and the central province of Baghlan and Ghore.

When the communists fell from power in 1992, their ethnically inspired activists joined their own ethnic Mujahideen and militia groups. Thus some Khalqis ended up with the *Hezb-i-Islami* of Hekmatyar and the Parchamis with the Jami'at Islami of Rabbani and *Shura-i-Nezar* of Masoud. The Hazarah and Uzbek army and party members joined their own warlords in *Hezb-i-Wahdat* and Junbish Shamal. This set the scene for the most vicious and barbaric ethnic conflict Afghanistan has ever experienced. If the communists slaughtered one another's activists, these Mujahideen and militias massacred anyone that belonged to another ethnic or political group. An American journalist who has written two books on Afghan resistance activists, after an extended tour of Afghanistan and Pakistan in 1997 reveals some of the horrors:

> Before we left Kabul, several interviews were conducted to learn of the terror that existed in Kabul under the administration of Rabbani and Massoud. We learned of people being forced to eat the flesh of the dead, of being forced to eat their own excrement, of the Hazarah beheading their victims with red-hot swords and axes to make the dead bodies convulse for their entertainment, while they gleefully referred to their victims as 'the dancing dead' [*raqs-e-marg*]. We examined excavations where women were kept for sexual pleasure, many were disfigured permanently, few were given any food or water and most were murdered by their captors. We were told of prisoners

having nails driven into their heads with hammers and of prisoners who were placed into cargo containers then lowered on to raging fires and burned to death. This horror was directed by the leadership of [Hazarah] *Hezb-i-Wahdat,* Junbish [Uzbeks] and Jamiat. [Hazarah] Combatants were told: 'If you kill one Sunni, you will go to Heaven, if you kill two Sunni, you will reach a higher place in Heaven, if you kill three Sunni and urinate in his mouth, you will receive a special house in Heaven'. I have not seen any Western media accounts of this barbarity by the anti-Taliban forces?.

(Bruce Richardson, 1997, *Afghanistan Mirror,* December issue)

Not only this, they raped women in front of their husbands, they abducted boys and girls for sexual pleasure, took by force other people's wives and looted private and public property with impunity.

Some similar Human Rights violations have been recorded by Amnesty International, Asia Watch and the United Nation Human Right reports between the fall of the communist government in April 1992 and the coming to power of the Taleban in Kabul in September 1996. Taleban were truly influenced by their Quranic education. They also strongly objected to infighting amongst the above ethno-political groups. They tried to steer clear of any action tying them to Pashtuns or any other ethnic group. Pashtun being the majority and the traditional ruling group do not fear other groups. They know that through democratic, Islamic or even Pashtunwali, their rights as a majority group cannot be denied. But it is not how other groups feel about the Pashtuns or about one another. Hence as the majority of Taleban rank and file members were from amongst the Pashtuns, they were accused of being the same as other militia and resistance groups. Thus the Taleban were accused of killing the Hazarahs and Uzbeks in the fight for taking Mazar in 1997. Western media and the United Nations also echoed such accusations. But according to the BBC's Kabul reporter, '500–1,000' were killed by local Pashtuns and Farsiwan. When in 1997 the Taleban army of POWs was massacred by the pro-Iranian *Hezb-i-Wahdat* and Uzbek General Malik militias, the local Shi'ah and Uzbeks then turned on the Pashtuns of Mazar, Balkh, Chamtal and other localities killing thousands and burning their houses for their support of the Taleban. Similarly, other people's property and businesses were seized on by these groups in Mazar. So when the Taleban conquered the stronghold of Uzbeks and Hazarahs a year later, it was these local people who joined the Taleban for this second attack killing Shi'ah Hazarah and followers of the main Uzbek warlord, General Dostum, motivated to take revenge for the wrong they suffered at the hands of Shi'ah and Uzbek militias.

The International Red Cross, who had access to all prisoners held by the Taleban, are on record saying that the POWs were treated humanely and were exchanged whenever possible, for their own prisoners. Taleban stated-policy was to avoid revenge killing and other ethnic mistakes of the warlords and in this way they tried to win the hearts and minds of ordinary Afghans. This policy at least superficially seemed to be working for them.

Despite there being a small Shi'ah population and almost a negligible number of the Wahhabist in Afghanistan, regional countries have exploited religious issues. Thus rivalry on religious grounds is another aspect of the politicisation of Afghan ethnicity. This is an area where Iran and Saudi Arabia and their supporters in the region have been at loggerheads for a long time. The Saudis who 'matched America dollar-for-dollar' during the 1980s are said to have helped the Taleban initially.[5] Olivier Roy sees Saudi Arabia and Iran as major ideological players on the Afghan scene.

> The failure of the Afghan Islamist Mujahideen to establish a stable regime after their capture of Kabul in April 1992 led to the return of a more traditional but exacerbated Islamic fundamentalism, that of Taleban ... This shift from Islamism to what I call neo-fundamentalism is pervasive amongst the Muslim World. In this sense the Saudi [Wahhabi] model is now prevailing over the Iranian [Shi'ah] one.
> (Roy 1998: 207–8)

Professor Ahadi notes that Iran fearing its ideological rivals, Saudi Arabia and Pakistan, may fill the gap left by Soviet withdrawal and American lack of interest, 'encouraged the Iran-based Shiite organisation to demand 25 per cent representation'. A demand rejected by 'the Sunni leadership [as] the Shiite had played an insignificant role in the war against the Soviet ... not least because Shiite constitutes' 9 per cent of Afghanistan's population (Ahadi 1988: 121). After the coming to power of Rabbani/Masoud 'both Saudi Arabia and Pakistan realised that Iran had played a major role in the formation and success of the Northern Alliance whose dominance in the Rabbani administration had tremendously increased Iranian influence in Afghanistan' (ibid., p. 123). Thus instead of confronting Iran itself, the Pakistanis and the Saudis developed the strategy of fighting Iran's supporters, Jam'iat, *Shura-i-Nezar*, *Hezb-i-Wahdat*, through their own Islamist supporters, headed by Hekmatyar, Sayyaf and Khales. After the coming to power of the Taleban, Iran's support for Afghan Shi'ah increased dramatically. Meanwhile the Taleban defeated Hekmatyar and Sayyaf. Hekmatyar had gone to exile in Iran and Sayyaf joined Masoud. Khales and his supporters accepted the Taleban, most of them joining the Taleban religious army. *Hezb-i-Wahdat*'s stronghold in Hazarajat and Mazar too fell to the Taleban in 1998. Iran then switched its support to the newly formed *United Northern Front* of Masoud and the remnants of Shi'ah groups.

Another major reason for the intensification of ethnic hatred in the post-communist era is the change of the political map in the region. With the breakdown of the Soviet Union, three countries have emerged on the northern border of Afghanistan, namely Tajikistan, Uzbekistan and Turkmenistan. Each has its own ethnic minority in Afghanistan. Iran to the west, being at loggerheads with the Pashtuns for centuries, has primarily supported the Shi'ahs. But after the fall of the communist government in 1992, it extended support to all non-Pashtun groups. Thus, all these minorities in an anti-Pashtun coalition (1992–94) at first made their wishes known for secession and when that was not going to be achieved they settled for federation. But federation is seen as a first step towards disintegration, thus all Pashtun parties have rejected that option too. Pashtun opposition was inadvertently strengthened by Mr Masoud, who between 1994 and 1996 repeatedly massacred Hazarahs, attacked the forces of communist Uzbek and Isma'ilia militia in Kabul, Baghlan and Kundoz provinces and contrary to international convention, he put their POWs to work, to build roads, caves for hiding arms and houses in his native Panjsher. Thus the ethnic minority coalition put together by Iran and Parcham party civilian and military activists broke down. Former enemies such as Hekmatyar joined forces in a new coalition with the Hazarahs and with this the demand for federation also declined.

An important reason for these and many other such coalitions falling apart is that none of these groups had the full support of the majority of their ethnic people. This is the reason why their 'strongholds' fell so rapidly to the Taleban. Further, *hoowiat-e-Afghani*, Afghan identity, being several centuries old, have more than sentimental value for them. They know that by joining these other countries, while their leaders might for the time be appointed to some high posts, they would end up at the bottom of those societies. Their high rates of illiteracy and unfamiliarity with modern industrial ways of life, that are taken for granted by most of the people of the former Soviet Union, would work unfavourably against them. This, apart from the general contempt they could face in their new environments. The Hazarahs, for example, though maintained with arms, money and international support by Iran are called '*Barbary*', barbarian, savages, by the Iranian public to this day. Uzbeks and Tajiks north of the Amu River reserve similar abuse for their Afghan kin.

The revitalisation of ethnic roots, as a result of foreign support is a typical ethnic phenomenon of the post-communist era. A shrewd anthropologist of the Cold War period some three decades ago commented.

> The exploitation of ethnicity in the informal articulation of political interests has been observed almost everywhere in the world ... Every political group ... mobilizes its resources in order to find solutions to a number of organizational problems: the problem of distinctiveness, of political communication, of decision making, of authority, of ideology and of discipline.
>
> (A. Cohen, 1969: 5)

In Afghanistan too, the sprinkling of foreign-trained ethnic leaders, who have formed parties and military/alliances, were later trained by the thousands by Soviet invading forces. When the Red Army withdrew in 1989, it left its entire ten year stockpile of arms not just for its surrogate communist government, but for its former militias. Thus the small Shi'ah Isma'ilia group of Kayan was awarded with the entire stockpile at Kailagai, a staging post in Central Afghanistan for arms shipments to all 155,000 Soviet forces during the ten years of war. Their leader, Jafer Naderi, in a BBC television interview was delighted with the gift, 'we were nothing before. So the coming of the Russians has been to our advantage'.[6] Dostum's militia inherited larger stocks at the Mazar airbase and other parts of the five northern provinces. The Tajik communist General Momin inherited the Port of Hiratan that had a large supply of arms, trucks and jeeps.

Russia, Iran, Uzbekistan, Tajikistan and Pakistan have kept up the flow of arms, in the post-Soviet occupation period to their client groups. In the process the communist militia leaders of yesterday (Uzbek and Isma'ilia) Hazarah and Tajik warlords, in exploiting their ethnic roots, exaggerated the Pashtun threat. On the other hand leaders who were either Pashtuns or had Pashtuns as the majority of their followers and party members (Appendix 12 A and B), headed six out of seven political parties based in Pakistan. None of these solely represented Pashtuns or worked for the Pashtun cause. On the contrary, the seventh and the only non-Pashtun party, *Jam'iat Islami* headed by a Tajik, Burhanuddin Rabbani from Badakhshan, and run by Ahmad Shah Masoud has campaigned on a 'single ethnic issue', solely for Tajik political power.[7] Its military campaign in its once stronghold of Kunduz, Takhar and Badakhshan, was amongst other things aimed at forcing local Pashtuns to flee.[8] They had turned into a slogan the Pashtun proverb, *ka zhrandah de plar dah, pu war dah,* 'if the mill belongs to one's father, turn should be observed'. Or taking the Pashtuns reference of regarding themselves as the *meshar woror,* the eldest brother, because of their historic position and number, by saying that the eldest brother is dead. Implying it is now the turn of the younger i.e. the Tajik to rule.[9] Through the use of such symbolic language, *Jam'iat* and its military extension the *Shura-i-Nezar* have been trying to change realities on the ground. Their verbosity continued by regarding themselves as *Tajik mafawq-e hama* Tajiks above all.

Tajiks are the victims of their own socio-historic position. They are a minority and, although significant as administrators and bureaucrats, nonetheless resentful of the Pashtun socio-political position. While the majority of the Tajik have accepted the Pashtun demographic and historic role, their present warlords have been trying to overlook and underestimate those ground realities. The Tajik have no modern historical figures like the Pashtuns with national and historic achievements to their credit. So in order to whip up support they have been turning the 'brigand' Bachai Saqaw the water carrier's son, into a hero, or elevating some of the present warlords to such a status. The Bachai Saqaw nine months of terror, in 1929, was ended by the Pashtuns. Supporters of Rabbani's Jam'iat Islami and more importantly the commanders of *Shura-i-Nezar* of Masoud had been downplaying the 1929 Pashtun stand and portraying Bachai Saqaw into a hero.

'Tajiks' are immigrants from Central Asia to the northeast provinces of Afghanistan. Masoud's forefathers, according to the Afghan exile press, come from *par-e-Darya* across the river (Amu) and that is probably why he has popularised the 'Tajik' identity and wished to divide Afghanistan to realise his 'greater Tajikistan' dream. The majority of Farsi or Dari-speakers who have been in Afghanistan for a long time call themselves after the area where they live like Kabuli, Herati, Ghaznichi and so on.

Two powerful supporters of the Tajik Jam'iat/*Shura-i-Nezar* are Iran and Russia. The political and economic interest of these two countries happens to coincide with 'Tajik nationalism'. Their support for the anti-Pashtun forces is therefore, one of the major causes of the exacerbation of ethnic conflict in the post-Soviet era. In October 1997 an Iranian twenty-two coach 'food aid' train was stopped by the Kazakh authorities. They found seventeen coaches full of arms, destined for anti-Taleban Masoud forces. The Russian Foreign Minister, Igor Ivanov, told a news conference in Moscow, 'Russia was supplying arms to Ahmad Shah Masoud and will continue to do so' (Interfax, 31 May 2000). After the Taleban captured Taloqan, Masoud centre in Takhar in August 2000, the Russian President Putin, Foreign Minister Ivanov and Defence Minister Igor Sergeyev, openly declared their support for Masoud. Sergeyev even met with Masoud in Tashkent on 26 October 2000 assuring him of support and continued opposition to the Taleban. Masoud joining with a country that invaded Afghanistan, killed an estimated 1.5 million Afghans, planted between ten and thirty million mines and destroyed 24,000 villages, is an act that will not be easily forgotten or forgiven by the majority of Afghans.

The Pakistani press in March 2000 ran a series of articles on how Iran in the winter (1999–2000) shared the expenses of providing arms to the anti-Taleban forces with Turkey, Uzbekistan, India and Russia supplying trainloads through Tajikistan to the Masoud/Rabbani forces. The Russians, who used to print money for the Kabul communist government, have continued printing the same currency for the anti-Taleban warlords in tonnes and 'through super-inflation, caused hardship for the people of incalculable proportion' (Richardson 1997: 11). Thus the inflation rate increased by over 6,000 per cent.

Russia and Iran's support for the former Rabbani/Masoud 'government' has wider implications:

1 The Russian policy has been to keep the war going so that a traditionalist, nationalist or an *ulema* group, like the Taleban could be stopped from coming to power and thus averting the 'Muslim Fundamentalist' threat to Central Asia.

2 The Russians wish to avoid or delay the day of being taken to the World Court, as the inheritor of the former Soviet Union, to pay reparation for the damage that could be assessed for ten years of occupation and its consequences.[10] Damage to life, and the country's infrastructure, their planting of millions of mines that injure and kill about seven to ten people every week and could be exploding, according to United Nation De-mining Agency, well into the twenty-first century.
3 Russia had 25,000 troops in Tajikistan, most of them were stationed on the border with Afghanistan. The Russian leaders, in order to keep their former Central Asian republics dependent on them, used the Taleban as a threat to the stability of these governments. Tajikistan as a poor former Soviet Republic, saw these troops as a stabilising factor, especially after the five years (1992–97) of Islamist-led revolt against the communist-led government.
4 Another important economic factor for both Russia and Iran was the averting of the proposed Central Asian oil and gas pipeline of neutral Turkmenistan, through Afghanistan to Pakistan, India and beyond, which would be a major blow to both countries' oil and gas industries.[11]
5 The Jam'iat leader, Rabbani, presumably out of gratitude for Russian arms and international support, is on record as assuring the Russians that he does not hold them responsible for the 'Soviet invasion'.[12]
6 Russian and Iranian policy had not changed in the post-Soviet invasion period. Both countries did not want a nationalist group such as the Taleban to come to power. For Russia the Taleban belong to the majority Pashtun, who in Pakistan and Afghanistan combined, number about forty million. The Russian aim, when in occupation in Afghanistan and later through its proxy communist government and militia, was to undermine the Pashtun cultural and historic position by carefully planned and orchestrated anti-Pashtun propaganda, through print and broadcast media. They did this in the first place by furthering and prioritising the rights of the minorities, by establishing 'unions' and 'societies' for them by writing an alphabet for languages, spoken by small groups of peoples, giving them airtime on radio and television. The Soviet aim in all this was to control Afghanistan. To do this they had first to control the Pashtuns. As the majority of political parties and fighters were Pashtuns the Russians decided on controlling the Pashtuns by force and intimidation. Thus bombing the Pashtun villages, forcing them to flee and infesting their areas with mines. Although its troops were forced to quit Afghanistan in February 1989, Russian plans of aiding Shi'ah, Isma'ilia, Uzbek and Tajik minorities against the Pashtuns have continued. Meanwhile they feared the Taleban's Islamic system and its capacity to spread their brand of Islamic 'fundamentalism' to Central Asia with its economic and strategic implications.

Iran, for the historic reason of always being at war with the Pashtuns, has actively been campaigning for the disintegration of Afghanistan. To this end Iran initially trained Afghan Shi'ah. Later they extended military and financial aid to other minorities such as Tajik, Uzbeks and Isma'ilia so that these groups can have a larger part in any future government than their percentage within the population deserved.

7 The Jam'iat/*Shura-i-Nezar* group was also helped by India, technically by keeping their helicopters and war planes in good repair. India also had mobile clinics in Masoud's area and had a military hospital for his wounded in the Kolab province of Tajikistan (www.sabawoon.com-Articles, 2001). Since the Taleban were pro-Pakistan, India had to support a group that would in the last analysis be opposed to Pakistan. India also feared that Taleban success might have encouraged Kashmir secessionists.

8 Tajikistan from across the border had given the Kulab airbase to Masoud's group. Their planes and supplies used to be shifted from Kulab to provinces under their control.[13] Tajikistan had also agreed to build 5,000 homes for the families of the commanders of Jam'iat/*Shura-i-Nezar* at Kulab, thus taking these commanders literally hostage, expecting them to fight to the end (Afghan On Line Press (AOP) June 1999). Two to three thousand refugees from Tajikistan, who were trained by this group also fought for them against the Taleban between 1994 and their repatriation at the end of 1997.

9 From all eyewitness and some written accounts, the military strong man of Jam'iat and the leader of *Shura-i-Nezar*, Ahmad Shah Masoud, has always been assisted in his decisions by French and British intelligence. The connection of these forces with Masoud goes back to the Soviet invasion. Two books published by key Soviet generals (Gromov – Commander of the Soviet 40th Army and Liakhovski, deputy Soviet advisor to Dr Najibullah) show how Masoud since 1982 has worked with the Soviets and has not fired a single shot in anger on Russian or Kabul forces.[14] Then the CIA picked others, some of whom were placed in Mujahideen interim governments and, channelled their aid through them to Mujahideen groups inside the country. So the British picked Masoud as the 'Tito of Afghanistan' (note 16) and passed him on to the French.

The Hazarah *Hezb-i-Wahdat* was formed and supported by the Iranian government, soon after the Soviet troops' withdrawal from the eight small Tehran-based Shi'ah groups. Russia, Uzbekistan and also Iran support the Junbish Shamal, Northern movement, which includes Uzbek, Isma'ilia, Tajik and Hazarah. The Taleban movement on the other hand at first relied on the Saudi and Pakistani support. Since 1998, Saudi Arabia downgraded its diplomatic relations on account of the Taleban refusal to hand over Saudi dissident, Osama bin Laden. That left Pakistan as their only supporter. The Pakistan military ruler General Musharaf, told newsmen that Pashtun are a major ethnic group [13 per cent] of Pakistan's 140 million population. It is in the interests of Pakistan 'to have good relations with Taleban who represent the Pashtuns majority' (*The News*, 29 May 2000).

The Taleban, unlike the Uzbeks and Hazarah Shi'ah or Jam'iat/*Shura-i-Nezar*, are not controlled by Pakistan or any other foreign power. Ahmed Rashid, a Pakistani journalist normally critically of his country's support for the Taleban writes: 'The Taleban have never been anyone's puppets and their strings are certainly not pulled in Islamabad' (Rashid 1998: 72). Rashid points to the various administrative, political and military factions within Pakistan and how the Taleban have taken advantage of such rifts. Unlike any other Mujahideen parties in the past, they knew Pakistan better and did not want to limit themselves either to the government, army, the military intelligence or specific private sectors. Both the Taleban and the Pakistanis gained from such contacts. Pakistani traders supplied oil, foodstuff, medicine and other goods. The Taleban taxed these items, earning them some revenue, they also taxed opium poppies that entered Pakistan. The Taleban also provided works for Pakistani engineers working on roads, bridges, micro telephone systems and electricity plants.

Dividing Afghanistan on ethnic lines

The Uzbeks and the Isma'ilia militia at the service of the Soviets continued to serve in the same capacity as the communist government in Kabul and, when that fell, they joined the anti-Pashtun Northern Alliance. Jam'iat militarist, Ahmad Shah Masoud, is on record as wanting to split Afghanistan and join his share with Tajikistan, creating 'Greater Tajikistan'.[15] In order to build Masoud as a legend, he has been presented by French and British intelligence as the 'Robin Hood of Salang Highway' or 'a Second Tito'.[16] These forces have since made Masoud famous in their media as the 'lion of Panjsher', the 'great strategist', a 'commander who defeated the Russians'. General Boris Gromov of the Soviet 40th Army, responding to Masoud's 'invincible' reputation poses this question.

> If there was such a very effective Afghan personality who was opposed to the revolutionary Kabul regime and the presence of Soviet forces, what would have prevented us from totally destroying him and his band ... It would be naïve to imagine that the powerful Fortieth Army could not have eliminated Ahmad Shah's band ... Masoud knew well what he could and what he could not do.
>
> (1997: 272–3)

General Liakhovski, deputy to the top Soviet advisor to Dr Najibullah, in a first encounter with Masoud's Panjsher base group made this observation:

> In our first operation against Masoud's band in 1980 lasting four days, we inflicted on him heavy losses of men and equipment. Masoud was not well known then and had no more than 1,000 local followers. That operation convinced him of entering into a secret agreement with the Limited Soviet Contingents.
>
> (2000: 453ff)

True to Liakhovski's prediction, soon after the Soviet invasion Masoud switched to the Soviet side. General Gromov writes:

> By 1982 we reached our objectives: we established firm links with Ahmad Shah, that lasted till the Soviet troops withdrawal [February 1989]. An agreement was reached between the Fortieth Army and the person of Masoud in 1982, according to which his bands would never attack Soviet convoys in Southern Salang that was solely under his control ... instead of fighting us and the government forces he ordered his men to fight [Hekmatyar's] Hezb-e Islami bands in the area.
>
> (1997: 266–7)

That is why Gromov says Masoud remained loyal to his commitment with us till our last soldier left Afghanistan. Bruce Richardson, an American journalist who interviewed many Soviet generals and soldiers writes:

> The constant reference to Massoud as a hero as in the following quote 'his bravery and astute defiance of the mighty Red Army' is false. The true image of Massoud can be found in the following books: 'You Have to Know Massoud', and [Masoud national hero or national traitor] by Brig. General Rahmatullah Safi; 'The Hand of Moscow', by Leonid Shebarshin, Director, First Dept. KGB; 'Limited Contingent', by General Boris Gromov Commanding General, Soviet Fortieth Army, and the second edition of my book: 'Afghanistan Ending the Reign of Soviet Terror' which cites 46 sources corroborating Massoud's treachery and collaboration. The sources include eyewitnesses, former KGB officials, Soviet generals and lower ranking soldiers, Chief of the Ukrainian Secret Service (FSB successor to the KGB) documents, books and articles from Afghan, Soviet, Finnish, British, American and Ukrainian writers ... Massoud ... using his military muscle, often in joint operations with the Soviet military to attack other resistance groups that were attempting to destroy Soviet targets.
>
> (6 August 1999, www.sabawoon.com)

The leader of *Hezb-i-Islami* Hekmatyar in his book *Hidden Conspiracies and Known Faces* (2000: 156–60) presents the above and many more sources of Masoud's collaboration with Soviet invaders and Afghan communists.

The Shi'ah Hazarah and the Uzbeks were two other noticeable ethnic military forces which demanded federation. 'The proposed federation or zoning of Afghanistan would be a step towards dissolving Afghanistan', became the slogan of most exile publications. The only common factor between the Pashtun Mujahideen of yesterday and the Taleban of today is their dogged opposition to secessionist movements.

In the struggle for power between the Taleban and the Northern Alliance, the Taleban, in May 1997 joined in their first and only alliance with an opposing faction of Uzbeks, headed by General Abdul Malik. The Taleban aim was to drive General Dostum out so that the remaining one-quarter of Afghanistan could also be united under them. In three days the joint forces of Malik and the Taleban conquered the whole of the north, reaching the city of Mazar. But Malik either bribed or threatened by the Iranian Consul in Mazar, Hazarahs and/or Jam'iat/*Shura-i-Nezar*, changed sides. As a result over 10,000 local Pashtuns and Taleban prisoners of war were massacred. The news of the massacre only reached the world when Dostum, who had taken refuge in Turkey, was called back by the Hazarahs who were growing impatient with Malik. Dostum, in order to clear his name announced that the killings were done by his rival and publicised the mass graves and wells full of bodies. Such carnage of one ethnic group by political activists of others has no precedence in Afghanistan. The UN has examined these mass graves and apart from writing a brief report and a watered-downed condemnation, has done nothing about it. Mr Malik the original perpetrator of this heinous crime paid an 'official visit' to the USA in 1998 and has since taken up residence in Iran.

Ethnicity revitalised

The ethnic stance of the warlords is also supported by most of their intellectuals in the West. The Hazarah newsletter *Wahdat* or Unity published from London supported *Hezb-i-Wahdat* till its fall in 1998. The weekly *Omaid* or Hope published in the USA employs several hardened secessionists and is financed allegedly by Masoud and Iranian authorities. There are numerous other such publications in France, Germany, Canada, India and Australia that tow the Masoud/Rabbani ethnic line. Amongst academics one other such advocate is Nazif Shahrani, an Afghan anthropologist in the USA. It can be said that Shahrani in his writing tends to take a one-sided approach when it comes to discussing the Afghan ethnic mosaic reserving his galling comments for the Pashtuns. For example, writing about the ancient Pashtun institution of *Loya Jirga* and the twentieth-century parliamentary process, he calls them a 'clever ploy' of 'Pashtun dominance'.

> The entire scheme of creating and using administrative unites as a basis for 'electing' representatives for the rubber-stamped parliaments (*majlis-e shura wa sana*) and for the equally meaningless so-called *Loya*

Jirga (Grand National Assembly) was another clever ploy used by the centralising state to assure Pashtun dominance of the political process of the nation.

(Shahrani 1998: 229)

The short history of parliamentary process can be traced to the country's first constitution in 1921. The Pashtun *Jirga* or its grander form *Loya Jirga*'s history can be traced back to the Aryan period (as noted in Chapter 2). While neither of these national institutions is a replica of Western democracy, they reflect Afghan traditional leadership, however flawed and limited that may seem from a Western perspective. Afghanistan has three types of traditional leaders: leaders of tribes and ethnic groups, the religious *ulema* leaders and the *rohanyon* spiritual leaders such as Sufi, Pirs and Hazrats (Misdaq 1990: 109–12).[17] These three categories of traditional leaders do represent and are chosen/elected by their district and sub-district constituencies. The fact that Pashtuns are 62.72 per cent of the country's population, meant naturally that more of them proportionally than any other ethnic group, were represented in *Parloman* parliament and on *Loya Jirgas*.

The *Loya Jirga* is the institution *par excellence* of the Pashtun, also recognised by other groups. As explained in Chapter 1 and elsewhere, *Loya Jirgas* are called upon in nearly all national emergencies to decide, sanction, adopt or reject proposals presented to them by central powers. The 1964 constitution turned the *Loya Jirga* into a functioning part of the country's two chamber *Parlomon: Wolesi Jirga* (Lower House) and *Meshrano Jirga* (Upper House).[18] To call *Loya Jirga*, 'a clever ploy' or a 'meaningless ... rubber-stamp' body is effectively to write off a unique and most respected Afghan institution, of which all Afghans – Pashtun and non-Pashtun, are proud. After the US invasion it was only two *Loya Jirgas* that were able to give legitimacy to the Karzai government they put together. Since the Soviet invasion, the majority of Afghans, have been in agreement that only by holding a truly representative *Loya Jirga* could a government representing the will of the people, rather than rule of the warlords, be formed. But warring factions within the country and their patrons in neighbouring countries, seeing the end of their influence through such a public platform, have refused to give in to such a demand.[19] The Islamist, Jam'iat Islami, for whose Peshawar-based press the Shahranis used to write during the Soviet occupation, had an ongoing campaign against the *Loya Jirga* as an 'archaic Pashtun Institution' that 'contradicts Islam', is a 'remnant of past feudal epoch' or even 'a fascist Pashtun tradition'. Jam'iat continued to oppose the *Loya Jirga* while in power (1992–96), but was demanding its convening because power was snatched from them by the Taleban.[20]

Jam'iat's aim ever since losing Kabul has been similar to that of Dr Najibullah's government of 1991, who after the fall of the Soviet Union also demanded the convening of, and their participation in, a *Loya Jirga*.

Both saw a chance of their rehabilitation and of regaining power through this backdoor. The Taleban for precisely this reason were against the *Loya Jirga* because they feared such a gathering would bring to power all those discredited warlords and their activists that they defeated on the battlefield and that they would not be able to live with one another and so the lawlessness of 1992–96 would be resumed. However, Jam'iat Islami and their *Shura-i-Nezar* have been actively campaigning since 1998, for the holding of a *Loya Jirga*. The Americans, Russians, British, French and Iranians have been helping with the cost and publicity in the hope of averting Taleban's 'danger' to the region and to protect Western investment in Central Asian energy sources.

It was hoped that through a *Loya Jirga* the king, who is a respected Afghan, would replace the Taleban.[21] [This is exactly what happened. After the fall of the Taleban the UN under pressure from the USA held a meeting in Bonn, Germany (2002) recommending the holding of a *Loya Jirga* both to approve the provisional government (June 2002) and to choose the leader of the transitional government. This leader by all accounts was supposed to be the former king, who was brought from Italy and guarded by the Italian police in Kabul, but was, just on the eve of the *Loya Jirga*, asked by President Bush's representative Dr Zalmai Khalilzad to stand down in favour of Mr Karzai. The *Loya Jirga* was also asked to ratify the new constitution in October 2003. The Jam'iat and *Shura-i-Nezar* who are at the forefront of this government were instrumental in this process].

What factors are responsible for such deeply felt dislike amongst the ethnic groups for one another? Although the communist period led to the politicisation of ethnicity, it did not create or invent ethnic differences. The smouldering of such dislike was present long before the present intensification and deep-felt hatred amongst the ethnic activists. In the eighteenth and nineteenth centuries, while the Pashtuns fought for the creation of Afghanistan and subsequently against foreign invaders, non-Pashtuns were expected to pay a poll tax as their contribution towards the expenses of such wars. Despite the dearth of ethnographic or historic evidence, one can guess that this could not have been to the liking of some ethnic groups. It was also perhaps short sighted, by doubting another ethnic group's commitment and ability to fight for Afghanistan. The Uzbeks, whose contingent came with Ahmad Shah Durrani to found modern Afghanistan, are a group in point. These Uzbeks, because of their own imperial past, had the experience and the stamina to have been included in Afghan/Pashtun fighting forces. Also troops could have been recruited from other groups to join the national *lashker* army in a time of emergencies. All these could have been reason for some ethnic groups' grudge against the Pashtuns, but it has never been seen in the form, shape and ferocity as has happened in the post-communist era. I have not seen any documentary evidence of Pashtun policy to deliberately not recruit them to the army and subsequent wars of conquests or defence.

One of the main reasons for ethnic awareness is first and foremost the deliberate attitude of the Soviets, in recruiting militias mostly from non-Pashtun groups. The Russians, through their closeness to the Parcham faction of the PDPA and their reading of history, knew that the Pashtun were unlikely to accept being merged into the Soviet Union's 15th republic. They therefore recruited from amongst those they could manipulate, both to establish themselves as a hegemonic force in Afghanistan and to fight against the Pashtuns. The Russian's dislike of strong groups, such as the Chechens, Volga Cossacks and other Turkik nations and their dispersal to the far-flung corners of their empire at a cost of some '14 to 20 million dead', is well-documented under Joseph Stalin and his chief of intelligence, Lavrenti Beria (*The Times*, 30 May 2000). They were equally familiar with small groups, whom they picked and made important by placing them in army, intelligence and civil jobs. Such previously neglected minorities in the Soviet Union gave the regime their total support. So it was not unusual for the Russians to repeat their well-tested Soviet experience in Afghanistan too. One of the reasons why it did not work in Afghanistan was the interest and interference of the West and of the Muslim world. These external forces aided resistance groups even amongst some of the minorities like the Tajik, Aimaq, Pash'i and Nuristani, who tried to blunt the Russians' ethnically devised cutting edge. However, the Russians did partially succeed in buying some commanders amongst the forces opposed to them and it was these men, as well as their loyal militia, who would be held responsible for the lengthening of the Soviet occupation and subsequent civil war.

With the dismantling of the Soviet state (1991), the USA and the West, having achieved their strategic goal, lost interest in Afghanistan. The Saudis, on the other hand, who were financially one of the major backers of the Afghan Mujahideen even after the Soviet departure, continued to support the resistance. The Saudis' aim in the post-Soviet withdrawal period was to safeguard their investment by favouring groups that were close to their Wahhabist school of Islam and opposed to Shi'ah Iran.

Pakistan, another important 'frontline state' during the occupation, is also close to the Saudis and opposed the increase in Iranian influence in Afghanistan. Pakistan consistently worked with groups it founded with the view of exerting influence over future central governments in Kabul. The backings of the newly independent countries for their 'kith and kin' on Afghanistan's northern border were other factors responsible for the exacerbation of ethnic tension.

So the vacuum the two superpowers, the United States and Soviet Union, left behind was filled by neighbouring and regional countries: Iran, Pakistan, Tajikistan, Uzbekistan, Turkmenistan, Saudi Arabia, India, Russia and Turkey. Every one of these countries, with the exception of neutral Turkmenistan, have been responsible for instigating groups close to it on religious, ethnic and/or political grounds. This has been the major reason for the continuation of the war. With arms, financial and international backing for their favoured groups, the ethnic flames were fanned, not just of the non-Pashtun against Pashtun, but of Tajik leaders against Hazarahs and Uzbeks and vice versa; of Pashtun leaders against *Shura-i-Nezar*, the *Hezb-i-Wahdat* and the Uzbek *Gilamjam* carpet stealers militia[22] and of the latter leaders against the Pashtuns and so on. Such intense political and military backing of various ethnic groups and interference in the internal affairs of Afghanistan by neighbouring and regional powers has no parallel in Afghan history.

Harmony and provocation

Is the feeling of hatred and distrust common to the majority amongst the ethnic groups or is it confined to the politically motivated armed leaders and activists? The majority amongst all Afghan ethnic groups, having lived in relative peace and security over the past centuries, is for the return of such peaceful times. Since the elimination of the Uzbek Khanets in northern Afghanistan in the mid-nineteenth century and the short-lived upheaval and civil war in 1929, the majority of Afghan ethnic groups have hardly been touched by major events such as the two world wars, the coming to power of the communists in Russia and in China or the partition of the subcontinent. The Taleban, having established their rule since 1998 in the former strongholds of Uzbek, Hazarah, Tajik and others, have shown no revenge or *en masse* killing of the opponents, despite these ethnic activists' barbarity in massacring one another, local Pashtuns in the north and the Taleban POWs. One reason why the public tolerated the Taleban for so long was because of their stand against ethnic cleansing. Local people who had seen the ethnic activists' hatred and bloodshed were content with the Taleban. Some Uzbeks in the cities of the north and Hazarah in Bamyan could not believe that such a 'God-fearing' and disciplined section of Afghan people had existed. On the other hand there is no deep-felt resentment amongst members of various ethnic groups against one another. Members of these ethnic groups who committed atrocities were in the employment of their warlords. At a time when state apparatus, trading and other normal businesses had completely collapsed the only employment and security that was on offer was to join an armed group. Most people therefore entered fighting not out of choice but out of necessity. But this was not the case with ethnic activists or their groups. The leaders of these groups received large sums of arms, cash and other assistance from abroad that envenomed the already deteriorated situation. They behaved in ways contrary to Afghan culture and detrimental to the sovereignty and independence of Afghanistan. Once these leaders identified with the interest of neighbouring powers then, for their own survival, they had to convince their ethnic followers of the legitimacy of their stance, whether autonomy or secession. From a national viewpoint, a strong central government would find such men traitors and collaborators, punishing them accordingly, while within their own ethnic groups they could claim hero status and the best guarantee of their lives and livelihood.

The Bolsheviks' invasion of Muslim lands in Central Asia in the early 1920s and China going communist in 1949 led to a million Tajiks, Uzbeks, Turkmen, Kirgiz, Qaraqelpak and others escaping to Afghanistan. Most of these were given land by King Amanullah in the 1920s and the Musaheban rulers in the 1930s in the north and north-east, next to their kith and kin across the international borders. Some came to Kabul and other cities to start businesses in hairdressing, patisserie or as chefs in restaurants. These Central Asian refugees in the decades up to the 1970s became very successful as traders, herders and carpet weavers.

A small number of these 'Basmachi' or 'thieves', as the Russian called them, continued their resistance against the Bolsheviks under their leader Ibrahim Beg from northern Afghanistan. The Red Army more than once crossed into Afghanistan in hot pursuit, making the new Afghan King, Nader Khan (1929–33) nervous, as the country was still recovering from the effects of the nine months' civil war in 1929. The king, having failed to convince the refugees of the seriousness of their actions for Afghanistan, sent his young brother, Shah Mahmud Khan, who chased Ibrahim Beg and his followers over the border into the Red Army's hands. This was a token resistance offered by the newly arrived refugees and did not affect either the rest of the refugees or other Afghan ethnic groups in the area. When Afghanistan went communist in 1978, and especially after the Soviet invasion, some of these latter day refugees became the invaders' militia within the Uzbek 'Junbish Shamal' northern movement, while others once again became refugees, first going to Pakistan and from there to the West and Turkey. Of these Kyrgyz and Kazakhs, who have been living in the Pamir since the early 1920s, went to Turkey as refugees under a special Turkish government plan in 1984. But after the collapse of the Soviet Union (1991), they returned not to the Pamir in Afghanistan but to their newly independent states of Kyrgyzstan and Kazakhstan.

It is important to draw a distinction between the armed political activists and the great majority of people in different ethnic groups who have long lived in close proximity to one another, inter-marrying, praying in the same mosques and burying their dead in the same cemeteries and learning one another's languages. Fortunately therefore, it would be virtually impossible to carry out a major ethnic cleansing policy, which would devastate and adversely affect long-established cross-ethnic relations. That is why the wider public is against the ethnically-spurred wars and wanton destruction practised by the political activists. Thus, elders and ethnic leaders from amongst the Tajiks, Hazarahs and Uzbeks have taken to refugee camps in neighbouring countries rather than associate themselves with what has been done in their name.[23] Hence in the period following the overthrow of the communists and the anarchy of the Mujahideen group's civil war (1992–96), although most of the north fell to the hands of these gunmen, large numbers of Uzbek and Turkmen refugees continued to remain in Quetta, Pakistan. When I visited these refugees on two occasions in 1994 and 1996, they told me they did not want to be killed for crimes committed by others in their name. They said they would only go when a central government, like that which existed before, was established in Kabul.

The armed political activists on the other hand, having been trained by outside interests and having pledged loyalty to them, have been acting in ways that are at variance with the wishes of the majority of their own people. That is why, without general popular support, they were wiped out one by one by the Taleban. This is the reason for the strong Uzbek militia, the Hazarah *Hezb-i-Wahdat* and the Tajik warlords in Herat, Kunduz, Kandahar and other parts of central and northern Afghanistan, who fell to the Taleban since 1994. Further, it was these local ethnic people who were guarding their areas, as part of the Taleban control of Afghanistan. The Taleban themselves did not have enough manpower or resources to man every village. Out of tens of Mujahideen resistance groups and a dozen political parties, only one major warlord, Ahmad Shah Masoud, remained, in less than 5 per cent of north-eastern Afghanistan. The Jam'iat Party of Masoud's boss, Rabbani, only remain in name as most of its commanders had abandoned it, left Afghanistan or joined *Shura-i-Nezar* or the Taleban.

Is there any parallel between what has happened since the 1980s to any period since the founding of modern Afghanistan?

Uncertainty, turmoil, a weak centre, physical and environmental factors are the main features of Afghan history. The major episodes of uncertainty and commotion in the period under study are the Declaration of Independence (1709 and 1747) and the last two decades of the Sadozai rule from the turn of the eighteenth century until power was transferred to the Barakzai dynasty in 1826.

The Declaration of Independence of Kandahar in 1709 and the founding of the state in 1747, were almost entirely issues between the two major Pashtun confederacies of Ghilzai and Durrani. As the struggle in these eras was about the national issues of fighting the Safavids, declaring the independence of the state or of choosing the kings, once these were resolved, all those involved, went back to their regions and villages to resume their ways of life. In other words there was no question of Afghan sovereignty and integrity being at stake afterwards from any internal forces. The struggle was about the changing of the guards, from the Safavids to the Ghilzai and Durrani and from the Sadozai to the Barakzai dynasty, of the same Durrani confederacy.

The next major period of commotion because of modernisation was the creation of the nation-state under Amir Abdur Rahman, the 'Iron Amir' (1880–1901) and his grandson Amir Amanullah (1919–29). The 'Iron Amir' and Amanullah, in their attempt to unite the fragmented and loosely held state under one central power, drove to introduce Western-style government and industry, and were met with opposition from most ethnic conservative groups. It took the 'Iron Amir', sixteen out of twenty-one years of his reign to achieve his aim of establishing a 'modern state' with a strong army and administrative centre. For this he fought Pashtun and non-Pashtun ethnic groups alike without exception until he achieved his aim (See Table 2.1).

The Pashtun Ghilzai, the Hazarah Shi'ah and the Nuristani *Kafir* or unbelievers, all of whom strongly resisted the 'Iron Amir' were not aiming to secede and join another country or even declare their own autonomy or independence. They wanted to avoid paying taxes or from being encroached on by government in other ways. The last two (Hazarah and Nuristani) in addition to maintaining their religious beliefs, wanted like all other rebellious groups to protect their local autonomy, by keeping their distance from what they saw as central government interference in their internal tribal and ethnic affairs.

In the case of Amanullah, nearly all ethnic groups opposed his cultural reforms. The main reason for this opposition was Amanullah's idealism. He failed to think through the implications of what the general public considered as 'un-Islamic' and 'un-Afghan' reforms. He was warned even by his 'blood-brother', Mustafa Kemal of Turkey during his legendary tour of seven months in 1927–28, to Europe, Turkey and Russia, not to undertake major social reforms without first training a strong national army. Kemal promised to help him by sending his best officers to Afghanistan. But Amanullah wanted Afghanistan to become a modern state based on the Western model, and although he agreed with Attaturk's advice, was not prepared to 'waste time' until such an army was in place.

The reason for resistance to Amanullah and his eventual overthrow was not to secede from Afghanistan, but to change the ruler, as so many times in the nineteenth century, thus wanting to return to the *status quo*. This is what happened. An illiterate Farsiwan from Shamali, thirty miles north of Kabul, replaced Amanullah. He did not declare a Tajik or any other state or express any wish to secede from Afghanistan. He thought he could run the country more in line with the aspirations and inspirations of the Afghan people.

The Hazarahs, after their subjugation to the central government in the 1880s, once again under Prime Minister Shah Mahmud (1946–53), threatened rebellion by asking for autonomy and sent a delegation to Kabul. The prime minister agreed to their wish, but told them that they were free to do what they wanted in their own Hazarajat, provided they would have nothing to do with anyone or any place outside their region. As Hazarahs are entirely dependent on trade especially with Kabul, they soon found out that their easily-won autonomy was not viable in practice. Soon they sent another delegation, 'denigrating the first one as unrepresentative and out of touch with the wishes of ordinary Hazarahs, declaring their loyalty to the central government and wanting to be treated like the people of the rest of the county'.[24] However, one thing that the Hazarahs learnt from this short-lived isolation was that they should not confine themselves just to mountainous Hazarajat, not being able even to provide for their own population. That is why they soon settled in Kabul, Ghazni, Balkh, Mazar and other towns, where their communities have grown since the late 1940s.

Iran then had no Shi'ah or Persian cultural aggrandisement plans as it does now after Khomeini's revolution, intervening in the Lebanese civil war through the Hizbullah, fighting the Sunni in Pakistan through the Ja'fary movement and the Pashtun in Afghanistan through *Hezb-i-Wahdat*. As the Farsi language spoken in Persia is a language of the region and an earlier Creole language, created from Pahlavi, Sughdi, Avesta and other regional languages, its different versions are spoken to this day in the countries of this part of the world. But Iran with its imperial past regards Farsi/Persian as its language[25] to have been exported to Afghanistan's parts of *Falat-e-Iran*, the Iranian Plateau, Central Asia and the subcontinent. Since the end of the Gulf War (1979–88) Iran has been spending millions on films, media and printed books to spread Iranian influence to non-Shi'ah *Dari* speakers in Afghanistan, *Farsi* speakers in Uzbekistan especially in the cities of Bokhara and Samarkand, and to *Tajiki* speakers in Tajikistan. Thus Iran through its religious link with the 9 per cent Hazarah and through its linguistic heritage with the 35 per cent who speak or have adopted Farsi as a *lingua franca* is exerting its national interest over Afghan sovereignty and supremacy in Afghanistan.

Briefly, after the communist coup of 1978, the ten years of Soviet invasion and the five years of post-communist Mujahideen infighting, attempts were made to re-write history. Regional and neighbouring countries seized upon the gap created by the collapse of the Soviet Union and the lack of interest of the USA. In their competition with one another, these countries have exacerbated the ethnic issue, an issue that never gave serious rise or concern to previous Afghan governments. Ethnicity also played no major role during the period of Soviet occupation amongst the resistance groups, tribes and ethnic communities. All Afghans criss-crossed one another's territory, shifting arms and spending nights in one another's villages without any fear or threat.

Conclusion

'Ethnicity ... in social anthropology refers to aspects of relationships between groups which consider themselves, and are regarded by others, as being culturally distinctive' (Erikson 1993: 4). Ethnicity includes groups from the level of clans and tribes to the more varied, socially heterogeneous, cultural and linguistic communities. Afghan ethnic groups distinguish themselves from one another on linguistic, cultural and sectarian grounds. Their boundaries are both cultural and territorial, depending whether they are 'tribal' or non-tribal. Even in these two categories hard-and-fast rules can not be drawn. The boundaries, of tribal Pashtuns and Turkmen, for example, are both territorial and cultural, while the boundaries of the Tajik are only cultural. These boundaries, despite biological, territorial and cultural perpetuity (Barth 1969a: 10), have been changing over the past two and a half centuries from emphasising ethnic distinction, to assimilation and then again to ethnic revitalisation and exclusiveness.

One line of research on Afghan ethnicity has tried 'to establish the "real" identity of ethnic groups by mapping their territorial distribution, tracing their origins and movements in time, and listing their "fundamental characteristics"' (R. Tapper 1988: 23). Soviet ethnographers, and later compilations, supplied such maps (Bruke 1955; Kislyakov and Pershits 1957). This 'mosaic' research model is criticised by Anderson, who disagrees with such focus on 'ethnogenesis' because such an 'approach tends to take diversity itself for granted, explaining it in reference to something else, rather than asking what sort of social "fact" it is'. An 'ethnic group' map cannot depict 'reality on the ground'. Swiss husband and wife team Pierre and Micheline Centivres-Demont, in their research in northern Afghanistan, come to the conclusion that 'groups commonly called "ethnic" and depicted in "ethnographic maps" are not comparable, since they share no common defining criterion – in one case it may be language, in another religion, or political or historical identity; maps simplify reality' (ibid.).

Most nineteenth and twentieth century rulers wanted to de-emphasise ethnicity. 'Afghanistan like other countries, has experienced the general trend of the present century, particularly as encouraged by the government policies, marked by a shift away from linguistic, descent, tribal and general ascribed identities, towards more achieved identities based on territorial, economic and political categories' (R. Tapper 1988: 30). But in the post-communist era, because of foreign interference, ascribed statuses have once again replaced achieved statuses. Political activists have revived old ethnic and cultural links in order to further their own agenda. Subsequently most urban, educated men and women who thought of themselves as 'Afghan' have discovered that they are 'Tajik', 'Pashtun' or one of many other ethnic configurations. Even those who have forgotten their descent or belong to the minor groups of Jat, Jugi and Mesali have been forced to align themselves with a group that would benefit them most. Such has been the force of an ethnically instituted civil war.

Ethnic nationalists have been campaigning for a 'broad based government', wanting leaders loyal to them to be included in such an administration. Nearly all governments in the past have been broad based. Non-Pashtun minorities manned the Afghan government's civil and military bureaucracy and it was they who for a long time were responsible for national policy issues (Ruben 1991: 73–100). But it is unlikely that the ethnic nationalists can ever work peacefully with one another. So the Taleban for the time when they were in power (September 1996–October 2001) seemed the only viable alternative on the Afghan political scene. Unlike in the former Yugoslavia or Rwanda, the Taleban did not kill a single Uzbek or Hazarah in revenge for the murder of over 10,000 Taleban POWs and local Pashtuns in Mazar. That is why despite the unprecedented ethnic politicisation there still is hope for Afghanistan. The period of Karzai government since November 2001 with no major wars amongst the former enemies, is a time for all to reflect and the two *Loya Jirgas* a platform for venting of pent-up feelings have served to some extent as a healing process. With the US and the West heavily involved in Afghanistan, only time will tell how they succeed in breaking the tradition of Afghan xenophobia by making their presence acceptable.

Conclusion

Introduction

My interest in writing this book was to understand why after the toppling of the monarchy in 1973, events have taken a turn completely different from that of any period in modern Afghan history. I soon realised that a full appreciation of the events of the past three decades needed a thorough examination of Afghan history, at least since the founding of the present state in the middle of the eighteenth century. Thus the first quarter of the book provides the background for such an investigation. My research led me to issues connected with tribe, state, Islam and the related topics of modernity, ethnicity and the various forms of evolving uncertainties and their underlying causes. From a long-term viewpoint, the uncertainties and associated problems, originate first from the physical nature of the country and second from its geopolitical location. The position of Afghanistan on the 'crossroads' between east and west has led to it becoming home to many different ethnic groups, intolerant of outsiders and fiercely conservative. So the *longue durée* or long-term patterns are the physical environment, the diversity of ethnic groups and the resistance to central control. These patterns have produced a people whose lifestyle has been at odds with modern central authority be it *dawlat* (state), *Milet* (nation) or *Mil-e dawlat* (nation-state), thus making the weakness of the state, another of the long-term factors. The *longue durée* of Afghanistan could therefore be summarised in terms of continuity and discontinuity. But the problem regarding constancy, which Afghanistan faced in the eighteenth and nineteenth centuries, is different from that of the last quarter of the twentieth century. However, all these uncertainties to a great extent go back to the original primordial factors: terrain and ecology.

Continuity and discontinuity

Terrain

The terrain has had structural implications for the people of the region and also for foreign invading armies. Large battlefield formations of imperial forces have proven ineffective. Firepower alone has not brought them long-term successes. None of these outside forces have been able to adapt to a terrain which the Afghans regard as their greatest asset in times of war.

The negative aspect of the terrain for the people themselves has been the setting of limits on communication, whether transport or contact between groups. Thus transportation over high mountain passes on mules, donkeys and camels limited what could be traded in the nearby markets. For most people within any valley and mountain-settlement such contact was on the periphery of their daily life. That is why it has taken a long time, even at the turn of the twenty-first century, for an awareness of others' needs to be registered or the necessity of a central authority above the plurality of the country to be accepted. The fact that such awareness has not been fully developed is the major underlying reason for the continuation of uncertainties. This is sometimes described as the characteristics of nomads and tribal societies and/or is conceived as an aspect of underdeveloped societies. In other words people are not bound together by a moral discourse of state or nation at this stage. However, there is plenty of myth and recorded history that they have acted together at crucial stages of their development, as if they were bound, not as they are in a vertical relation of individual to his tribe/group and their homeland, but horizontally as a relation between developed states and their citizens.

The ecological conditions, part of the physical terrain, determine what animals of burden (donkey, mule, buffalo and camel) can be locally reared and what animals (sheep, goats and cattle) can be had as sources of food. Ecological conditions are also responsible for crops and agriculture, thus the exchange of surplus produce for what cannot be grown locally. This barter-trade arrangement is an old trading pattern used in limited amounts, in some of the villages in central, south and northeast Afghanistan even today.

Tribe as a cornerstone of governance

Physical environment and ecological factors are in-built situations which determine the nature of the people and their approach and reaction to central authority. The earliest groupings of such people in Afghanistan are *qawm* the tribe, which though not under one leader, are unified through kinship and common descent. *Qawm*, therefore, is the most common form of social organisation. With the exception of the Tajik, most other ethnic groups (Hazarah, Baluch, Pash'i, Aimaq) see themselves as *qawmunah* (plural of *qawm*). The largest of such a tribal group is the Pashtun who form 62.73 per cent of the country's population, and one of the smallest, the Turkman 2.69 per cent. However defined, modern Afghanistan's governance problem has been one of struggle and dilemma of tribe and state developing to one of tribe and nation in the eighteenth and nineteenth centuries, and eventually to one of tribe/ethnic groups and the nation-state, since the 1880s.

As we have seen, the Pashtun tribes by serving in the imperial armies of the Persians, Turkmen and Moghuls were familiar with states and centrally organised forms of government. It was because of this long practical experience of contact with strong armies that they themselves were first able to establish their own principalities and kingdoms in the subcontinent and later in the eighteenth century their own governments. Thus the Ghilzai tribal confederacy, whose members have served in many western and eastern imperial forces, established themselves as masters of Kandahar in 1709 and within a decade brought down the two-century-old Persian Safavid dynasty, extending their rule over the whole of present-day Iran. Again within a period of eleven years it was yet another western Pashtun confederacy, the Durranis, who through a tribal *jirga* established the modern state or *dawlat* of Afghanistan in 1747.

In the eighteenth and most of the nineteenth century the problem of Afghanistan was one of struggle between tribe and state. Since tribes founded the state, its governmental machinery was expected to be an extension of the tribal way of life. Though this could not be an exact replica, all governments at least for the first one hundred years tried to pacify the tribes by making them feel as an integral part of the state. That is why from 1709 to the turn of the nineteenth century, tribes were officially represented in government decision-making machinery as in the tribal *jirgas* and councils of Mir Wais, his son Mahmud and his paternal nephew Ashraf, Ahmad Shah Durrani and his son Timur Shah. The long established rival claimants to the throne used the tribal grip over the government to their own advantage. This was one of the main reasons for the uncertainties of the government in the centre and the tribe on the periphery. Winners and losers in competition for power both influenced and used tribes as their backers. The state and its central authority, therefore, were seen as being a relationship across the tribes.

The two expansionist imperial powers, British India and Tsarist Russia, taking advantage of this ongoing turmoil chipped at the borders of the country from the east and from the north (see Map 5). They laid their own conditions on the governments of the time, thus leading to restricting Afghan freedom, which in turn led to repeated wars and the distrust of forces outside the tribal world. Thus from the period between the turn of the nineteenth century till 1826 despite half a dozen rulers following closely on the heels of one another in Kabul, most provincial centres remained in the hands of other tribal claimants to the throne. This uncertainty, mainly amongst the ruling Pashtun tribes, led to the first period of civil war (1818–26). As disputes over legitimate claims at the centre made Kabul weak, the provincial centres in control of men connected to different disputants at the centre, were not strong enough, either to pose much harm to the centre or to withstand foreign invading forces.

The emergence of the modern Afghan nation-state

These uncertainties regarding state and tribe were dramatically redressed by Amir Abdur Rahman (1880–1901), who like no other ruler before him succeeded in establishing a discourse between state and all the ethnic groups in the country. This horizontal relation of the state and its citizens established by the Amir as an 'icon of resoluteness' (Edwards 1996: 2) is seen as the founding of the 'nation-state' in Afghanistan. The futile rivalries between the grandsons of Ahmad Shah led to civil war and the transfer of rule from Sadozai's (Popalzay sub-tribe) to the Barakzai (Mohammadzai sub-tribe) of the Durrani. The feeble restoration of order under Dost Mohammad's second rule (1842–63) accompanied by the inter-Barakzai rivalries that followed, further divided the country and left its people up in arms. The 'Iron Amir' not only succeeded in eliminating inter-Barakzai and dynastic rivalries, he also swept aside all claimants to the throne and those ethnic warlords who had become used to ruling their regions independent of Kabul. However, despite establishing the nation-state and the subduing of the royal rivals and other ambitions men, the Amir was not able to curb Tsarist Russia which took thousands of square miles of Afghan land in the north (Punjdeh, Wakhan and Zulfiqar) by force. Neither was he able to obtain British Imperial India's support, which used Afghanistan as a buffer between India and Russia, to regain these lost territories. Thus despite firm central control and a disciplined army, the newly established nation-state because of its comparative military weakness was no challenge to the dominant rival empires. Meanwhile, British India by concluding the treaty of Gandomak (1873) obtained control of Afghanistan's foreign policy and demarcating their sphere of influence, they drew the 1893 Durand Line, separating and often dividing the Pashtun tribes from one other, which had already made Afghanistan similar to a dependent state.

The horizontal relations of people and nation-state replacing traditional vertical relation, of coexistence between tribe and state, was further developed by defining the borders of the country with the Russians in the north and British India in the east. The establishment of an extensive bureaucracy and the employment of personnel to run the machinery of government from across the ethnic gamut and the extension of government's core services to all regions further developed the nation-state in the twentieth century. However, this new relationship at best was unable to replace the traditional code of upbringing that has been used by all groups to guide them in their relations to one another and to any outside forces. These are seen by one observer as contradictions 'deeply rooted... in Afghan culture, but they have come to the fore in the last one hundred years, since the advent of the nation-state' (Edwards 1996: 216).

In fact cultural and ethnic differences and their preservation is a common feature of people in most societies. The reason why the nation-state has not taken firm root in Afghanistan is partly due to lack of such forces as industrialisation, universal education, mobility and the development of an urban lifestyle. The presence of external forces that have used Afghanistan as their battleground, both in the nineteenth century and also during the twentieth-century Cold War and, since 1979, 'Hot War', is another reason pertinent to the roots of the nation-state. Internally the tribe has been around for a long time and has viewed the state, since its inception, to be on its periphery. While the borders of the tribe are fixed, those of the state have been shifting, depending on the strength or weakness of the rulers. Under such circumstances it is not unusual, as in former Yugoslavia, Somalia and Yemen, for people to fall back on their traditional morals and customary maps. That is why the evolution of state to nation or nation-state, while externally keeping them from prominence, did not necessarily mean the elimination of these ethnic and religious forces, which came to the surface in 1929 and again since 1982.

Resistance to modernity

Developmental factors (industrialisation, education, urbanisation, mobility), needed careful handling if they were to be accepted by the people of the predominantly tribal Afghan state. On the contrary, the Amir's grandson King Amanullah's youthful enthusiasm to provide the educational, social and industrial base of the nation-state was seen by the religious and traditional leadership in the country more as the weakening of religion and the breaking of cultural norms and barriers. No ethnic group wanted this to happen. The 1,000-strong *Loya Jirga* members, representing all ethnic groups, meeting in 1923, instead of approving his constitution, rejected those sections that were aimed at women's emancipation, co-education and an emphasis on modern education at the cost of Islam. The Pashtuns who had been the backbone of all previous governments, not only abandoned Amanullah, in fact the eastern *Shinwari* tribe rose against him. While the government sent its forces in 1929 against the *Shinwari*, an illiterate 'brigand', the Bachai Saqaw, with a small band of his supporters attacked and toppled the king.

The problems that Amanullah faced were not of his entire making. The state bureaucracy had not done its job of convincing the public that modern education was an essential part of modern life and that to develop a country, men and women were required to make their contributions, that education would take people away from their immediate tribe and village and that this would be to the benefit of the country as well as the individual concerned and so on. Since such a state of development had not been reached by the time of Amanullah's reign, a second, though brief spell, of nine months' civil war, was to follow in 1929.

To the Pashtuns, whose frugal lifestyle depends on the number of males in the family, both to earn the family's livelihood and to be counted against *terburs* or cousins, schooling meant losing a member of the family to the *Payendah kahole* or their extended family, i.e. the government. (Payendah Mohammad Khan being the ancestor of the Musaheban ruling family 1929–78). That is why even in the 1930s, the perception of the state continues to be seen in patrimonial terms. Demands are made similar to that within an extended family. For example, after the defeat of the usurper, Bachai Saqaw, and the crowning of Nader Khan, their replacement for Amanullah, these Pashtuns' first condition for continuous support of the government was that the latter should not build schools, roads or enlist them into the army without their consent. All governments, down to 1973 (Daoud's republic) honoured this pledge. But by the 1970s the Pashtun attitude had changed significantly enough to demand roads, schools and hospitals. Even when Daoud's government started conscripting school and university Pashtun graduates into the six-month customary army service, the government met no resistance. This change of attitude towards modernisation was even more pronounced amongst some other smaller ethnic groups. They made excessive demands for the development of their languages, cultures and regions. Demands that the governments' restricted budgetary means and egalitarian approach regarding tribal linkage and ethnicity could not meet.

The decade of the constitution

The decade of the constitution gave Afghans opportunities to express themselves not just in a village or tribal *jirga* to one another but through the media to the whole country. Thus demands and grudges were brought into the open in the 'decade of democracy, 1963–73', as in no other time in Afghan history. Tens of daily, weekly and monthly papers and magazines sprang up. All debates in parliament were broadcast live. The communist and other leftists as well as the Islamists, made hay while the sun shone. As a result, violations on linguistic, ethnic and regional bases that were simmering or had been overlooked by previous governments were not just openly aired, but fanned and exacerbated. These splits also took ideological forms. The pro-Moscow Khalq and Parcham factions were opposed on the one hand to the pro-Peking *Shola Jawed* or eternal flame and *Setam-i-Meli* or national operation and on the other hand to the Islamists. The Parcham faction of mainly urban non-Pashtun Kabulis, while claiming 'internationalism' and 'world proletarian rights' sided with the *Setam-i-meli* on ethnic lines while Khalq and Parcham, despite their common stand against others also confronted one another. Lastly the Islamists, while opposed to all communists, also challenged the country's traditional *ulama*. These divisions were to reverberate long after some of these original parties had left the scene, at least as organised groups: *Shola*, Khalq, Parcham and *Setam-i-meli*.

All these parties and groups that had started appearing on the Afghan scene since the mid 1960s had equal opportunities to develop ideologically in the 'decade of democracy'. These times of free-for-all expression of opinions and opportunities ended with the toppling of the monarchy. When Daoud came to power in 1973 his very first act was to do away with the free press. The communists in 1978 replaced and renamed Daoud's republican publications in their own name, forbidding any other publications. The Mujahideen parties who appeared on the scene after 1992 abolished communist publications, accusing rival publications of being 'communist' and 'anti-Islam'. Lastly the Taleban after taking Kabul in 1996 stopped publications that were connected to previous parties or groups, regarding them as divisive and damaging to the national interest. They started their own modest quarterlies and weeklies in Kabul and in the provinces.

Ethnicity and ideology in contemporary Afghanistan

The ethnic, religious and political ideologies in Afghanistan are a reflection of the world at large. Ethnicity was not as important in the eighteenth and nineteenth centuries as it has become towards the end of the twentieth century. Ethnicity was locally viewed as a primary aspect of identity. This identifying factor under local conditions of internal migration, urbanisation and subsequent social interaction has changed. Over 7 per cent of Pashtuns, and a small percentage of most other ethnic groups have changed their identity to Dari-speaking *Farsiwan* people, though when pressed hard, they will not identify themselves with Tajiks, whose language is Dari. Barth argues that under certain circumstances ethnic change can happen and that ethnicity is not fixed and primordial. However, he does not neglect the stability of ethnic identity by pointing 'to the organising and canalising effects of ethnic distinctions' (Barth 1969: 10). That is why in Afghanistan we have an ethnic identity that is both fixed and changing. For example, those 7 per cent of Pashtuns who had lost their language and were termed *Parsiban* or *Farsiwan* were seen by the majority of Pashtuns to have changed their ethnic identity. However, during the Soviet occupation and in the subsequent years Tajiks, Hazarahs and Uzbeks tried to ethnically cleanse them from most of the north and northeast. So their revival of their original Pashtun roots became a matter of life and death for them. In the same way Dari speakers who did not know about their origin redefined themselves as 'Tajik'. Also, members of some smaller groups who have either lost their genealogy or wanted to upgrade themselves have also started calling themselves Pashtun, Tajik or Uzbek.

The civil war that followed the withdrawal of the Soviet forces led to armed members of larger ethnic groups committing a level of atrocities against each other, unknown before in Afghan history. Thus the Tajik activists, who acquired the upper hand, indiscriminately bombed and massacred Hazarah, Pashtuns and Uzbeks. Uzbeks and Tajiks rose against one another. Hazarah and Uzbeks militants also turned on the Pashtuns and Tajik and vice versa. All this, from the fall of the communist government in April 1992 to the fall of Mujahideen resistance parties in September 1996. When the Taleban took Kabul at the latter date, the Tajik, Hazarah and Uzbek armed groups, under pressure especially from Iran and Russia, patched up their differences and stood as one against the Pashtun-dominated Taleban. However, the situation has changed since 1997, in that Uzbek and Hazarah have loosened their ties with Tajik leaders headed by Masoud and Rabbani. So the fixed ethnic distinctions of A, B and C were temporarily overlooked by their joint opposition to D, creating temporarily a new identity of divergent ethnic groups opposing the much larger dominant Pashtuns. But when faced with external dangers, such as foreign invasion, all A, B, C and D join together, forming a national 'Afghan identity' to avert the danger. Also, at the other end of the spectrum, each component of the above A, B, C and D form alliances on kinship and myths of origin to form opposition to other groupings, down to the level of village and extended family. When all such emergencies are over, they revert to assume their own distinguished local, cultural and linguistic characteristics. Thus my fluctuating ethnic model (fixed and changing), could neatly fit into a four-part definition put forward by Jenkins (1996: 810) that:

i ethnicity is about cultural differentiation;
ii although ethnicity is centrally concerned with culture it is also rooted in, and to some extent the outcome of, social interaction;
iii ethnicity is no more fixed or changing than the culture of which it is a component;
iv ethnicity is a social identity, which is both collective and individual, externalized in social interaction and internalized in personal self-awareness.

Afghan political parties and groups when in power used their ethnic roots and links to recruit new members, and favoured those that they could trust and identify with. Thus Daoud favoured and recruited only from the Parcham faction. Though himself not communist or Tajik, he closely identified with these metropolitan Dari speakers. The communists Khalq and Parcham in turn recruited from within their own ethnic boundaries for their factions within the PDPA. The Mujahideen in turn, at least overtly, removed all the communists and their 'repugnant' ideology but nonetheless, could not avoid relying on their own ethnic members to hold sensitive posts, both as guerrilla groups and also when in power. The Taleban, despite their determination not to fall in the trap of the previous groups and their announcement from day one that 'Afghanistan belongs to all the people who live in this country', were unable to convince the political activists of some other ethnic minorities of their real intentions.

Since the majority of *madrassa* or seminary graduates and undergraduates are Pashtuns and it is they who spearheaded the Taleban movement, they continued to be accused of favouring Pashtuns. Though six out of fourteen ministers and eleven out of twenty-five provincial governors (November 2000) were non-Pashtuns; tens of commanders belonging to ethnic minorities manned their regions for the Taleban as well as fighting against the forces of the then last remaining warlord, Ahmad Shah Masoud.

Overtly each ruling group has justified its action according to its philosophy. Daoud as a nationalist considered all other groups' activities as opposed to national interest. However, he was to learn at the cost of his and his entire family's life that the most dangerous group from a national standpoint was the Parchamis with long-established relations with the Soviet intelligence. 'That the leading Afghan Communists worked with the KGB prior to taking power comes as no surprise' (Metrokhin 2000: 5) The Parchamis rank and file in turn, without perhaps knowing the extent of Soviet global ambitions, threw their lot in with them.

The communists regarded other groups either as 'subversives' or as opposed to 'modernisation and progress'. When they were in 'power' (1978–92), although for the most part, under direct Soviet influence and occupation this already fractured national picture further deteriorated, sharpening linguistic, ethnic and regional divisions. The Khalqis covertly emphasised Pashtun dominance, and the Parchamis when in power implemented ethnic cleansing plans which physically attempted to reduce the size of the Pashtun majority. Thus after the fall of the communists from power in 1992, the scene was set for the *setam-i-meli*, the Uzbek and Isma'ilia communist militias and Parcham military and civilian activists to join with the Jam'iat and *Shura-i-Nezar* and the Shi'ah *Hezb-i-Wahdat*, to directly challenge the Pashtun grip over political leadership. Thus the four years and seven months of fratricidal war among the Mujahideen, with the communist generals and their militias siding with their ethnic factions, has unleashed the worst and most vicious civil war ever experienced in Afghan history.

Lastly, the Taleban whose platform was Islam, regard all 'parties' as opposed to Quranic edicts. They said that such organised groupings bring disunity and rupture to the ranks of the Muslim *ummah* and should not be tolerated. They had their own small-scale national and provincial publications, which articulated their policy and Islamic philosophy. However, their restrictions on men, women, music and filming that are considered as 'draconian' by most Muslim and non-Muslim press, made them thoroughly unpopular abroad. But they viewed such Western inspired criticism as the West's opposition to the forming of an Islamic state. They qualified their suspicion of the West as follows: Islam forbids bank interest and usury. This has national and international implications. In Islam the *ummah* has no frontier. This is bound to give the West the feeling that the probability of such a large Islamic state, with a population of 1.2 billion, as an explosive threat. Modesty in clothes and life style is emphasised in Islam. This would deprive the multi-billion dollar fashion industry of the West of the millions it makes from this trade in Muslim countries, and so on. So according to the Taleban it is their fundamental approach to life that is disliked by the West. They saw the West as using Afghan women and their education, or men's beards or the fact that they are not agreeable to a 'broad based' government as excuses to cover the West's real opposition. No government today, they said could be correctly classified as 'broad based' in the sense of including representatives from all ethnic and tribal groups in the country within it. And so they argued, why should such an unrealistic demand be made of them.

Comparative and theoretical issues: tribe and state

The Pashtun experience of imperial states, both as their soldiers and subjects, connected them to a much wider world system. Their attempts to form their own governments were very much modelled on these systems external to their own tribal mechanism, although they tried to make the former fit into the mould of the latter. My thesis, therefore, is that contact with the wider world, i.e. globalisation over the ages, has been responsible for the enhanced feeling of localisation and that the two are interlinked. At the same time locality and ethnicity are closely interconnected. However, in Afghanistan, because of migration, such ethnic identification is not always solely confined within one group in one region; locality and ethnicity mould and shape themselves depending on the external demands that they face.

The Afghan state came into being in 1747 through a *Loya Jirga*, a Grand Assembly of the tribes, which appointed a charismatic leader, Ahmad Shah, to head its first government. Since Afghanistan is by and large a tribal society, it has not developed along the lines of Western nations and states, in that the tribesmen transfer their tribal and kinship loyalties to that of the central authority. Such a Western-like state has not been possible so far owing to Afghanistan's long-term factors. Indeed Afghanistan's four distinguished kings, Ahmad Shah Durrani (1747–73) who turned the tribal kingdom into an empire, Dost Mohammad (1833–63), who transferred the dynasty from Sadozai to his Barakzai and nominally united the country, Abur Rahman (1880–1901), the 'Iron Amir' who overtly limited the tribal grip on central power and Amanullah (1919–29) who attempted comprehensive programmes of socio-political and economic reforms, each tried in their own way to found a lasting central power. They also accepted tribal reality, and tried to coexist with it. But the struggle for power between the centre and the periphery, as explained in this book, is inter-related with a number of factors, some favouring the tribes, others central authority. The well-developed social code of behaviour, such as

Pashtunwali and the isolation of the tribes have been two important assets of the tribes. The rivalry and claims to the throne, depending on tribal assistance is another factor favouring the autonomy of the tribes. Meanwhile, discord and disunity, a prominent feature of the Afghan tribes, coupled with their meagre existence and economic dependence have been used to the advantage of central governments in imposing their will. Thus the recent history of Afghanistan is a balancing act between the tribes and central authority. Any imbalance in this equilibrium has led to tribal rebellions or civil wars. The two and a half centuries of Afghan history show that such imbalances have occurred either because of kings' and rulers' ineptitude or because of foreign provocation. So, generally speaking, when the weakness of the state is sensed the tribes make their demands and, conversely, when discord and disunity are sensed amongst the tribes, the rulers and states have been imposing their conditions. Thus both state and tribe have been driven to mould themselves to this state of flux.

Afghan identity and the sense of belonging to the part of the world they call theirs is well established and strongly felt. If we ask the question what does a state or a nation-state do, the answer may be that it works for the wellbeing of all people within its borders and preserves its territory and sovereignty. This is what a state is expected to do in the West and this is what is accomplished sometimes by the tribes and sometimes by the state in Afghanistan. When the concept of nation and state is viewed from such a pragmatic angle, then the claim to statehood and nationhood in Afghanistan is no different from that elsewhere.

Islam

In Afghan society the delicate balance, instanced above, between tribe and state concerns legitimacy. While state and tribe can question one another's legitimacy, Islam as a sacred religious tradition is above such suspicions and, therefore, has been a powerful unifying force in times of crisis. Thus *ulama*, *Pirs*, Sufis, Saints and other religious leaders have always played a role of unifying people across sectarian, tribal and ethnic boundaries. The influence and prestige of such leaders is only second to the *amirs*. In 'Afghanistan, where the concept of the nation has developed but recently, where the state is seen as external to society and where people's allegiance is directed primarily towards their local community, the only thing which all Afghans have in common is Islam' (Roy 1986: 30). However, Islam as an ideology or concept of belief varies according to the understanding and the image that a believer has of it. Thus, the general view held by the masses is different from the legalistic view of the *ulama* which in turn is different from that of the various schools of Islamists and their interpretation of Islam.

Islam is usually invoked when the country is facing danger externally or when adjudication is required to quell the fire of discontent between warring tribes. When such an emergency is over, Islamic fealty also recedes into the background. Why is this so? From a tribal perspective, Islam, like tribal ideology, is deeply embedded in Afghan culture and is invoked as and when necessary. From an Islamic point of view, the reason for this is two-fold. The failure to assimilate local Afghan culture within an Islamic purview and the modern pre-occupation of Afghans, like other Muslims, with 'nations and states'. These issues have taken their attention away from the wider responsibility to the *ummah* where borders and frontiers, parts of the building blocks of nations and states, are dispensed with. In other words, Islamic ideology like *qawmwali* or tribal ideology is deeply rooted in the minds of the people and cannot be physically taken or overrun like the occupation of tribal or ethnic lands. For Afghans the Islamic heritage constitutes one of their main shared cultures and ideologies with the rest of the Muslim world. Thus, like a tribe, Islam has had historic continuity for the past fourteen centuries. However, any political discourse aimed at encompassing the tribe has to articulate the shared values of the tribe. Any discourse on the other hand, which is expected to reach the majority, will have to integrate those common Islamic ideologies that are understood and regarded as fundamental to Islam. The appeal of Islam in everyday matters is also paramount. Dying for Islam is, for example, felt to be much more worthy than dying in a tribal squabble. For death in upholding Islamic values is *jihad*, holy war, and those taking part in it can either gain the status of *ghazi* warrior or *shahid* martyr. Both are highly desirable: the first gains blessing and respect in this world and the second earns an eternal place in Heaven. While dying in a tribal war as a result of greed, or a display of power and revenge, according to Islam, may well qualify the tribesman for a period in hellfire in the hereafter.

The Taleban said there had never been a serious attempt in the past to establish a pure Islamic state on the model of the *Kholafa-e-Rashedin*, or the rule of the four rightful caliphs that followed the death of the Prophet. The Taleban were the first group to try to establish a state on that ideal model. Although the attempt was ridiculed in the West and also by those Muslim rulers who, according to the Taleban, depend for their survival on Western support, the Taleban vowed they were determined to make that dream come true. If the Taleban in Afghanistan had succeeded, other countries such as Pakistan, Bangladesh and Central Asia might have followed. This would have led to the establishment of yet another ideological bloc, which Americans had feared as a replacement for communism. In August 1997, when on a visit to Kandahar, I met the Taleban leader, Mullah Muhammad Omar. During our conversation he said, 'if we allow our women not to observe Islamic rules, would the Christian West be pleased with us?' I said 'no'. He then said 'if we water down our Islamic way of life a little, would that please the West?' I said 'not necessarily'. He then said, 'why should we change our Islamic way of life, if it does not even please the west?' Other Taleban leaders said that even if they were to open up nightclubs, the West would still have other axes to grind. They named the Arab oil Sheikhs and the rulers of Jordan, Egypt and Turkey, saying that these rulers, despite overlooking Islamic pronouncements, are not any closer to the West. So how could a small and economically unimportant country like Afghanistan ever become closer to the materialistic West?

The way ahead

The socio-political changes within the Afghan ethnic scene since the 1960s, especially since 1992 and the Mujahideen scramble for power, has awakened sleeping dogs as never before. Historically, the possession of arms and fighting wars was the exclusive domain of the Pashtuns. Pashtuns fought wars, shedding their blood while most other ethnic groups paid a poll tax towards the expenses of those wars. This traditional arrangement was for the first time changed in the ten years of Soviet occupation. The Soviet invasion provided an opportunity for all other ethnic groups to arm themselves and to learn armed warfare training and experience. As a consequence, politically active members of nearly all-ethnic groups have been exaggerating their importance and numerical count, making demands for secession, federations or greater local autonomy. All such demands would inevitably further weaken the traditionally feeble centre. The end result would be the inevitable disintegration of the country. The group that stands to lose most is the Pashtuns; because the country they have put together and kept from rival empires and internal upheavals in the past two and a half centuries would be lost. As most of the gas, oil and some other minerals are in the north, politically and economically, the loss of the north would be unacceptable and would entail the toughest fight yet to keep the country together. That is one reason why all Pashtun Mujahideen groups and the Taleban stood firm against federalism or any other move that would be considered as the first step to the disintegration of Afghan territorial entity. But there are still powerful regional forces, who despite pledges to the UN and other world bodies not to interfere in the internal affairs of the country, continually pour money and arms into the country in their desire to see a dismembered Afghanistan. What should be done to foil these avaricious regional and neighbouring plans?

1   After the restoration of peace, whether by the USA or through a *Loya Jirga*, Afghanistan needs a proper and scientifically based census so that each ethnic group can gauge their own numerical strength and assess their position within the total population. There is the excellent census issued by the WAK Foundation for Afghanistan and also the World Population (Brook 1981: 377). But the first is the work of an NGO carried out under their own auspices and the second two decades old. The future government should involve the relevant UN

bodies in this exercise, for no other reason than to give it an aura of respectability. However, Afghans, through their long experience of the UN, know that the UN is both a toothless tiger and an instrument of the five veto nations and therefore, have no great faith in this world body. Nevertheless, scientifically amassed statistics with UN blessings have a good chance of winning the approval of ethnic groups. The need for such a census is urgent, as all previous population statistics are at best guesswork and more often misleading.

2   The Tajiks, through their language Dari, have almost had a monopoly over the country's bureaucracy since its inception. The reason for this is the ready availability of literate personnel and their long association with *Farsi* as the dominant language of the region. Their long experience in urbanisation and educational qualifications has traditionally best suited them for the running of government machinery. The other factor inadvertently working to their advantage is their non-tribal mode of existence posing no threat or challenge to central authorities. As the one-time domination of the region by *Farsi* has long been replaced by other national languages (in the case of Afghanistan by Pashto) other Afghan ethnic groups, therefore, must be trained so that they too, in accordance with their qualifications and suitability, could fill such vacancies.

3   The country needs roads and railways to criss-cross tribal and ethnic lands, so that in this way trade and mobility can be ensured. Such modern means of transport would provide those living in isolated and so far excluded valleys with a better opportunity to meet and trade with others. In other words, through transport, administrative infrastructure and related urbanisation an attempt could be made to tackle the problems of a multi-ethnic state like Afghanistan. The problem with a plural society like Afghanistan is that groups within it, because of their cultural variation, have been and would like to continue to operate in accordance with their own rules and norms. Since social living requires the understanding of others' national culture, transport and trade are one set of tools which could deal with the problems of high level localisation facing Afghan society.

4   The government must uphold previous laws making it possible for members of any ethnic group to move freely in Afghanistan to buy and sell land and property. In this way most of the people, who in the civil wars of the last twenty-three years, have been entrenched in their own valleys and mountains, would be encouraged to disperse from their strongholds and provide opportunities for others to move in. This might take some time, but with legal backing the scheme could break the back of stubborn resistance to central authority, which has been the hallmark of the past two and a half centuries and one of the main causes of the last two decades of civil war. There is an enormous capacity for expansion in Afghanistan. The agricultural, urban and

industrial sectors still occupy a fraction of the total land. Nearly all rivers flow to surrounding countries without much use being made of them. Despite the country's rich mineral and energy sources, Afghan export is still confined to fruit, rugs and hides.

5   The central government, in order to gain the trust of its citizens, must develop the country's major languages and provide the opportunity for different linguistic groups to have schooling in the language of those whose number exceeds 50 per cent in any province. Where there is no such clear-cut majority, education should be in either of the two formal languages, Pashto or Dari. This would be expensive for a developing country like Afghanistan, but the people themselves should be given the opportunity to decide whether they want to remain truly bilingual, trilingual or multilingual. However, since Pashto is spoken by 55 per cent and Dari by 33 per cent of the total population, education therefore should be in Pashto and Dari bilingual form with which the majority is familiar. Only in two districts (not a province) of Turkmens, one district of Uzbeks and the district of Nuristan, over 50 per cent of their tiny populations speak their own languages (WAKFA, 1999 census).

Learning both national languages should be compulsory for all students, so that by the time children progress to secondary schools and above, they would be fluent in both languages, regardless of what sort of primary language education they might have had. While in Pashto or Dari-speaking areas, education should be in their own tongues, making the other language part of the compulsory syllabus.

6   Major industrial plants must be close to their raw materials so that the government is not accused of paternalism or favouring one ethnic group over another. However, recruitment for skilled white-collar or blue-collar labour should be on a national level and in accordance with skills and qualifications. This could be justified economically by placing industry where the raw materials are and recruiting personnel according to their expertise. Is it possible for Afghanistan to be a plural society and can the multiplicity of ethnic and tribal groups live together? At what point could the Afghan state command legitimacy? Was the Taleban able to achieve this and would they have replaced the proverbially weak state with a strong one?

If the above points can not be acted upon over the next decades, because of the pace of change in the world and in the region, it is unlikely that the traditional isolation of Afghan society will be maintained. Afghanistan has the misfortune to have people from neighbouring countries within its population. Iran, as the only Shi'ah state in the world, aggressively aids and abets the Shi'ahs in the region. It has been spending about $5 million a day, to prop up opposition since September 1996, the date when the

Taleban over-ran Kabul. In Central Asia, where there are few Shi'ahs, Iran uses its cultural and linguistic card to further its national and sectarian aims. At present the newly independent states of the former Soviet Union, such as Turkmenistan, Uzbekistan and Tajikistan on the northern borders of Afghanistan are too busy coming to terms, after over fifty years of Soviet communism, with their own independence and statehood. In time these countries could become reasonably well off and might follow Iran in spreading their ethnic, partisan ideology and culture amongst their scattered people. So if the Afghan government does not foresee that eventuality, further regional and ethnic wars might follow.

In the end, members of all ethnic groups, if they want to live within a plural society must know that they have to be realistic, to accept one another's differences and the devices of social control, including control from a unitary centre. As in a power relation between tribes, ethnic group and government, it must be the latter that should dominate and the former that should be subordinated. This is not to say that the desire for power will be eliminated. 'All the evidence shows that the struggle for power is universal in time and space and is an undeniable fact of existence' (Roucek 1967: 12). But in the case of Afghanistan the hope is to take the struggle for power from the domain of armed resistance and civil war to a peaceful competition for power on the national level, as is the case with such competition within tribes and ethnic politics.

Afghanistan is over 99 per cent Muslim. Afghan identity and tradition is well established. The world is moving more and more in the direction of Western democracies. So the rules of Islam, democracy and the Afghan tradition must be reflected in any future scheme. Western democracy alone is no answer. As experience after the 1940s shows, Western democracy has brought nothing but corruption and misuse of power to most underdeveloped countries. The Afghans have to accept that a majority group would have a larger share of the educated classes than a minority group and so would have more of a presence than any minor ethnic group. As long as jobs are allocated according to educational qualifications and experience, no one should mind who is holding a position of authority. However, judging by the experience of other countries, such as the Russian residents of Muslim Central Asian republics, the Indian pledge to safeguard the interests of the British after the 1947 partition or Whites' interest in post-apartheid South Africa, opposition and conflicts will not end. However, present Western demands, also repeated by the UN, that all ethnic groups should share in the running of a 'broad-based' government in Afghanistan are impractical. There are more than 100 ethnic groups in the USA. They are certainly not all explicitly represented in the government. Similarly, Britain, France and other countries have not given an allocated share to the ethnic and social groups that live in their countries. The leaders of the ethnic groups who tried to form alliances and governments (1992–96 in Kabul) and in exile in 1980s, before the

Taleban seized control, could not make such arrangements work. The end result was the killing of over 50,000 Kabul residents, the destruction of the historic city of Kabul and the absence of any semblance of government or national authority. No Afghan wants to revert to such chaos and anarchy. But some regional governments and forces beyond the neighbouring countries overtly and covertly interfere in Afghanistan's affairs and have made it plain that the establishment of any regime would not be just a matter of Afghan choice. The Russian defence minister, Igor Sergeyev, for example, meeting with the last of the warlords Masoud, in Dushanbe, on 26 October said, 'even if the fundamentalist Taleban take the whole of Afghanistan we will not recognise them and will work for their elimination' (BBC and world press reports). The reactions of others and the US government were no different from the Russians. Whether the Taleban, by adopting an Islamic approach, or the US-installed Karzai government could achieve international legitimacy and establish a strong Islamic or democratic state would to a great extent depend on the repercussion of forces, far and beyond the borders of Afghanistan.

Epilogue
America's and Afghanistan's 9/11

Introduction

So far, I have been concerned with explaining how the social and historic events of the past two and a half centuries have impacted on Pashtuns and the various minority ethnic groups in the country, and how this socio-historic and political interplay landed these groups in the Soviet War and subsequent vicious civil war, resulting in the loss of thousands of lives and the almost total destruction of the country and collapse of its infrastructure. During the interval between completing the work and final publication, however, the calamitous events of September 11 2001 (9/11) occurred, and have since have led to the occupation of Afghanistan by yet another superpower, this time the United States of America. It is of utmost historic and political importance to try to shed light on why events took such a course, one which saw a shift in the US role from helping to liberate Afghanistan from the clutches of the Soviet Union to becoming the occupier itself. In this final part of the book I want to examine why and how the US reached such a conclusion in policy, how it has been handling its occupation and what its consequences are, not only for Afghanistan but also the United States.

Background to the US occupation: the Osama bin Laden affair

In the post-9/11 aftermath, US intelligence sources consider Saudi financier Osama bin Laden and his al-Qaeda group to have been behind most anti-American terrorist attacks since 1992. Richard Clarke, who was appointed in May 1998 as National Co-ordinator for Security and Counterterrorism by President Clinton and served in the same capacity under George W. Bush till March 2004, writes, 'it just seemed unlikely to us that this man who had his hand in so many seemingly unconnected organisations was just a donor, a philanthropist of terror' (Clark 2004: 135). According to the CIA and FBI, the co-ordinated bombings of the American embassies in Kenya and Tanzania on 7 August 1998 connected the dots leading to a picture of bin Laden as the culprit. Of the two embassies, the damage in life and property was most extensive in the Kenyan attack, 'two hundred fifty-seven were dead and five thousand wounded' (Clarke 2004: 181). Now American authorities are also of the opinion that bin Laden was behind attacks on American and UN forces in Somalia, such as the shooting down of a Blackhawk helicopter and desecration of troops killed there in 1994. He is also alleged to have been connected to the failed attack on an American destroyer in Aden Port in 1992; the Ramsi Yousef attack on the World Trade Center in New York in 1993; Yousef's and 'blind Sheikh' Abdur Rahman's attack on a New York tunnel and bridge the same year; the attack on the USS Cole in Aden in October 2000 which killed seventeen sailors; and of course, the New York and Washington attacks on 11 September 2001 with around 3,000 dead and the subsequent attacks within Saudi Arabia on American, foreign and Saudi government targets.

Bin Laden belongs to an extremely wealthy Saudi construction family. He was recruited by the CIA in the mid 1980s to help the Afghan *Jihad* against Soviet occupation. Bin Laden used his contacts and financial resources to recruit Arab fighters who won the respect of Afghan Mujahideen for their fearlessness. When the Soviets withdrew in 1989, bin Laden went back to Saudi Arabia and there he tried to persuade the ruling family to ask the Americans to leave their country, home of Islam's two holiest places, Mecca and Medina. 'In 1991 the Saudi government had given up trying to persuade Usama bin Laden to stop his criticism of the royal family, its military alliance with the United States, and the continuing presence of US forces ... A frustrated Saudi government told him to leave the country' (Clarke 2004: 135). Bin Laden chose to live in the Sudan, where a religious scholar Hasan al-Turabi and his National Islamic Front were in charge of the government. Both men were known to each other through their international network of growing radical Islamists. It is said that bin Laden used his wealth to invest in joint projects like the Sudanese Commodities Market, a new airport, a road between the two largest cities and a leather factory. From there it is said that bin Laden funded arms shipments to Bosnia as well as support for Islamist opposition movements in Egypt, the Philippines and Morocco. In the summer of 1995, bin Laden wrote a public letter to King Fahd denouncing the presence of US troops in Saudi Arabia. Indeed, in June 1995 when Egyptian president Hosni Mubarak was in Ethiopia for the conference of the Organisation of African Unity, he had to be heavily protected in his armoured limousine lest he also be assassinated, like his predecessor Anwar Sadat, by an Egyptian opposition now linked to bin Laden and his Afghan-Arab veterans, many of whom lived with him in Sudan.

Concerned at the ever increasing influence of bin Laden in Sudan, America and its allies, especially Egypt, put pressure on the Sudanese government who finally asked bin Laden to leave in 1996. Bin Laden decided it was time he returned to Afghanistan; to try his influence with the Mujahedeen leaders in his bid to establish an Islamic khilafat (Caliphate)-based government in Kabul. Thus, bin Laden and his Afghan-Arabs returned to Afghanistan where the Northern Alliance chief Burhanuddin Rabbani was the nominal head of the fraction-ridden 'government' in Kabul.[1] Rabbani placed bin Laden in the eastern province of Kunar. When the Taleban swept to power six months later, bin Laden came to Kabul and also built a residence for his large family in Kandahar.

The CIA, who had a 'golden opportunity' to capture or bomb bin Laden's plane on its way from Sudan to Pakistan, did nothing. In fact, before the tragedy of 9/11, the US never mounted a serious attack against bin Laden or his men in Afghanistan. Yet after the tragic events in New York and Washington in 2001, it was this man who was the most wanted person by American authorities, with a $30 million reward on his head.

Bin Laden was popular with all seven Mujahideen groups who operated from Pakistan during the ten years of Soviet occupation. But for the Taleban, most of whom were commanders of some of those seven parties, his name and fame carried even greater weight. The Soviet defeat left a power vacuum in Afghanistan and the warring groups were only too pleased to find a source to help them win their cause. For the Taleban, bin Laden was not just a rich man, he had a proven record of being able to train, arm and mobilise large numbers of fighting men, which would be a great asset to them. The Taleban government won diplomatic recognition from only one of the six countries that border Afghanistan (Pakistan). The two other countries that also gave recognition to the regime were Saudi Arabia and the United Arab Emirates.

When the US started putting pressure on the Taleban to expel bin Laden and close his training camps, the Taleban always denied the existence of such camps and asked for proof of bin Laden's involvement in the East African embassy bombings, the USS Cole attack and others. Although the training camps' aerial photos were with the Americans, and one such camp in Khost was bombed by Clinton, they somehow never made them public before 9/11. It was only in January 2002 that *Time Magazine* published some of these photographs.

The Taleban always used Pashtun tradition and Islam as reasons for not handing bin Laden to the Americans. As for the Pashtun code of honour, they stated their argument along the lines of *Pashtunwali*, which prohibits the handing over of one's guests to his enemy. Arguing their case on Islamic grounds, they proposed to try bin Laden by a *Shari'ah* Afghan court or other such Islamic court with judges from Afghanistan, Pakistan and one Muslim country nominated by the USA. They even proposed for a trial by satellite, but the US always refused, insisting on his being handed over to America to stand trial there. America was exerting its power and influence to have its way and this behaviour looked bullying to most onlookers, since there was no diplomatic relation between the two countries, no extradition treaty, no concrete proof of guilt that had ever been made public and most annoying to Muslims, the blank refusal to accept from amongst the choices presented, thus giving the impression that it did not care about the sacred *Shari'ah* law or its implication in such a case.

In the summer of 2001, the Taleban organised a meeting of their Islamic scholars to decide the fate of bin Laden. These *ulama* issued a fatwa stating that bin Laden should be asked to leave of his own accord, which avoided going against both Afghan tradition and Islamic edicts in such a matter. A few days after that meeting, the Taleban said that bin Laden would indeed be leaving. They even told the Americans that bin Laden is no longer under our protection, meaning come and get him and we won't stop you. However, the US either did not understand this hint or deliberately ignored it. To make the matter worse, the State Department's spokesman in Washington said that bin Laden's leaving alone wouldn't be enough to win the Taleban America's diplomatic recognition. The Taleban then concluded that bin Laden was simply an excuse and that America was basically against their regime and what they stood for. 'The Taleban rightly believed that if they evicted bin Laden, as Sudan had done, the US would then have other objections that would block aid. American would want the Taleban to insure women's rights and would insist on varying an end to the opium production' [the Central Asian oil pipeline through Afghanistan to Pakistan; the setting up of a broad based government and so on] (Clarke 2004: 208).

It was this atmosphere of such tension between the Taleban and the US in the aftermath of the events of 9/11 that lead to the bombing and subsequent defeat of the Taleban and the occupation of Afghanistan by the US in October 2001.

American bombing and occupation

The decision by the Bush government to replace the Taleban can be traced to a secret conference in Berlin in July 2001. That gathering was attended by America's closest allies and it was decided that if the Taleban did not expel bin Laden, allow the oil pipeline from Central Asia through Afghanistan to Pakistan, and agree to a broad-based government, and so on, they would be carpet bombed in October of that year. That meeting was made public by a former Pakistani foreign minister, Niaz Naik in an interview with the BBC on 18 September, and was then covered by the *Guardian* newspaper, CNN and other media sources. Naik said that President Clinton's Under Secretary of State Karl Inderfurth, told him of this meeting, adding that the Saudi ambassador to Germany was also present. Little wonder then, that when the WTC and Pentagon were attacked on September 11, before the dust had settled the finger was pointed at bin Laden and the fate of his Afghan hosts was thus also sealed.

In its war in Afghanistan the US did not want to repeat the mistakes of the Soviets by invading with a large land force, which would have been doomed. Instead they sent in CIA men and Special Forces agents to use the loosely held together Northern Alliance, especially Masoud's opposition forces to prepare the ground situation for aerial bombings. The opposition Northern Alliance, who had by then been cornered by the Taleban into 5 per cent of Afghanistan's land in the remote north-east considered the possibility of an American invasion as a God-sent opportunity to save them from extinction.

The CIA team was headed by one who became known as 'Gary' and his team as 'the jawbreakers'. They stuffed a briefcase with three million dollars in $100 bills, intending to buy the loyalty and commitment of the opposition commanders. CIA Special Operation Chief Hunk (one name only) said to the *Washington Post* correspondent Bob Woodward, 'money talked in Afghanistan and they had millions in covert action money ... warlords or sub-commanders with dozens or hundreds of fighters could be bought off for as little as $50,000 in cash' (Woodward 2004: 194).

After landing on 26 September at 3pm local time within an area controlled by Masoud's faction, the Shura-e-Nezar, the team was received by Mohammad Arif Sarwari, who was in charge of their security. Gary 'placed a bundle of cash on the table: $500,000 in ten one foot stacks of $100 bills [in front of Arif and told him] "buy food, weapons, whatever you need to build your forces up" ... [Gary told his host] there was money available and much more ... [not long after that] Gary would ask CIA headquarters for and receive $10 million in cash ... [having seen the manna from heaven] Arif said, "the Northern Alliance welcomes you"' (Woodward 2004: 142–3).

The following day Gary and his 'Jawbreaker' team met with General Fahim, commander of the Northern Alliance forces and Abdullah Abdullah the Northern Alliance foreign minister. Gary 'put $1 million on the table, explaining that they could use it as they saw fit [adding] the president [George Bush] is interested in our mission. He wants you to know that the US forces are coming and we want your cooperation' (Woodward 2004: 155).

The CIA has been under a great deal of pressure in the post-9/11 months for not knowing of the attack and also failing to co-ordinate properly with dozens of other US security organisations. CIA Director George Tenet, who has since resigned, told the 9/11 Congressional Commission on 14 April 2004, that the agency had set up seventy-five new centres, twenty-five of which were in Afghanistan and they included eight different tribes or ethnic groups.

After their restructuring within the Department of Homeland Security, the CIA and Special Forces on the ground co-operated in sending a report about the presence of some 8,000 Taleban troops in the North and also possible targets for bombings. From his thirty-plus years of experience as a CIA agent, Gary knew that the intelligence and the military back in

Washington were of the opinion that 'the Taleban would be a tenacious enemy in a fight and that the US strikes would bring out its sympathisers in Afghanistan and in the region, especially in Pakistan ... Gary saw it differently. He believed that massive, heavy bombing of the Taleban front lines, "really good stuff", as he called it – would cause the Taleban to break and would change the picture' (Woodward 2004: 184).

At a meeting on 2 October 2001 the Pentagon presented their plan of attack to President Bush. 'We will use the cruise missiles, B-1s, B-2s, B-52s, TAC air in the south, Rumsfeld [Donald, Secretary of Defense] said. And just to be clear, he added, "all targets will get the preferred weapons in the south. North, will get all targets but without the preferred weapons"' (Woodward 2004: 188).

The war on the Taleban fronts started on 7 October 2001 after they refused to give in to President Bush's ultimatum of surrendering bin Laden and his followers and destroying his training camps. President Bush appeared on American television networks at 1 pm announcing, 'on my orders the United States military has began strikes against al-Qaeda terrorist training camps and military installations of the Taleban regime in Afghanistan (Woodward 2004: 209). After thirty-four days of carpet bombing, the Taleban evacuated Kabul and took to the mountains from where they continued to fight. Their forces in the north also laid down their arms after Tajik and Uzbek warlords promised them safe passage to their homes. A promise these former enemies never intended to honour. In order to win the war, America not only needed to place its submarines and aircraft carriers in the Indian Ocean, but also required the support of the former communist states like Russia, Uzbekistan and Tajikistan, as well as Pakistan, for use of their airspace and the placing of troops and airpower in their airports and bases.

The relentless bombing of the Kabul Front brought the Northern Alliance troops within ten miles of Kabul. But despite days of bombings, the Northern Alliance could not over-run the Taleban frontline. Fahim urged Gary, 'just hit the front lines for me ... I can take Kabul, I can take Kunduz if you break the line for me ... Fahim was short and stocky, looked like a thug, seemed to have had his nose broken about three times' (Woodward 2004: 238). Soon it became a joke in the US Congress that 'the Northern Alliance has no shoes'. Fahim, a former driver with the communist government in Kabul, is not known for his courage or his military prowess. The Americans were soon to find that out. While the Bush administration's intelligence and military had set up the date for the start of the bombings, Fahim went to Tajikistan. CIA director, George Tenet reported to a meeting of the principles at the White House, 'we are going to move ahead without waiting for Fahim'. It was a dramatic decision since Fahim was the overall leader of the loose affiliation of warlords' forces in the Northern Alliance.... A US Defense Agency memo called Fahim 'a wimp who would talk and talk, then not show up for battle. Fahim was never quite ready, always declaring his need for more money, more bullets' (Woodward 2004: 267–8).

The Northern Alliance has never suffered from a shortage of arms. 'Iran and Russia had both supported the Northern Alliance with millions of dollars over the years. Iran was probably the biggest contributor, providing money to support thousands of Alliances troops' (Woodward 2004: 225). During America's attack on the Taleban, 'the Russians were willing to send weapons to the Northern Alliance. They had some distribution networks, but somebody would have to pay for the arms. It was ... decided that the CIA would pay. They would give the former enemy about $10 million' (Woodward 2004: 290). The arrangement for this transfer was to be made by Condoleezza Rice and the Russian Defence Minister. This was 'peanuts' in comparison to what the CIA spent during the 1980s on its proxy Afghan War. 'By 1985 the Afghan programme was getting 50 percent of the CIA's Operations budget. Within a year it ... became almost 70 percent' (Crile 2002: 339). Then 'the CIA secretly armed and trained several hundred thousand fundamentalists warriors to fight against our common Soviet enemy; and that many of those who now targeted America were veterans of that early CIA-sponsored *jihad*' (Crile 2002: 508).

In the eight weeks of bombing against the Taleban and al-Qaeda forces, America used many of its most devastating weapons. Amongst these were smart bombs, uranium tipped warheads and the most terrifying, BLU-82 'Daisy cutter' 15,000 lbs bombs each of which left a radius of 600 yards devastated, killing everyone within and rupturing lungs and eardrums of those not killed. America spends more on its military then the rest of the seven G-8 nations put together. Hence in military technology America has kept abreast of every nation, including the former Soviet Union. The following extract gives an idea of the efficiency of this war machine that was engaged against the Taleban.

> A U.S. special forces soldier, sitting on horseback, spots a Taleban target. He types out the information on his laptop computer and transmits the data to a predator, a new unmanned drone flying 25,000 feet overhead. The predator relays the data to the commanders in Saudi Arabia, who direct the drone to the target for a closer look – and take a look themselves through its real time video transmission. The commanders then send the target's coordinates to a U.S. bomber pilot in the area, who punches the coordinates into the computer of a 'smart bomb.' The bomb is fired and explodes within three feet of the target. This sounds like a science fiction but it is really happening, said William M. Arkin, a defense consultant and adjunct professor at the U.S. Air Force School of Advanced Air Power Studies. More striking still, the whole process – from finding the target to dropping the bomb – take 19 minutes. During the Gulf War assigning a particular bomb to a particular target took three days.
>
> (Al Franken 2003: 222)

248 *Epilogue*

The purpose of all this relentless bombing was to break the Taleban apart and split them up as the CIA's Gary and Pentagon hawks had urged. But in a cable from a CIA station in Islamabad it was becoming apparent that, 'based on multiple sources, including the new intelligence chief, said that the bombings had so far been a big political disappointment and were not dividing the Taleban. 'Taleban leadership remains united and defiant around Mullah Omar' ... 'in other words, splitting the Taleban was a fantasy. It was very sobering, the enemy was stronger than they imagined' (Woodward 2004: 234). The next day in a televised news conference the Joint Chief of Staff General Richard Myers also admitted 'the Taleban are resilient'. However, 'in all, the US commitment to overthrow the Taleban had been about 110 CIA officers and 316 Special Forces personnel, plus massive airpower' (Woodward 2004: 314). Bob Woodward disregards the participation of countless mercenaries paid for by the CIA, the ragtag Northern Alliance troops in their thousands, the tribes paid to fight alongside Hamed Karzai and Pacha Khan, just to name a few.

Karzai and the new government

After the Taleban were bombed into retreat and then hiding, the US began to appreciate their need for a compliant government in Kabul to see their occupation through. One thing was clear; the US authorities did not want the Northern Alliance to fill this vacuum. In a White House meeting, Secretary of Defense Donald Rumsfeld said, 'we are going to apply airpower, we are going to allow the Northern Alliance to move towards the outskirts of the town [Kabul], and we will tell them to hold short of the town. Any Taleban military that try to leave, we are going to hit them' (Woodward 2004: 308–9). Thus on 11 November 2001, twenty-five air strikes were called in to bomb the hills above the Bagram airbase. American sources put the number of Taleban casualties in this massive attack at 2,200 with some thirty tanks and half a dozen command posts also knocked down. It was then made possible for the Northern Alliance troops to move towards Bagram and the hills above it, a position they had lost in September 1996 to the Taleban and had hitherto not dreamt of recapturing, which again placed them at the gates of Kabul.

Meanwhile the US leadership was fully preoccupied with the beginning of their process of 'nation-building', something Mr Bush had months earlier announced that America was not interested in. Colin Powell, the secretary of state, at a White House meeting of the principles said,

> there had to be a leadership in Kabul after the Taleban defeat that represented all the Afghan people. Richard Hass, his policy planning director, would go to Rome to visit with the former king, who said he would help the transition to the post-Taleban government but wanted no formal role in the new regime. 'Even Musharaf [president of

Pakistan] wants to talk about the post-Taleban Afghanistan' Rice [Condoleezza-National Security Advisor] said. 'We need to exploit that'. 'In the short term it would be useful to be obscure on the future of Taleban' [Dick] Cheney [vise president] suggested ... 'but in the long term – we need the Taleban to be gone'.

(Woodward 2004: 191–2)

One thing the Bush administration was unanimous about was that the Northern Alliance should not fill this void in Kabul. One month into the war, at a meeting of the principles President Bush said, ' "we need to think through how we are going to get some victory before the snow falls. And we need to think through Kabul". "Do we want to take it?" asked Powell. "Do we want to hold it? If we want to hold it, what are we going to do with it?" "May be the U.N. should handle Kabul", the President said. "Yeah, the U.N. is the best way to handle it", Powell agreed' (Woodward 2004: 219). However, CIA director George Tenet warned Bush's principles 'the Northern Alliance will want to take Kabul, and it would be hard to control ... we need a non-Taleban Pashtun to cooperate with the Northern Alliance on Kabul' (Woodward 2004: 223). Also, at a meeting in the White House General Musharaf, the Pakistani military leader, asked about the Northern Alliance taking Kabul, ' "We will encourage our friends to head south, across the Shamali Plains, but not into the city of Kabul", Bush said. "politically, we need to send a signal that the Northern alliance will not run post-Taleban Afghanistan ... it will be governed by a broadly representative group, as well as the rest of the country" ' (Woodward 2003: 304, 306).

As far as the Bush administration was concerned there were two elements in Afghanistan, the Northern Alliance which they still use as their proxy soldiers and the over 60 per cent majority Pashtuns, a group to which most of the Taleban also belonged. The Americans can use the minorities, the Uzbeks, Tajiks, Shi'ah and others, but they cannot bring peace in the long term without Pashtun participation. This is what the history of Afghanistan has illustrated time and again. Some elements in the minorities have often joined the invaders in the past helping them to take Afghanistan, but in the long term, all these invaders have had to come to terms with the Pashtuns.[2] It was this lesson of Afghan history that the Bush principles were coming to grips with. But to do this they had to make contact with Pashtuns in the south, east and south-west.

> tribal leaders in southern Afghanistan maintained ties with the Taleban, Tenet was not prepared to send teams into the south. It simply was not secure. Nor was there a definable front line as there was in the north.... 'We need to get the Pashtuns to play with us, we need to calm the Paks down ... We need to tell the southern tribes what the political scenario is. We need the vision. We need to make it

clear that we are there for the long term' Tenet summed up ... the CIA briefs repeated how important it would be to offer incentives to the Pashtuns to withdraw support from Taleban.

(Woodward 2004: 226–7)

The Americans were aware of the hostile interplay between Pashtuns and the dishevelled Northern Alliance, which was put together by the Iranians after the collapse of the communist government back in April 1992. It was then joked that the 'Northern Alliance' was neither northern nor an alliance, as it had in it groups who operated from the east and south-west, not to mention that the different groups were, and still frequently are, at each others' throats, the eruption of violent skirmishes between them becoming the norm. Hardly what one could term an 'alliance'. Thus the CIA, from its ten years of contact during the Soviet invasion, had this to say.

'The Pashtuns are anti-Northern Alliance – they could be anti-Taleban. They are not anti-U.S.' said Tenet. In other words their allegiances were negotiable-just like every body else's in Afghanistan. 'They only want to control their shuras', referring to an Islamic principle of self-governance. 'The Northern Alliance is not monolithic. They could easily fragment. They could go against each other ... We have an Iranian dimension in the west and a Russian influence in the north', tenet said of Northern Alliance. 'We need a vision of Kabul', Rice reiterated. 'The vision for Kabul is important to avoid alienating the Pashtuns' ... Look, we do not need to take Kabul to show results ... we need to figure out Kabul, the Pashtuns, the Northern Alliance', Cheney said.

(Woodward 2004: 230, 233)

In the course of two months of bombing it became clear to the Bush team that they could not, in the short term, bring Pashtuns on board without forsaking the Northern Alliance. They had to work out a compromise which would, to a certain extent, satisfy both of the above elements. The Northern Alliance leaders were known to them.[3] They needed a Pashtun that would also be acceptable, or at least tolerable, to the Northern Alliance. One such person was Hamed Karzai, a Pashtun from Kandahar who had been, according to Mujahideen sources, in contact with American authorities since the Soviet war period. During Soviet occupation, Hamed Karzai was working for Sebghatullah Mujadeddi and his National Front, which was the smallest of the seven Peshawar-based groups. He was also one of a number of deputies in the foreign ministry to Rabbani and Masoud in the mid 1990s. While at that job, Karzai escaped an assassination attempt at the hands of Masoud's men. He told me of this in an interview while I was working for the BBC. He was fortunate that the building where he was imprisoned came under rocket attack and while the guards ran for cover, he escaped through a window, cutting himself with broken glass. Karzai only returned to Kabul when the Taleban came to power in September 1996. While not given a specific formal position, it is said that he indirectly worked for the Taleban. He says he left the movement because he no longer agreed with their policies. He left Kabul for Quetta in Pakistan where his father was also living. There, he kept a low profile during the Taleban's remaining years, only surfacing again when the US bombing of the Taleban was in its second or third week. He went to the mountains of Oruzgon to organise some elements in his own tribe against the Taleban. He had CIA officers with him in the mountains of Oruzgon who evacuated him to Pakistan when the Taleban got too close.

The CIA, in south-west Afghanistan only had Karzai to count on. Four weeks into the bombings, the Taleban were still putting up tough resistance. In another of the hurriedly assembled White House meetings, '"we can't afford to lose", Rice said. "The Taleban proved tougher than we thought". Tenet said they had dropped supplies to Dostum and Attah, but in the south the only person doing much – and that wasn't a whole lot – was Karzai, who had 400 to 500 fighters. Rumsfeld lamented that in Mazar the Taleban had at least double and perhaps triple the forces of the Northern Alliance. Powell took the floor to argue against Americanising the war. "I would rule out the United States going after the Afghans, who have been there 5,000 years"' (Woodward 2004: 275).

Karzai as America's leader for Afghanistan

The job of finding the next Afghan leader was given to an old hand at the state department, James Dobbins. Dobbins knew the division of labour for the region was split among three state department bureaus in charge of Afghanistan, Pakistan and India, Central Asia and Iran. It was these bureaus plus the CIA that had to be consulted.

> He first went to the CIA, where several officials mentioned Hamid Karzai, the moderate Pashtun, as a leader who had broad appeal ... General Frank [commander of the war on Taleban] also recommended him. Dobbins joined a conference in Bonn, brokered by the U.N. where factions of the Afghan Opposition were trying to see if they could agree on a leader. The new head of the Pakistan intelligence service said Karzai was a possible, and the Russian representative told Dobbins, 'Yes, he has been to Moscow, we know him well, we think he is a good person.' Iranian Deputy Foreign Minister Mohammad Javad Zarif told Dobbins at the mention of Karzai, 'he lived in Iran for a while and we think well of him'. Dobbins was nation-building. He found Karzai had communication skills, empathy and an ability to forge personal relationships rapidly. [the Bonn opposition delegate chose Karzai, although he was not even there] Karzai took

the oath of office in Kabul on December 22. Regime change had been accomplished 102 days after the terrorist attack in the United States.

(Woodward 2004: 314–15)

Karzai was not well known in Afghanistan. Those who know him say that often when they went to see his father he would be listening, not participating. Karzai was not a prominent figure among the Mujahideen nor did he hold any significant post in the Mujahideen exile governments or in the post-Soviet/communist period. He has not spent an extended period in Moscow or Tehran nor did he go there as a Mujahideen government representative. It is therefore questionable that a nameless Russian representative to Germany could recognise and give Karzai his approval. Beside, Dobbins had never met Karzai at that time and so it is not clear how he could describe his personal qualities. It is even questionable that an Iranian deputy foreign minister could recognise such an Afghan and 'think well of him'. To my knowledge Karzai never spent an extended period in Iran, either privately or on an official capacity. Dobbins, on a PBS documentary has said that Karzai was introduced to them 'by ISI [Inter Service Intelligence] the military intelligence of Pakistan'. Karzai was known to some American authorities and had CIA officers placed with him in the mountains of southern Afghanistan. Karzai himself in a televised speech to the joint houses of the US congress on 15 June 2004 told a story 'on the day I was chosen as head of Afghanistan's government, a stray bomb landed near me, killing four American and about twenty Afghans'.

Despite long contact and Karzai's track record with US authorities, the Bush administration did not put all their eggs in Karzai's basket. They had for all intents and purposes divided Afghanistan three ways. The north was given to an infamous Uzbek warlord, Rashid Dostum; the west to another warlord, Ismail Khan and Kabul to Karzai. That is why, three years after the Taleban there is no Afghan army or policy of any significance to talk about. 'The goal the Pentagon approved was only a 4,800-man Afghan national army by 2004. Some regional warlords count their strength at ten thousand men under arm. The initial units of the new force were trained by the US, but we soon stopped support and provision. Many of the new recruits departed the force, taking their equipment with them' (Clarke 2004: 278).

Karzai has been totally powerless to extend his rule to the rest of the country.

> As a result, the new Afghan Government of President Karzai was given little authority outside the capital city of Kabul. There was an opportunity to end the factional fighting and impose an integrated national government. Yet after initial efforts to unite the country, American interest waned and the warlords returned to their old ways. Afghanistan was a nation raped by war and factional fighting for twenty years ... but in contrast to funds sought for Iraq [$87 billion

for Iraq and $2 billion for Afghanistan] U.S. economic and development aid to Afghanistan was inadequate and slowly delivered.

(Clarke 2004: 278)

While visiting Afghanistan, the US Defense Secretary Rumsfeld and other American officials also paid visits to the two warlords in the north and west of the country as well as Karzai in Kabul. Many have started calling Karzai the mayor of Kabul. Even concerning the release of some Pakistani prisoners in the north (June 2003) Karzai would request Dostum rather than order him. Also, while 90 per cent of Afghans are unemployed and $4.5 billion in foreign aid has vanished over the past two and half years, Karzai only claims to have built an army of about 6,000 out of a projected 70,000. Kabul and the rest of the country are still 'policed' by warlords militias. Only in May 2004, the Uzbek warlord's forces chased the governor and the army chief of Karzai from a northern province accusing them of 'pestering local people'. Both these warlords are collecting excise taxes amounting to hundreds of millions of dollars for themselves, despite Karzai's insistence that such revenue collection should be the job of the central government.

Winning hearts and minds?

America had been talking to the Taleban from the time they came to power in Kabul in September 1996. In fact, having witnessed the warlords and their destructive actions in the previous four and a half years, the US was relieved, as was the UN, at the emergence of a group who were committed to restoring law and order and to putting an end to factional fighting and widespread drug cultivation. The state department under President Clinton is on record as having said that they are working with the Saudi law and can also work with some *Shari'ah* of the Taleban. However, the Taleban's strict interpretation of Islam created many enemies for them both within and outside the Islamic world. Thus the events of 9/11 provided the grounds for an American intervention. The Bush administration, informed by the support of an emotional US public and the US' status as the sole world superpower, quickly gathered the moral aid of many governments to respond. After all, it was a foreign attack on its soil. Mr Bush first spoke about a 'crusade' against terrorists, saying that 'those who are not with us are against us'. The term 'crusade', for many Muslims, invoked thoughts of the Crusaders and the 200 year wars. He quickly replaced it by what the Pentagon called *Operation Infinite Justice*, again displaying an astonishing disregard for the religious lobby, who pointed out that 'infinite justice' was something that only God, not the US military, was capable of delivering. Following this second *faux pas* in selling the war to the public, the process was subsequently named *Operation Enduring Freedom*, thus giving less of an impression of sheer vengeance, and keeping in line with the president's assertion that the reason for anti-American terrorism was that 'they're jealous of our freedoms'. The suggestion that those who were not with the administration were against them, which also came under scrutiny, was also gradually dropped by the White House.

In the attack that was planned, the US set itself the following aims: to destroy al-Qaeda's infrastructure in Afghanistan and to eliminate or capture its leaders; to bring down the Taleban regime; to strengthen forces within Afghanistan hostile to the Taleban; to arrest or kill leaders of the Taleban's military and civil administration; to set up a US-friendly government in its place; to create a broad-based government; to involve the UN in giving legitimacy to American occupation and finally to deploy American, coalition and Afghan forces to achieve these objectives.

Diplomatically the US had already laid the groundwork by imposing its sanctions on the Taleban and following it by imposing similar sanctions through the UN security council; freezing Taleban assets in America; putting pressure on the three countries – Pakistan, United Arab Emirate and Saudi Arabia – who recognised the regime to sever relations, who obliged shortly, one by one.

From the Bush administration's viewpoint, the war in Afghanistan was multidimensional. For the US domestic consumption it was meant to assure the public that the terrorist infrastructure was gone, its leaders and their Taleban hosts replaced. Furthermore, they had been made to pay the price and America was once again safe. For the international community the message was that anyone daring to oppose the world's sole superpower would face similar consequences. And for the Afghans, it was meant to bring peace, stability and democracy by chasing away al-Qaeda and their hosts, the Taleban regime.

However, with the advent of President Bush's 'adventure' into Iraq, all the above objectives were jeopardised. The American people do not feel any safer. According to the state department (corrected version of their 2004 report,) terrorist attacks were higher in 2003 than at any time before. Most of the countries that supported Mr Bush in Afghanistan have turned against him. The opposition to the Iraq adventure brought over ten million people in some 1,000 cities around the world onto the streets in protest. For the Afghans, the US policy of working with the various notorious warlords, paying them and their militias and including them in the Karzai government and its military operations, killing thousands of innocent Afghans, has done nothing but give way to discontent and disillusionment with America's approach. The feeling on the ground is that *Operation Enduring Freedom* was yet another phase in the two and a half decades of war, insecurity and destruction in the country.

Since I am writing about Afghanistan, I want to explore some of the Afghan disgruntlement with the Bush administration's policies, especially their use of military power.

Seymore M. Hersh, a Pulitzer Prize-winning journalist quotes from a report for the Pentagon, by Hy Rothstein, an expert in unconventional warfare and a veteran of the Special Forces, who now teaches at the Navy Postgraduate School, in Monterey, California, which contains a military study of what is happening in Afghanistan.

> They decided that he would look at the unconventional side of the war. As part of his research, he went to Afghanistan, and spent a lot of time in the field with various commanders and troops. And his report, when it was delivered in January [2004] was a quite devastating account of a war that wasn't won, and why it wasn't won, and why it's not going to be. What makes that document so interesting to me is that it reflects what I've heard privately from aid people, other government people, intelligence people, and special-operations people. But here it was in writing, which might make it harder for the Administration to walk away from it.
>
> (*The New Yorker*, 6 April 2004)

Over the past three years there have been daily clashes with some 20,000 mainly US troops in south, east and south-west of Afghanistan. On 15 March 2004, the Chinese news agency, Xinhua reported:

> While the United States-led coalition forces in Afghanistan are trying to win people's support in the ongoing war on the Taliban and al-Qaeda network, local people's complaints against the troops' behavior are growing. 'Contrary to our culture and tradition, the troops search our houses in villages and even occupy them for as long as 15 to 20 days and arrest and terrify the innocent locals on wrong intelligence reports', Gul Rahman, a member of a tribal delegation, told. 'Neither they allow us to go out of our houses nor permit any one to visit us', another delegate, Malik Zari Khan said. 'We are not Taliban or al-Qaeda rather we are law-obeying citizens and our demand for the Americans as well as for the [Karzai] government is to honor our cultural values and not to harass us arbitrarily', another tribal elder Jahangir Wazir Khan told Xinhua. In the meantime US military spokesman Lt. Col. Bryan Hilferty downplayed their concerns, saying 'spending one night in cold weather is better than living in 23 years of war.' He was referring to over two decades of civil war and Afghan people's miseries.

This is not the view of a couple of disgruntled tribal elders. Most Human Rights organisations have also written about abuses by troops. The New York-based Human Rights Watch in one of its many reports on 'Afghanistan: Abuses by US Forces', written well before abuse revelations of Iraqi prisoners, concludes, 'US Forces operating in Afghanistan have arbitrarily detained civilians, used excessive force during arrests of non-combatants, and mistreated detainees'. The report said that the US administered system of arrest and detention in Afghanistan 'is outside the rule of law'.

'The United States is setting a terrible example in Afghanistan on detention practices', said Brad Adams, executive director of the Asia division of Human Rights Watch. 'Civilians are being held in a legal black hole – with no tribunals, no legal counsel, no family visits and no basic legal protections'. 'There is compelling evidence suggesting that US personnel have committed acts against detainees amounting to torture or cruel, inhumane, or degrading treatment', said Adams.

The US has created twenty detention centres in their major military bases. The International Committee of the Red Cross (ICRC) is not allowed into nineteen of these twenty detention facilities. Only after the Iraqi prisoner abuse blew up were the ICRC allowed to visit prisoners in Kandahar as well as in Bagram, north of Kabul.

Human Rights Watch conclude that the US-administered system of arrest and detention in Afghanistan exists outside of the rule of law. The fifty-nine-page report also details mistreatment. Released detainees have said that US forces severely beat them, doused them with cold water and subjected them to freezing temperatures. Many said they were forced to stay awake, or to stand or kneel in painful positions for extended periods of time (New York, Human Rights Watch, 8 March 2004). After Iraqi prisoner of war photographs were published, twenty former detainees came forward to the Afghan Human Rights Commission, saying they had been subjected to similar degradations. It is now clear that the US troops practiced such acts contrary to the Geneva Accord on Prisoners of War, first in Afghanistan and subsequently Guantanamo Bay. Some Afghan translators, who objected to the US troops stripping prisoners naked during interrogations, were told that these were methods approved by the Pentagon and the White House.

The abuses are not just confined to the US troops. Their surrogate partners, the Northern Alliance militias, also operate with complete impunity. They have been raping Pashtun women, beating and killing their men and then stealing whatever they could lay their hands on in the north of Afghanistan. Mary Robinson, the former Irish President, then Head of the UN Human Rights Commission was appalled when she came across such abuses by Shi'ah, Uzbek and Tajik militias of the Northern Alliance. After her visit to northern Afghanistan, she told reporters in a news conference in Islamabad about 'sexual excesses on both men and women, beatings, even killings and stealing of the Pashtuns property, this is very serious. In one village a Pashtun flock of thousands of sheep was taken by force' (Mrs Robinson, Islamabad, March 2002).

Mary Robinson's findings were corroborated by Northern Alliance militia in the Turkmen capital of Ashgabat. 'We even sexually abused eight years old girls, whose bodies were like boys and they did not know what we were doing. We have been told that instead of killing the Pashtuns, abuse them sexually, so that they can carry the guilt and shame feelings for all their lives'. These militias did not divulge their identities (Sabawoon on line, 16 September 2002).

The disillusionment of Afghans with US policy started with the killing of some 3,000 Taleban prisoners of war in the north of Afghanistan. The Irish film producer, Jamie Doran, has captured this massacre on film, which was shown to the European parliament before being broadcast on national TV networks in Italy, France and Australia amongst other countries. No national American network will show it. When the former BBC film producer, Mr Jamie Doran asked one of his contacts at a large US network why they couldn't show it, he was told, 'not now Jamie, not now'. The film shows the presence of CIA officers, Special Forces and other American military personnel. Although there have been no allegations that American forces were responsible for committing the massacre itself, they are believed to have been aware of what was being carried out. Jamie Duran was asked by World Socialist Web Site:

> *WSWS*: In your opinion, in such an operation involving the transportation and elimination of up to 3,000 people, is it possible that the American troops did not have knowledge or give their consent?
>
> *JD*: You want my opinion? My answer is no. One hundred and fifty Americans soldiers were present at Sheberghan prison. That does not include CIA personnel. In my opinion, it would be highly unlikely that they could remain unaware of something taking place of such magnitude.
> (http://www.wsws.org/articles/2002/jun2002/dora-j17.shtml)

'Witnesses say ... US Special Forces re-directed the containers carrying the living and dead into the desert [of Laili] and stood by as survivors were shot and buried. Now, up to three thousand bodies lie buried in a mass grave' (SANA, 15 August 2002).

Other prisoners were trucked off in sealed containers, witnessed by a number of Afghans present. When the European parliament pushed for a trial of the abusers, the UN representative in Kabul, Lakhdar Brahimi, poured cold water over the idea, claiming that Afghanistan did not have the proper legal infrastructure and also that it wasn't possible to guarantee the safety of the witnesses. The fact that venues such as Nuremburg and The Hague could be found for Afghan genocide perpetrators was never even entertained.

Another mass killing was the aerial bombardment of a prisoner-of-war fortress, Qala-e-Jangi in Sheberghan, near the city of Mazar. Instead of surrounding the prison and cutting off water and other facilities and then trying the mutineers, the American jets in November 2001 bombed to death most of the 470 prisoners. This savagery was witnessed on television by people around the world. The 'American Talib' John Walker Lindh was amongst eighty-six who survived.

The UN did not raise its voice over the killing of prisoners by American jet fighters nor about the perpetrators of the 'caravan of death'. These latter were 3,015 from among the 8,000 who surrendered to the US military's Afghan allies (Northern Alliance) after the siege of Konduz in the north. 'In Doran's film, Amir Jahn, an ally of Northern Alliance leader General Rashid Dostum, states that the Islamic soldiers who surrendered at Konduz did so only on the condition that their lives would be spared', WSWS, above).

Soon after they handed over their weapons, the prisoners were forced into six 40-ft sealed containers, packed like sardines. When the prisoners began shouting for air, US allied Afghan soldiers fired directly into the truck, killing many of them. The rest suffered an appalling road trip lasting up to four days, so thirsty they clawed at the skin of their fellow prisoners as they licked perspiration and even drank blood from open wounds. After four days the containers arrived at their destination, the stronghold of the Uzbek warlord, Rashid Dostum, in Sheberghan. An eyewitness, a former member of Dostum's militia takes up the story:

> Opening of first container was like a ceremony of triumph. All of us, God forgive me, were proud of our handiwork. We counted 293 dead and two alive when the first container was emptied.
>
> I opened the padlock with my own hands. I removed the padlock, turned the heavy handle and pulled the door toward me with my full might. The heavy door of the container suddenly opened with a jerk and dead bodies of bearded Taliban began spilling out of the container as if they were trying to launch one last attack on us.
>
> In a haste to run away from the macabre spectacle, I tripped and fell down on the ground, buried under the spilling, rotting bodies of our prisoners. I shall never forget the sensation as long as I live. It was the most revolting and most powerful stench you could ever imagine. A mixture of feces, urine, blood, vomit and rotting flesh, it was a smell to make you forget all other smells you ever experienced in your life. It was the smell of death – death of humanity, death of values, death of justice.

Cargo containers are designed for cargo and not for human beings. There is no ventilation once the door is closed. The air inside is not enough to sustain a sparrow for a week. One can imagine the situation when about 300 young adults are stuffed alive in one such metallic box.

I crawled from under the falling bodies of Taliban and got to my feet. My colleagues laughed tauntingly when I could not control my stomach and began vomiting all over my shirt and over the dead bodies of container-dwellers.

Our prisoners were more eloquent in death than they had ever been alive. Their faces were frozen in various expressions of horror and pain. Their bodies were locked stiff in different postures of a macabre dance. In their frenzy to get a gulp of breath, they had clawed each other faces and bodies. Blood had oozed and dried around their mouths, eyes, ears and noses. Most of them had lost control of their body orifices and their bodies were smeared liberally with their own feces and urine, most of it petrified and putrefied. Only two of the 295 prisoners from the first containers were alive when we dragged them out. Those two were also on the verge of death so our commander put bullets in their heads to hasten them on their way to join their colleagues.

I handed the bunch of keys to someone and rushed away from the scene.

That very same day I decided to run away from Afghanistan and now I am going to pray every day and night. I seek forgiveness of God for being a part of this crime.

(SANA, 15 August 2002)

After Jamie Doran's film accounts were heard in Afghanistan, two other witnesses were killed by Dostum's men and others have fled to Kabul and Central Asia.

America in the aftermath of 9/11 is still too sensitive for politicians in the US and Human Rights organisations to demand an enquiry and the trial of those amongst Dostum's men, CIA, Special Forces who were present while these prisoners were forced into these metallic containers in Konduz and its arrival 400 miles away in Sheberghan.

Andy McEntee, former chairman of Amnesty International, who saw the film footage in Berlin and read the transcript, told DPA news agency that he believed 'there was prima facie evidence of serious war crimes having been committed by US soldiers in Afghanistan'. Mr. McEntee said he believed the war crimes had been committed not only under international law but also under US law'. 'No functioning criminal justice system can choose to ignore this evidence', he said.

(17 June 2002 SWSW)

The *Sydney Morning Herald* in a headline: 'Massacre row: does UN have blood on its hands?' criticised the UN for 'the scant action over Afghan massacres' (3 February 2002).

The massacre and Duran's film have featured widely in some of the main French and German newspapers (*Le Monde, Suddeutsche Zeitung, Die*

Welt). Yet the existence of the film has not even been reported by such leading newspapers as the *New York Times*, the *Los Angeles Times* and the *Washington Post* (WSWS, 17 June 2002).

The Pentagon issued a statement 13 June denying the allegations of US complicity in the torture and murder of POWs, and the US state department followed suit with a formal denial on 14 June.

Another aspect of the war that will be in the news for years to come is the use of 'Depleted Uranium' (DU) warheads that the US and its allies, especially Britain, dropped in thousands of tons over the Kabul and Konduz Taleban frontlines and also on the Tora Bora forests and mountains, over al-Qaeda and its leadership. Reports are already coming out of its massive effects on flora, fauna and more importantly on Afghan civilians. So far, two separate studies have been made public: one in November 2002 at Jalalabad, Kabul and the Bagram frontline, the second a revisit of Kabul and Jalalabad a year later by an Afghan scientist, Dr Mohammed Daud Miraki (Mdmiraki@ameritech.net) Director of the 'Afghan DU & Recovery Fund' entitled 'The Silent Genocide from America', in which he also gives details of Dr Asaf Durakovic's study http://www.umrc.net/AfghanistanOEF.asp. Dr Durakovic is a professor of nuclear medicine and radiology and a former science advisor to the US military, who set up the independent Uranium Medical Research Center (UMRC), testing US, British and Canadian troops and civilians for DU and uranium poisoning over the past few years.

I now quote at length from Dr Miraki's report on the use of DU and other heavy metals used in the war against the Taleban and al-Qaeda in the Pashtun-dominated south and east of Afghanistan.

> 'When Bush Jr. said, "we will smoke them out ..." he lived up to his promise, making life an unattainable reality for the unborn and unsustainable reality for the living sentencing the Afghan people and their future generations to a predetermined death sentence'.

> > 'When I saw my deformed grandson, I realized that my hopes of the future have vanished for good, different from the hopelessness of the Russian barbarism, even though at that time I lost my older son Shafiqullah. This time, however, I know we are part of the invisible genocide brought on us by America, a silence death from which I know we will not escape'.
> > (Jooma Khan of Laghman province, March 2003)

These words were uttered by an aggrieved Afghan grandfather, who saw his own and that of others' familial extinction at the hands of the United States of America and her allies. Another Afghan, who also saw his demise, said':

> > I realized this slow, yet certain death, when I saw blood in my urine and developed severe pain in my kidneys along with breath-

ing problems I never had before. Many of my family members started to complain from confusion and the pregnant women miscarried their babies while others gave birth to disabled infants'.

(Akbar Khan from Paktika province, February 2003)

DU weapons system use has been reported in the *Guardian*, *The Boston Globe*, the BBC and many other media sources.

> The DU explosive charges in the guided bomb systems used in Afghanistan can weigh as much as one and a half metric tons (as in Raytheon's Bunker Buster – GBU-28).
>
> *Le Monde* March 2002

The usage of new generation weapons was also confirmed by the Uranium Medical Research Center (UMRC) in Canada:

> US military health warnings to OEF [Operation Enduring Freedom] personnel indicate the presence of radiological contaminants; recommending troops take protection measures. OEF's forward targeting personnel, Special Forces and post-bombing, site inspection teams have been given radiation protection instructions, radiation detectors and protective equipment prior to and since entering Afghanistan.

In addition to the bombs and rockets, the US air force relies heavily on AC-130 flying gunships which are equipped with the 25mm GAU-12 Gatling gun (1,800 rounds per minute) with DU ammunition further adding to the contamination of the environment in Afghanistan. Furthermore, US ground forces rely heavily on the A-10 'tank killer' that uses 30mm rounds of depleted uranium ammunitions. These two weapon systems contribute on a daily basis to the misery of the people there.

This disaster will haunt Afghan children, women and men for generations to come. Dr. Michael H. Repacholi of the World Health Organization reported:

> DU [deleted uranium] is released from fired weapons in the form of small particles that may be inhaled, ingested or remain in the environment.

He added further:

> Children rather than adults may be considered to be more at risk of DU exposure when returning to normal activities within a war zone through contaminated food and water, since typical

> hand-to-mouth activity of inquisitive play could lead to high DU ingestion from contaminated soil.
>
> (*The Laissez Faire City Times*, vol. 5, no. 44, 29 October 2001)

At the defense department briefing, Dr. Ross Anthony, from the Rand Corporation had said the following about depleted uranium: 'The kidney is the part that is the most susceptible' (*The Laissez Faire City Times*, vol. 5, no. 44, 29 October 2001).

Steve Fetter and Frank von Hippel wrote in the *Bulletin of the Atomic Scientists* (1999).

> Radiation doses for soldiers with embedded fragments of depleted uranium may be troublesome ... The ground the DU-contaminated plumes passed over would be coated with a thin layer of DU dust, some of which would be later kicked up by wind and human activity.... The munitions could deposit a layer of [depleted uranium] dust on crops that could be eaten directly by humans or by animals later consumed by humans.... However, rough estimates suggest that there is a cancer risk from consumption.

What this translates into is more deformities, diseases and deaths for the Afghans. As I also stated in my previous report http://www.rense.com/general35/perp.htm, it took on average five years for various deformities to emerge in Iraq after the first Gulf War. However, in Afghanistan, people started to complain from various health problems within weeks of the initial bombing. This means only one thing, the magnitude of uranium-based weapons used in Afghanistan is much higher than that in Iraq during the first Gulf War. This fact is reinforced by the news that in the first few months of the bombing more 6,600 J-dams/smart bombs have been dropped on Afghanistan, making the size of the uranium contamination much higher than in Iraq during the first Gulf War.

The emergence of excessive health problems increased curiosity and concerns among scientists world-wide of the usage of depleted uranium. The first scientific undertaking was led by the Uranium Medical Research Center (UMRC) which consisted of two consecutive trips to Jalalabad and Kabul. The preliminary findings by the UMRC research teams concluded:

- Radiological measurements of Afghan civilians' have high concentrations of uranium in a range beginning at 4× and reaching to over 20× normal populations. This is 400 per cent to 2,000 per cent higher than the study controls and normal population baselines of the concentrations of monograms of uranium per liter of urine in a twenty-four-hour sample.

- The isotopic ratios of the uranium contaminant measured in Afghan civilians show that it is not Depleted Uranium (DU). The isotopes of uranium found in the Afghan civilians' urine is Non-Depleted Uranium.
- UMRC investigated the possible origins of this contamination. The preliminary results of the radiological urine analysis are corroborated by radiological measurements of debris and weapons' fragment samples at OEF (Operation Enduring Freedom) target sites and bomb-craters.
- UMRC's Field Team found several hundred civilians with acute symptoms and reportedly developing chronic symptoms of uranium internal contamination (including congenital problems in newborns). All subjects' on-set of symptoms are reported to coincide with the calendar dates of the bombing and were not present prior to the bombing.
- Radiological measurements of any populations' urine specimens identify, as a standard practice, the abundance of each of the three naturally occurring isotopes of uranium (U234, 235, 238). These isotopes' abundances (quantities) are measured as a fraction of the uranium released in a twenty-four-hour sample of urine. The isotopic ratios (proportions) of the uranium in the urine collected in Afghanistan has the unmistakable signature of Non-Depleted Uranium. It does not express the isotopic ratio of DU. Depleted Uranium and Non-depleted Uranium are both species of uranium. UMRC is reporting the isotopic signatures of the uranium found in the Afghan civilians' urine. (UMRC Preliminary Findings from Afghanistan & Operation Enduring Freedom, http://www.umrc.net/ AfghanistanOEF.asp).

After collecting samples of urine, soil from blast sites and surrounding areas in Kabul and Jalalabad and other areas, UMRC carried out detailed scientific analysis of these samples and released their findings on 21 May 2003', http://www.umrc.net/AfghanistanOEF.asp:

- UMRC's findings, May 2003, reveal a wider scope of human and environmental contamination in Afghan civilians, corroborating the November 2002 Jalalabad findings.
- Jalalabad area: New reference levels based on recent collections of samples and controls have revised the Jalalabad results upward to uranium values 45× normal.
- New bioassay studies identify uranium internal contamination in Spin Gar (Tora Bora) area and the City of Kabul are up to 200× the Reference Level of the unexposed population (Mdmiraki@ameritech.net,).
- Surface water, rice fields and catch-basins adjacent to and

> surrounding the bombsites have high values of uranium, up to 27× normal.
> - Field and laboratory data show that samples with elevated uranium levels, civilian health problems, and weapons exposure histories correspond spatially and chronologically to ordnance deployed by Operation Enduring Freedom.

Along the lines of the UMRC findings, I instructed two groups of field surveyors to comb eastern and southeastern Afghanistan as well as Kabul for effects on uranium on local populations, they have found many dreadful conditions.

They targeted wide areas all over Afghanistan, however, the depth of the contamination is situated in the Pashtun dominated areas, east, southeast, south and southwestern Afghanistan ... thousands tons of non-depleted uranium along with depleted uranium (mostly from A-10 and AC-130 Gatling guns) has been used by the US and her allies against the defenceless people of Afghanistan.

The bulk of the contamination is in Tora Bora, Bagram frontline – north of Kabul, Shaikoot, Paktia, Paktika, Mazar-i-sharif and Konduz frontline (field surveyors).

Data collected by field surveyors: Subsequent to the contamination, several newborn children have physical deformities and those that do not have physical deformities suffer from mental retardation. These cases are reported from Paktia, Nangrahar, Bagram, Mazar-e-Sharif and Konduz.

During the bombardments of Tora Bora, Bagram front lines, Konduz and Mazar-e-Sharif, many Taleban soldiers were seen with blood coming out from their mouths, noses and ears. Meanwhile, those Taleban soldiers who returned to their respective villages started to vomit blood and had bloody stools. Subsequently, many have died from their conditions.

During the bombardment of Kuram village, in the Surkhrod district of Nangarhar, the village was completely destroyed and many people were killed without any physical injuries.

After the bombardment of Khost, public health workers have reported the occurrence of skin lesions in several civilians. Those that developed the skin lesions died after their conditions deteriorated. My team also reported that many children are born with no limbs, no eyes, or tumours protruding out from their mouths and their eyes.

Every week cases of deformed births are recorded in the six areas of heavy DU usuage. However, local officials are putting them down to stress and adverse living conditions of women being refugees of war. America's battle to win over the hearts and minds of the Afghans is far from over, and has had limited success thus far. The details of the prisoner of war massacres and the use of radioactive weapons systems have not yet fully reached the Afghan public or the outside world. The picture of the Afghan conflict over the past three years, for most people, has been one of daily civilian toll and the talk of how terrorism is being eliminated slowly but surely by coalition troops. Mr Bush launched the attack on al-Qaeda and the Taleban in October 2001. Three years on, the leaders of these groups are still freely issuing orders to their supporters, and if anything they operate with ever increasing impunity as a public weary of waiting for tangible improvements in their lives grows ever more disillusioned. The main casualty of the US and its coalition bombings in Afghanistan have been civilians who, in most cases, had nothing to do with either al-Qaeda or the Taleban. The US-installed government in Kabul is widely regarded as re-playing the Afghan communists' role, vis-à-vis their Soviet masters. Let us examine one such instance, a report, nine months into the war, from the Voice of America Radio of 22 July 2002.

> 7/22/2002 (VOA): A U.S.-based human rights group says U.S. air strikes in Afghanistan aimed at al-Qaida and Taleban fighters have mistakenly killed more than 800 civilians since last October. The group Global Exchange says the death count comes from six months of surveys in Afghan towns and villages.
>
> However, Afghan President Hamed Karzai disputes the group's figure. Speaking on Sunday with the BBC, a spokesman for Mr. Karzai said the strikes have killed fewer than 500 civilians, and that that number is low given the size of the U.S.-led military campaign. The spokesman, Tayeb Jawad (now Afghan ambassador to Washington), said the United States and Afghanistan are fighting the same war on terrorism.
>
> The *New York Times* newspaper quotes Global Exchange workers as attributing the deaths to U.S. reliance on incomplete or misleading information when launching air strikes. The paper also quotes Afghans who say warlords sometimes provide the Americans with false or misleading information to provoke an attack on an enemy town or village.

A professor at New Hampshire University, Marc Herold, puts the death toll of Afghan civilians by the end of December 2001 at 3,500. Japanese Long Shore Workers Resist the War write:

> Despite the lies in the American corporate media and lies of the U.S. government we now know through European and other foreign mainstream media that over 3,500 civilians have died in the U.S. bombing of Afghanistan. These Afghani civilians had nothing to do with September 11th. This civilian death count was meticulously tabulated by

Prof. Marc Harold of the University of New Hampshire who compiled the information from the foreign press up until Dec. 10th, 2001. (24 December 2001).

Also see: A report on the number of civilian casualties in Afghanistan, by Marc W. Herold.

Craig Borowiak in an article, 'Translating accountability: from the global economy to violence and back again. Last December, Mark Herold, Professor of Economics and Women Studies at the University of New Hampshire, reported that the number of civilian deaths in Afghanistan resulting from US bombing had exceeded 3,500. Today, estimated deaths exceed 4,000. There is significance in these numbers' http://www.duke.edu/~jad2/borowiak.htm.

Marc Herold, working from authenticated press reports, put the figure of Afghan deaths after three months of bombing at over 3,500 which is higher than the 9/11 tragedy in America. However, casualty figures are difficult to collect for the simple reason that the American forces do not accept figures given by the local villagers and the government in Kabul has no intention of systematically corroborating such disputed figures, nor is there any other human rights organisation, to my knowledge, dedicated to discovering the truth in this area.

Long-term consequences of American occupation

President Bush, like any other American president would, went after the men who attacked the symbols of America's economy and military power. However, without pausing to reflect on why there is so much anger towards America in the wider world, the Bush administration launched their global 'War on Terror' to supposedly eliminate terrorists everywhere and forever. The dislike of America is not uniform for people around the world. American foreign policy makers should understand this and tackle it. The Latino world's dislike of America is not the same as that of Arabs or Persians. The grudging coexistence of some Far Eastern nation with America is not the same as that of the Russians, Germans or French. The Muslim dislike of America is largely based on its one sided support of Israel in the Palestinian issue and its support for repressive leaders in the Arab world who are not popular with their own people. There is also the dislike of America as a wasteful consumer society, devouring one third of the world's resources, by a mere three hundred million of its people, while the rest of world's six billion population fights an unequal war over the remainder. In political and military terms, America is now the world's only superpower and frequently flexes its muscles, to the almost universal distaste of people around the world. Some examples of this 'might is right' attitude to interacting with the rest of the world include the hugely unpopular invasion of Iraq in the face of world opposition, the refusal to sign the Mine Ban Treaty already adopted by some 100 countries, the opposition to the setting up of an international criminal court, the refusal to sign the Kyoto agreement on global warming and so on and so forth.

Each of the above topics alone would be a possible title for a book, some already written, others that could be published. Here I am only concerned with Afghanistan and what the implication of present America foreign and military policy may be to Afghans and Americans. Afghanistan is an ancient land, whose history can be traced back 5,000 years. As the 'crossroads of Asia', it has seen many invaders come and go. For most Afghans, the American occupation, coming on the heels of the Soviet invasion, is but another such intrusion.

Afghanistan has a reputation as being the last nail in the coffin of empires that have overstretched themselves. Going back only three centuries, we notice that Afghans were the main cause of the Moghul Empire's fall through their stubborn resistance to Moghul dominance of the region, culminating in the invasion of India by Afghans. The Afghans also put an end to the 200-year-old Safavid Persian Empire in 1709, not just by expelling them from Afghanistan, but by taking the whole of Iran, thus becoming neighbours with Turkey, Armenia and Azerbaijan. By putting up tough resistance to the British Indian empire in 1839, 1879 and 1919 (the three Anglo-Afghan Wars) the Afghans consider themselves to have been an important element in ending the British Empire. By forcing the British to accept their independence, the Afghans claim they opened the possibility for the Indian subcontinent and later Africa to also demand independence. And due to the fierce resistance to the communist Soviet empire for ten years between 1979 and 1989, Afghanistan is regarded as the catalyst for its economic, political and military collapse and implosion.

Currently, the Afghans consider themselves amongst the causes of the Islamic revival in the present age. The invasion of Afghanistan by an atheist 'evil empire' awakened forces that had been dormant for a long time. Such resistance against the Soviet Union brought together Islamic forces from many parts of the world. This also gave birth to al-Qaeda who in turn carried their violent manifesto to Arab and non-Arab Muslim nations. Now that the Afghans, and to some extent al-Qaeda, are in the background, their sympathisers in other countries under other names are taking their struggle to new fronts. It is 'like a smashing pod of seeds that spreads around the world, allowing them to step back out of the picture and have the regional organisations they created take their generation-long struggle to the next level' (Clarke 2004: 287).

One imagines President Bush crossing off, on his chart of photographs, the faces of such men as bin Laden, Ayman al-Zawhiri, Mullah Omar, Hekmatyar and others as they are eliminated, rather than confronting the root of this terrible problem, the hatred and readiness of thousands of others in 'the back alleys of dark warrens of Baghdad, Cairo, Jakarta, Karachi, Riyadh,

Khartoum, Tehran, Damascus, Detroit and Newark, using the scene from Iraq (war and prisoner abuse) to stock the hatred of America even further, recruiting thousands whose names we will know, whose face will never be (crossed by Mr Bush), not until it is again too late' (Clarke 2004: 287). Even a tiny percentage being the most 'extremist Islamic terrorists' out of a Muslim population of over a billion, could attract some potential 'suicide seekers' to their cause. Such numbers could take this war on terror well into the twenty-second century and lead to the fall of most pro-Western governments in the region. Al-Qaeda and its clones around the world cannot be eliminated by the brute force of arms, i.e. fighting fire with fire. America must adopt a more balanced foreign policy and work to reach out to the people themselves, not just their pro-American governments. The American administration must work to change its view of ordinary Muslims from one of animosity and suspicion to one of tolerance and coexistence with the West. The approach should not be one of inflexibility and stubbornness in wiping out the fundamentalists and replacing them with a Jeffersonian Democracy. The approach should be of winning the hearts and minds of Muslims by the great deal that the West has on offer in terms of improving their agriculture, housing, education and health, indeed their entire standard of life. This is not going to be achieved quickly, in time for good approval ratings before the next election. Such a shift in policy would require a great deal of forward thinking, planning and patience. It requires first of all a change in the US foreign policy of supporting dictators, rather than their citizens; sharing and exploiting Muslim resources with their people, rather than distributing the profit amongst their rulers; being just and realistic in the Palestinian-Israeli case rather than supporting, financing and arming Israel to saturation point. If America adopts such an approach to world issues, it could remain a superpower 'with a humane face' and would not be as disliked or opposed as it currently is.

We have two recent examples of former imperial states, who were helped by America to make fundamental changes in their foreign policy ambitions and are today the richest nations in their parts of the world. These are Japan and Germany. They do not have bases and soldiers stationed around the world and yet they are almost universally respected and trade with all races and all cultures. America needs to practice some of what it passed on to these two countries. Also, instead of going to war in Iraq and Afghanistan and wasting human life and billions of dollars, America could have turned those countries into close allies by spending a fraction of the 'war chest' on working with the Iraqis and Afghans in a developmental capacity.

By the time talk of war was in the air, the Taleban were isolated, suffering from sanctions placed on them by the US, and through US influence by the UNSC. They were starved of any sources of funds, and more isolated internationally than ever. Were they expected to put their hands up in the air and simply 'throw in the towel', despite the initial encouragement from Bill Clinton's administration and the UN for bringing relative peace, mass disarmament programmes and a huge decrease in land used to cultivate opium? At that critical juncture, they had little choice other than to cling to bin Laden because he was a (perhaps their only) source of financial and military support and thanks to the CIA, had a proven track record from his years fighting the Soviet Red Army. The Afghan people do not like foreign rule or rulers chosen for them by outsiders. In time, the Taleban would have presumably given in to pressure from their moderates within the movement and from the Afghan population without. This change, however, would have to occur naturally over a number of years, and not as the result of a sustained bombing campaign of a country, already reduced to rubble, by the most advanced military power ever known to man. Afghanistan is ungovernable without the consent of its people, who will simply not tolerate a government whose composition owes more to foreign states and backroom power sharing deals than to a homegrown, authentic Afghan governance. Such a government would inevitably find getting to grips with ruling a country suffering from such incomparable devastation very difficult, but with time they would surely rise to the challenge. In view of such historic, and political realities, if the Bush administration, instead of simply eliminating the Taleban, had spent a tenth of the war-chest billions on reconstruction and redevelopment programmes in Afghanistan, the Taleban and the Pashtuns, who have a track record of centuries of wars in the region, would have become America's surrogate troops and through them, the US could have exerted great influence not just in Afghanistan but over the whole region. This cannot be said of either the fractious Northern Alliance or the Karzai government which they installed.

Conclusion

America's invasion of Afghanistan has not brought the security, prosperity or democracy it promised. Three years on, and the presence of some 20,000 American and coalition forces plus 6,500 UN now NATO peace keeping forces have had little impression outside the city of Kabul. Thousands of innocent people have been killed. $4.5 billion raised by international sources for the first three years of the Karzai government has vanished without making a cent's worth of change to the lives of ordinary people. Power is deliberately shared between Karzai and the warlords. Initial efforts to unite the country have waned, which is why Karzai has little control outside Kabul and the warlords retain absolute rule over their fiefdoms in the provinces. The opportunity to unite the country and form an integrated government after two and a half decades of war has been missed. It is not, therefore, surprising, that forces loyal to the Taleban, Hekmatyar and remnants of al-Qaeda have resurfaced and enjoy support, especially in the south and east of the country.

Instead of working with Muslim governments and their people to isolate the extremists, Mr Bush has handed the 'enemy precisely what it wanted and needed, proof that America was at war with Islam, that we were the new crusaders and had come to occupy Muslim lands' (Clarke 2002: 246).

Now that America is in Afghanistan, it will not be able to extract itself quickly. I recall President Clinton saying he would have American troops out of Bosnia by Christmas 1998. However, eight years on they are still there, and Bosnia is comparatively a much simpler and less volatile land than Afghanistan.

So long as the warlords are around, arms are not collected and Afghanistan's peace-time army of 70,000 and police force is not trained and put in place, security can not be guaranteed. When there is no security, no durable improvement can be made in the lives of the Afghan people and thus the vicious cycle continues.

Karzai is not personally corrupt, nor has he any preconceptions about such important issues as ethnicity, language or religion in Afghanistan. He can exert a great deal of influence with the Bush administration, the US military in Afghanistan, as well as the NATO forces there, however all too often he seems to be unwilling, or perhaps unable, to 'show his teeth'. Whether this is due to his lack of experience as an administrator, or perhaps his well-documented personal safety issues, he has not accomplished a great deal so far in terms of progress for the Afghan people as a whole. A country which has been through nearly three decades of war requires firmness and resoluteness. It must be said that so far, Karzai has lost the support of much of his own Popalzai tribe, various other Pashtun tribes, and perhaps most noticeably he has still not gained the trust of the non-Pashtun groups who dominate his government.

The presence of America in Afghanistan should be utilised to rebuild the country and to unite its people across ethnic and religious barriers. If America has its own interests in mind with regards to its presence in Afghanistan, Afghans themselves should be intelligent enough to use that presence to simultaneously further their own interests as best they can. This is an opportunity which will not last for long. If America is committed to bringing democracy from the outside-in, then the Pashtuns, who are the majority and are now (like always in the past) providing tough resistance against the occupation, should take the opportunity to gather around one of their own parties or movements, win those elections and form their own kind of governments, all the time making good use of American resources and know-how to change the standard of living for all people in Afghanistan. The Afghans should learn from the experiences of Japan post-WWII: A Japanese intellectual once said: 'America is like a wild cow, we are stuck to its udders sucking its milk, you Afghans are holding it by its horns'.

Appendix 1: categorising books on Afghanistan

1. British writers of the nineteenth century who have written general historical accounts of the Pashtun/Afghans and have been consulted are: Caroe, O. 1959, *The Pathans 550 BC–AD 1995*; Ferrier, J.P. 1858, *History of the Afghans*; Burns, A. 1973. *Cabool. A personal narrative in the years 1836, 1837 and 1838*; Bellow, H.W. 1880, *The Races of Afghanistan*; Malleson, G.B. 1879, *History of Afghanistan from the Earliest Period to 1878*.
2. Specialised books on the eighteenth and nineteenth centuries: Robertson, G.S. 1974, *The Kafirs of Hindu-Kush*; Gommans, J.J.L. 1995, *The Rise of the Indo-Afghan Empire* (Economic History); Brown, L. 1791, *Battle of Panipat*. Books on the first and second Anglo-Afghan wars (1839–42, 1879–81) and biographies, especially on the subjects of Ahmad Shah, Amir Abdur Rahman and his predecessor, Amir Dost Mohammad; Mousavi, S.A. 1998, *The Hazarah of Afghanistan*; L.B. Pullada, 1973, *Reform and Rebellion in Afghanistan 1919–1929*; A. Hyman, *Afghanistan Under Soviet Domination, 1946–83*; Elmi and Majrooh, 1988, *The Sovietisation of Afghanistan*.
3. Afghan writers (in English and their own languages) covering the eighteenth and nineteenth centuries and early history include: Al-Afghani, S.J. 1938, *History of Afghanistan* (originally in Arabic); Ghubar, M.G.M. 1944, *Ahmad Shah Baba-i-Afghan* (Dari); Jalali, G.J. 1967, *Ahmad Shah the Great's letter to Sultan Mustafa III Usmani* (Dari); Wajdi, A.J. 1986, *The Today and Tomorrow of Traditional Jirgas* (Pashto); Fizad, M.A. 1989, *Loya Jirgas* (Dari); Reshtia, S.Q. 1984, *Between Two Giants* (English); Tabibi, A.H. 1985, *A Nation in Love With Liberty* (English); Kakar, M.H. 1971, *Afghanistan 1880–1896*.
4. Anglophone books on the nineteenth and twentieth centuries: Noelle, C.1997, *State and Tribe in Nineteenth Century Afghanistan*; Fletcher, A. 1965, Afghanistan – Highway of Conquests; Fraser-Tytler, W.K. 1967, *Afghanistan*; Dupree, L.1980, *Afghanistan*; Sykes, P. 1915, *A History of Persia, Vol. II.*; Lockhart, L. 1938, *Nader Shah, A Critical Study*; Gregorian, V. 1969, *The Emergence of Modern Afghanistan 1880–1946*.
5. Political books, mostly of the twentieth century: Rubin, B. 1995, *The Fragmentation of Afghanistan*; Rubin, B. 1995, *The Search for Peace in*

Afghanistan; Cordovez and Harrison, 1995, *Out of Afghanistan*; Amastutz, J.B. 1986, *Afghanistan – the First Five Years of Soviet Occupation*; Arney, G. 1990, *Afghanistan*; Urban, M.1990, *War in Afghanistan*; Adamec, W.L. 1974, *Afghanistan Foreign Affairs*.

6 Books on Islam and Islam in Afghanistan: Roy, O. 1986, *Islam and Resistance;* Olesen, A. 1995, *Islam and Politics in Afghanistan;* Asad, M.1985, *The Principle of State and Government in Islam*; Maududi, S.A. 1968, *First Principles of the Islamic State*; Maududi, S.A. 1976, *Political Theory of Islam.*

7 Books on Pashtun and Afghan anthropology: Barth, F. 1959, *Political Leadership amongst the Swat Pathan*; Edwards, D.B. 1996, *Heroes of the Age*; Ahmed, A. 1976, *Millennium and Charisma Amongst the Swat Pathan*; Ahmed, A. 1983, *Religion and Politics in Muslim Society*; Tapper, R. 1983. (ed.) *Tribe and State in Iran and Afghanistan*; Tapper, N. 1991, *Bartered Brides*; Sharani and Canfield (eds) *Revolution and Rebellion in Afghanistan.*

Articles cited in the thesis by: Anderson, J., Barfield, T.J., Canfield, R.L., Glatzer, B., Hager, R., Katz, D.J., Shahrani, M.N. and Strand, R.F.

Appendix 2: the institutions of Pashtunwali

A. *Melmastia* or hospitality is the requirement *Pashtunwali* places on all its tribesmen towards others, whether they are strangers or members of one's own tribe. Elphinstone in the first decade of the nineteenth century observed: 'The most remarkable characteristic of the Afghans is their hospitality. The practice of this virtue is so much a point of national honour, that their reproach to an inhospitable man is that he has no Pushtoonwali' (Elphinston 1969: 226). Hospitality to strangers is offered free, without expecting any reciprocity. But hospitality to one's kinsmen or tribesmen puts the recipient under reciprocal obligation, accompanied by the 'fear that he will not be in the position to return it adequately when the occasion demands' (Spain 1962: 64). For the Pashtuns there are many reasons why they should abide by the requirements of *melmastia*:

1. It is the way of their ancestors.
2. It is an integral part of the code of honour and shame.
3. Hospitality increases one's fame and thus makes a person more honourable in the eyes of his community. Through hospitality one gains support and followers (Barth 1959: 11–12).
4. The prestige thus gained places him higher than his peers. This gives him an aura of authority; others will listen and seek his advice, and the process will help prevent threats of dishonour to his achieved prestige.

B. *Badal*, or revenge/retribution under *Pashtunwali*, is the right of every Pashtun, regardless of its consequences. Revenge is both individual and collective. If one is wronged within one's own lineage, as among the Nuer in Sudan, one is expected to take the 'law into his own hands'. When one's cattle are stolen or taken by force, this expectation is met by taking back his cattle or their equivalent. Similarly, in cases of forceful capture of property among the Pashtuns, honour is only reinstated when restoration takes place. In the case of adultery or murder, the honour of the victim and that of his family and kinsmen are only restored by killing the offender.

Badal allows no limitation in time and space and the obligation remains as long as a single individual of his lineage survives. 'Occasionally killing in such non-Pashtun environments like Calcutta [Middle East] or Singapore are found to be the result of a feud which had its beginnings in some distant years' (Spain 1962). The Pashtun saying 'I took my revenge after a hundred years and people say I hurried' epitomises the constant fear that hangs over the head of the wrongdoer and his family.

C. *Badraga*, escort or safe passage through one's tribal land, is another aspect of Pashtun hospitality. Anyone in fear of being robbed or shot may ask a host for *Badraga* and he is then under obligation to freely escort the man out of his territory. Should anyone reprimand him, they will face not only the wrath of the escorted person but that of his host as well, a price few would want to entertain. Hence, those who ask for *Badraga* are always mindful of choosing someone who can deliver them safely out of their area, not choosing a man who has the blood of someone a few villages down the road on his hands. Prominent families in adjacent tribes sometimes work out reciprocal *Badraga* arrangements and escort one another whenever needed.

D. *Nanawatai*, or asylum, is from the Pashto word *nanah watel*, entering, which could be translated as asylum or sanctuary. In other words, the act of giving up oneself to the person whose protection is asked. The person asking for *Nanawatai* signifies his inferior position with respect to the protector. Thus, unlike *Melmastia* or *Badraga*, the request for *Nanawatai* puts the protégé in a permanently inferior position vis-à-vis his patron. One would only ask for such a disgrace in the following situations:

1 When one is in debt and wishes to avoid payment for whatever reason.
2 When homicide is involved and the murderer has no courage to face the consequences of his actions, either he himself or an elder or female member of his family is sent to take *Nanawatai* in the bereaved house. *Pashtunwali* dictates that instead of lynching the person, he is given food, immunity, and his appeal accepted. After the acceptance of his *Nanawatai*, blood compensation may be arranged through elders without the presence of either party. Since no amount can restore the last life, the amount is usually small and the injured party often refuses to take it.
3 When one has dealings with another clan or tribe and cannot handle it on one's own. In this case the suppliant will take a goat or a sheep and kill it at the door of the protector as a sign of offering. In such cases asylum, according to *Pashtunwali*, cannot be denied or else 'the honour of the party thus solicited will incur a stain if he does not grant the favour asked of him' (Elphinstone 1965: 226).

The consequences of *Nanawatai* are dire for the asylum seeker. The humiliation and the sense of dependence and inferiority that the suppliant and his family feel towards the protector may eventually become too much, giving them no alternative but to leave and start elsewhere afresh. It can be said that *Nanawatai* is an option similar to the English legal system, about which a judge once said that the courts of law in England are open to all like the Ritz Hotel. While only the rich can stay at the Ritz, in *Nanawatai* it is only the poor, desperate, weak and dependent who will forgo their honour and social status to ask for asylum. Since blood feuds are a prominent feature of Pashtun tribes, it indicates that despite dangerous consequences, not every one is prepared to ask for *Nanawatai*.

Islam and Pashtunwali

Islam, as a universal religion, transcends other values and permeates every individual and group. Islam has been the unifying factor in Afghanistan for centuries, but in the post-Soviet withdrawal period, political groups have made use of Islam in a divisive way. The belief and adherence to Islam also tends to be ignored when some aspect of social organisation is considered separately. In Pashtun areas, Islam is sometimes in conflict with the much older customary tribal code, the *Pashtunwali*, also collectively referred to as *'azat/sharm*, honour/shame. Thus, conflict with religion is particularly noticeable in matters concerning honour and shame. John Anderson (1983), who carried out fieldwork among the Ghilzai Pashtun, speaks of the dialectics of Pashtun (Ghilzai) tribalism and sees three cognate distinctions at work: tribalism (*qawmwali*) versus factionalism (*gundi*); tribal countryside (*atrap*) versus city (*shaher*); and the land of the rebels (*yaghistan*) versus the seat, or domain, of the government (*hukumat*). These contrasting spheres articulate tension in Pashtun society, but also demonstrate that there are Pashtun ways of coming to terms with them. It also further indicates that Islam is not the only institution that regulates everyday affairs. Instead, Islam coexists with other traditional sources that have been around from times well before the coming of Islam. So, in order to resolve any tension between the opposite spheres mentioned above, Pashtun common-law experts, or *merakchian*, integrate and articulate those shared ideological elements that are the product of centuries old political discourse with a view to resolving or neutralising antagonistic approaches, whether between these opposites or in tribal conflicts. In Islam, for example, a woman's consent is necessary for marriage. In *Pashtunwali* if a girl's scarf is snatched from her head, or a man starts firing into the air, announcing his engagement to a girl, she has to be given to him in marriage. But normally the high bride price and the years it would take for a father to agree in such cases deters most men from such bravado. Also in *Pashtunwali*, a woman whose husband dies may be remarried to the man's brother or another close relative. This is justified by the payment of bride wealth, which gives right of possession, as long as she lives. But in Islam, a woman cannot be re-married without her consent and her husband's family has no right of possession of her. In Islam, A must die for unjustly killing B and that is the end of the matter. In *Pashtunwali* revenge killing continues for generations. In short, for the rural Pashtun restoration of honour, and in order to not give the impression of being weak, redress is preferable when it is in accordance with *Pashtunwali* rather than Islam. Asking for justice under Islamic injunctions would indicate a man's weakness and thus leave him wide-open to further encroachments by his rivals. However, in non-Pashtun areas, Islamic decisions often override local customs, *rawaj* or *adat.*

Appendix 3: state and Islamic jurisprudence

Islam's view of the state differs from the Western view in a number of ways. Any state that is occupied by Muslims, however homogeneous the population, coextensive or congruent in their evolution, will not necessarily count as an 'Islamic state', even when almost the entire population of such a state is Muslim, as in Afghanistan, Saudi Arabia or Libya. It can only become an Islamic state by consciously applying the socio-political tenets of Islam to the everyday life of the *umma* and their state apparatus. These are Quranic injunctions, the traditions of the Prophet, the convention of the four Right-Guided Caliphs, and the ruling of the great jurists. The Quran is the book of Allah, where everything good, which is desirable, and everything bad, which is undesirable, is explained. These 'dos and don'ts' in Islamic jurisprudence are called *nass* or *nusus* (in plural). The *nusus*, ordinances, are unambiguous and, therefore, not subject to conflicting interpretations. The Traditions (*Ahadith*) and Sunnah are the sayings and doings of the Prophet Mohammad. As the Quran says, 'the Prophet does not speak of his own volition'; in other words, Allah inspires him and what he says is what Allah wishes him to say. How the four Caliphs managed the Islamic state after the passing away of the Prophet is recorded in the books on *Sahabah*, the contemporaries of the Prophet. Great jurists over the next several centuries explained and interpreted the above three sources and are regarded as the best guidance for a proper understanding of the principles of Islam (Maududi 1986: 3–5). All these taken together make up the Shari'ah. The Shari'ah, in its entirety, either refers to obligatory acts (*fard*), the omission of which constitutes a sin; forbidden acts (*haram*), the commission of which constitutes a sin; or to allowed acts (*mubah*), the commission or omission of which does not make a man a sinner (Ibn Hazm 1926: 62–4).

As the situation of Muslims since the time of the Prophet has changed, an amplification of the Islamic legal corpus has also become necessary. This is done through *Ijtihad*, or independent reasoning. *Qiyas*, or deduction through analogy and *Ijma*, are the consensus or united will of the people. These mechanisms of Islamic jurisprudence became necessary because most Muslims believe that the Islamic state of the time of the

Prophet, and subsequently that of his Right-Guided four disciples, could never be reproduced because 'any deviation from that model must necessarily detract from the "Islamic" character of the state. Nothing could be more erroneous than this idea' (Asad 1985: 22). According to Asad, the Quran and Sunnah do not lay down any specific form of state. 'For every one of you We have ordained a Divine Law and an open road' (Quran 5: 48). The Divine Law (*Shari'ah*) outlines areas within which Muslim life may develop; the Law-Giver (Allah) has conceded to us within this area, an 'open road' for temporal legislation, which could cover those contingencies that are deliberately left untouched by the *nusus* of the Quran and Sunnah. Mohammad Asad writes that there is nothing in Sharia to prescribe any definite pattern to which an Islamic state must conform nor any detailed elaboration of constitutional theory. However, the law that emerges from the Quran and Sunnah gives a vivid and concrete outline of a political scheme capable of realisation at any time in history and under all social and political conditions. Because it was meant to be realised at all times and under all human conditions, the Shari'ah has been offered in outline only and not in detail, perhaps for the obvious reason that man's social conditions are time-bound and therefore variable.

> That is why the Shar'ia does not attempt the impossible. Being a Divine Ordinance, it duly anticipated the fact of historical evolution, and confronts the believer with no more than a very limited number of broad political principles. Beyond that it leaves a vast field of constitutional-making activity, of government methods and day-to-day legislation to the *Ijtehad* of the time concerned.
>
> (Asad 1985: 23)

An Amir or ruler of an Islamic state, is chosen from among the *ulama* by religious scholars and his peers and can only be removed by them. Thus, the legitimacy of an Islamic state is ordained in the Quranic injunction of: 'O you faithful! Obey Allah and obey the Apostle and those in authority from among you' (Quran 4: 59). In this short verse, several important principles relating to the essence of an Islamic state are established. Firstly, that such a state must enforce Shari'ah ordinance in its territory. That is, it must enshrine Islamic principles in its constitution and enforce them. Thus Shari'ah should, in all matters of public concern, form the inviolable basis of all state legislation. Secondly, since Shari'ah cannot supply all relevant laws for state administration, it therefore has to be supplemented by temporal and amendable laws with the proviso that these will not at any time contradict or run counter to the spirit of Shari'ah. Thirdly, verse 59 from Chapter Four of the Quran makes it an obligation to obey Allah and obey the prophet and those chosen to authority from among you (Maududi 1968: 27–8).

While obeying Allah and his Prophet is unequivocal and unwavering, obedience to the *amir* is contingent on his following the Shari'ah Canon of Law to the letter. This principle, which is also ordained in the Sunnah, clearly indicates that the *umma* must take an active part in the running of the state and its government. It must support it when it is in accordance with *Shari'ah* and oppose it when its pronouncements are contrary to the spirit of the Divine Law. Such active participation by believers in the affairs of the state is asked for in another verse of the Quran, '*amruhum shura baynuhum*, their [the believer's] communal business is to be [transacted in] consultation amongst themselves' (Quran 42: 38). Islamic scholars regard this *nas*, injunction, as fundamental to all state business and the way the government of an Islamic state is established and run. The believers are asked to undertake the affairs of 'their communal business in consultation among themselves'. This includes the political business of the state, which must be carried out in the *shura* or assembly. The example for such an assembly goes back to the four Rightly-Guided Caliphs. The Arabian tribes of their time had highly developed tribal structures and assemblies in which chiefs settled their inter and intra-tribal differences. The Rightly-Guided Caliphs used these chiefs and their assemblies to gauge the feelings of the populace. The logical conclusion of this *amruhum baynuhum shura* through *Ijtihad* was that had the Prophet and his disciples held elections amongst those tribes, the people would probably have chosen the same chiefs to represent them. Akbar Ahmed calls this 'the primordial model, one which is associated with early Islam and continues until today, is "tribal segmentary Islam". This category may include the Bedouin, the Berber, and the Pukhtun'. Among these North African and Pashtun tribes 'the world is seen in relationship to one's place in the genealogical charter' (Ahmed 1988: 61). Thus a Pashtun *jirga*, or assembly, can also be regarded as a consultative assembly, like Arabian tribal assemblies in the time of the Prophet, through which public opinion could be measured.

Hence, from an Islamic viewpoint, the elections for today's parliaments, assemblies, or *shuras* are an extension of those tribal assemblies. As the majority of people no longer live in tribal confines, general elections nation-wide are expected to bring out leaders and representatives similar to the Arabian tribal chiefs of 1,400 years ago or the Pashtun Khans of modern times.

Thus 'the intellectual leaders of the community are morally bound to bring forward whatever new ideas they may have relating to communal progress, and to advocate such ideas in public; and for this reason the right to the free expression of one's opinions in speech and in writing is one of the fundamental rights of the citizens of an Islamic state' (Asad 1985: 83). Such freedom of opinion or its expression in the media must not run contrary to the Laws of Islam. Briefly then, only a state that is organised and administered in accordance with the Shari'ah can qualify as an Islamic state.

Appendix 4: struggle against Persians in the West

The attitude of the Persian emperors to the western Pashtuns, as historical records show, was always hostile. 'Shah Abbas the Great (1588–1624), in order to break the power of the Abdalis [one of the two important tribal confederacies in the region], transferred a large section of this tribe [away from its Kandahar base] to Herat' (Misdaq 1997: 39). Although Afghans have served in Persian armies as mercenaries, regular soldiers and conscripted troops from the earliest recorded history, the Persians have always been jealous and distrustful of them.[1] As in the east, it was the Pashtuns in the west who rose to challenge Persian rule. Like the Moghuls, the Persians too played off one tribe and its leader against the other. But the Pashtuns saw through this and, after falling for these Persian tricks on a number of occasions, rose first in 1709, gaining the independence of Kandahar and its environs, and then again in 1747, uniting under one leader to cast off Persian hegemony.

Appendix 5: Abdali uprising, intrigue and deception

The Abdali, to whom the founder of Afghanistan, Ahmad Shah Abdali (1722–72) belonged, are one of the two major tribal confederacies of southwest Afghanistan and the Kandahar region. In the seventeenth century Kandahar was a province of Persia. 'The measures taken by Shah Abbas the Great and his successors ... to ensure [the subjugation] of the Afghan tribes were relaxed under the rule of Sultan Hussain' with the inevitable result that the subject 'tribes were not slow to betray their discontent' (Malleson 1879: 211). The Abdali returned to their homeland in Kandahar during the reign of the above Safavid king, united under Ahmad Shah Abdali's grandfather, Dawlat Khan, and refused to accept Persian suzerainty. The Persian court was furious at Dawlat Khan and dispatched armies to quell his rebellion. But Dawlat Khan 'defeated in two battles the Persian expeditionary forces sent against him, and won name and fame for himself amongst the Afghans' (Ganda Singh 1959: 3). Having failed militarily, the Persians overtly changed their tone, recalling their governor and sending another, a Georgian Christian who had recently converted to Islam, in 1702. This man was renamed Shah Nawaz by the Persians, but became known to Afghans as Gorgin (The Georgian). Gorgin presented Dawlat Khan with some valuable presents and entered into friendly negotiations with him. But he soon covertly contacted elements within the Abdali opposed to Dawlat Khan, and thus eliminated him in time.[1] Gorgin then offered to accept Dawlat Khan's eldest son, Rustam Khan, as the leader of the Abdali, provided he handed over his young brother, Zaman Khan, as a hostage and guarantor of good behaviour by the Abdali. Rustam consulted the Abdali elders and, even at this testing hour, they agreed to Gorgin's demand for two reasons: to keep the leadership of the Pashtuns among the Abdali, thus foiling the attempts of the rival Ghilzai Hotek tribesmen, and to prevent the traitors who had helped Gorgin from assuming leadership of the Abdali. Gorgin sent Zaman Khan, the father of Ahmad Shah Abdali, to Kerman in Persia, where he could be watched closely.

Soon after this the Baluchis revolted. Gorgin sent Rustam Khan to pacify them, but the latter was defeated and had to return to Kandahar.

Rustam's former enemies accused him of siding with the Baluchi. Gorgin, who was looking for an excuse, threw Rustam Khan in prison and asked Atel (who had helped Gorgin kill Dawlat Khan) to also kill Rustam Khan for him, in return for being recognised as the leader of the Abdali.[2] Gorgin, whose plan for the Abdali was not yet complete, undertook to fulfil his promise to his henchman, Atel, provided that he could bring his Sadozai (a sub-tribe of the Abdali) to live in the outskirts of Kandahar. The governor also recognised Amir Khan as Mir Wais, the leader of all the Pashtuns. Atel, after threatening his Sadozai tribesmen with dreadful consequences if they refused to move to the city's outskirts, managed to settle the majority of them there. Gorgin, who wanted to punish this Abdali sub-tribe once and for all, sent his troops one dark night in 1707, massacring the Sadozai. Those who escaped the massacre were exiled to the province of Kerman. With this the Abdali in Kandahar receded into the background, and the Ghilzai appeared on the stage (Ganda Singh 1959: 6). With the Sadozai no longer a problem, Gorgin turned his attention to Mir Wais, who had already written a letter to the Persian monarch, complaining of Gorgin's oppression and cruelty, to which the Shah did not respond. When Gorgin heard about this letter, he handcuffed Mir Wais and sent him as prisoner to the Persian court in Isfahan, 'knowing well that once he too is out of the way, the Pashtuns in Kandahar will no longer be a challenge to the Persian rule' (Al-Afghani 1938: 17).

Appendix 6: the early life of Ahmad Shah, king in waiting

After the death of the infant Ahmad's (Ahmad Shah's) father, Zaman Khan, in 1722, his mother, Zarghuna of the Alikozai subtribe of Abdali, feared for her sons. She married her daughter to Haji Isma'il Khan, a well-known leader, and left the turmoil of Herat, with her two sons, for the relative peace of Farah. It was from there that the two brothers went to their imprisonment in Kandahar ten years later.

In 1738 the Persian ruler Nader Shah, after laying siege for a year, finally took Kandahar. The young Ahmad's brother-in-law, Haji Isma'il Khan, who had joined Nader Shah's service as an officer, recommended the release of the two brothers and they were among the first prisoners to gain their freedom. Nader Shah not only released them, but also gave them a grant of money from the imperial treasury and awarded the elder brother the governorship of Mazendaran.[1]

Nader Shah, who had already raised a 16,000 strong army of Pashtuns (12,000 Abdali and 4,000 Ghilzai), together with 80,000 of his own Persian troops, left for India, conquering Ghazni, Kabul and Peshawar on the way.[2] Nader Shah employed Ahmad Khan on his personal staff first as *Yasawal*, or orderly officer,[3] later as *Yasawal Suhbat*, or protocol officer, and then *Bonk Boshi*, or treasury officer (Malleson 1879: 272; Ghobar 1944: 81). Nader Shah's other *Yasawals*, like Ahmad Khan, were the sons of well-known chiefs and rulers throughout Persia. Recruitment to this rank around the king was thus based on family pedigree and some understanding of court etiquette. As *Yasawal Suhbat*, Ahmad Khan kept order in the court and ensured smooth operation of the appointment system for an audience with the king. It was because of his 'impeccable character' that he was later put in charge of the imperial treasury as the *Bonk Boshi*. Nader Shah is on record saying that he had not seen any man of such laudable talents as Ahmad Abdali in Iran, Turan, Turkistan, or India (Ganda Singh 1959: 18). On Nader Shah's first campaign to India, a former prime minister of the Moghul court, who was well known as an expert physionomist, saw in Ahmad Khan's face 'greatness and predicted that he was destined to become a king'. When this news was reported to Nader Shah, he summoned Ahmad Khan, telling him, 'Remember Ahmad

Khan Abdali, that after me the kingship shall pass on to you, but you should treat the descendants of Nadir with kindness' (Ganda Singh 1959: 19). Ahmad Shah and his son Timur Shah kept their word to Nader's descendants, saving the family after Nader's assassination (Appendix 7) and making sure they continued to stay in power in Khorasan.

Ahmad Khan was among the commanders of the 12,000 Sadozai troops accompanying Nader Shah to India. It was in the army, during Nader Shah's numerous military campaigns in the Caucasus, Central Asia and India, that Ahmad Khan excelled. In the Daghistan (Caucasus) campaign, the Abdali fought with such vigour that Nader Shah promised, after the battle, to grant them anything they asked. The Abdali troops, through their commanders, asked him to allow their people to return back from exile in Iran and Herat to their homeland in Kandahar. The king granted their request.

Ahmad Khan was in the service of Nader Shah from the age of sixteen to twenty-five. These nine years of service in the Persian court gave Ahmad Khan a thorough knowledge of government, administration, conquest, and, most importantly, a better understanding of Persia and the Shi'ah religion than most of his predecessors. It was because of such understanding that, when he came to power, he never attempted to launch campaigns beyond Khorasan and Kerman, regions the Afghans considered part of Afghanistan.[4] It was the knowledge and experience gained during his formative years with Nader Shah, together with the rule and experience of his own forefathers, that Ahmad Khan put to good use when he himself became king.

Appendix 7: Nader Shah's assassination, formation of the Afghan state

Nader Shah, an Afshar tribesman born in Mashhad, began life as a cameldriver, rose to robber baron, and finally became a king, ruling over a vast empire for eleven years and three months (1736–47) as King of Persia (Wilber 1958: 74). Nader Shah was highly temperamental by nature; in a terrible rage, he gouged out the eyes of his own son and later punished all those who were present for not appealing to his better nature and stopping him. In the last year of his rule his mind became even more deranged.[1] He suspected the Persians of conspiracy and disloyalty and inflicted cruelty on his subjects everywhere.[2] It was because of this oppressive and inhuman attitude that his own nephew, Ali Quli, rose against him in Sistan. Ali Quli was quickly supported by the Kurds in Khabushan and, covertly, by some of Nader Shah's own officers. Of all the Persian nobles at his court, Mohammad Quli, commander of his inner guards, and his relative, Salih Khan, the superintendent of his household, were the most active and discontented (Lockhart 1938: 259–61).

In his outer guard camp 'he had ... a corps of 4,000 Afghan; these foreign troops were entirely devoted to him and hostile to the Persians. On the night of 19–20 June, he summoned their chiefs: "I am not satisfied with my guards ... your loyalty and your courage are known to me. I order you to arrest all their officers tomorrow morning and place them in irons ... It is a question of my personal security and I trust the preservation of my life to you alone". Nader emphasised to the Afghan guards "not to spare anyone if they dare to resist you"' (ibid.: 261).[3]

The commander of these guards was Ahmad Khan Abdali. He assured the king that he would immediately implement his orders and went to prepare his guards for the morning's task. A spy who overheard the conversation informed Mohammad Quli, who in consultation with Salih Khan had hatched the plan of killing the king that night.[4] The conspirators' next plan was to keep the news of the king's murder secret and prepare to take the Abdali troops by surprise. But one of Nader Shah's wives, through a maid, informed Ahmad Khan of the murder and the need to safeguard the royal household. Ahmad Khan, in the dead of the night, prepared some 3,000 fully armed troops for the coming encounter and also assigned a group of his men to guard Nader's household/harem.[5] One of Nader's widows, known to the Abdali troops as Bibi Sahiba, sent the famous *Koh-i-Noor*[6] diamond, along with other presents, to commander Ahmad Khan that morning, in return for protecting the *harem* from the mob (Ghubar 1944: 84). Ahmad Khan, having assured the security of the royal household, left for Kandahar with the Ghilzai commander of these troops, Noor Mohammad Khan, who brought the cavalry and artillery, followed by Ahmad Khan's foot soldiers.

The Afghan troops, on their way to Kandahar, informed people everywhere about the murder of Nader Shah and invited their elders to the coming *jirga* in Kandahar, where an Afghan king would be elected.

Appendix 8: Britain's Forward Policy and the 'great game'

Britain continued to develop the concept of 'Forward Policy' from about the middle of the nineteenth century, especially after the seizure of Punjab, which they captured from the Sikhs. The frontier that they inherited from the Sikhs, who since the 1760s had effectively guarded it against repeated Afghan invasions, somehow became 'unscientific' in the sense that invaders could still come over it and threaten India:

> The Forward Policy formulated by Malcolm (d.1833) in the early nineteenth century indeed aimed at extending British influence into the areas lying between the dominions of Britain and Russia in order to create buffer zones between the spheres of interest of the two imperial powers.
> (Noel 1998: 40)

But the idea of a Forward Policy was not accepted in all quarters. Thus the 'controversy led to the emergence of two distinct schools, commonly called the "Forward and the Stationary"' (Ghaus 1960: 3). The Stationary school argued in favour of the present frontier, which lay at the foothills of mountains, and regarded the occupation of India by Russia as 'quixotic'. The Forward followers, seeing the fall of Tashkent, Samarkand, Khieva and other Khanates to Russia as a real threat to India, were in favour of steadily shifting the border westward.

The first two Anglo-Afghan wars (1839–42 and 1879–81) were primarily fought with the Forward Policy in mind; they aimed to extend the border of India to the Amu River (which formed the border between Afghanistan and Russia) or to have the kings and Amirs in Afghanistan subservient to British demands. This Afghan historians call *hers-i-jahangiri*, or greed for capturing the world. The 1876 Treaty of Gandomak, which handed Afghan foreign policy to the British, was a product of such thinking. Reviewing this treaty, Lord Lytton, the Viceroy of India, wrote that the second Afghan war

> was fought to secure two main objects: first, the exclusion of all foreign influence from Afghanistan, and secondly, such a rectification

of the Afghan frontier as would suffice to render impossible for the future the exclusion of British influence from that state.

(Ghaus 1960: 22)

Britain, as a consequence of the first Anglo-Afghan war, learned that, despite their superior forces, they could not impose a puppet, such as Shah Shuja, whom they had brought from retirement in India, on the Afghans. Russia also learned in the 1880s that despite their hospitality to the 'Iron Amir', who was their guest of honour for twelve years, Abdur Rahman was not prepared to go along with their designs. The Amir writes in his autobiography:

> I am under great obligation [to the Russians] and shall never forget their kindness, because ingratitude is the very worst of sins. But ... I am not entitled to sell my country and my people to the Russians in compensation for my personal gratitude towards them.
>
> (Munshi 1900)

This scramble for land was part of a gigantic game played by both countries at the expense of south and central Asia. British intelligence, some 140 years ago, coined the phrase 'the great game' to describe the activities of its rival Tsarist intelligence to the northwest of India and in the steppes of Turkistan. Later in the nineteenth century, the Forward Policy was also seen by Kipling and others as a 'game' played by these European imperial powers using their intelligence, diplomatic and military skills to outsmart one another (Klass 1987: 1). Lord Curzon, the British Viceroy in India (1899–1905) described it as hardly anything but a 'game':

> Turkistan, Afghanistan, Transcaucasia, Persia – to many these words breathes only a sense of utter remoteness or a memory of a strange vicissitudes and a moribund romance. To me, I confess, they are pieces on a chessboards upon which is being played out the game for the domination of the World.
>
> (Quoted in Sikorski 1987: 13)

General Roberts, who later headed a British force in the second Anglo-Afghan war as Lord Roberts, defended the Forward Policy in a speech in the House of Lords on 7 March 1898, as one that would secure 'political control over the robber-haunted no-man's land which lies on our immediate frontier' with a view to forestalling any European power from striking at the gates of India or destroying the integrity of neighbouring Afghanistan, for which 'we have made ourselves responsible' (Ghaus 1999: 24).

The Forward Policy coined by the British was in effect the policy of both Britain and Russia, one of a slow and steady spread of colonial power. While the British attempted to use the Forward Policy to secure a strong and defendable frontier for India, the Russians, according to many sources, wanted to eventually reach the warm waters of the Indian Ocean and enjoy all-year-round access to the sea. From the many nations in the region that were merged within the borders of these empires, the Afghans were the only ones who maintained, at tremendous odds, their battered independence. Afghanistan had been the victim of long-term imperial plans devised by Catherine the Great as early as 1791, and then by the British shortly thereafter.

Correspondence between top British officials of the time (Lytton, Salisbury, Biddulph, Lyall and others) 'at different times admitted that Pishin and Sibi [in Baluchestan] formed part of the Afghan Kingdom'. As for northwest frontier Pashtun tribes, it had to be 'admitted on all hands, the Pathans of the Indian borderland belong to the same ethnological groups as did the Pathans of Afghanistan' (Ghaus 1960: 23; Fraser-Tytler 1967: 48; Bellew 1880: 13). However, these and other colonialists of the time argued that these Pashtuns were somewhat different, that these tribes had no sympathy for those of their kinsmen inside Afghanistan, or that they were not effectively ruled by Kabul.

Both imperial countries, in their propaganda, impressed on their own people that they were giving the benefit of superior Western civilisation to the backward and 'semi-barbarous' states. The contest for imperialist possession in Asia compelled both countries to maintain political and military balance elsewhere. Afghanistan, as a victim of the Forward Policy, saved itself by the sheer determination of its people to cling to their independence and freedom. Only when Afghan sovereignty, and what Afghans were prepared to do in its defence, became clear to the British in 1919 and eventually to the Soviets in 1989, were the two powers ready to set limits on their imperialist aims in Afghanistan. Afghan historians consider their last war against the British (1919) and their ten-year (1979–89) freedom fight against the Soviets as the major reasons for the disintegration of these two superpowers. The independence of Afghanistan from Britain encouraged freedom movements in the subcontinent during the 1940s, and in Africa in the 1960s. The stand against the Soviet war machine had a similar effect on Eastern Europe and the republics of the Soviet Union.

Appendix 9: British and Soviet/Russian interest in Afghanistan

The Russians since the time of Peter the Great (1682–1725), had been interested in warm-water ports in the Indian Ocean; their activities in Central Asia in the nineteenth century were interpreted as part of that scheme. The first Russian interest in Afghanistan dates back to the middle of the nineteenth century. Afghanistan and Iran, in their centuries-long rivalry, provided an opportunity for the British and Tsarist forces to come face to face for the first time. This was in 1837, when a Russian-backed Persian military force wanted to take Herat. The British, fearful of a Russian presence in Afghanistan and its eventual threat to India, helped the Herat authorities diplomatically and militarily, enabling the Afghans to repulse the incursion (Amastutz 1986: 4). Two years later, the British, fearing another attack on Afghanistan by Russia, wanted to take Afghanistan for themselves and thus embarked on the first Anglo-Afghan war (1839–42). Despite 'the ... considerable subsidies [by the British] to the tribal [Pashtun] chiefs ... the Afghan rallied ... to eject the invaders' with disastrous defeat and the loss of 15,000 troops and camp followers (Tapper 1973: 32). The war cost to the Indian treasury was nearly fourteen million pounds. Historians later derided this British adventure as a 'signal catastrophe', the 'disastrous Afghan adventure', 'Auckland's folly', and the 'retreat from Kabul' (Norris 1967).

When, in 1869, the Khan of Bokhara (in today's Uzbekistan) became a vassal of Russia, the Afghan king, Sher Ali, turned to the British for aid in case the Russians tried to cross the Amu River, which then (as today) formed the border. The British refused. London specifically informed India that Russia was not threatening the Amir and that no treaty should be concluded with him.[1]

> Sher Ali was bitterly disappointed. 'The English', he wrote, 'look to nothing but their own interests and bide their time. Whoever's side they see strongest at the time they turn to him as their friend. I will not waste precious life entertaining false hopes from the English and will enter into friendships with other governments'.
>
> (Rawlinson 1875: 283, quoted in Fletcher 1965: 127)

The Amir was under pressure because he had been sent several letters by the aggressive governor of the newly conquered Turkistan, General Kaufmann, who already had the Amir's exiled brother's son, Abdur Rahman, with him. The Afghan king, in order to appear friendly to the Russians, agreed to receive their mission in Kabul. The British, in their rivalry with Russia, also wanted to send an envoy for the first time since the 1839–42 war. The Amir, knowing the strong feelings of his people could not guarantee the protection of such an envoy, wrote a letter politely refusing the suggestion. Lord Lytton, the Viceroy, then gave him a written ultimatum.[2] The Viceroy's proposal, considering the Afghan mood, was unrealistic and Sher Ali could not accept it. In a desperate attempt to avoid being squeezed between the two imperial powers, Amir Sher Ali sent his vizier, or first minister, to India to calm British fears, but to no avail.

Auckland, the Viceroy, then organised a group of officers and armed soldiers to go to Kabul. The Afghan border guard 'courteously but adamantly told them that they could not proceed until he had received approval from Kabul' (Fletcher 1965: 132).[3] The British then sent three armies from three directions. Sher Ali, seeing this, put his son, Yaqob Khan, on the throne and went north to travel through Russia to put his case to the Congress of Berlin. As General Kaufmann did not allow him to cross the Amu River, Sher Ali had no opportunity to test European sincerity and died of a broken heart in northern Afghanistan (21 February 1879). His son, fearful of Russian designs because they maintained that the Hindu Kush mountain range in central Afghanistan was the natural border of Russia's Turkistan rather than the Amu River, called for negotiations with the British, who then made him sign the Gandomak Treaty (20 May 1879). In this treaty, Britain assumed control of Afghanistan's foreign policy and allowed itself free access to the country. The British 'resident' agents who arrived in Kabul did not liaise between the two countries; they ran Afghanistan's affairs. The British political agent Cavagnari, now Sir Louis, was subsequently housed with a dozen officers and seventy-five Sepoys near the king's palace.

Not long after the arrival of the British agents, Afghan soldiers, who had not been paid for months, came to demonstrate in front of the palace and then moved 250 yards to continue their demonstration in front of the British residents, who opened fire on them. The soldiers went to their barracks and came back with their rifles; in a few hours Cavagnari and all the other British officers and troops were dead.

This act precipitated the Second Anglo-Afghan War (1879–81). The British armies occupied Kandahar and Kabul. Abdur Rahman's paternal cousin, Ayob Khan, who was in charge of Herat, headed for Kandahar. In Maiwand, together with the armies of the local tribes, he defeated the British army to the last soldier. Some 1,130 troops were missing and 250,000 rounds of ammunition and all heavy cannon fell into the hands of the Afghans. This battle, known as the Battle of Maiwand, is celebrated in the Afghan annals of battles as a sensational victory.[4] The war cost Britain £20 million and over 3,000 soldiers, in comparison with the 1839–42 war, which cost £13.8 million and about 15,000 deaths. Afghanistan suffered more, 'for its dead were the best and bravest among those who had matched their stones and knives against foreign rifles'. The war officially ended on 21 April 1881, when all British troops left Afghanistan, despite 'Queen Victoria's conviction that the Kandahari wished to retain "the benefit of Christian rule [!]"' (Fletcher 1965: 141).

Appendix 10: the Pashtunistan issue

The question of Pashtunistan can be traced back to the late nineteenth century, when Afghanistan was threatened from the north by Tsarist Russia who had approached the Amu River, and from the south and east by Imperial Britain occupying the Peshawar basin and most of Baluchestan. Amir Abdur Rahman, according to Afghan accounts, had no choice but to agree to Sir Mortimer Durand's proposal in drawing a line across the 1,700 miles border separating and dividing Pashtun tribes on India's north-western frontier. Working mainly from a map, the two sides signed the Durand Agreement in 1893 after only two weeks of surveying. However, the Amir with ambitions going far beyond his borders did not realise that such an agreement would take permanent shape.

> As Commander of the Faithful [*Amirul Mo'menin*], the Amir of Afghanistan was looked on as the spiritual head of Islam not only in his own country but also to a large extent in north-western India as well, and Abdur Rahman, though anxious to settle his south-east boundaries, was also anxious to include under his temporal as well as his spiritual authority as much as possible of the territory occupied by his Islamic followers.
>
> (Fraser-Tytler 1967: 187)

Throughout the 1880s the expansion of the British towards Afghanistan, by building roads, command posts and laying railway lines had been deeply resented by the Amir. But the British always posed as friends. The Amir writes:

> The only thing that surprised me was, that on the one hand the Indian Government said: 'We do not require any more country towards Afghanistan; we only desire to see Afghanistan a strong independent Kingdom', and on the other hand having cut a tunnel through the Khojak hills, were pushing the railway line into my country, just like pushing a knife into my vitals.
>
> (Munshi vol. 2, 1900: 159)

The Amir, in order to show his displeasure, started to help the Pashtun tribes of Wazir, Afridi, Mohmand and the Kurum Turi, who would harass the British Indian bases in their areas. He also took the District of Asmar in northeast Afghanistan and the Dir and Bajawar principalities, despite his previous undertaking not to meddle in these autonomous territory affairs. In order to stop further deterioration in the area, the British decided to demarcate theirs and the Amir's spheres of influence. Thus, according to Article Six of the Durand Agreement, a 'full and satisfactory settlement of all the principle differences of opinion which have arisen between them in regard to the frontier.'

After the partition of the sub-continent in 1947, the North West Frontier tribal belt, along with other settled Pashtun regions, was passed on to the newly created Muslim state of Pakistan. The Afghans questioned the legality of such a transfer and the issue of 'Pashtunistan', the land of Pashtun, has ever since remained unresolved. For the purpose of this book, the issue of Pashtunistan requires the clarification of the following points:

1   Why was the Durand Line Agreement signed?
2   Did the British drawing of this line incorporate all the tribes?
3   Could the 1947 partition legally pass these lands and their people to a 'Successor state'?
4   What are the claims of Afghanistan and Pakistan over this area?

1. Why was the Durand Agreement signed?

Amir Abdur Rahman was of the opinion that by signing the Durand Agreement he was separating his and the British spheres of influence. Lord Curzon and his other contemporaries in British India reiterated his impression. That is why the agreement was named as a Durand 'Line' not boundary, or border. According to Afghan historians the agreement was signed under threat of war and economic blockade (Ali 1959: 140–1; Kakar 1971: 111–12; Ghobar 1982: 687–94). British historians maintain that Durand was a negotiated settlement, pointing to the Amir's own writings. 'I requested the Viceroy to send me a map, having marked up the boundary line as they proposed' (Munshi, vol. 2. 1900: 157), but these accounts do not mention that on the same page the Amir was horrified to see,

> in the map sent to me by the Viceroy all the countries of the Wazir, New Chaman, and the railway station there, Chegheh, Bulund Khel, the whole of Mohmand, Asmar and Chatral, other countries lying in between, were marked as belonging to India. I accordingly wrote to the Viceroy a long letter of predictions about the tribes ... but my advice was not appreciated, and the Indian Government was so

anxious to get these tribes from me, that they expelled my officials [from these areas].

(ibid., pp. 157–8)

The 'long letter' explained to the British authorities, that if he were left in charge of these tribes he would bring them under his control (as he had most the Afghan tribes and ethnic groups in sixteen years of campaigns) and thus turn them into the best friends of the British, should they one day be threatened in this area. If, however, they insisted on separating them from his kingdom, they would be of no use to him or to the British. It was this advice that the British ignored. Some half a century later:

Sir William Barton, a frontier officer of long experience, wrote: 'For more than a century [the Pashtun lands east of the Durand Line] had formed part of the Afghan Kingdom to which they were united by sentiment and loyalty as well as by race ... the expectation that the British official hierarchy would wean them from a ruler who embodied Afghan or Pathan nationalism was based upon the flimsiest grounds'.

(Fletcher 1965: 247)

Arnold Fletcher, commenting on the disregard to the people in the border area, writes: The 'Durand Line itself was an ethnological monstrosity, drawn with bland and lofty disregard for the bifurcation of the tribes, and even of particular villages that would – and did – result from its creation' (Fletcher 1965: 247)

The Durand Line that stretches from Pamir in north-east Afghanistan to the desert of Iran in south-west Afghanistan was not completely surveyed by Sir Mortimer Durand and his team. At best only 300 out of 1,700 miles of this border were surveyed and even there often the villagers were asked to decide which side of the border they wanted to be. If it took long to decide, the surveyors' team would go hunting, asking them to be told of their decision on their return.

2. The British drawing of this line did not incorporate all the tribes

In fact those along the line were considered autonomous and were ruled by a combination of treaties and local tribal *jirgas*. The presence of government officials was and still is minimal, often consisting of a political agent, aided by local tribal militias. These autonomous tribal areas in the nineteenth century were known as *Yaghistan* or the land of the unruly, now called *'Alaq-e-ghair*, i.e. area outside [Pakistan] government regulations. The whole of the frontier tribal area 'may be divided into two categories: (1) acephalous, egalitarian groups, living in low-production zones and (2) those with ranked society living on irrigated lands, usually within larger state systems. *Nang* ('honor') is the foremost symbol of the former society, as *qalang* ('taxes', 'rent') is of the latter' (Ahmed 1983: 8). The *Nang*, honour or acephalous tribes, despite the Durand Agreement and the disputes over it, have maintained their autonomous status to this day.[1] It is the settled Pashtun, the *Qalang* areas, where land is registered and taxes are collected which formed part of British India. These latter Pashtuns accepted the British in the nineteenth century as they have Pakistan since partition. So from a legal point of view, if the acephalous tribal areas were not incorporated into British India, how could they be passed on to Pakistan, as a successor state? Pakistan has continued more or less in the same way as the British, with the exception of reserving certain seats in the Senate and National Assembly for persons chosen by the tribes themselves and not elected as in the rest of Pakistan. Even today the Pakistan government cannot undertake any project in the *'Alaq-e-ghair'* without local consent. So the attitude of Pakistan towards these Pashtuns is not very different from that of British India. As for the tribes themselves, they have benefited from their location in the disputes between Afghanistan and Pakistan, as they had benefited from the claims of British India and the Afghan Kingdom in the nineteenth century. In the nineteenth century they drew 7.5 million pounds in annual subsidies from the British plus collecting tolls on their roads and passes, and since 1947 they have used their position to obtain concessions from Afghan governments and have been engaging in contrabands on both sides of the border.

3. Could partition of British India legally pass on these tribes to the successor state of Pakistan?

An Afghan diplomat and former president of the UN General Assembly, Abdur Rahman Pazhwak, in his book *Pashtunistan, The Khyber Pass as the Focus of the New State of Pakhtunistan*, writes that such succession is 'legally unacceptable' and that Pakistan could not legally inherit any of the British controlled Pashtun territory between the river Indus and the Durand Line:

> (a) The *ipso facto* incorporation of the territories concerned in the State of Pakistan would constitute a novation which as such has no basis in law. (b) The theory of 'State Succession', in itself very debatable, could not of its very nature bring about the desired result ... disputed territories were not, up to the time of British leaving India, constituted as 'state-like' territories. Some were [*qalang*] administered territories while others were judicially independent [*nang*] tribal areas, neither formed an integral or definite part of ... British State, the Indian State, or Pakistani State.
>
> (Pazhwak 1953: 147)

It is an accepted principle of international law 'that in case of total annexation or of fusion of States, the treaties and agreements of these States which have disappeared [e.g. British Indian state], themselves disappear in principle' (Pazhwak 1953: 148). Other international lawyers also support the illegitimacy of the 'succession state'.

Brazilian statesman Professor Accioly, in his treatise on international law points out that a '...new State constitutes a new personality and it is not with it that such treaties or agreements were contracted'. Another such lawyer, Anzilotti, writes, 'International treaties are contracted *intuitu personae* and are not transferable in law. The extinction of one of the contracting parties causes the extinction of bilateral treaties'. Professor Francois of the academy of international law at the Hague declares, 'the rights and obligations flowing from treaties do not in general pass to the successor state ... To infer this continuity in the will of the successor state is to misconceive the essential principles of all succession'. Professor Cavaglieri 'admits in principle that in the case of the disappearance of a pre-existing state, its obligation and rights disappear with it and that in cases of dismemberment, the newly constituted states negotiate and conclude their treaties freely'.[2]

How then could the Pashtun territories east of the Durand Line, both settled and tribal, become part of Pakistan? To answer this question we have to turn to our final point:

4. What constitutes the claim over this territory and its people by the two disputing countries, Afghanistan and Pakistan?

Afghanistan's claim is apparent from its long association with the area on historical, linguistic, genealogical, and cultural lines. To Pakistan, the Pashtun area, as claimed by Afghanistan, comprises about half its territory and one eighth of its population. Therefore, whatever the legal arguments, Pakistan has never seriously entertained abandoning control of this area. In 1947 the British before leaving proposed a plebiscite to give the people of the sub-continent an opportunity to opt for either a Hindu or a Muslim state. 'To this the Afghan Government promptly protested, asking that two additional choices be offered in the North West Frontier Province [NWFP] – union with Afghanistan or the establishment of a separate Pushtoon nation. Their request brought curt refusal; and a second request was met with silence' (Fletcher 1965: 249). Being Muslims the Pashtuns naturally voted (289,244 votes) for union with Muslim Pakistan and only (2,074 votes) for union with India. As only a fraction of those entitled cast their votes, the result of this plebiscite was used by successive Afghan governments to argue its invalidity.

Two years after partition the Afridi tribesmen in a *Loya Jirga* declared their independence. Their proclamation in part reads:

> We of the national assembly of Pakhtunistan having formed the first nucleus of a free and independent Muslim government ... support the freedom loving Pakhtuns ... which will not only benefit Pukhtunistan (from Chitral to Baluchestan and from Khyber and Bolan to the banks of the Indus) but will also fulfil its obligation to the cause of progress and world peace.[3]
>
> (Islah, 12 April 1949)

In the years following partition many such meetings were held and declarations announced. The press and radio propaganda war between the two countries in the 1950s and early 1960s reached frenzy pitch, leading to the closure of the border and the port of Karachi three times to Afghan import and export (1952, 1955 and 1961–63). Pakistan's embassy and its consulates were attacked by government-orchestrated demonstrators in Afghanistan, with Pakistan replying in kind.

The dispute with Pakistan in time took on a regional dimension. Pakistan's enemy, India signed an 'eternal friendship' treaty with Afghanistan in 1950 also acknowledging like Kabul, 'Pashtunistan Days' despite Pakistan's protests. Soviet leaders too, taking advantage of the dispute, in 1955 loaned $100 million to the Afghans at 2 per cent interest rate repayable over thirty years, typical of Cold War loans, and also provided a route through their territory for Afghan goods to the outside world as an alternative to Pakistan. They also sided with Afghanistan, asking for a plebiscite to test the will of the Pashtuns to the east of the Durand Line and thus began to draw Afghanistan closer to itself.

The closure of the border with Pakistan for over two years (1961–63) had immediate repercussions for the perishable seasonal Afghan fresh and dry fruit exported to Pakistan and India, two important traditional markets. With the usual land route closed, Daoud's government decided to airlift the seasonal grapes to India. The Soviets also intervened to replace Pakistan as a market for the Afghan fruit trade. Thus from 1961 to 1962 five Afghan planes airlifted 1,500 tonnes of grapes to India and thirteen Soviet aircraft airlifted 7,250 tonnes to the Soviet Union. From 1962 to 1963 the Afghan tonnage to India almost doubled (2,797 tonnes) with the Russians airlifting 11,000 tonnes. But unlike Afghan trade with India, the Soviet increased tonnage did not match the price they paid. 'So contrary to the situation in 1961–62 when the Afghan gained a $1,468,000 credit from the Soviet Union, only $1,430,000 resulted during 1962–63 airlift for more tonnage' (Dupree 1980: 552). The Russians argued that the reduced price was as a result of 'damaged goods', though it was clear to the Afghans that 4,000 out of 11,000 tonnes could not be put down to 'damaged goods'. However, despite the relative success of the airlift to India and Russia, the planes, on grounds of cost and convenience were unlikely in the long run to replace some 100 trucks, that used to transport daily several thousand tonnes by road to the sub-continent. Since dry and fresh fruit used to count as important export items, the government realised that if the border were to remain closed, soon Afghanistan would not be able to earn enough to repay its dollar loans from the Soviets and others.

Appendix 11: the initial months of communists in power

1978

17 April: Assassination of Parcham ideologue, Mir Akbar Khyber
25–26 April: Arrest of Taraki, Karmal and others by Daoud
27 April: Daoud killed in a coup organised by the Khalq group
30 April: Communist government, its president and revolutionary council announced
May–June: Armed tribal rebellion in Kunar and Nuristan
Early July: Karmal and other Parchamis posted abroad
8 July: Amin appointed secretary to the central committee and deputy prime minister
12 July: Decree No. 6 on land reform announced
15 August: Colonel Abdul Qader, defence minister, arrested on coup charges
19 August: Taraki assumes the duties of the minister of defence
23 August: Arrests of some Parchamis for the Eid conspiracy
6 September: Karmal and others posted abroad were dismissed and summoned to Kabul
19 October: New red flag was introduced in place of the tricolour
27 November: Karmal and his Parchamis expelled from the PDPA
30 November: Official party organ *De Saur Inqilab* April revolution printed
5 December: Taraki and Brezhnev signed treaty of friendship and good neighbourliness

1979

16 January: Taraki's publicised 62nd birthday
14 February: US ambassador kidnapped by *Setam* members and killed in rescue attempt
19 March: Fighting in Herat and Paktia, killing of Soviet and communist officials
27 March: Hafizullah Amin appointed prime minister

5 April: Soviet military delegation headed by Gen. Epishev, head of political directorate of Soviet army and navy, arrived in Kabul
23 June: Demonstrations in Kabul suppressed by the army
25 June: Nineteen officers and men killed in Herat army mutiny
5 August: Army mutiny in Bala Hissar in Kabul
10 September: Taraki on return from non-aligned conference in Cuba met with Soviet leaders in Moscow
14 September: In a conspiracy to kill Amin, Taraki is wounded
17 September: Kabul Radio announces Amin as chairman of the revolutionary council
9 October: Taraki's death (who was smothered) is announced
14–15 October: Further Army mutiny in Kabul
8 November: Soviet ambassador Puzanov involved in conspiracy to kill Amin leaves for Moscow
2 December: Lieutenant General V.S. Paputin first head of the Soviet interior ministry, arrives in Kabul and meets with Amin
4 December: Soviet leadership sends Amin cordial messages on the anniversary of Afghan-Soviet friendship treaty
Early December: 2,500 Soviet strike forces land at Bagram airbase
24–25 December: Soviet transport planes begin landing with increased frequency, bringing troops and equipment
27 December: 19.15 local time, Soviet troops seize ministry of interior, neutralise Kabul, garrison Afghan troops and immobilise vehicles
20.15 Karmal's statement from Termez in Uzbekistan on Kabul Radio frequencies issued on change in leadership
21.00 Kabul Radio station hitherto guarded by Afghan troops attacked by Soviet forces
21.45 Soviet News Agency Tass carries text of Karmal's radio announcement
21.53 Moscow Radio, Home Service transmits the text of Karmal announcement
22.30 Moscow Radio Serbo-Croat service announces Amin's liquidation
23.10 Kabul Radio, list of new revolutionary council members, headed by Karmal. An announcement that the 'revolutionary tribunal' has executed Amin
28 December: 02.40 Karmal government requests urgent political and military assistance from the USSR on treaty of friendship basis. Later that day Karmal is 'unanimously' elected as secretary general of the central committee of PDPA.

Appendix 12: Mujahideen resistance parties

A. Islamist

1. *Hezb-i-Islami Hekmatyar.* Gulbodin Hekmatyar, a Pashtun Kharoti from a sub-tribe of the Ghilzai, heads *Hezb-i-Islami*, or the Party of Islam. Hekmatyar is a charismatic leader known among the resistance as a 'fire brand'. His academic history is marred by expulsion and changes between schools in his hometown of Imamsahib, in Kundoz province and Kabul. Hekmatyar was expelled from *Harbi Showanzai* (military school) in Kabul, but after completing high school he went to Kabul University and completed his first year in the engineering faculty. He was active in Kabul University student union affairs, participated in the student union congress of 1970 and was an elected member of student union executive council (1971–72). The young Hekmatyar was charged with the murder of a student and imprisoned (1972–73). The Daoud government also accused him of a coup attempt in 1974 and he escaped to Peshawar 1975. His party's followers were mainly Pashtuns, but also included minorities such as Tajiks, Uzbeks, Hazarahs and Turkmen as its field commanders and fighters. These, however, were with Hekmatyar not out of conviction, as it turned out later, but because they received better arms and ammunition by joining his Hezb. Hekmatyar was very close to Pakistan's inter service intelligence (ISI) and throughout the Soviet occupation received the lion's share of all outside aid, both in cash and arms.

2. *Hezb-i-Islami Khalis.* This faction of Hezb headed by Muhammad Yonus Khales, who broke away from Hekmatyar in 1979; the two Hezb parties became known as Hezb Hekmatyar and Hezb Khalis. Hezb Khalis is a smaller party organised on tribal and Islamic lines. Muhammad Yonus Khalis belongs to the Khogyani tribe of Nangarhar and nearly all his party members and followers were Pashtuns. He was a graduate of the traditional madrassa and for some years worked on the ministry of justice's monthly magazine. He was also a contributor to *Gahiz* newspaper in the 1960s. Khalis, unlike Hekmatyar, had good relations with both moderate and Islamist parties. Khalis was also the first leader to travel inside Afghanistan to meet with his fighters. Such courage and close contact with his followers brought him more support.

3. Abdur Rasul Sayyaf, a graduate of Abu Hanifa Madrassa in his hometown of Paghman (1963), heads *Itehad-e-Islami*, or Unity of Islam. On his mother's side Sayyaf belongs to the Kharoti tribe of Ghilzai. He entered the Faculty of Shari'ah at Kabul University for a four-year degree course and then went to Al-Azhar University in Cairo, completing his MA in 1972. He then taught at the Faculty of Shari'ah but was arrested in 1974 and spent more than five years in prison. His co-tribesman, Khalqi leader Hafizullah Amin, spared his life and, when Babrak Karmal released Sayyaf like other prisoners in the general amnesty of 1980, he went to Pakistan and formed his own party. His following, like that of Khalis, is almost entirely Pashtun. He speaks good Arabic and, because of his contact with Saudis and other wealthy Arabs, receives far more financial and military aid than the size of his party warranted. He put his financial resources to good use by 'purchasing' commanders and fighters from other parties as well as recruiting new ones.

4. Burhanuddin Rabbani, a descendant of the Yephtalite or White Huns Tajik from Badakhshan province, heads *Jam'iat Islami*, or the Islamic Association. Rabbani, several years senior to Sayyaf, also attended the Abu Hanifa Madrassa in Paghman. Like Sayyaf, he entered the Faculty of Shari'ah at Kabul University and taught there after graduation from 1963–66. In 1968 he got his MA from Al-Azhar. The resistance leadership regards Rabbani as an almost reluctant member of the Islamic movement since its beginning in 1957. Rabbani was appointed as the second leader of the Mujahideen to take in turn the presidency of Afghanistan for four months in July 1992, but he unilaterally renewed his term of office four times and held the post for a total of forty months, until he was overthrown by the Taleban in September 1996. The Jam'iat Party is predominantly Tajik, though some idealistic Pashtuns who didn't believe in ethnic division also joined it during Soviet occupation. But when the Jam'iat's, and its leaders Rabbani and Masoud's, ethnic activities became apparent during Rabbani's overly-extended presidency, nearly all these Pashtun fighters abandoned him.

B. Moderate parties

1. Muhammad Nabi Muhammadi headed *Harakat-i-Inqilab-i-Islami*, or the Revolutionary Islamic Movement, from Logar province (south of Kabul). Muhammadi, an Ahmadzai Ghilzai, was madrassa educated and a well-known Islamic scholar. He was a member of the *Wolesi Jirga* (lower house of parliament) in the 1960s and a strong opponent of the communist MPs. Muhammadi left for Pakistan in 1978 and, after gathering a small group of like-minded madrassa educated scholars, he founded the party and soon turned it into the largest resistance group during the Soviet occupation. Muhammadi's followers were mainly Pashtuns from amongst the mosques and madrasses. The majority of Taleban also belonged to this

party. But Muhammadi's party was the least organised within the resistance and commanders exercised a great deal of autonomy. Muhammadi had good relations with all parties and their leaders; this was marred when his party became involved in long and bloody wars over opium poppies in Helmand province with Hekmatyar and Sayyaf followers. He died of natural causes in May 2002.

2. *Jabh-i-Nejat Meli*, or the National Liberation Front (NLF), led by Sebghatullah Mujadedi. He was one of two Sufis among the resistance leadership and belongs to the Naqshbandi order. The Mujadedi family has been important in the twentieth century both for sanctioning kings and opposing them. The communists, upon coming to power in 1978, killed most members of this family. Daoud imprisoned Sebghatullah, also know as *Hazrat*, for his opposition to the Khruschev and Bulganin visit to Afghanistan in 1955. He spoke ardently against Russian influence in Afghanistan. He has an MA in Islamic law and jurisprudence from Al-Azhar in Cairo (1953) and was a lecturer at Kabul University. Since his exile in Pakistan, like Rabbani and Sayyaf, he too has assumed the title of 'professor'; none of these three were actually professors while teaching at Kabul University. Mujadedi's *murids*, or spiritual followers, were overwhelmingly Pashtuns from the South and East. Mujadedi was not liked by Pakistani authorities and as a result received the smallest share of aid during the occupation. He, like Gailani (see below), sold truckloads of weapons in the arms markets of Pakistan. Both argued that they had followers to pay and rent for the many houses their party officials occupied in Peshawar; few accepted this justification of selling arms that were supposed to be used against the Soviet occupying forces. After the fall of the communist government, the resistance leaders in Pakistan, according to an agreement amongst them, appointed Mujadedi as the first resistance president in Kabul for two months (April and May 1992). After two short months in office, he was reluctant to vacate but an ultimatum from Masoud, Sayyaf and Hekmatyar persuaded him to step down.

3. *Mahaz-i-Meli Islami Afghanistan*, or the National Islamic Front of Afghanistan (NIFA), headed by another Sufi leader, Sayed Ahmad Gailani, who claims to be the descendant of Sayed Qader Gailan in Iraq. The Soviet 40th Army commander in Afghanistan, General Gromov, in his book *The Red Army*, states that Gailani's father, Sayed Hassan Gailani, was married to a Martha Richter, the daughter of a German police officer, thus casting doubt on his spiritual ancestry and giving the impression that his father, also known as *Naqib Saheb*, may have been planted amongst the eastern Pashtuns. Gailani had more *murids* than Mujadedi and these too were nearly all Pashtuns from the south and east of Afghanistan. These two spiritual parties also provided an opportunity for most educated Afghans, who did not want to be identified with either their ethnic group/region or the 'fundamentalists', to participate in the *jihad* against the Soviets.

C. Shi'ah parties

1. The above seven parties were known as the 'Peshawar Seven' and so Iran, in competition with both Pakistan and the Sunni majority in Afghanistan, formed eight parties from the country's 9 per cent Shi'ah, naming them mostly after their own parties such as *Pasadena, Hizbullah, Feda'ian, Mustaz'fin, Naser*, etc. Soon after the collapse of the communist government in Kabul these eight parties, some with only a few members, were put together in Tehran under one name: *Hezb-i-Wahdat*, or Party of Unity. The most important of the eight was called *Sazman Naser Islami*, or the Organisation of Islamic Victory; the leader of this party headed the new Wahdat party. Wahdat membership was not just 100 per cent confined to Shi'ah Hazarah, but to those Hazarah who were fanatically pro-Iran. Since Hazarajat in central Afghanistan could not be physically joined to Iran, they advocated federalism and complete autonomy from the centre in Kabul. They also overstated their population, claiming to be 23 per cent of the country's total population. Only Mujadedi, who was looking for allies outside the moderates, agreed to grant them a 23 per cent share in future governments. Gailani never made his opposition clear to this Wahdat demand, but all the other Peshawar parties rejected it.

2. Sheikh Asef Mohseni, a Qizelbash Shi'ah from Kandahar, headed *Harakat-e-Islami Afghanistan*, or Islamic Movement of Afghanistan. Educated in Najaf, Iraq, he was the only Afghan calling himself 'Ayatollah', the highest Shi'ah clergy authority. While much smaller in comparison to Naser, the men in its ranks were more educated than those in Naser. At first *Harakat-e-Islami Afghanistan* was more of an Afghan nationalist party than one just adhering to the Iranian line; it was for this reason that Mohseni and his party were expelled from Tehran during the last years of the Soviet occupation. However, after the Soviets left Afghanistan, Iran's aid in arms and finance to Mohseni's group resumed.

3. Sayed Beheshti, educated in Shi'ah schools in Iran and Iraq, headed *Shorai Enqelabe Etefaqe Afghanistan*, or United Revolutionary Council of Afghanistan. He was an Afghan nationalist and his party was in line with those of Peshawar. For this reason, its members were respected and moved freely to all parts of Afghanistan and through the Pashtun areas to Pakistan. However, this was not to the liking of the pro-Iranian Naser and its leader Abdul Ali Mazari. In the continuous fighting that raged in most parts of Hazarajat, many of Beheshti's followers were either killed or made to join Naser. The party had to move its headquarters to Quetta in Baluchestan, where two other smaller Shi'ah groups followed. After the fall of communists, Naser did not allow *Shorai Etefaq* and other Iran-based groups to return or play any role in Hazarajat.

Appendix 13: Geneva negotiations

The Geneva Talks that started on 15 June 1982 were concluded after twelve 'proximity' or 'indirect' rounds of talks on 7 September 1987. The talks took one and a half years of shuttle diplomacy by the United Nations to set up. The urgency and the seriousness of the situation that called for these talks and had involved the UN from the beginning are described by an under secretary-general of the UN for political affairs as follows:

> The invasion of Afghanistan sent shock waves through the chambers and corridors of the United Nations ... An emergency session of the General Assembly was then convened on January 14 [1980]. With only a few exceptions, the more than seventy delegations that spoke condemned the invasion as a blatant violation of the UN Charter and of International law. A resolution 'strongly deploring' the invasion and calling for the immediate, unconditional and total withdrawal of the 'foreign troops' – a euphemism that was to be relentlessly ridiculed by the press – was adopted on January 14, 1980, by a vote of 104 to 8 with 18 abstentions.
>
> (Cordovez and Harrison 1995: 73–4)

Background to the talks

The UN sponsored talks were throughout conducted between the governments of Pakistan and Afghanistan. Pakistan was the second-best choice for the Soviets. It had turned to a frontline state, after the Soviet invasion of Afghanistan. Pakistan was a centre for the Mujahideen resistance groups and, also by then, home to over one million refugees (this figure grew to three million in Pakistan alone by the end of the Soviet occupation). Pakistan, although never officially admitted, was the conduit of arms to the resistance, but the Soviets never ignored its role. The Soviets also knew that an agreement reached with Pakistan might be acceptable to the resistance.

Through behind-the-scene activities between the two superpowers and other regional states, the Kabul communists were agreed on, as another party to the talks for similar reasons. From the Soviet point of view, Kabul was the 'legitimate' government of the people of Afghanistan. From the Western [the USA, Europe, Islamic and the Free World] viewpoint, the first and most urgent situation that needed to be dealt with was the invasion by the Red Army. Once the Russians had left Afghanistan, they were all convinced the communist government in Kabul would fall.

From the resistance point of view, any talk with the Kabul government implied its recognition. 'The Geneva dialogue is giving an air of legitimacy to the unrepresentative puppet regime of Kabul and providing justification for prolonging the stay of the Red Army in Afghanistan' (editorial, *Mujahideen Monthly*, p. 5, March–April 1987). Kabul on the other hand also refused to talk to the resistance, incessantly calling them 'bands of thieves', 'counter-revolutionaries', 'puppets of Pakistan and western imperialism'. The official position of the resistance was to reject the Geneva Talks and not to be held by it, as they were not a party to the negotiation. The interim Prime Minister, Rasul Sayyaf's party announcement that 'talks have started in Geneva, no one has consulted the resistance's and neither would these talks be acceptable to the Mujahideen' spoke for them all (Hiwad 16 June 1982). Yet they did nothing to stop Pakistan negotiating on their behalf. The resistance official line was that they were ready to talk to the Soviets, who had invaded the country and were the enemy they were fighting, but not the Kabul 'installed' government.

The mechanism for the talks

There were a multiplicity of views and reservations about the Geneva Processes. The two parties to the talks, the Kabul government headed by Babrak Karmal and the Pakistan government of General Zia-ul Haq, were not on the best of terms. The UN representative, Diego Cordovez, in view of the varied expectations suggested a formula.

> I suggested holding 'proximity talks'-a format in which the interlocutors never meet face to face-aimed at concluding a 'comprehensive settlement' that would contain a set of interrelated provisions designed to resolve all the issues involved. I proposed that the talks be held in the sedate environment of Geneva.
> (Cordovez and Harrison 1995: 81)

The Pakistan foreign minister preferred to call them 'indirect talks', which was then adopted. The delegates in all the twelve rounds of 'indirect talks' met at the UN Centre, *Palais des Nations*, in Geneva, with one delegate coming in the morning and another in the afternoon. Later in the process, in order to 'speed up' the talks process, the delegates used to sit in different rooms in the same building, with the UN representative shuttling between them. The UN officials exercised great care so that the two delegates never ran into one another during the talks. In between as well as before starting the talks, the UN representative undertook extensive travels to the region and to the capitals of countries involved. These talks, because of the length of time and the reluctance of the Soviet Union to commit itself to a realistic timetable for withdrawal, often left the impression that they were not going anywhere.

Throughout the six years United Nation kept Iran, the United States, Soviet Union and Saudi Arabia informed of the progress of the talks. By the end of the Soviet occupation some two million refugees had taken shelter in Iran. Though invited to be party to these talks, Iran refused and made its participation conditional on the Afghan resistance being made a party to the talks. This as Iran knew was unacceptable to the Soviets and the Kabul government. But Iran, despite the Ayatollah's rhetoric in Tehran, was never really interested in playing an important part in these talks. Firstly, it had its own war with Iraq to cope with. Secondly, Iran needed arms from the Soviet Union, and so was not going to jeopardise that source at such a crucial time by making an issue of the Afghan resistance participation in the talks. Thirdly, because of the Islamic credentials of the regime in Tehran, neither Iran nor the Soviet Union was ever open about these covert politico-economic relationships. The Soviets on the other hand needed Iran's petro-dollars and covert neutrality. That is why time and again Soviet officials, when criticised by Iran, would say, 'Iran is an Islamic country, we understand how they feel'.

As for keeping the Soviet Union informed, it had its own man at the talks and knew more about what was going on than even the parties to the talks. Cordovez explains.

> An important event had taken place in New York a few days before I left for Geneva. Vladimir Shustov, one of the ambassadors at the Soviet mission ... gave me a paper with a name hand-written on it: Stanislav P. Gavrilov. Shustov told me that Gavrilov would be at Geneva 'to maintain liaison' with me. Gavrilov, he added, was an expert on the region and the highest-ranking diplomat in Kabul. Since the ambassador in Kabul was a party man, 'we consider [Gavrilov] our ambassador and he will report this assignment directly to Gromyko', said Shustov with institutional pride ... I met Gavrilov ... on the eve of the talks. I thus started a formal working relationship with the Soviet Government ... it involved an implicit understanding not to tell the Afghans what we had discussed, very often not even the fact that we have met.
>
> (Cordovez and Harrison 1995: 85)

The United States through its mission at Geneva and at the UN was continuously kept informed; although wanting to punish the Soviet Union for its role in the Vietnam War it gave the impression of not wishing to see the war end too soon. Cordovez says, Ambassador George Sherman, one of the US permanent representatives to the UN 'officially told me that while supporting a negotiated solution, the United States was not, and did not wish to be, involved in any diplomatic efforts to solve the conflict'.

> Upon my arrival in Geneva, I was invited for lunch by Ambassador Herman Swaebe, a close friend of President Reagan ... I told Swaebe that President Reagan's name would be associated with a Soviet withdrawal no matter what and that the U.S. should therefore, support my efforts. He said he would talk with the President at Christmas.
> (Cordovez and Harrison: 85)

The United States, once convinced that the Soviets were not in hurry to leave, changed its stand and also at the end of the Geneva process, together with the USSR became one of the two international guarantors of the Accord.

The agenda for negotiation

The 'package' that the UN put together for the talks included the withdrawal of Soviet forces; the non-interference in one another's (Pakistan/Afghanistan's) internal affairs from the date of the agreement; the guarantee of Afghanistan's sovereignty and non-aligned status as before; the return of the refugees and the international guarantees of the agreement. The question of 'interference' took a long time to resolve. The Kabul government and the Soviets accused Pakistan and the West of arming and training guerrillas for operations against the Kabul forces. Pakistan pointed to the invasion as the most blatant form of interference. Then, there was the question of symmetry – both superpowers, deciding to render aid to their Afghan side, comparable to that of the other. However, by 1987 the Soviet leaders repeatedly declared that 'with or without Geneva their troops were going to leave'. It was then possible for both superpowers to put their weight behind the Geneva talks and concurrently sign the Accord and to stand as international guarantors of the Accord. Thus the four Accords below that were signed in Geneva on 14 April 1988 contained all the above points:

> (1) Bilateral Agreement between the Republic of Afghanistan and the Islamic Republic of Pakistan on the Principle of Mutual Relations, in Particular on non-interference and non-intervention. (2) Declaration of International Guarantees. (3) Bilateral Agreement between the Republic of Afghanistan and the Islamic Republic of Pakistan on the Voluntary Return of Refugees. (4) Agreement on the Interrelationships for the Settlement of the Situation Relating to Afghanistan.

Appendix 14: Russian designs on Afghanistan

Year	Ruler	Russian/Soviet involvement
1682–1725	Peter the Great	Advocates Russian territorial expansion in Central Asia
1837	Durrani in Herat and Kabul	Russian backed Iranian attack on Herat
1839	Khan of Khiva	Russian manifesto justifying Khiva's occupation
1864	Prince Gorchakov	Justifies expansion into 'half-savage wandering tribes'
1869	Khan of Bokhara	This Central Asian Khannet turned into a Tsarist vassal
1878	Amir Sher Ali	Russian diplomatic mission to Kabul accepted
1885	Amir Abdur Rahman	Russian occupation of Afghan Punjdeh
1889	Amir Abdur Rahman	Russia and Britain agree not to occupy Afghan lands
1896	Amir Abdur Rahman	Russia and Britain signed comprehensive border settlement
1907	Amir Habibullah	Rejected St Petersburg convention
1919	Amir Amanullah	Diplomatic relation with USSR established
1921	Amir Amanullah	Treaty of friendship with the USSR signed
1929	Amir Amanullah deposed	Russian abortive attempt to restore him to power
1933	Nader Shah	Renewed 1921 treaty with Soviet Union
1952	Zaher Shah	Soviet objects to foreigners in northern Afghanistan
1955	Zaher Shah	Russian $100m credit aid
1956	Zaher Shah	$32m. Russian concessionary loan for weapon purchase
1977	Zaher Shah	Daoud's walk-out from the Kremlin
1978	Mohammad Daoud	Russian aid expanded to $1,265 m
1978	Nur Mohammad Taraki	Communist coup and takeover
1979	Hafizullah Amin	Russian invade Afghanistan and bring in Karmal
1989	Najibullah	Russian troops withdraw from Afghanistan
1992	Mujhideen	Internal war between groups for power. Russia supporting the Northern Alliance
1996	Taleban	Controlling 95 per cent of Afghanistan. Russia's support of opposition intensifies
2001	Karzai	Came to power with American aid. Taleban defeat also Russia's objective

Notes

Introduction

1 Pashtun eight million or 52 per cent; Tajik three million or 19.8 per cent; Hazarah and Uzbek each 1.3 million or 8.6 per cent; Char Aimaq 450,000 or 3 per cent; Turkmen 300,000 or 2 per cent; Nuristani 200,000 or 1.9 per cent; Baluch 130,000 or 0.8 per cent; Afshar/Qizelbash 30,000 or 0.2 per cent (Franz 1981: 106). The remaining 2.1 per cent, according to Jang Newspaper Group, 26 November 2001, quoting (Brook 1981: 377) are other smaller groups.

2 According to partial government census in 1977–78, the population of Afghanistan was estimated at sixteen million, with 3 per cent growth (Smith *et al.* 1973: 59; Nyrope and Seekins (1986: 85–7). Louis Dupree using the *Kabul Times Annual 1967* adds together linguistic and ethnic groups to arrive at the population of the country (1980: 57–64). UNIDATA, going by languages in Tajik-dominated provinces has given yet different figures for people who speak languages other than Dari/Farsi.

3 The Afghan writer Sa'duddin Shpoon's family migrated from Khogiani (eastern Afghanistan) to Kundoz (north-east). In his novel *Shintaghai* or Blue-tit, Shpoon quotes his father, 'our tribal-land is the abode of pashtunwali, we can not sleep in our bus there, or else we would be mocked' (Shpoon 1999: 26). The Tappers also found that the immigrant Pashtuns in the north, even after a century, though they do not admit it, still uphold the major requirements of pashtunwali.

4 A recent timely survey of Afghanistan's population 'over a period of six years from 1991 to 1996', in all the districts of Afghan provinces, by WAKFA, concentrating on: ethnic identity and language, puts the population of Pashtuns at 62.73 per cent.

5 The second word in the stone inscription by Shapur I at Naqsh-e-Rustam 'Gundifer Agban Rismund' according to Olaf Caroe, cannot be anything but 'Afghan' (Caroe 1959: 79–80). Also the Chinese traveller Hsuan Tsang travelling in the region in the seventh century refers to 'A-p'o'Kien' as the resident of the Suliman Mountains [a Pashtun region] (Gregorian 1969: 29). The Moroccan traveller, Ibn-Battuta, writes of a fierce tribe of Persians called Afghans (Fraser-Tytler 1953: 50; Caroe 1959: 136).

6 The river Amu or Oxus (known to the Greeks) forms the natural border of Afghanistan with Central Asia.

7 Attak the banks of River Indus, is historically considered as the frontier that separates Pashtuns from India.

8 There are three types of Shi'ah in Afghanistan. The Hazarah, who have Mongoloid features, lived in Afghanistan long before Chengis (Genghis) Khan entered Afghanistan in the thirteenth century. The origin of the Hazarah is

unknown, neither is it known where they picked up the *Hazaragi* version of the Farsi language nor when they became Shi'ah. They number about 1.5 million.

Because of their different physical features and religion, the Hazarahs have been mocked, like the Sikhs in India or the Irish in Britain by the rest of the population including the Shi'ah Qizelbash. Hazarahs in turn are hostile towards the rest and are resentful towards the Pashtuns: a) for being the ruling majority and b) because Pashtun nomad or *kochi* compete with them for the '*alafcher*', grazing area.

The second group of Shi'ah, the Qizelbash (Red Hat) are Iranian Shi'ah who came with Nader Shah (d.1747) and later with the first Afghan king, Ahmad Shah Durrani, to serve in the subsequent Afghan armies and governments as clerks, teachers and commissioners. The Qizelbash number about 140,000. The third group, the Isma'ilia, the followers of the Agha Khan, number about 100,000.

The Shi'ah, despite their long residence in Afghanistan, have not been particularly loyal to the Afghan state. The Qizelbash, for example, collaborated with the British invading forces in the 1839 war showing them how to enter the city of Kabul; the Hazarahs joined the British forces in the 1879 war fighting against other Afghans. During the Soviet occupation a Hazarah Prime Minister and other influential Hazarah officials made sure the Hazarahs did not enter the war with the Russians. The Russians in turn did not drop a single bomb nor lay any mines in their area. After the rise of the Taleban, Qizelbash refugee women in the USA with the help of Feminine Majority Movement and some Hollywood actors and actresses, have mounted propaganda campaigns to denounce the Taleban. After the fall of Taleban (October 2001) the US special forces have recruited Hazrahs to help them locate members of the Taleban and Al Qaidah.

9 The largest and most significant re-capture was from the Uzbek and Shi'ah pro-Iran groups in the northern provinces, which fell in to the hands of the Taleban in September 1998. A BBC correspondent was the first to be allowed in to Mazar. He reported that 'Mazar the capital of the north is quiet but tense. Local people are relieved that by the coming of the Taleban, factional fighting [amongst Uzbek, Shi'ah and Tajik] and insecurity would end, though they are nervous about the implementation of the strict Shari'ah Islamic code by the Taleban'. The reporter, William Reeves, also said that reports of mass killings were exaggerated and that people in Mazar told him 500–800 were killed in the battle for the city of Mazar (BBC World Service: 10 December 1998).

10 Afghanistan, though devoutly Muslim, never produced a *khalifa*. The only time when this became likely was during the reign of King Amanullah (1919–29). The young Amanullah, achieving Afghan independence in the years preceding the abolition of the last *khalifa* in Turkey, was present at an opportune time, but with his overthrow the hope for an Afghan *khalifa* also disappeared.

1 Formation of the Afghan state: 1747–72

1 These imperial competitions and conquests in recorded history extend from Achaemenid, Bactrian, Kushan, Sasanid, Umayad and Abasids to Ghaznawids, Mongol, Timurid, Safavid and Moghul. Pashtun tribes fought with Timur against the Pashtun-supported Delhi Sultanate. They fought with Babur when his Moghuls overthrew the Lodi Pashtun rulers of Delhi. They fought with Nadir Shah Afshar when he defeated the Ghilzai Pashtun rulers of Iran and Kandahar. Pashtuns were also caught between Moghul and Safavid competition in the sixteenth and seventeenth centuries, and in the nineteenth century's 'great game' played by Britain and Russia 'for which Afghanistan and

the Pashtun were the main arena' (Hager 1983: 93). In the twentieth century they were caught between the USA and the USSR, culminating in the Soviet invasion of the 1980s.
2 The Abdali and Ghilzai tribal confederacy and the eastern Pashtun tribal confederacy, as in the war against the Moghuls in the sixteenth century, acted like other tribal confederacies such as the Zulu or early Hausa-Fulani tribes in Africa and the Mongol hordes of Chengis (Genghis) Khan and his descendants in the thirteenth century.
3 Some Ghilzai are settled in western Iran and others amongst the Uzbeks in Central Asia. However, it is not clear whether they had gone to Central Asia or Iran of their own accord or were exiled by the Persians and Shabanid Uzbeks (Elphinstone 1969: 436).
4 Babur conquered Kabul in 1504 and wanted to open up the Kuram and Zazi route as an alternative to the Khyber Pass, which from time immemorial has been costly for all emperors as they had to pay high tolls to the resident Pashtun tribes. However, this Central Asian ruler, from the Ferghana valley, despite transferring his capital to Delhi and ruling from there, wished to be buried in Kabul. His battered grave and the surrounding garden still exist in central Kabul. For details of the Afghan country and its people see Babur's own autobiography, Tuzek-e-Baburi, trans. Beveridge, A.S. *The Babur Nama*, London, 1922.
5 The movement that started in Hashtnagar (NWFP) initially had the support of the Khalil, Afridis and Oraksais. It reached its height during the lifetime of Bayazid's two sons, Sheikh Umer (died 1591) and Jalal-uddin (died 1599/1600). In 1583 Moghul forces suffered a major military defeat in a battle with the Yosufzai. In 1586–87 the Mohmand under Jalal-uddin repeatedly attacked Peshawar. In the period 1593–94 the Roshanis killed the governor of Kabul province. Just before his death, Jalal-uddin attacked Moghul forces in Ghazni. In 1611 Sheikh Umer's son, Ahdad, attempted to take over the city of Kabul from Moghul rule. Ahdad died fourteen years later battling Moghuls in the Tira district. Between 1626–28 Ahdad's son Abdul Qadir fought Moghuls in Khyber and Peshawar with an army of local tribes, Khalil, Mohmand, Yosufzai and Khattak (Aslanov 1981: 29–31; Raverty 1888: 45–6; Spain 1985: 32–4).
6 Mohammad Waliullah, Tarikh-e-Farrukhabad, BM.OR.1718. For a brief account of Bangesh history and genealogy also see Gommans 1995: 171–4.
7 Mahmud Ghaznawi's (AD 998) mother was a Tukhi from Zabul province. Tukhi is a sub-tribe of Ghilzai (*Khybari*, Dawat journal, issue 101 and 102, May–June 1999, p. 7).
8 This historic *Loya Jirga* was held thirty miles to the north of Kandahar in the village of Maanja. Representatives from other provinces (Farah, Sistan, Baluchestan, Kandahar and southwestern Afghanistan) were invited. Haji Mir Wais read the letter of the Makkan *ulema* to the *jirga*, convincing them that the Islamic world was with them. The war strategy of how to take on the 23,000 Persian troops was finalised at this meeting.
9 The main reason for Ashraf's defeat was that the Sadozai, who ruled in Heart, and the Ghilzai Sultan Hussian, who was in charge of Kandahar, not only refused to come to the aid of Ashraf but went to war against him from the east. In fact Ashraf was killed in the battle against his own Ghilzai troops from Kandahar.
10 Shir-e-Surkh or Sheik-e-Surkh is the mausoleum of an unknown holy-man two miles to the southeast of Kandahar city. The date of the coronation varies between July and October 1747. Ganda Singh says, 'there is a letter of Ahmad Shah to Muhammad Husain Afraid, dated.... 15 July 1747, in

Tazkirah-i-Anandram, which refers to his having been crowned'. Putting all accounts together, Singh (1959) and Ghubar (1944) are of the opinion that it was in October 1747.

11 Al-Afghani in *History of Afghanistan* (1938) quoting from *Tajo Tawarikh*, maintains that the change of name from Sadozai to Durrani by Ahmad Shah was in accordance with a dream of *Mian Omar Saheb of Chamkani*. Fletcher, confirming the story of the dream says, 'although the name may simply have originated from the pearl earrings that had been worn by the royal guards of Nader Shah, which Ahmad had led' (1965: 43–4).

12 For a complete contemporary account of the reign of Ahmad Shah, see *Shahnamah*, by Hafiz (Pashto text), BM. MS. OR. 4231. Judging from his style of Pashto writing, Hafiz, was probably an Afridi. He was present in the battle of Panipat. The work is in Pashto verse. Also see Ahmad Shah's biographers: Ganda Singh (1959) and Mir Gholam Mohammad Ghobar (1944). For an analysis of Ahmad Shah and the Pashtuns, see Misdaq 1997.

13 In the battle that ensued early in the morning of 13 January 1761, 60,000 (some say 95,000) Afghans faced three times their number over a battle line which was eight miles long. In the butchery that followed, some 10,000 Afghans and local Muslim forces were killed. The casualties of the Mahratta and Jat forces were much higher. Before the end of the day the enemies were defeated running in all directions.

14 The Afghans have been eastward looking for many centuries. They have been traders, merchants, settlers and rulers in the subcontinent since the tenth century. Mahmud of Ghazni, from AD 1000, on an almost annual basis, used to mount military expeditions, normally to temple cities, where vast amounts of wealth in jewellery and cash were stored for safe-keeping (Tapper 1966: 231–5). The Ghaznawids were followed in India by the Ghurids, who in turn were followed by Lodies and Suries (though not necessarily in succession). All these different Afghan ruling dynasties were accompanied by settlements, which started in the north, spreading slowly to the lowlands and helped the armies of their kinsmen at times of war. So the Pashtuns had had experience of government for a very long time and it was no surprise that in the sixteenth and seventeenth centuries, religious and nationalistic movements started in earnest for establishing a government of their own.

2 State to nation: 1773–1973

1 1818: Ata Muhammad Khan Bamizai holds Kabul in the name of the grandson of Shah Mahmud; later in 1818, Dost Muhammad Khan occupies Kabul, but crowns Timur Shah's other son Sultan Ali (1818–23): Muhammad Azam Khan deposes Sultan Ali and rules in the name of yet another of Timur Shah's sons – Shazadah Ayob; it is only in 1823 when Muhammad Azam is succeeded by his son Habibullah Khan who imprisons Shahzadah Ayob, thus ending seventy-six years of rule by the Sadozai dynasty. However, in the same year another of the Barakzai brothers, Sherdel Khan, deposes the said Habibullah in 1823; in 1824 Yar Muhammad Khan replaces him. In the same year Sultan Muhammad assumes power and continues until 1826. It is after 1826 that Dost Muhammad Khan, known amongst his brothers as 'Gorgak', the little wolf, assumes power in the first of his two terms of rule. Dost played the sectarian card, by siding with his maternal uncle's Qizelbash Shi'ah, while Sultan Muhammad took the side of the Sunni orthodoxy. The latter, after accepting the sum of 100,000 rupees from the state treasury as his annual stipend, agreed to Dost Muhammad's rule.

2 Despite struggling for power over Kabul, the Barakzai brothers had similar problems in ruling over Kandahar, Ghazni and Peshawar.

3 The British deliberately created the narrow strip of land over a mountainous area, stretching out into China so that India would not have a border with imperial Russia (see Map 4).
4 The last paragraph in this agreement of 12 November 1893 is also vague (Caroe 1965: 463). Article 1, Paragraph 2: 'The Government of India will at no time exercise interference in the territory lying beyond this line on the side of Afghanistan and His Highness the Amir will at no time exercise interference in the territory beyond this line on the side of India.' The article speaks of a 'line', and not a 'boundary' or 'border', as is the case of all other such agreements.
5 The Afghan historian Hassan Kakar and others who read his account express doubt about the authenticity of Abdur Rahman's autobiography. They consider it the work of his biographer Mir Munshi Sultan Muhammad Khan, but Munshi in vol. I (1900: vii–viii) admits that the Amir at first himself wrote but later dictated to him. The shrewd Amir used to test Munshi by asking him days later to translate back from the English. Sir Mortimer Durand in *The Amir* (Sykes 1926: 5) attests to the autobiography's authenticity. Lord Curzon, in *India and Afghanistan* by Singhall (1963: 176n) commenting on Abdur Rahman's autobiography, also dismisses any such doubts, 'the whole book bears upon it the stamp of one of unquestionable authenticity ... a great many of the stories ... identical with what he said to me when I was in Kabul six years ago'.
6 Many within the royal family were accused of his murder, including Amanullah. But the Russians identified the murderer as Mustafa Saghir, a British agent, and this was also the version accepted by the Afghan government. Saghir was eventually caught in Turkey and hanged by Attaturk.
7 The first *hijra*, emigration, was when the Prophet Muhammad had to move from Makkah to Madinah in AD 622, from which date the Muslim calendar begins. These sub-continent Muslims were repeating that *hijra*, by moving from amongst the unbelievers to the land of Islam.
8 My own father was the construction contractor for the building of the Dar-ul Aman, an imposing parliament building for his new capital. Everyone had to wear a hat, suit and shoes (without nails) within the building. My father remarked that he never wore the hat and spent all day holding it in his hand. His suit, comprising a woollen jacket and trousers, never needing ironing but it was 'uncomfortable to pray in'.
9 The family was given asylum in India. When the British heard of Karim breaking the rules of asylum, they did not want him back in India and he went to Burma where he was killed.
10 Shah Wali Khan in his memoirs writes, 'it is eight months since we left France and our stay in Zazi has also lengthened. Without this small spot, Zazi, nearly the whole of Paktia and the rest of the country have fallen to the hands of the enemy. The Zazi are a business people and they too are unable to go about their works and are suffering. The Gardez refugees have added to their economic misery' (Shah Wali Khan 1940: 76).
11 My father was an *arbakai*, a tribal military leader of his section of the Zazi *lashkar*, fighting alongside Shah Wali Khan, one of Musaheban brothers, all the way to Kabul.
12 While they were being taken to the gallows, one of Bachai Saqaw's ministers turned to Shah Wali Khan, the brother of the king and said, 'You had sworn on the Quran not to kill us. Why are you hanging us now?' Shah Wali retorted, 'The king had taken the oath with you, but it is me who is hanging you' (Quote from Dr Abdul Latif Rashid, an eyewitness).

3 Daoud's republic: 1973–78

1 The number of teachers at the start of the first five-year plan in 1956, was 4,000 increasing to 13,200 by the end of the second five-year plan in 1967.
2 Some Afghan elders with knowledge of the royal family say that when the Musaheban brothers came to power in 1929 they agreed to have the king from among the sons of Payendah Khan second wife, mother of: Nader Khan, Hashem Khan, Shah Wali and Shah Mahmud and the prime minister from amongst the sons of his oldest wife, mother of: Muhammad Aziz who was father to Daoud and Naim. Daoud's expectations of coming back to power and later rebelling against the king were because of the formers' breaking of this understanding.
3 Louis Dupree (1980: 620) gives accounts of thirty strikes in Kabul and the provinces between April and July 1968.
4 The king is said to have asked two former ministers, who both refused the post. He then turned to his minister of Mines and Industry, Dr Mohammad Yosuf, PhD in physics, educated at Gottingen, Germany, who accepted the post.
5 By the Treaty of Gandomak 'the Amir [Yaqob Khan] agreed to conduct his foreign relations in accordance with the advice and wishes of the British government and to countenance a British representative in Kabul. The British government, on its part, undertook that its agents should never in anyway interfere with the Amir's administration. . . . But after the unfortunate assassination of Cavagnari [a British Political Agent in Kabul] and the second Anglo-Afghan war (1881), the Treaty of Gandomak was abrogated' (Ghose 1960: 21–2). Ever since the partition of the Indian subcontinent between Hindus and Muslims Afghan governments have been arguing that just as Indian Muslims were given the chance to opt for either remaining with India or joining Pakistan, the Pashtuns of the North West Frontier and Baluchestan should also be given the choice in a plebiscite or referendum as to whether they want to remain with Pakistan, join Afghanistan or form their own state. As this would effectively mean the partitioning of Pakistan, the latter has never given in to such demands.

But Afghanistan missed three chances of recovering its lost lands, east of the Durand Line. In 1857 during the Indian Mutiny, when all Muslims were ready to rise against the British and so an Afghan initiative would have been decisive; during the First World War (1914–18) when Turkey, an old ally of Afghanistan, was a co-belligerent and so Afghanistan could have joined the *Jihad* against the British, and during the Second World War when the Germans in alliance with the Russians 'created a potential opportunity for Afghanistan to re-conquer the historical Afghan lands in the NWF . . . adding to the temptation was an explicit German promise to guarantee Afghan borders up to the limits of the eighteenth-century Afghan Durrani empire . . . as well as the port of Karachi' (Arnold 1985: 24–5).

The issue of Pashtunistan came to the fore when Britain refused to entertain the idea of returning the border area back to Afghanistan after its announcement of withdrawal from the Subcontinent. Britain had already reinforced the 1893 Durand Agreement by the subsequent treaties of 1919 and 1921 with Afghanistan and offered a plebiscite to the Frontier Pashtuns, either to go with Hindu India or with Muslim Pakistan. The Afghan authorities considered this unrealistic since as Muslims they would vote for Muslim Pakistan. They demanded a separate plebiscite of staying with Pakistan, joining Afghanistan or declaring their separate state, which neither Britain then, nor up to now Pakistan, had heeded 'as it would mean losing 190,000 square miles of Pakistan's territory' (Caroe 1965: 435–6; Dupree 1973: 485–90; Frazer-Tytler 1953:

306–10). Also Mohammad Naim, the Foreign Minister and his delegation visiting London in 1946 put, unsuccessfully, these Afghan proposals to the British government.

6 Wazir Mohammad Gul Khan, a nationalist Pashtun minister, conveyed this story to me in Kabul when I was still at school and received me at his home after hearing of my part in a school drama, for which I also received rewards of books, pens and writing exercise books from the Deputy Minister of Education, Abdul Ahmad (Punjsheri).

7 Mr Aziz Naim, nephew of Daoud, maintained that such meetings with Karmal and other left-wingers never took place and that these 'seminars' were no more than receiving dignitaries, as is the custom in Afghanistan.

8 One *tankist*, while losing control of his tank, plunged into the Kabul River and five to seven soldiers, whose guns went off by mistake were killed.

9 Hassan Sharq, from an unknown background of Anar Dara in Farah province, was in charge of Daoud's prime ministry office 1963–73 and was one of his close confidants in retirement and his minister 1973–78. All this time it is said, he was a KGB plant and kept the Russians informed. In his book, *Karbas Posh-i-Berhanah Pa*, he paints a different picture of himself, but does not explain why his 'parents' had no relatives in the area or where they were from originally.

10 The Helmand River Water Agreement with Iran was criticised by most Afghans as an issue of political convenience for Musa Shafiq, as being excessive by agreeing to guarantee 64 sq. cu. metres of water per second, measured in an area many hundreds of miles inside Afghanistan. The water of the river, after forming the border for a short distance with Iran, pours into a lake inside Afghanistan, from where it seeps into the sandy desert of Iranian Baluchestan. Daoud eventually ratified this agreement in 1977. The agreement with Pakistan entailed the dropping of any insistence on the Pashtunistan issue in return for opening the Karachi port and the frontiers to Afghan trade.

11 When Taraki was in power he made this public, saying Daoud 'foolishly' turned down his offer. Sultan Sabir, the editor of *Hiwad, Nation*, weekly in Baluchestan, once told me that when he met Daoud and talked about the presence of Parcham communists in his government he asked Daoud why he did not bring in the Khalqis. Daoud told him, '. . . the Parchamis are good nationalists' implying that the Pashtun dominated Khalqis was not? (Personal communication with Sabir 1984).

12 Speech to graduates of Kabul Polytechnic on 27 February 1974, at the presidential Gul Khana Palace. Pages 2–3, of President Daoud's Speeches, Messages, Interviews and Official Visits (17 July 1973 to 15 July 1975) Ministry of Information and Culture.

13 For a full list of these papers, the language they were published in and their policy see (Dupree 1980: 602–7).

14 Pacha Gul Wafadar, an air force officer and ambassador who had grown up in his household, told me that Daoud's brother Mohammad Naim and Daoud's eldest son Mustafa asked him to kill Daoud, which he refused on the grounds that he considered Daoud as 'father'. Both argued with him, one saying 'he is my only brother' and the other 'he is my father and would anyone want to kill his father for no reason, but he is going to destroy us all' (Author's discussion with Wafadar in Brighton, October 1999).

15 Mohammad Khan Jalaler, like Hassan Sharq and Ali Ahmad Khan and half a dozen others who reached high offices and held them through coups and regime changes, are said to be KGB implants, brought to Afghanistan at an early age. Having changed their identities, they all seem to have been brought up by rich business families in Kabul. Jalaler, for example, was Finance Minister for twenty-one years under the king, under Daoud's republic, under the Khalq

and Parcham communists; H. Sharq was Daoud's number two (1953–63), ambassador (1973–78) and prime minister under the communists.

16 In October 1974, Iran gave Afghanistan $10 million for a feasibility study of the railway project and some other projects; Saudi Arabia offered a $55 million interest free loan; Iraq earmarked a $10 million loan and a $2 million grant; Kuwait and other Gulf States making similar gestures. However, after the ratification of Helmand Water Agreement, Iran announced that it was cutting back on foreign aid and, despite comprehensive Afghan discussion with them, Iran defaulted on its promises in 1977.

17 Author's conversation with the former Defence Minister, General Mohammad A'ref Khan, 1978 in Kabul.

18 This story was told to me by Daoud's nephew, Aziz Naim and also in private conversations by the former Minister of Education Ali Ahmad Popal and also repeated by Abdul Samad Ghaus, an Afghan Foreign Ministry official, in his book, *The Fall of Afghanistan*. (Another version says that Daoud thumped the conference table and walked out of the meeting; yet others say he stayed to the end of the meeting, which continued in a tense atmosphere.) Some Afghan diplomats hearing of this exchange later concluded that Daoud by losing his temper had probably signed his death certificate. Exactly one year later, the communists gunned down Daoud and his entire family.

19 The king's son-in-law and cousin, General Abdul Wali, was Daoud's bitterest rival within the royal family. In 1963 when Daoud was dismissed from the premiership, Shah Wali Khan, the only Musaheban brother still alive, suggested to the king that it was time this post was given to his son General Abdul Wali. General Abdul Wali, equally hot-tempered, used to call Daoud 'hot-head', and by some other uncomplimentary adjectives. After the coup of 17 July when Abdul Wali was chained so that his head touched his knees and was presented to Daoud, the latter told him, 'who is a hot-head, you or I'? Author's conversation with General Abdul Wali in Rome, May 1994.

4 Afghan communist parties and personalities

1 Sayed Jamaludin Afghani, known to the Arabs and the outside world as Al-Afghani, was born in As'd abad, Konar Province, where his descendants still live. He was especially gifted in languages and a prolific writer. He submitted a programme of reform to Amir Sher Ali who later exiled him because of Jamaludin close contact with his rival, Azam khan. Jamaludin travelled to Russia, London, Paris, Istanbul and Cairo, publishing and preaching Pan-Islamism as a counter force against European imperialism. In Paris he brought out one of the first Arabic language newspapers, *Aruwatul uthwqa*, The Firmest Bond, which was circulated widely within the Arab World.

2 Anahita Ratebzad was the wife of the royal surgeon Dr Qamaruddin and was a trained nurse. As a political activist she attracted many school and university girls to Parcham, held regular meetings with them, which ended in disco dances.

3 After the Red Army invasion and the atrocities that were daily committed by the Russians and the communists, the underground activists in Kabul used to taunt the Parchamis for their hypocrisies, by blowing the *third of 'Aqrab* event out of proportion, while remaining silent on the cruelty that was meted out to the people under their own rule.

4 The rivalry between Khalq and Parcham was highlighted in the relationships between Hafizullah Amin and Babrak Karmal; Taraki and Mir Akbar Khyber, Taher Badakhshi (an Isma'ilia Shi'ah), the founder of the anti-Pashtun, National Oppression Party. Amin and Taraki and their junior supporters

headed the inter-party rivalry in the Khalq faction, and in the Parcham faction it was between Gholam Dastagir Punjsheri and Karmal and also to a lesser extent between Keshtmand and Karmal.
5 'The poem to the glory of the land of Lenin"and the miracles of the life-bearing revolution" ended thus: For this matchless achiever We send DOROUD to that pioneer par excellence. And to the heroic people we send DOROUD to that great leader The Great Lenin' (Hyman 1984: 61).
6 *Farsi to* which present-day Dari and Persian are related is a relatively recent Creole language made up of *Pahlawi, Sughdi, Avesta* and other local languages. Like present-day Urdu or Swahili, it soon became the language of the region and was used as the court language by Turks, Uzbeks, Pashtuns and the Moghul rulers. It is only in the past eighty years, after *Fars* changed its name to 'Iran', indicating a connection with the *Aryans*, that it has for nationalistic purposes been claimed as 'the language of Iran', thus making Turks, Afghan and others conscious of developing their own languages.
7 I was in Kabul then when he invited amongst others my father-in-law and his brother Mr Baqa'ee.
8 Amin's conversation with the author in June 1965 at his Gower Street Hotel in London.
9 Personal communication with Amin in London, 1965.
10 When Amin came to power he sent Asadullah Amin, his son-in-law and the head of intelligence, to Mr Ghulam Ali Ayeen, a former Hazarah colleague at the faculty of science, who was also in America and subsequently in prison in Kabul to ask him just one question. 'Why did the CIA not recruit me like Ayeen and some other Afghan students'? Mr Ayeen said, 'they (CIA) told us never to mention anything to Amin who was an extreme nationalist'. Author's conversation with Amin's nephew, Zalmay in Brighton, October 1999.
11 Karmal has privately said on a number of occasions that he is a Pashtun belonging to minor branches of the Ghilzai confederacy. Since he has mentioned different tribes to different people at different times, there is doubt about his true origins. Raja Anwar, a Pakistani communist sympathiser, also questions his Pashtun origin. 'Karmal himself claims to be a Pashtun, but the author's research has established that he is a Tajik ... he has no close or even distant relationship with any Pashtun family. It was probably his father who began to identify himself as a Pashtun' (1988: 62).
12 Personal correspondence with military officials who had come to Pakistan as refugees.

5 Events leading to the Soviet invasion

1 These are called *Ahmad Shahi* colours, referring to the colour of the flags of Ahmad Shah Durrani's various regiments. These are also the most popular colours worn by Afghan women. King Amanullah officially adopted the tricolour with the explanation that Black stands for occupation, Red, for shedding blood and Green for achieving independence.
2 A Parchami, by the name of Abdul Qodus Ghorbandi, at Amin's request before the meeting had crossed the Floor and voted with the Khalq. Karmal paid him back after coming to power, in January 1980 by imprisoning him.
3 Babrak Karmal was posted to Czechoslovakia, Anahita Ratebzad to Yugoslavia, Karmal's half brother Mahmud Baryalay to Pakistan, Abdul Wakil to London, Nur Ahmad Nur to Washington and Dr Najibullah to Tehran. Others like Engineer Nazer Mohammad, Abdul Aziz Mohtat and Pachagul Wafadar also followed.
4 BBC (SWB Part 3, 19 July 1978; 27 September 1979).

5 Other leading conspirators were Abdul Qader, General Shapur Ahmadzai, Dr Mir Akbar, Head of Jamhooriat Hospital and the *Setam-i-Meli* leader, Taher Badakhshi.
6 Most of them first went to Prague to meet Karmal and from there the Russians brought them to Moscow. (Author's personal conversation with many Khalq and Parcham members).
7 My wife Arian Misdaq was Amin's daughter's school mate at Rabia Balkhi Girls School in Kabul.
8 Author's private conversations with Khalqis, confirming this story.
9 According to the statements of their friends and relatives, Gulabzoy, started army service as a non-commissioned officer and was dyslexic; Mazdoryar had read nothing of significance on Marxism or Leninism; Watanjar had only read the translation of Maxim Gorky's novel *Mother* and also another pamphlet, '100 Questions and Answers About Communism'; Sarwari known as the 'Butcher of Kabul' had read nothing about communism. Personal communication with relatives and friends of Gulabzoy, Watanjar and Sarwari.
10 An Afghan historian writes, 'the conspirators first stayed at the villa of the TASS correspondent' and were later smuggled to the Soviet Union (Kakar 1995: 39). My brother owned that villa and we lived next door. The two-floor villa has no basement and we went in and out as we knew the TASS man, his cook and most of the others who worked with the TASS Bureau Chief. We would have certainly known about the presence of these fugitives, who were the talk of the town.
11 For the first time the Pashto term *Lomray Wazir*, literally, first minister or prime minister was used. Kakar writes 'Amin was promoted to the position of first minister, not Prime Minister, as is generally understood' (Kakar 1995: 35). This is not correct because firstly, no one else served as prime minister at the time and secondly, in the first weeks of Amin's appointment to this position, Kabul papers were bracketing *Lomray Wazir* as 'prime minister'.
12 Aziz Akbari was a refugee living in Tours, France in 1995. When in August that year he had heard of my traffic accident in Tours he came to visit me at my hospital saying, 'We have not met but I know of your name'.
13 Mrs Taraki told this story in Pul-i-Charkhi prison to Anwar.
14 Newspaper reports of these treaties suggest that the basic text is the same. The Soviet Foreign Ministry just made minor changes to make it relevant to this or that country.
15 Text of the treaty in *Afghanistan – A Nation in Love With Freedom* (Tabibi 1985: 185–6).
16 I was in Kabul at the time and saw this huge Illusion plane taking the Khalq leaders to Moscow.
17 In July 1979 Amin sent a letter to President Carter's National Security advisor. The Afghan official 'personally handed the letter to Mr Zbigniew Brezinski but received no reply' (Kakar 1995 fn. pp. 329–30).
18 NATO countries also knew Soviet preparation and from October onwards they knew that the Soviets were massing forces on the other side of Amu River (*Spies Nest* vol. 29).
19 Salih Muhammad Zairay, cabinet minister and head of NFF confirmed this story to me. He said 'all reports we were getting pointed to a joint Pakistani-Chinese and American invasion' (Personal communication).
20 Telephone conversation between Taraki and Kosygin, 18 March 1979 at the time of the Herat uprising, *Journal of South Asia and Middle Eastern Studies*, 1994, vol. 17, no. 2.
21 Telephone conversation in London with Salih Muhammad Zairay, 8 June 1997.
22 Another version is that Amin was giving a party for Ghulam Dastagir Punjsheri,

Notes   321

a founding member of the PDPA (a double agent for the KGB and the CIA, later moved to Origan in the USA) who had come from Moscow after a long stay; the cook was a KGB colonel, Mikhail Talebov, native of Azerbaijan (Kakar 1995: 23).
23 The official exchange rate then was 91 Kopeck to a dollar.

6 Afghan resistance: 1975–92

1 *Arbakai* leaders are tribesmen who are appointed in accordance with the influence and population of the section of the tribe they represent. For battlefield purposes, these leaders then appoint a *Mir* or *Khan* under whose orders they fight.
2 There are some 2,000 registered *madrassas* in Pakistan, with some also dotted on the Afghan side of the border. The most famous *madrassa* is *Deoband* in the town of that name in northern India to which most of the traditional Afghan *ulama* has been. Another prominent *madrassa* is that of *Haqania* in Peshawar from which many resistance commanders graduated.
3 Most Shi'ah Afghan scholars went for higher education to Qom in Iran or Najaf in Iraq, two well-known centres for Shi'ah religious study.
4 For more detail on state and private *madrassas* see *Islam and Resistance* (Roy 1986: 70–4), *The Fragmentation of Afghanistan* (Rubins 1995: 184–95).
5 There is a great deal of literature on the Islamist movement, since it became a crucial factor in the war against the Red Army. Their own literature emphasises present leadership and their role more than those who started the movement. For general information see (Rubin 1995: 83–4), (Reshtia 1984: 61–8), (Brigot and Roy 1988: 88–91ff), (Olesen 1995: 227–55).
6 The *ustaz* campaign of recruitment, like that of the communists, started at Kabul University where most of them taught. Thus Hekmatyar and Emad were recruited from the faculty of engineering, Masoud and Habibur Rahman from Kabul Polytechnic. A large cadre of the Islamists came from the secondary and high schools. 'The young Islamists inaugurated a campaign of politico-religious preaching throughout the country, with branches called *Da'wat–o-tanzim* (preaching and organisation) as its spearhead' (Roy 1986: 73). The provinces that produced most of the radical *ulama* and Islamists were the three Pashtun provinces of Kunar, Laghman and Nangarhar. These provinces are also known as *Mashreqi*, eastern. 'The fundamentalism of the Mashreqi *ulama* had always been more radical and anti-traditionalist than in other regions. From 1950 onwards the movements inspired by Wahhabist had shaken the region. Such as *Punjpir* movement . . . a certain 'Sayed Mullah' influenced the Shinwari of Kunar towards both Wahhabism and *Hezb-i-Islami*' (Roy 1986: 72). Also Badakhshan in the north-east and Herat in the west contributed to the reserves of the Islamists. The Pashtun provinces because of their proximity to Pakistan and their long historical link with the sub-continent were either trained in *Punjpir* (an Islamist madrassa in Pakistan), or *Deoband*, *Haqania* and other madrassas.
7 *Islam wa 'adalat-i-ijtima'i*, Islam and social justice.
8 The Hazrat of Shorbazar (an area of Kabul), is a saintly family belonging to the *Sufi Naqshbandi tariqat* (a Sufi brotherhood) which is one of the three main *tariqas* in Afghanistan. This family has played a key religious role in the twentieth century in the sanctioning, enthroning and dethroning of monarchs. Because of these close relationships with the ruling families, they have always used their influence to further religious causes without themselves coming to the forefront, in ways such as helping with the papers Nida-i-Haq, Khaddam al-Furqan and also the establishment of Afghanistan's *Jam'iat ulama* in the 1930s.
9 I met Faizani's son at a conference in Tehran in 1988. He told me his father

322 *Notes*

'was arrested by Daoud and is still missing'. Since the body was never returned nor had the authorities admitted to the killing, he gave the impression that his father was still alive and probably had been sent to Siberia, by the communists, as rumoured, together with thousands of other Afghans who started disappearing after the communists came to power in 1978. Faizani's son spoke of a 'mobile university' educating Mujahideen in the front lines. The son like his father is politically active and was on a peace mission with his sister, a medical doctor, to the United States and Germany in April 1998.

10 'Good Muslims' was a phrase coined by the UN referring to those moderates, relatively well known Muslims in Kabul that the UN wanted to share power with the resistance in a coalition.

11 I was in Kabul for six months in 1976. I could sense the fear and uncertainty, because of Daoud's regular announcements of coups against himself. The public, having become disillusioned with the monarchy, was prepared at first to give Daoud a chance. But his selection of little known and inexperienced ministers, their assignment of important roles to army officers and communists for playing a key role in the coup of 26 *Sarathan* (17 April) and his autocratic and paternalistic approach, he had soon lost all the support he had initially been given.

12 There were numerous landowners and Khans who were killed or arrested after the decree on land reform was passed, limiting their holdings, or confiscating their properties such as cinemas and hotels, or cancelling their trading arrangements with foreign companies and firms.

13 Some forty members of the Hazrat of Shurbazar, the Mujadedi family, were killed and their property confiscated. Another *Pir Gailani* party, belonging to the *Qaderi* order, fled in 1988 to Pakistan when I was in Kabul. Both started their moderate resistance parties during the Soviet occupation.

14 Up to 1986 the 'total number of lecturers at Kabul University was 750'. Of these 318 have been lost: Jailed (6), executed (36) and fled abroad (276), *The Sovietization of Afghanistan*, pp. 79–80 and pp. 73–141.

15 The 'Iron Amir', Abdur Rahman, also held this view back in the 1880s. He compared the Russian move into a new territory to the careful attention of an elephant in stepping forward. He writes 'the elephant weighs where it places its hoof and once it steps forward, does not go back'.

16 Record of UN General Assembly annual votes on Afghanistan

Year	For	Against	Abstentions
1980 (Emergency)	104	18	18
1980	111	22	12
1981	116	23	12
1982	114	21	13
1983	116	20	17
1984	119	20	14
1985	122	19	12
1986	122	20	11
1987	123	19	11

17 The information on these dates is given by numerous publications. For quick reference see: 1987, *A Chronology of Events*, Agency Afghan Press, London; 1985, *Afghanistan Chronology 1978–1985*, United States Information Agency, Washington, DC, *War in Afghanistan: 1978–1989*, Mark Urban, 1990. This book is written from the perspective of the Soviets and the Kabul government.

18 Sayyaf is Pashtun on his mother's side. He also altered his name, Abdul [slave of] Rasul [the Prophet], to Abdur-Rab [slave of God] Rasul Sayyaf to gain Arab

acceptance. As Afghans do not speak Arabic, most names are chosen by their 'sound' rather than by their Arabic meaning.
19 Iraq paid $9 million a year to only one of the minor resistance leaders, Sayed Ahmad Gailani, who claimed Iraqi ancestry connecting him to the *Qaderi* Sufi Order. (Private communication with General Rahmatullah Safi, a wartime military commander of Gailani's NIFA group).
20 I saw eleven of these missiles in 1990 when I was in Kandahar. They belonged to a commander of Hezb Khalis, who later joined the Taleban. [A similar number was also with Mullah Rocketi, a Sayyaf commander who too joined the Taleban.] The missiles were about 30 kg in weight and the batteries still showed active pink, contrary to the CIA's disinformation that the batteries went flat after two years. After Soviet withdrawal in February 1989, the US was anxious to collect these missiles, and to prevent them from falling into the 'wrong hands'. Some of Hezb Khalis' men sold these missiles to Iran for $500,000 each and some were even seen at the official army parade of Qatar in 1990. The CIA did buy some back, but over 120 were never accounted for.
21 These were 1. Sazman Naser, 2. Sepah-i-Pasdaran, 3. Hizbullah, 4. Jabh-i-Mutahed, 5. Da'wat, 6. Nuhzat-i-Islami, 7. Nair`i Islami, and 8. Harakat-i-Islami. After the overthrow of the communist regime, the Iranians amalgamated the first seven into Wahdat-i-Wahdat, the Party of Unity. Harakat-i-Islami, having lost favour with Iran, remained separate.
22 *The Ethnic Composition of Afghanistan* (WAKFA 199: 57).
23 After Iran's presidency of the OIC for 1998/99, the relation between the two countries normalised and their foreign ministers exchanged visits to one another's capitals.
24 BBC Pashto Service interviews with Hekmatyar in 1989. The underestimation of the Kabul communist forces became a fashionable theme. The final fall of Kabul proved to be a tough problem and was not solved till April 1992. Kabul authorities according to a UN plan were to hand over power to a neutral body of Afghan technocrats. Once Dr Najibullah announced his acceptance of this plan, Masoud and Jam'iat joined with Uzbek militia and the Hazarah Shi'ah forces and marched on Kabul, foiling the UN plan of a peaceful handover. Hekmatyar resisted them and this was the beginning of the internecine war between Islamist groups that continued for over four years and seven months.
25 Barnet Rubin and Olivier Roy ignored Masoud's duplicity despite numerous sources, which reveal that Masoud never fought against the Russians. (*The Red Army* by General Gromov, commander of the Soviet 40th army in Afghanistan; *What Really Happened in Afghanistan* by Alexander Mayorev; *The Russian Elite* by Cary Schofield; *Afghanistan Ending the Reign of Soviet Terror* by Bruce Richardson; Afghan *Heroism and Tragedy* by Alexander Liakhovsky and numerous other Afghan and non-Afghan sources).
26 Mazdak's brother Khan Muhammad, the deputy of WAD, killed the security minister Ya'qubi, minutes after Dr Najibullah's failed attempt to escape under UN escort to Delhi. Khan Mohammad was one of a large number of those generals that the regime began producing from 1986, after only six months of training in military tactics and strategies. These two brothers closely worked with the KGB and held crucial party and state jobs.
27 Ya'qobi's deputy was Mazdak's brother, Khan Mohammad (see above note) who like his brother had secretly joined the alliance of the northern militias. He rang the BBC Persian Service from Moscow, asking for his whereabouts not to be mentioned on the programme, proudly explaining how Najibullah was prevented from fleeing to India and how the minister of WAD had 'committed suicide' (BBC Interview April 1992).
28 The hardy Afghan people could survive on a minimum of subsistence rations.

324 *Notes*

But at all times they cursed the resistance parties and their leaders, whom they accused of corruption and nepotism. Such disillusionment was the main reason why the general public never took any serious interest in the internecine war that followed the Soviet withdrawal. Outside the Mujahideen party membership, certain individuals only fought for this or that party for a few months at a time, not out of commitment, but in order to make enough money to meet their family expenses.

29 Afghan gas had been exported to the Soviet Union since 1968. According to a trading protocol, the Soviets had been officially receiving 2.5 billion cubic metres up to 1985. Afghan officials, even within the PDPA used to complain about the positioning and manning of the meters on the Soviet side of the border, believing that more than twice the above amount went to Russia. However, even the revenue from the sale of that amount was not handed to the Afghans. The proceeds were part payment for the import of arms and repayment of outstanding capital and interests on debts. After '1980 the Soviet took the step of crediting its import of Afghan natural gas against the cost of maintaining the friendly fraternal assistance"of its limited military contingent in Afghanistan" (Kakar 1995: 239, n25).

30 This is probably an underestimation. Soviet forces were present in all twenty-nine provinces. If we put their losses at twenty a day, it comes to 7,300 per year and to over 70,000 for ten years. This, measured against 1.5 million Afghans killed in the war, 55,000 US troops killed in Vietnam, is not an unrealistic figure. '...Official losses put at 13,310 dead, 35,478 wounded, and 311 missing (the real number of dead may be four times greater...') (AIC, Monthly Bulletin, p. 1, No. 93, Dec. 1988).

7 From common cause to internal war and the rise of Taleban

1 I came to know the king well during the war. He gave his first ever post-exile interview to me for the BBC (May 1984). The king has consistently said that he does not want restoration of the monarchy but is ready to serve his people in 'whatever capacity that is asked of me'. King Muhammad Zahier was born in 1915. Since 1973 he has been living on Saudi pension in Rome. A soft spoken, gentle person, who in four decades of his reign never signed an execution order; his chief justice would sign on his behalf. The Islamists accuse him of amassing a lot of wealth, but his friend the Shah of Iran bought the king a flat in Rome and there has been no indication of hidden riches. The king is a cautious person. He has never had the enthusiasm of Cambodia's Sihonauk or France's De Gaulle, with whom he is sometimes compared. He remains popular with the public, who remember his reign through the happier eyes of a people at peace. Every day since the communist coup back in 1978 has been a missed opportunity for the king. In all these years, had the king wanted to come back, the majority of Afghans across the ethnic and tribal spectrum would have supported him. I wrote these words in 1999. After the fall of the Taleban in October 2001, the West and the UN persuaded the king to go to Afghanistan and in the *Loya Jirga* stand as a candidate to lead the country. However, when the said *Loya Jirga* was held in June 2002, the king was dissuaded by the Americans through President Bush's special envoy Dr Zalmay Khalilzad, to the utter disappointment of the majority of *Loya Jirga* and the Afghan nation, to stand down in favour of Mr Hamed Karzay.

2 Professor Majrooh was gunned down a few months later by the Islamists because of his survey. His survey showed that the leaders of the resistance were low down on the popularity list for most Afghans. Majrooh told me that the

actual figure for the king was 85 per cent and if he had announced that figure some might not have believed it. So he said he reduced it to 73 per cent.

3 To date, there have been eight UN special representatives for Afghanistan: Perez de Cuellar, Diego Cordovez, Benon Sevan, Satirios Mousoris, Mahmud Mestiri, Norbert Hall, Lakhdar Ibrahimi and Frances Vendrell. After the fall of Taleban, Lakhdar Ibrahimi once again surfaced to work with Karzay warlord dominated administration.

4 Details of the coup against the UN were given in *Mujahed Woles* (an exile paper) by Dr Hassan Kakar 1992, November/December Issue. Also see 'Saudi Arabia, Iran and the conflict in Afghanistan', by Professor Ahadi (1998).

5 For details of the coup in Mazar, amongst other sources also see: Afghan Information Centre (AIC) 11th year, March–June 1992 issues; *Mujahed Woles* (also see note 4 above). It was Uzbek militias and fallen communist Parcham factional forces that were the real power in Kabul. Parcham Party members: Mahmud Baryalai (Karmal's half brother), Farid Mazdak, Najmudin Kawyani, Paigir and many of its generals came into the open, by joining the anti-Pashtun Islamists and militias.

6 These eight Shi'ah parties were: Harakat Islami, Nohzat Islami, Jabh-i-Islami, Jabh-i-Mutahid Islami, Hizb-i-Da'wat Islami, Sazman Naser, Sazman Pasdaran and Hizbullah. Two Afghan Nationalist Shi'ah parties preceded these: Shura-i-Inqlab-i-Islami and Shura-i-Itefaq. These were completely wiped out by the pro-Iranian parties.

7 Hekmatyar passed the job to a Tajik member of his party, Abdul Sabor Farid, to impress on the Northern Alliance that he did not believe in an ethnicisation policy (Hekmatyar 2000: 108–9).

8 All the major parties opposed this gathering, declaring its decision unacceptable. The smaller groups that joined Rabbani were Sayyaf's Itehad-i-Islami (pro-Wahhabi), Sheikh Asef Mohseny's Qizelbash Shi'ah Harakat Inqilab. I sent BBC's Kabul stringer Hamed Elmi to cover the meeting for the Pashto Service. He told me, 'Rabbani has collected people from the streets of Kabul, such as drivers, shop-keepers etc. with the instruction to vote for him. All these people are paid to stay put when the council is in session'.

9 It is this government that the West continued to recognise, although it had no cabinet or fixed address.

10 Hekmatyar regarded Dostum as a Soviet and communist stooge and saw no place for him in an Islamic government. He also opposed Hezb-i-Wahdat, but not as vehemently as he opposed the Uzbeks. When he later joined in an alliance with these two he was accused of lacking principles. Hekmatyar writes that since peace was not possible with Masoud/Rabbani, by joining the Uzbek and Shi'ah I stopped them attacking us and also prevented the fanning of an ethnic war (Hekmatyar 2000: 150–3).

11 Hekmatyar waged five years of war against the Masoud/Rabbani 'government' and the Taleban. The BBC stringer, Hamed Elmi, quoted him to me saying, 'I have not spent so far a penny of my own money'. Meaning that he was paying for his expenses of running a TV and radio station as well some 10,000 fighters 'out of the interest on his money in foreign banks'.

The Afghan currency that was printed in Russia for the communists continued to be printed for Rabbani/Masoud. Uzbekistan produced perfect imitations of these notes for Dostum. The Iranians had been pumping oil-money to Hezb-i-Wahdat up to May 1996 to continue fighting in Kabul and, after their forceful expulsion from Kabul by Masoud, the Shi'ah have been receiving similar amounts from Iran to continue to wage war from their stronghold of Bamyan and Mazar against the Taleban.

12 In addition to these major Islamist and militia forces, other armed groups

included the former regime's forces of Kabul garrison, Harakat Islami of Mohseni, Harakat Inqilab Islami of Muhammadi, Hezb Khalis of Haqqani, Mahaz Milli of Gailani and Jabh-i-Nijat of Mujadedi. The position of these forces in Kabul was as follows: to the south the two Hezbs; to the east Muhammad, Mujadedi, Gailani and Sayyaf; to the south-east Mohseni, Sayyaf, Gailani, Mazari and Khales, to the west Sayyaf, Masoud/Rabbani, Muhammadi, Gailani, Mohseni, Khales and Hekmatyar and to the north Masoud/Rabbani, Hekmatyar, Sayyaf and Dostum. 'Besides the above forces, inside and outside Kabul, there are thousands of underground armed men of KHAD in Kabul...' (AIC, No. 132–5, March–June 1992).

13 The real number of those killed will never be known, as Afghans in accordance with Muslim practice, bury the dead as soon as possible. The Red Cross figures are based on those who had come to the hospital and died because of their injuries. It does not include those who died instantly in such bombing and were buried.

14 This is the version that was relayed to me in Kandahar in April 1997. Kandahar was the stronghold of the Taleban, and where Mullah Muhammad Omar was based, although their government continued to operate from Kabul, the capital of Afghanistan.

15 Mansur was the son of Haji Maghash, a well-known commander of Mujadedi's National Front in Kandahar, who died from natural causes in May 1995. I met Mansur in 1993 on a visit to Kandahar. He was in charge of the Kandahar International Airport and several MiG fighter jets. He was a drug addict and often high and incoherent, which is why I was never able to use his interviews for the BBC. His Achakzai tribesmen camping in the lounge and corridors of the airport and drinking tea all day, surrounded him.

16 Other commanders who helped the Taleban at this initial stage were Haji Bashir, commander of Hezb Khalis in Maiwand district, and drug baron Mullah Abdul Ghafar Akhundzadah of Helmand. Soon after the episode, Mullah Muhammad Rabbani (number two to Mullah Muhammad Omar) is reported to have gone to Kabul to ask president Rabbani for help. The president, who said that the Taleban were his 'soldiers', asked his Kandahar commander Mullah Naqib to support them.

17 These were the ambassadors of the US, UK, China, Italy, South Korea and Spain who were said to be interested in funding such a project. As there was no government in western Afghanistan, rumours were rife that Pakistan was treating western Afghanistan as part of its territory. In a telephone interview with General Babur I asked him, 'who gave you the visa to travel to Afghanistan'. This annoyed him intensely saying, 'we don't ask of millions of Afghan refugees coming to Pakistan. How come you ask such a question?' I told him that 'they are helpless people seeking refuge from the war while you are a government minister. You and your guest's trip cannot be equalled to the refugees entering Pakistan'. The next day his Interior Ministry in Islamabad put out a statement saying that Rabbani's representative in Quetta had issued the visas, which was not the case.

18 Ahmed Rashid quotes these figures in his paper (1998 ed. Maley).

19 I was in Kandahar airport in July 1994 and was pleasantly surprised to see the airport building in a good state of repair. However, there was no proper maintenance of the planes. Although Mansur offered to fly me back to Quetta, I turned his offer down. He assured me, saying that 'we fly our planes every Wednesday like the Pakistani military, to keep them in good flying condition'. I knew of several instances of planes in the hands of warlords that had crashed due to technical problems.

20 The Jami'at commander Mullah Naqib was later asked by Rabbani to hand over

his arms to the Taleban. The Taleban lulled Rabbani into thinking that they were fighting for him and so there was no need to have two forces in Kandahar. After the handover, Mullah Naqib was given twelve Kalashnikovs for his personal safety and asked to withdraw to his home village in Helmand. Later, the Taleban informed me that 'we told Naqib we assure you of your safety like anyone else, there is no need for you to have arms', thus we took the arms from his bodyguards'.

21 Masoud gave the impression that he only feared Hekmatyar and the Hazarah leader Mazari, both of whom he accused of working for foreign countries against the interests of Afghanistan. Once these two were disarmed, he would hand in his arms, putting his pistol in front of Mullah Mesher saying, 'like this'. (Interviews with Taleban Ministers, April 1997, Kabul).

22 Taleban commander Mullah Nekmal, who was present at that meeting, told me 'our plans were to detain both Masoud and Sayyaf, but before we knew it they were gone'.

23 Hekmatyar's plight was publicised by Masoud's brother, Wali Masoud, in an embassy newsletter in London.

24 Davis' figure of 2,000 in *How the Taleban Became a Military Force* (ed. Maley 1998: 59) is also confirmed by Masoud and Isma'il Khan.

25 Isma'il Khan's interview published in *Omaid*, a weekly in the USA, by Masoud/Rabbani supporters. Isma'il Khan later told the same story to the BBC. In both he blamed his defeat on the followers of the defeated Kandahari warlords who joined him.

26 Mullah Abbas gave me this account in Kabul in April 1997. He said that only after one of Masoud's men recognised one of his men was the highly charged atmosphere defused

27 One Hazarah was hit by a shovel breaking both his arms. When we at the BBC asked, Mr Qanooni, Masoud's man 'responsible' for security in Kabul about this, he denied it. Even though our correspondent had been a witness to the crime. In view of the personal danger involved, the correspondent suggested we covered the story from London. This was not the first time Masoud had massacred the Hazarahs. This had occurred twice before, once in 1993 when he had totally obliterated the Shi'ah quarters of Chendawoll, and again in 1994, when he had massacred them in Qala-i-Berchi, where mostly Hazarahs lived.

28 'Our forces were shaken by the losses over the minefields. No one had the energy to continue, but Mullah Abdul Razaq, another front-line commander, said 'I will drive a bit further to see what was happening. Razaq said he kept on driving without seeing a single Masoud or Hekmatyar man. When he reached the Harb-i-Pohantunn (Military University), he thought that it was the Arg (Presidential Palace), as he had never been to Kabul before. He was trying to radio the rest when he saw two pickups full of Taleban passing him heading for the Microrayon area of Kabul, proceeding to occupy the empty Presidential Palace' (Conversation with Mullah Abbas, Minister of Health, Kabul, April 1997).

29 Also see *The Times*, page 9 for the same story and more, under the heading 'Taleban poised to Eliminate Forces of Former Army Chief' (i.e. Masoud), 2 October 1997.

30 Isma'il Khan escaped prison (May 2000) after three years by bribing a prison guard.

31 I was told the full story of the failure of the Taleban in Mazar by two of their acting ministers who would not wish to be named.

32 When I asked Taleban ex-Foreign Minister, Mullah Muhammad Ghaus, about these casualties, as Taleban were still battling in the north, he underestimated

their casualties, saying that 'only about 500 of our Taleban got killed. The rest were all local people and those who went from the neighbouring provinces to see Mazar and pay a visit to the shrine of Ali there. Most of our Taleban made their way, like me, to Kunduz to join other Taleban under him', pointing to Muttaqi, Minister of Information, next to him. (February 1998 London).
33 I asked Muttaqi, 'how could you trust a Masoud commander like Bashir Salangi, to join you?' He replied, 'we knew Salang would be closed after we crossed. Our aim both then and now is to unite Central and Northern Afghanistan. Bashir himself volunteered to join us and we knew from the inaccurate firing that Masoud was subjecting the hills around us, that Bashir might do what he was told to do' (February 1998 London).
34 Rahimullah Yosufzai, News Bureau Chief in Peshawar, writes, 'Mujahideen Commanders had been committing excess against their people and looting the public exchequer, they fear that the Taleban won't spare them if they capture them' (*The News*, 3 Oct. 1997). This is one reason that these commanders, especially in the north, will not be willing to hand over their arms to the Taleban.
35 Hekmatyar, having been pursued from Kabul in September 1997 by the Taleban, went to Mazar and from there to Iran. The Iranians gave him a residence in north Tehran.
36 I interviewed Dr Najibullah twice in Pashto by satellite for the BBC. Most of my colleagues, who went to Kabul, if any, came back with Dari interviews.

8 Post communist ethnicity

1 Amir Koror and his family ruled over Ghore as *Amirs* in AD 712. Koror is also remembered for his poetry. His poem is the earliest recorded in the Pashto language.
2 When the Pashtun migrated to the north-eastern province of Kundoz, for example, they did not replace existing Uzbek, Arab or Tajik settlers, they reclaimed *Dasht-e-* (desert) *Archi* for their settlement and agriculture (Barfield 1978: 31). The Pashtun did the same in the nineteenth century when they were sent by the 'Iron Amir' to guard the border in the north. Later they reclaimed desert and semi-desert areas (Nancy Tapper 1973). When the Pashtun settled in northern India from the tenth century onward, they brought new lands under plough by piercing tunnels in the mountains for irrigation (Gommans 1995: 145ff).
3 After the Taleban declared the currency of the Uzbek warlord, Abdur Rashid Dostum illegal, according to local traders in Mazar (December 1996–January 1997), Iran spent some $40 million in purchasing the Uzbek warlord's worthless currency to stabilise its exchange rate. Money for this warlord was printed in Tashkent. On the military front hundreds of planes, trucks and even trainloads of arms from Iran, Uzbekistan and Russia have been reaching the anti-Taleban warlords. Pakistan is alleged to have done the same for the Taleban.
4 I have spoken to three former government officials who confirmed this story. Keshtmand was attacked and shot in the mouth by the Khalqis for his anti-Pashtun sentiments. The *Independent on Sunday* (1995) in a front-page article expressed astonishment that Mr Keshtmand, whom the West fought for ten years, is now receiving state benefits in North London.
5 The warm relationship ended when the Taleban refused the extradition of Osama Bin Laden, accused of the bombing of Riyadh and Dhahran [and later of 9/11]. The Saudi Minister of the Interior, in a news conference in Qatar in July 1998, exonerated Bin Laden of having had any hand in those bombings. As he had been deprived of his Saudi nationality, 'he is nothing to us, we are

responsible for Saudi nationals only'. The Americans, in addition to those bombings also accuse him of the 1998 East African embassy bombings and have asked the Taleban for his expulsion. The Taleban gave the US two months to present its evidence to the High Court in Kabul, so that Bin Laden could be tried under Islamic Shari'ah law. The Americans failed to do so. The Taleban then suggested he should be tried by a group of *ulama* from Afghanistan, Saudi Arabia and one more Muslim country nominated by the US, the Americans rejected that idea too. The Taleban then asked the Organisation of Islamic Countries (OIC) to send a team to monitor Bin Laden to American satisfaction. This Saudi-based organisation, presumably under pressure from the US, made no response. Furthermore, the Taleban said it's against the *Pashtunwali* rules to hand over one's guest to a non-Muslim country, like the USA, with whom they have no extradition treaty.

6 BBC TV interview with Naderi in February 1989.

7 Hekmatyar quotes his Tajik Prime Minister, Mr Farid, saying: 'President Rabbani was anxious to see me alone. After his third try, when he got me on my own he said. We have been blessed by a special historic occasion: I am the President, you are the Prime Minister and Masoud is the Defence Minister. Such historic occasions are rare to come by. Why don't we jointly work for our deprived [Tajik] people". Farid said, I told him, *ustaz* this is not the solution, neither Islam nor our country's social system would allow us to benefit from such a stand."Mr Farid adds, 'I was amazed how a Muslim who considers himself an Islamic scholar, could have such un-Islamic mentality' (Hekmatyar, 2000: 109).

8 The refugees from these provinces I have seen in NWFP and Baluchestan on a number of occasions sent representatives, at great personal danger, to ask if they could return to their land and villages. They were all, without exception, abused and threatened. The Tajik refugees from Tajikistan, who also lived in their houses and villages in Takhar and Kunduz provinces, were then given most of their land. After Kunduz and the southern province of Baghlan fell to the Taleban, all land and houses previously occupied illegally were returned to their rightful owners regardless of their ethnic affiliation

9 These have become the slogans of the weekly *Omaid*, published in California and, according to numerous Afghan sources, funded by Ahmad Shah Masoud and since the fall of Kabul (1996) by Iran. This and a great deal more is revealed by Dr Rostar Taraki, a former Afghan Minister of Education, who is now teaching and researching in Leyon, France, in *Afghan Melat* (Organ of the Afghan Social Democratic Party), issues 72–5, May and June 1998.

10 An Afghan, M. Sedidiq Noorzoy, Emeritus Professor of Economics at the University of Alberta, Research Associate, Centre for Middle East Studies, University of California, Berkley, has worked out in detail a case for the World Court as to how loss of life, earnings for an average life-span, loss of years of the country's income, damage to infrastructure, etc. could be assessed. This report was serialised in the Journal of Afghan exiles, the *Afghanistan Mirror*, in Los Angeles, 1987–88.

11 Professor Anwar ul-Haq Ahadi, of Providence College in the USA, told me that soon after the Taleban took Kabul on 26 September 1996, American intelligence sources reported that Iran supplied twenty plane loads of war material to Masoud and Russia, forty-two planeloads to General Dostum's militia. According to these and other sources, Ahadi is of the opinion that Iran alone is spending some $5 million a day in Afghanistan to keep the anti-Taleban Northern Alliance intact.

12 Rabbani is reported to have told Russian officials in 1994 in a meeting of the Central Asian Nations Economic Forum, held in Dushanbe (Tajikistan), of which Afghanistan, Pakistan, Turkey and Iran are also members, that their war

was with the Soviet Union and not with the Russian Federation. Ignoring the fact that most of the soldiers who fought in Afghanistan were Russian and when Russia inherited the assets of the Soviet Union, it also held itself responsible for its liabilities and international obligations.

13 These four provinces in January 2000 were parts of Parwan, Kapisa, Takhar and the whole of Badakhshan. Though most of Parwan and parts of Kapisa and Takhar were in the hands of the Taleban. Badakhshan's centre Fizabad was in the hands of other warlords.

14 General Boris Gromov, Commander of the Soviet 40th Army *The Red Army in Afghanistan* translated by Pardis Musafer into Pashto; General Liakhovski, deputy to General Veranikov (advisor to Dr Najibullah), *The Bravery and Tragedy of Afghans*, translated by Muhebur Rahman into Pashto.

15 Masoud wanted the six provinces of Parwan, Kapisa, Baghlan, Kunduz, Takhar and Badakhshan to join with Tajikistan. This plan was spoken about in public in 1989 by the then Soviet and French Foreign Ministers. It has also been documented by numerous writers including, the American writer Bruce Richardson in 1994; Soviet 40th Army Commander in Afghanistan, General Boris Gromov 1997; the document of 'agreement between the Soviet Fortieth Army and Ahmad Shah Masood 1982', and many Afghan sources.

16 The ITV news presenter, Sandy Gall, in his book *News From the Front Line*, Chapter 8, tells the story of how British Intelligence asked him to popularise the war in Afghanistan together with the young commander, Ahmad Shah Masoud. His narration starts after British Foreign Secretary Lord Carrington's failed visit to Moscow in 1980 'to try to persuade Brezhnev to withdraw his troops from Afghanistan, arguing that the British had made the same mistake three times in the past 140 years and lived to regret it' (p. 116). Sandy Gall then writes: 'Not very long after that I received a call from a friend in British Intelligence telling me that the Foreign Secretary remained particularly concerned about Afghanistan and was anxious to keep the war in front of the British public', how could that be done? Would I talk to someone from his office and give him, and Lord Carrington, the benefit of my advice?' ... A meeting was arranged with a man from MI6 intelligence. 'We met for lunch at Stone's Chop House in Piccadilly, an old-fashioned eating-house in the English style'. They then discussed, marketing such TV footage; Sandy assuring the MI6 man that either the ITN or BBC would show it. 'The matter rested until 1982 when, deciding it was time the world should be told just what was going on ... in Afghanistan. I rang the same friend in intelligence, told him my plan ... We met again in Stone's and had a very similar sort of lunch'. The man from MI6 then advised Sandy to 'go to Paris and talk to one or two people there', 'Which people?' 'Well, he said, there was a very knowledgeable and much-travelled scholar called Olivier Roy, and another man, also deeply interested in the subject and well-travelled too, called Jean-Jose Puig ... there is, however, one young Afghan guerrilla leader who we think is exceptional. He's called Masud – Ahmad Shah Masud – he's in his twenties and operates from a place called the Panjsher valley'. 'He paused then looked at me very seriously. Because, you see, we think he has all the makings of a second Tito" (Gall 1994: 116–18 &ff.). Also see a detailed review of this book in the *Guardian*, by Richard Gott, '*Playing the Great Game With Incredible Gall*', 12 Feb. 1994. Also *The Times*, same date '*The Virtual Reality of War*', by Ian McIntyre.

17 'Traditional Leadership in Afghan Society and the Issue of National Unity', was the title of a paper I presented to a conference in Bonn (Koenigswinter, September 1990) on *Afghanistan: Problems of Pacification, Repatriation and Reconstruction*. Papers for this conference were published in a volume by Ingo Marenbach (Publisher) with a Foreword by Jachim Herudk (Orig. D), AZK Manuscripts,

Koenigswinter, September 1990. This paper was also published in *Central Asian Survey*, vol. 9, no. 4, pp. 109–12, Pergamon Press, UK.

18 The 1964 constitution, Chapter 5, accepted the *Loya Jirga* as part of the constitution. In 1975 Daoud's Republic and in 1980 Karmal's communist government maintained the constitutional status of *Loya Jirgas*. In 1987 Dr Najibullah's communist government called upon the *Loya Jirga* to abolish the temporary constitution of Babrak Karmal, known as the *Fundamental Principles*, replacing it by his new constitution, explaining the functions of the *Loya Jirga* in Chapter 4, section 66–7, as a reflection of the will of the people.

19 In 1982 the tribes of south-west and south-east Afghanistan called for a *Loya Jirga* near Quetta in Pakistan. Pakistan fearing Pashtun nationalism over Pashtunistan irredentism disrupted this body, threatening its convenors with Hekmatyar and Rabbani's supporters. Another such attempt in Baluchestan also faced a similar fate.

20 The Tajik party, Jam'iat Islami, and its military wing, the *Shura-i-Nezar* supervisory council, even tried to belittle the *Loya Jirga* by coining their own Dari terms for such gatherings: *Shoray Buzerg Islami*, the Great Islamic Council; *Shoray Ahle-Hal-wa-Aqd* the Council of Religious Leaders; *Shoray Qiadi* the Leadership Council; *Shoray Mashwarati*, the Consultative Council; *Shoray Tafahum* the Council of Discernment and so on.

Though *Shura* is Islamic and is a gathering of religious and pious leaders, none of the above *Shuras* had such background or composition. They were all political and sectarian, using the Islamic term *Shura* to give them Islamic credence and to avoid the Pashto term *Jirga* assembly/gathering.

21 These Western and Iranian backed anti-Taleban groups have held meetings of small groups of their supporters in Isfahan (Iran), Istanbul, Bonn, Frankfurt, London and Cyprus, in order to prepare the ground for the convening of a *Loya Jirga*. Parallel to these resistance and warlords' groups, the supporters of the former (87 years old) King Muhammad Zahir, who has been living in exile in Rome since 1973 and is supported by the US state department, has held meetings in Rome and Bonn with a view to convening an 'emergency *Loya Jirga*'. Never in the past has a *Loya Jirga* been organised by exiles or held abroad or supported by foreign powers. Afghans are always suspicious of men who have foreign support. Furthermore, the two groups' approaches and aims in holding a *Loya Jirga* are also different. While the former resistance leaders and warlords wish to be rehabilitated and to share power with the Taleban, the second group would like themselves to replace the Taleban, using the king's name and fame to achieve this.

22 The term Gilamjam was coined during the Soviet occupation for the Uzbek militia, who on entering peoples' homes, used to put every item which was to their liking inside carpet or *gilam* (woven from goat hair), folding it and taking it away.

23 Sayed Jagran, a famous nationalist Hazarah commander, who kept his distance from the excesses of the Iranian backed *Hezb-i-Wahdat* is reported on the Taleban's capture of Bamyan, as saying 'the thing they have done in the name of Hazarahs', meaning it was not according to the wishes of the Shi'ah Hazarahs that *Hezb-i-Wahdat* undertook such barbaric actions against the Sunnis in general, and Pashtun in particular.

24 This recent episode in Afghan ethnic awareness is well known. The quotation comes from Dr Abdul Latif Rashid, the French educated, deputy mayor of Kabul in the early 1950s.

25 Historically Persia was trilingual: Old Persian, Elamite and Akkadian. Later Aramaic 'was employed throughout the empire for imperial administration and also for diplomatic correspondence (Encyclopaedia Britannica, vol. 17, p. 661).

Epilogue

1 Bin Laden later claimed to have given $10 million to Rabbani to find ways of stopping the factional fighting. Taleban also produced written records of Rabbani government granting over 600 Afghan passports to the Arab fighters.
2 The Qizel Bash Shi'ah helped the British forces enter Kabul in 1839; the Hazarahs Shi'ah joined British forces in the Second Anglo-Afghan War in 1879; elements of the Uzbek, Isma'ilia and Tajik joined the Soviets and it is these same groups who threw their weight behind the present occupation by the US.
3 In fact, since the Soviets invasion, the CIA had links and paid millions to Ahmed Shah Masoud and his brother Wali Masoud in London. It is said that there is presently some $300 million in the Morgan Stanley bank in New York belonging to Masoud, over which Fahim, the present military leader, has differences with the Masoud family. These dollars are probably from the money paid to Masoud by the CIA for action against bin Laden, al-Qaeda or the Taleban. It has recently come out into the open that the Masoud brothers regard the money as theirs while Fahim says it belongs to the faction – the Shura-e-Nezar.

Appendix 4: Struggle against Persians in the West

1 Persian emperors, from the time of Darius the Great in 550 BC to the conquests of Alexander in 330 BC, regularly recruited Afghan troops from among the hill Pashtuns in the south and west, as well as Uzbeks from the Kingdom of Bactria (modern Balkh in northern Afghanistan). See: Herodotus, *The Histories*, Book Seven, Penguin edition (1966: 439); Fletcher, A. *Afghanistan: Highway of Conquest*, New York (1965: 28). Herodotus, who is assumed to have been born between 490–480 BC, after talking with the Persian emperor Xeroxes' soldiers, speaks of the Pashtuns as *Gandarians* and of their country as *Pactyca*. *Gandahara* was the name of the region occupied by eastern Pashtuns, which included the Peshawar Valley and its environs, and *Pactyca* is the Province of Paktika (Paktia) in southern Afghanistan to this day (Herodotus 1966: 215).

Appendix 5: Abdali uprising, intrigue and deception

1 The elimination of Dawlat Khan was achieved with the aid of two men, known as Ezat and Atel, and also the assistance of Mir Wais himself, among others of the rival Ghilzai tribe (Ferrier 1858: 24). With the aid of these dissident elements, Dawlat Khan, his son, and his bodyguard were arrested one night and handed over to the Persian governor, who immediately put them to death.
2 The conspirators from the rival Ghilzai Hotak tribe included Mir Wais himself and, from the Sadozai Abdali, two men known to history as Ezat and Atel. According to Ganda Singh, Mir Wais, after showing the Persian governor how to bring down Rustam Khan, withdrew to the background for fear of tribal revenge. Even Ezat, at the last minute, could not make himself shed the innocent blood of his tribal elder and refused. Only Atel, blinded by the glory of leading the Sadozai, went ahead and killed Rustam Khan. The Persian governor's tactic was to make the Pashtuns accountable for one another's murder. However, everyone knew these men were no challenge to Rustam Khan and that he could not have been brought down without the governor's tacit understanding.

Appendix 6: The early life of Ahmad Shah, king in waiting

1 Mazendaran was also the place where Sultan Husain Hotek, the jailer of Ahmad and Zulfiqar and the Ghilzai governor of Kandahar, and his family were exiled by Nader Afshar (Misdaq 1997: 46–8).

2 One version of history is that three years later, when Nader Shah returned to his capital Meshhad, Ahmad Khan went to pay his respects and it was at this time that he was recruited to Nader Shah's forces.
3 Ghanda Singh maintains that Ahmad Khan also accompanied Nader Shah to India. He writes 'After Nader's victory over ... Delhi (9 March 1739) Ahmad Khan was once seen by Nizam-ul-Mulk Chin Qalich Khan Asafjah, a former prime minister of the empire ... sit outside the jail gate near Diwan-i-Am' (1959: 19).
4 Khorasan was the name given to the area from Mashhad and Kerman in the west to Khiwa in the north and Herat and Kandahar in the east. For most of the Safavids' 200-year-rule, this formed a single province; this province changed hands many times between the Persians, Uzbeks and Afghans. See, among others, Al-Afghani (1938: 26–7 and 47) and Gommans (1995: 53 and FN).

Appendix 7: Nader Shah's Assassination, formation of the Afghan

1 For a full account of Nader Shah's cruelty also see: BM. Ms. OR. 3350; and for an account of his reign, see *Shahnameh Naderi*, BM. Ms. ADD. 26285; for an explanation of how Ahmad Shah and his heirs helped Nader's descendants, see Mohammed Ul-Husaini, *Tarikh Ahmad Shahi* (Dari Text) BM. Ms. OR. 196.
2 In January 1747, Nader Shah left Isfahan for Yazd and Kerman. 'Wherever he halted, he had many people tortured and put to death and had towers of their heads erected'. After the Nau-roz celebrations in Kerman, he left for Mashhad where he behaved 'in an even more brutal and inhuman manner than he had done at Isfahan and Kirman' (Ganda Singh 1959: 20).
3 This is an eyewitness account by a Jesuit priest, Rev. Pere Louis Bazin, in the Shah's service, as quoted from his memoirs by Lockhart. Bazin writes that Nader Shah had a premonition of being killed and was determined to leave for 'his headquarters in the impregnable natural fortress of Kalat-i-Naderi in Khorasan' (Wilber 1958: 74), but that his guards assured him of their loyalty to the last man and he decided to remain.
4 About seventy Persian officers, headed by Salih Khan and Mohammed Quli, set out at midnight to execute the plan. Fifty-seven of them disappeared on the way out of terror. Nevertheless, the two coup leaders entered his tent, and Salih Khan struck the king on his hand with his sword and, before Nader could jump to his feet to return the blow, Mohammad Quli struck him on the neck, severing his head (Lockhart 1938: 261).
5 Ahmad Khan and some of his men, who still could not believe the news, rushed to inspect the tent. Seeing the king's body and the looting that was being carried out by the Persian soldiers, Ahmad Khan removed the seal from his dead master's finger, and, saluting the corpse, left with the mass of men who accompanied him back to his quarters. In a matter of four hours the royal tent and all its possession were plundered by the Persian troops.
6 The *Koh-i-Noor* diamond is first mentioned in Babur's autobiography. He maintains that it belonged to the Afghan king, Alaoudin Ghori (1296–1316). It came to Babur's son from the Bikramajit, a raja family, in 1526. It stayed with the Moghuls for the next 200 years, until Nader took possession of it in his first attack on Delhi in 1739. In 1747 it was presented to Ahmad Khan by Nader's wife and remained with Ahmad Shah's family until 1813, when it was extorted from Ahmad Shah's grandson, Shah Shuja, by the Sikh ruler of Punjab, Ranjit Singh. After the capture of Punjab by the British East India Company (EIC) in 1849, the diamond came into the hands of the British and in 1850 they presented it to Queen Victoria. It is now part of the British crown jewels.

Appendix 9: British and Soviet/Russian interest in Afghanistan

1 After the murder by an Afghan prisoner of the Viceroy of India, Lord Mayo, in the Andaman Islands, Lord Northbrook was appointed his successor. Although Northbrook wanted to make an alliance with the Amir, the Gladstone government stopped him from doing so. In 1949 an Afghan from the Zadran tribe in Paktia, who had been expelled from Afghanistan, shot the Prime Minister of Pakistan, Liaqat Ali, in a public gathering for uttering harsh words about Afghanistan.
2 Leyon, despite protests from some of his own cabinet members, wrote: 1) the British would aid Afghanistan in the face of unprovoked attack (the British were to be the judge of the necessity); 2) the British would recognise Abdullah Jan as his heir, as the Amir wished; 3) that Afghanistan was to be open to all English men; and 4) that Afghans were to refrain from any foreign communications without British consent. Privately, Lytton had also spoken of the position of Sher Ali as 'that of an earthen pipkin between two iron pots'.
3 Lord Cranbrook, the Secretary of State for India in London, wrote that Lord Lytton and the 'war party' took this as an excuse to invade Afghanistan for the second time. However, it is very likely that the Amir, after hearing of this armed mission's presence at the Khyber, would have allowed them to proceed to Kabul. The British papers incorrectly wrote that Afghan border guards attacked the British political agent Cavagnari. Lytton also did not follow London's instructions to send the mission through a route other than the Khyber.
4 The British press, once again, had stories of bloodthirsty Afghans cutting the bodies of fallen soldiers to pieces and other such atrocities. But when Major Mitford was assigned to go and bury the bodies, he wrote that the 'bodies had not been mutilated as reported ... I never heard of one authenticated instance of the preparation of such loathsome barbarities as were related by some correspondents' (Fletcher 1965: 140).

Appendix 10: The Pashtunistan issue

1 The acephalous tribes include Bajawar, Mohmand, Khyber, Kurum, Northern and Southern Wazirestan, Orakzai.
2 All quoted in Pazhwak (1953: 148–9) referencing the *Encyclopaedia Britannica*, Encyclopaedia Aryana and Yearbook of Institute of International Law, 1931.
3 Afghan daily Islah, 12 April 1949; Fletcher (1965: 254–5) also quotes the same source.

Bibliography

Manuscripts, newspapers and radio monitoring reports

Afghan Information Centre (AIC) 1988, Monthly Bulletin, no. 93, Peshawar
Afghan Information Centre (AIC) 1989, February, no. 95, Peshawar
Afghanistan Mirror, Published monthly in Los Angeles since 1988
BBC, *Summary of World Broadcast* (SWB), 1979, 11 October
BBC, *Summary of World Broadcast* (SWB) for 1980 (as cited in the text)
BBC, *Summary of World Broadcast* (SWB) Part 3, The Far East, FE/6219/C1/3
BBC, *Summary of World Broadcast* (SWB), FE/6461/C/1, 3 July 1980
BBC, *Summary of World Broadcast* (SWB), FE/6497/C/3, 14 August 1980
BBC, *Summary of World Broadcast* (SWB), FE/6495/C/2, 16 August 1980
BBC, *Summary of World Broadcast* (SWB), FE/6502/C/1, 20 August 1980
BBC, *Summary of World Broadcast* (SWB), FE/6509/C/1, 29 August 1980
Bruce, R. 1997, *Afghanistan Field Report*, December, serial no. 67, vol. 9, pp. 9–15
Daily Telegraph, 1997, 31 July, p. 12
FBIS/US, 1980, 11 February
FBIS/SU, 1980, 13 February
Guardian, 1996, 2 October, p. 11
Hafiz. *Shahnamah* (In Pashto Poetry) BM. Ms. OR. 4231
Hiwad Daily, 1982, 16 June, Peshawar
Journal of South Asia and Middle Eastern Studies, 1994, vol. 17, no. 2
Islah Daily, 1949, 12 April, Kabul
Kabul Radio, 1978, 25 May (Taraki's speech on arrest of opponents)
Mujahed Woles, 1992, November and December, issue
Mujahideen Monthly, 1987, March and April, p. 5, Peshawar
Newsweek, 1980, 12 December
Nader Shah's reign: *Shahnamah Naderi*, BM. Ms. ADD 26285 (Farsi Text)
Nader Shah's cruelty: BM. Ms. OR. 3550 (Farsi Text)
Shahadat, 1997, Organ of Hezb Hekmatyar, published in Peshawar
State Department, Washington, Document No. 789.11/6-2751
The Times, 1996, p. 9, 2 October
Ul-Husaini, Mohammed, *Tarikh Ahmad Shahi*, BM. Ms. OR. 196
Waliullah, Mohammad, *Tarikh-e-Farukhabad*, BM. OR. 1718
Washington Post, 1996, A23, 26 September

Printed books

Adamec, W. Ludwig, 1974, *Afghanistan's Foreign Affair to Mid-Twentieth Century: Relation with the USSR, Germany and Britain*, The University of Arizona Press, Tuscon Arizona.

Adamec W. Ludwig, 1991, *Historical Dictionary of Afghanistan*, The Scarecrow Press Inc. Metuchen, New Jersey, USA.

Afghan Mujahed, March and April 1989, *Eighth Year*, published by Peshawar based interim Government.

Afghan Samsur, 1998, *The Second Saqaw Era* (Pashto text), published by Afghan Cultural Association in Germany.

Afghanistan Chronology 1978–85, United States Information Agency, Washington.

Ahadi, Anwarul Haq, 1988, 'Saudi Arabia, Iran and the conflict in Afghanistan' in ed. Maley *Fundamentalism reborn, Afghanistan under the Taleban*, Hurst and Company, London.

Ahmed Akbar, 1976, *Millennium and Charisma among Pathan – A Critical Essay in Social Anthropology*, Routledge and Kegan Paul, London.

Ahmed Akbar, 1988, *Towards Islamic Anthropology, Definition, Dogma and Directions*, International Institute of Islamic Thought, Virginia, USA.

Ahmed Akbar, 1999, *Islam Today, A Short Introduction to the Muslim World*, IB Tauris Press, London.

Ahmed, Akbar, 1983, *Religion and Politics in Muslim Society*, Cambridge University Press, London.

Akhramovish, R.T., 1966, *Outline History of Afghanistan the Second World War*, Nauka Publication House, Moscow.

Akram, Asem, 2001, *Sardar Mohammad Doud*, Mizan Publishing, Virginia (Dari text) USA.

Al-Afghani, Sayyed Jamal-udin, 1938, *History of Afghanistan* (Trans. from Arabic, 1901, into Dari by Mohammad Amin Khogiani), Kabul.

Amstutz J. Bruce, 1986, *Afghanistan, the First Five Year of Soviet Occupation*, National Defence University, Washington, DC.

Anderson, Benedict, 1983, *Imagined Communities. Reflection on the Origin and Spread of Nationalism*, Published by Verso, London.

Anderson, J., 1978, *Introduction and Overview* in *Ethnic Processes and Intergroup Relations in Contemporary Afghanistan*, Occasional Papers no. 15 of the Afghanistan Council of Asia Society, Summer, New York.

Anwar Raja, 1988, *The Tragedy of Afghanistan, A First Hand Account*, Verso, London and New York.

Arnold Anthony, 1983, *Afghanistan's Two Party Communism: Parcham and Khalq*, Stanford University Press, California.

Arnold Anthony, 1985, *Afghanistan: The Soviet Invasion in Perspective*, Hoover Institute Press, Stamford, California.

Arney, George, 1990, *Afghanistan, the Definitive Account of a Country At a Crossroads*, Mandarin Paperbacks, London.

Asad, Mohammad, 1985, *The Principles of State and Government in Islam*, Dar Al-Andalus, Gibraltar.

Asad, Muhammad, 1975, *The Spirit of Islam*, Islamic Council of Europe, London.

Asia Society, Afghanistan Council, vol. V11, no. 1, January 1979, New York.

Aslanov, M.G., E.G. Gafferberg, N.A. Kisliakov, K.L. Badykhina and G.P. Vasilyeva, 1969, in *Ethnography of Afghanistan: A Russian Study*, eds. G. Grassmuck, L.W.

Bibliography 337

Adamec and F.H. Irwin, *Afghanistan Some New Approaches*, Michigan University Press, Ann Arbor.

Asta Olsen, 1995, *Islam and Politics in Afghanistan*, Curzen Press, London.

Ayoub, Mohaoud M., 1987, *Theology of Islamic History*, Fryer Stowasser Barbara ed., in *The Islamic Impulse*, Centre for Contemporary Arab Studies, Georgetown University, Washington, DC.

Auboyer, J., 1965, *The Art of Afghanistan*, Paul Hamlyn, London,

Bailey, F.G., 1970, *Stratagems and Spoils: A Social Anthropology of Politics*, Blackwell, Oxford.

Banks, Marcus, 1996, *Ethnicity: Anthropological Constructions*, Routledge, London.

Barfield, J. Thomas, 1978, *The Impact of Pashtun Immigration on Nomadic Pastoralism in Northeastern Afghanistan*, in eds. Anderson and Strand, *Ethnic Processes and Intergroup Relations in Contemporary Afghanistan*, Occasional Paper no. 15 of the Afghanistan Council of Asia Society, New York.

Barth, F., 1959, *Segmentary Opposition and the Theory of Games: a Study of Pathan Organisation*, in *JRAI*, Jan–Jun, vol. 89, no. 1, pp. 5–21.

Barth, F., 1959, *Political Leadership Amongst the Swat Pathan*, The Athlone Press, University of London.

Barth, Fredrik, 1969a, ed. *Introduction, Ethnic Groups and Boundaries*, George Allen and Unwin, London.

Berman, Marshall, 1988, *All That is Solid Melts into Air: The Experience of Modernity*, Penguin Books, London.

Bellew, H.W., reprinted 1979, *The Races of Afghanistan: A Brief Account of the Principle Nations Inhabiting that Country*, sang-e-Meel Publications, Lahore.

Beveradge, A.S., 1922, Trans. *The Babur Namah*, London.

Borovek, Artyom, 1990, *The Hidden War – A Russian Journalist's Account of the Soviet War in Afghanistan*, Faber and Faber, London and Boston.

Bradsher, S. Henry, 1985, *Afghanistan and the Soviet Union*, Duke University Press, Durham.

Braudel, Fernand, 1995, *History and the Social Sciences: The Longue Durée*, 1958 trans. Sarah Mattews in *Histories: French Construction of the Past*, in Arthur Goldhammer et al., Romana Naddff series, The New Press, New York.

Brook, S., 1977, *The World Population Today, Ethnographic Processes, Problems of the Contemporary World Series*, 46, Trans. Sam Sheiman, USSR Academy of Sciences, Moscow.

Brown, J. Lieu, Col., 1926, trans. *Battle of Paniput*, 1791, Oxford University Press.

Burke, Peter, 1990, *The French Historical Revolution: The Annales School, 1929–89* Stanford University Press, California.

Burke, Peter, 1992, *History and Social Theory*, Polity Press, England.

Burns, Alexander, 1842, reprint 1973, *Cabool: Being A Personal narrative of a Journey to, and Residence in the City, in the Years 1836, 1837 and 1838*, Akademische Druck-u Verlagsanstalt, Graz, Austria.

Caroe, O., 1965, *The Pathan*, Macmillan & Co, London.

Chronology of Events, 1987, Agency Afghan Press, London.

Clarke, A. Richard, 2004, *Against all Lies, Inside America's War on Terror*, Free Press, New York.

Crile, George, 2003, *Charlie Wilson's War*, Atlantic Monthly Press, New York.

Cohen, Abner, 1969, *Custom and Politics in Urban Africa, A Study of Hausa Migrants in Yoroba Towns*, Routledge and Kegan Paul, London.

Cordovez and Selig Harrison, 1995, *Out of Afghanistan, The Inside Story of the Soviet Withdrawal*, Oxford University Press.
Daoud, M., 1973, *Republic of Afghanistan*, President Daoud Speeches, Messages, interviews and Official Visits. (17 July 1973–15 July 1975), Government Press, Kabul.
Davis, Anthony, 1988, *How the Taleban became a Military Force*, in Maley ed. *Fundamentalism Reborn, Afghanistan under the Taleban*, Hurst and Company, London.
Dupree, Louis, 1980, *Afghanistan*, Princeton University Press, New Jersey, USA.
Dupree, Nancy Hatch, 1984, in Shahrani M. Nazif and Canfield Robert L. eds. *Revolutionary Rhetoric and Afghan Women*, pp. 306–40. *Institute of International Studies*, University of California, Berkeley.
Durrand, Sir H. Mortimer, 1907, 6 November, *The Amir Abdur Rahman Khan*, in the *Proceeding of the Central Asian Society*, London.
Edwards, David B., 1996, *Heroes of the Age: Moral Fault Line on the Afghan Frontier*, University of California Press, Berkley and London.
Elmi, Yosuf, ed. 1988, *Afghanistan – A Decade of Sovietisation*, Peshawar Pakistan, Golden Printing Press.
Elphinstone, M.S., 1965, *An Account of the Kingdom of Caubol*, Graze, Akademische Druck-U. Verllagsanstalt.
Erikson, Thomas Hylland, 1993, *Ethnicity and Nationalism: Anthropological Perspectives* Pluto Press, London and Boulder, Colorado.
Evans-Pritchard, 1940, *The Nuer, A Description of the Modes of Livelihood and Political Institution of a Nilotic People*, Clarendon Press, London.
Faizad, Mohammad 'Alam, 1989, *National Loya Jirgas in Afghanistan* (Dari text), Lahor-Pakistan.
Ferrier, J.P., 1858, *History of the Afghans*, London.
Fletcher, Arnold, 1965, *Afghanistan: Highway of Conquest*, Cornell University Press.
Forgas, David, 1988, *A Gramsci Reader*, Lawrence and Wishart, London.
Fortes and Evans-Pritchard, 1940, *African Political System*, Oxford University Press.
Fox Robin, 1967, *Kinship and Marriage, An Anthropological Perspective*, Penguin Books, London.
Frazer-Tytler, W.K., 1967, *Afghanistan: A Study of Political Developments in Central and Southern Asia*, Oxford University Press.
Franken, Al, 2003, *Lies and the Lying Liars Who Tell Them, a Fair and Balanced Look at the Right*, Dutton, a member of Penguin Group, USA.
Gall, Sandy, 1994, *News from the Front, a Television Reporter's Life*, Heinemann, London.
Ganda, Singh, 1959, *Ahmad Shah Durrani*, Asia Publication House, Bombay.
Gellner, E., 1964, *Thought and Change*, Weidenfeld and Nicholson, London.
Gellner, E., 1994, *Encounter with Nationalism*, Basil Blackwell, Oxford.
Gellner, E., 1983, *Nations and Nationalism*, Basil Blackwell, Oxford.
Ghaus, Abdul Samad, 1999, *The Fall of Afghanistan*, Trans. into Pashto by Dr. S.Z. Th'zai, Danish Bookshop, Peshawar.
Ghose, Dilip Kumar, 1960, *England and Afghanistan: A Phase in Their Relations*, The World Press Private Ltd, Calcutta.
Ghubar, Mir Gholam Mohammad, 1944, *Ahmad Shah Baba-i-Afghan*, Kabul, Government Press (Dari Text).
Giddens, A., 1990, *The Consequences of Modernity*, Polity Press, Cambridge University.

Glazer, Brent, 1997, *Afghanistan on the Brink of Ethnic and Tribal Disintegration*, in Maley ed. *Fundamentalism Reborn? Afghanistan and the Taleban*, Hurst and Co., London.

Glucman, M., 1955, *Custom and Conflict in Africa*, Blackwell, Oxford.

Gommans, J.L., 1995, *The Rise of the Indo-Afghan Empire, c.1710–80*, E.J. Brill, Leiden, Holland.

Goode J. William, 1964, *The Family*, Columbia University, Prentice-Hall, Inc. New Jersey.

Grassmuck, *et al.*, 1969, *Afghanistan: Some New Approaches*, University of Michigan, Ann Arbor, USA.

Gregorian, Vartan, 1969, *The Emergence of Modern Afghanistan, Politics of Reform and Modernization, 1880–1946*, Stanford University Press, USA.

Gromov, Boris, 1997, *Red Army In Afghanistan*, Pashto trans. by Pardais Mosafer, Danish Bookshop, Peshawar.

Grillo, Ralph, 1998, *Pluralism and the Politics of Difference: State, Culture, And Ethnicity in Comparative Perspective*, Clarendon Press, Oxford.

Hager, Rob, 1983, *State, Tribe and Empire in Afghan Inter-Polity Relations* in Tapper ed. *The Conflict of Tribe and State in Iran and Afghanistan*, Croom Helm, London.

Haroon, A., 1996, *Daoud Khan Da KGB Pa Loma Ki*, or *Daoud Khan in KGB's Trap* (Pashto Text), Khyber Publications, Peshawar.

Hastings, Adrian, 1977, *The Construction of Nationhood: Ethnicity, Religion and Nationalism*, Cambridge University Press.

Haviland, 1997, *Anthropology*, University of Vermont, Harcourt Brace College Publishers, USA.

Heikal, Mohammed, 1976, *The Road to Ramadan*, Fontana/Collins, London.

Hekmatyar, G., 2000, *Barbandai Cairai, Patai Dasisay* or *Hidden Conspiracies, Known Faces* (Pashto Text), Peshawar.

Herawi, Mohammad Anwar, 1969, *The Expeditions of Ahmad Shah Durrani* (Dari text), Government Press, Kabul.

Herodotus, 1966, *The Histories*, Book Seven, Penguin, London.

Hobsbawm, E.J., 1990, *Nations and Nationalism Since 1780: Programme, Myth and Reality*, Cambridge University Press, Cambridge.

Hopkirk, Peter, 1994, *On Secrete Service East of Constantinople: The Plot to Bring Down the British Empire*, John Murray, London.

Hyman, Anthony, 1984, *Afghanistan Under Soviet Domination*, Macmillan Press, London.

Ibn Hazam, 1980, *Al-Muhalla, on Fard, Haram and Mubah* quoted in *State and Government in Islam*, by Assad, Dar Al-Andalus, Gibraltar.

Isby, C. David, 1989, *War in a Distant Country, Afghanistan: Invasion and Resistance*, Arms and Armour Press, London.

Jalali, Gulam Jailani, 1967, (commentary and notes), *Ahmad Shah the Great's letter to Sultan Mustafa III Usmani* (Farsi text), the Historical Society of Afghanistan, Kabul.

Jenkins, R., 1996, *Ethnicity etcetera: Social Anthropological Points of View*, in *Ethnic and Racial Studies*, vol. 19. no. 4. October, Routledge, London.

Kakar, M. Hassan, 1995, *Afghanistan, The Soviet Invasion and the Afghan Response, 1979–1982*, University of California Press.

Kakar, Hassan, 1971, *Afghanistan: A Study in International Political Development*, Punjab Educational Press, Lahore.

Bibliography

Kakar, Mohammad Hassan, 1988, *De Afghanistan pu bab de Genev Jorah*, or *Geneva settlement about Afghanistan* (Pashto text), Writers Union of Free Afghanistan (WUFA) Publications, Peshawar.

Klass, Rosanne, ed., 1987, *Afghanistan: The Great Game Revisited*, Freedom House, New York.

Kushkaki, Sabahuddin, 1986, *Dah-e-Qanune Asasi: Ghaflat Zadagi Afghanha Wa Fursat Talabi Rusha* (Dari Text) The Decade of the Constitution: the Unawareness of the Afghans and the Opportunism of the Russians, Published by the Cultural Council of Afghan Jihad, Pashawar.

Latour, Bruno, 1993, *We Have Never Been Modern*, Trans. Catherine Porter, Prentice Hall, London.

Levi-Strauss, Claude, 1969, *The Elementary Structure of Kinship*, Social Science Paperbacks, London.

Liakhovski, Alexander, 2000, *Afghan Heroism and Tragedy*, Pashto trans. by Muhebur Rahman, Afghan Cultural Association, Germany.

Lockhart, L., 1938, *Nader Shah: A Critical Study, Based Mainly Upon Contemporary Sources*, London.

Mackenzie, D.N., 1965, trans. *Poem from the Diwan of Khoshal Khan Khattak*, George Allen and Unwin Ltd.

Majrooh, S.B. and Elmi, S.M.Y., 1986, *The Sovietisation of Afghanistan*, Printed Corporation of Frontier Limited, Peshawar.

Male, Beverly, 1982, *Revolutionary Afghanistan – A Reappraisal*, Croom Helm, London.

Maley, Williams (ed.), 1998, *Fundamentalism Reborn? Afghanistan and the Taleban*, Hurst and Company, London.

Malleson, G.B., 1879, *History of Afghanistan from the Earliest Period to 1878*, London.

Marsden, Peter, 1998, *The Taliban, War, Religion and the New Order in Afghanistan*, Oxford University Press.

Maududi, S. Abdul 'Ala, 1968, *First Principle of the Islamic State*, Islamic Publications Ltd, Lahore, Pakistan.

Maududi, S. Abdul 'Ala, 1976, *Fundamentals of Islam*, Islamic Publication Limited, Lahore, Pakistan.

Mitrokhin, Vasiliy, 2002, *The KGB in Afghanistan*, working paper no. 40 introduced and edited by Christian F. Ostermann and Odd Arne Westad, Cold War International History Project, Washington, DC.

Misdaq, N., 1997, *Ahmad Shah Durrani Founder and First King of Modern Afghanistan*, Irfan publication, Delhi.

Misdaq, N., 2000, *Afghan Foreign Policy in 20th Century*, in *Afghanistan in the 20th Century*, Afghanistan Cultural Association (Pashto text) Germany.

Misdaq, N., 1997, *Nationhood in the make-up of Contemporary Afghanistan*, Pashtunkhwa Publication (Pashto Text) Peshawar.

Mohammad, Yasien, 1995, *Fitra: the Islamic Concept of Human Nature*, Ta Ha Publishers, London.

Mohammad, Yosuf and Mark Adkin, 1992, *The Bear Trap, Afghanistan's Untold Story*, Leo Copper, London.

Mohammad, Ali, 1959, *The Mohammadzai Period*, Government Publication, Kabul.

Mousavi, S.A., 1998, *The Hazarahs of Afghanistan, An Historic Cultural and Economic Study*, Curzon Press.

Munshi, Mir ed., 1900, two vols. *The Life of Abdur Rahman, Amir of Afghanistan*, John Murray, London.

Noelle, Christine, 1997, *State and Tribe in the Nineteenth-Century Afghanistan, the Reign of Amir Dost Mohammad Khan (1826–1863)*, Curzon Press.
Norris, J.A., 1967, *The First Afghan War-1838–1842*, Cambridge University Press.
Nyrop, Richard F. and Donald M. Seekins eds., 1986, *Afghanistan: A Country Study, Foreign Area Studies*, The American University, Washington, DC.
Olesen, Asta, 1995, *Islam and Politics in Afghanistan*, Curzon Press.
Pazhwak, Abdur Raman, 1953(?), *Pakhtunistan: The Khyber Pass as the Focus of the New State of Pakhtunistan*, Afghan Embassy, London.
Pazhwak, Abdur Rahman, 1987, *Muzakerate Genev or Geneva Talks, Collection of Essays of Afghan Mujahed Information Centre*, Peshawar.
Petrokhin, Vasiliy, 2002, *The KGB in Afghanistan*, Working paper no. 40 introduced and edited by Christian F. Ostermann and Odd Arne Westad. Printed by Woodrow Wilson International Center for Scholars, Washington, DC.
Poulada, B. Leon, 1973, *Reform and Rebellion in Afghanistan, 1919–29*, Cornell University, USA.
Poulada, B. Leon, 1962, *Problems of Social Development in Afghanistan*, JRCAS, January.
Rahim, M.A., 1961, *History of the Afghans in India AD 1545–1631*, Pakistan Publishing House, Karachi.
Rashid, Abdul, 1987, *The Afghan Resistance: Its Background, Its Nature, and the Problem of Unity*, in *Afghanistan the Great Game Revisited*, ed. Klass, Freedom House, New York.
Rashid, Ahmed, 1998, *Pakistan and the Taleban*, in ed. Maley, *Fundamentalism reborn, Afghanistan under the Taleban*, Hurst and Company, London.
Rashid, Ahmed, 2000, *Taliban, Islam, Oil and the New Great Game in Central Asia*, Yale University Press, New Haven, CT.
Rashid, Ahmed, 2001, *Taliban: Islam, Oil and the New Great Game in Central Asia*, Pan Macmillan, London.
Reshtia, Sayed Qasem, 1984, *The Price of Liberty: The Tragedy of Afghanistan*, Bardi Editore, Rome, Italy.
Reshtia, Sayed Qasem, 1990, *Between Two Giants: Political History of Afghanistan in the Nineteenth-Century*, Afghan Jihad Works Translations, Peshawar, Pakistan.
Richardson, Bruce, 1996, *Intimidation, subversion and Pacification: Russian Policy in Transcaucasia, Central Asia and Afghanistan*, Afghanistan Mirror, California.
Richardson, Bruce, 1996, *Afghanistan Ending the Reign of Terror*, Maverick Publications, Bend, Oregon.
Robertson, G. S. 1896, (reprint 1974), *The Kafirs of the Hindu-Kush*, Oxford University Press.
Roucek, S. Joseph, 1967, *Minority-Majority Relations in Their Power Aspects* in Harry A. Bailey ed. *Negro Politics in America*, Temple University, Charles E. Merrill Books Inc. Columbus, Ohaio.
Roy, Olivier, 1986, *Islam and Resistance in Afghanistan*, Cambridge University Press.
Roy, Olivier, 1989, *Afghanistan back to Tribalism or on to Lebanon? Third World Quarterly, Ethnicity in World Politics*, pp. 70–82, October, vol. 11, no. 4, London.
Roy, Olivier, 1988, *Has Islamism a Future in Afghanistan From Traditionalism to Fundamentalism to Islamism ... and Back*, in ed. Maley, *Fundamentalism Reborn? Afghanistan and the Taliban*, Hurst and Company, London.
Rubin, Barnet, R., 1991, *Old Regime in Afghanistan: Recruitment and Training of a State Elite*. Central Asian Survey, vol. 10, no. 3. Society for Central Asian Studies, Pergaman Press.

Rubin, Barnet, R., 1995, *The Fragmentation of Afghanistan*, Yale University Press.
Rubin, Barnet, R., 1995, *The Search for Peace in Afghanistan, From Buffer State to Failed State*, Yale University Press.
Sahi (no first name), 1994, *Yak Dah-e-Democarasi Der Afghanistan* (Dari Text), A decade of Democracy in Afghanistan, Peshawar, 1994.
Sharq, M. Hassan, 1996, *Karbas Posh-i-Berahnah Pa, Raz haye Nohoftah-Jeryanat Pushte Pardah wa Inkeshafate Takan Dehendah, 1310–1370*, Saba Ketabkhanah, Peshawar. [Memoir of Hassan Sharq, 1932–92 in Dari].
Shahrani, M. Nazif and Canfield, L. Roberts, 1984, *Revolution and Rebellion in Afghanistan: Anthropological Perspective*, Berkley, California.
Sikorski, Radek, 1987, *Moscow's Afghan War: Soviet Motives and Western Interests*, Institute for European Defence and Strategic Studies, Occasional Paper no. 27, London.
Silverman, Marlin and P.H. Gulliver, 1996, *Inside Historic Anthropology: Scale-reduction and Context*, Focal no. 26/27, London.
Singhal, D.P., 1963, *India and Afghanistan: A Study in Diplomatic Relations, 1876–1907*, University of Queensland Press, Australia.
Smith, D. Anthony, 1986, *The Ethnic Origins of Nations*, Basil Blackwell, Oxford.
Southall, A., 1956, *Alur Society*, Heffer, Cambridge.
Sykes, Percy, 1915, *A History of Persia*, vol. II. Macmillan, London.
Tabibi, Abdul Hakim, 1985, *A Nation in Love with Freedom*, Igram Press, Los Angeles, USA.
Tahir, Amin, 1984, *Afghan Resistance, Past, Present and Future*, In *Asian Survey*, vol. 24, no. 3: 373–99, Islamabad, Pakistan.
Tapper, Nancy, 1991, *Bartered Brides, Politics, Gender and Marriage in an Afghan Tribal Society*, in *Cambridge Studies in Social and Cultural Anthropology*, Cambridge University Press.
Tapper, Richard, 1988, *Ethnicity, Order and Meaning in the Anthropology of Iran and Afghanistan*, in Colloques internationaux Le fait ethnique en Iran et Afghanistan, editions du CNRS, Paris.
Tapper, Richard, ed., 1983, *Introduction* in: *The Conflict of Tribe and State in Iran and Afghanistan*, Croom Helm, London.
Tapper, Nancy, 1983, *Abd Al-Rahman's NorthWest frontier: the Pashtun Colonisation of Afghan Turkistan* in R. Tapper ed. *Conflict of Tribe and State in Iran and Afghanistan*, Croom Helm.
Taraki, Nur Mohammad, 1960, *De Bang Mosafery*, The Travels of Bang (Pashto text), Pashto Academy, Kabul.
Thapar, Romila, 1966, *A History of India*, vol. I. Penguin Books.
Tytler-Fraser, W. Kerr, 1953, *Afghanistan: A Study of Political Development in Central and Southern Asia*, Oxford, London.
Urban, Mark, 1990, *War in Afghanistan*, Macmillan Press, London.
(US Embassy papers), *Spies Nest*, 1980, vol. 29, Tehran, Iran.
Varma, B., 1968, *English East India Company and the Afghans, 1757–1800*, Punthi Pustak, Calcutta.
Wajdi, Abdul Jalil, 1986, *De Afghanistan de `Ana`nawi Jirgo Nan aw Saba* or *The Today and Tomorrow of Traditional Jirgas in Afghanistan* (Pashto text), Aman Books, Peshawar-Pakistan.
Wak, M. Inamuddin, 1998, *The Ethnic Composition of Afghanistan*, WAK Foundation for Afghanistan, Printed by Sapi Centre, Peshawar, Pakistan.

Wakman, Mohammad Amin, 1985, *Afghanistan at the Crossroad*, New Delhi, ABC Publishing House.
Weber, Max, 1947, *From Max Weber, Essays in Sociology* eds H. Gerth and C.W. Mills, Routledge and Kegan Paul, London.
Weber, Max, 1973, in *Elite Against Democracy, Leadership Ideals in Bourgeois Political Thought in Germany 1890–1933*, by Walter Struve, Princeton University, Princeton New Jersey.
Weber, Max, 1978, *Economy and Society, An Outline of Interpretive Sociology*, eds. Guenther Roth and Claus Wittich, London.
Weber, Max, 1964, *The Theory of Social and Economic Organisation*, Translated by A.M. Henderson and Talcott Parsons, ed. with an introduction by Talcott Parsons, The Free Press, New York.
Whitteridge, Gordon, 1986, *Charls Masson of Afghanistan: Early Explorer, Archaeologist, Numismatist and Intelligence Agent*, Aris and Philips Ltd, Warminster, England.
Woodward, Bob, 2004, *Bush at War*, Simon & Schuster, New York.
Wolesmal, M.H. ed., 1988, *Geneva Talks, Collection of Essays by AR Pazhwak*, Published by Afghan Mujahed Information Centre, Peshawar.
Wilber, N. Donald, 1962, *Afghanistan: its People its Society its Culture*, Hraf Press, New Haven, USA.
Wilber, N. Donald, 1958, *Iran: Past and Present*, Princeton University Press.
Writer's Union of Free Afghanistan (WUFA), Series no. 77, Peshawar, Pakistan.
Yosufzai, M. Baqai, 1337 (1958–59), *Gross National Product of Afghanistan*, Kabul.

Index

Abdali tribe 40–4, 53, 281–2
Abdal-Wahhab, Muhammad ibn 145
Abdullah, Abdullah 245
Abdullah, Wahid 91, 93
Abdullelah, Sayed 91
Abdur Rahman, Amir 4–5, 49–50, 52–61, 68–9, 150, 219–20, 227, 233
Achak, Jumu'ah 171
Achekzai, Mansur 180
'Achekzai Militia' 162
Adams, Brad 256
advisors, Soviet 129–30, 135, 138–9
'Afghan Arabs' 242–3
Afghan–Soviet treaty 69
Afridi tribe 37, 294, 297, 313, 314
Afshar tribe 41
Ahadi, Anwarul Haq 205
Ahmad Noor, Noor 83
Ahmad Shah Durrani (Ahmad Khan) 3, 19, 21, 26, 39, 43–9, 45, 53, 55; early life of 283–4
Ahmadzai, Shapur 90, 121
Ahmed, Akbar 10, 14–15, 18
Akbari, Aziz 124, 130
Akhramovich, R.T. 98
Akram, Asem 79, 82
Al-Afghani, Sayed Jamaludin 46, 98
Ala'udin Khan 182
Al-Azhar University 81, 145, 146–7
Ali, Nawab 124–5
Alizai, Nur Mohammad Khan 42–3
al-Qaeda 241, 246–7, 254, 260, 264–9
Alur people 22–3
Amanullah, King 14, 61–9, 76–7, 147, 218–20, 228, 233
Amin, Hafizullah 93–4, 102–4, 107–13, 118–38
Amin, Tahir 150, 154
Amnesty International 204
Amstutz, J. Bruce 125

Amu Darya 208
Anas, Mohammad 110
Andarabi militia 162
Anderson, Benedict 24–7
Anderson, J. 222
Angar, Faiz Mohammad 98
Ansari, Bayazid (Pir Roshan) 36–7
Anthony, Ross 262
Anwar, Raja 118, 121, 125, 127, 130, 134, 136
Aqa, Gul 156
arms supplies 207–8
Arney, George 96
Arnold, Anthony 83, 85–6, 101, 104, 108–9
Asad, Muhammad 149
Ashraf, Shah 41, 226
Attaturk, Kemal 64
Auboyer, J. 35
Awakened Youth movement *see Wish Zalmyan*
Azher, Samad 90, 120
Azimi, Nabi 171
Aziz, Mir Abdul 41

Babur, General Nasirullah 150, 180
Babur, Zahir ud-Deen Mohammed 36
Bachai Saqaw 64–5, 207–8, 228–9
Badakhshi, Taher 105
Baghlani, Bashir 188
Balkhi, Sayyed Ismail 147
Baluchestan 29, 62, 170, 177–80, 289, 293, 305, 316, 317
Baluchi tribe 37
Bamyan 217, 325, 331
Bangash 37, 38
Banks, Marcus 26
Barakzai dynasty 53–4
Barth, Fredrik 14, 97, 200, 230
Baryali, Mahmud 121

Batrayev, B.N. 121
Battle of Maiwand 291
Beg, Ibrahim 66, 218
Begum, Mughlani 47
Beria, Lavrenti 216
Berman, Marshall 115–16
Bhutto, Benazir 179–80
Bhutto, Zulfiqar Ali 131, 149
bin Laden, Osama 72, 196, 210–11, 241–6, 268
Bolshevik 70
Borowiak, Craig 265
boundaries, territorial and cultural 222
Bradsher, S. Henry 92, 94, 124, 127–9, 132
Brahimi, Laskhdar 257
Braudel, Fernand 5–6
Brezhnev, Leonid 70, 84, 91, 93, 111, 124–5
Britain and the British Empire 4, 13–14, 18, 29, 54, 56, 60–72, 77, 155, 210–11, 226–7, 239, 267, 287–92
Bulganin, Nikolai 84, 91
Burjon, Mullah 180, 184
Bush, George (senior) 160
Bush, George W. 215, 241–54, 260, 264–70

Caroe, Olaf 11–12
Carrington, Lord 155
Carter, Jimmy 159
census-taking 236–7
Centivres-Demont, Pierre and Micheline 222
Central Intelligence Agency (CIA) 111, 159, 163, 187, 196, 210, 241–52, 259, 268
Chaliand, Gerard 150–2
Charkhi family 67
Cheney, Richard 249–50
China 106, 159, 165, 218
Chishti Order 153
civil wars, Afghan 3–4, 30, 53–4, 65, 173–4, 226–7, 241
Clarke, Richard 241–2, 244, 252–3, 267–9
Clinton, Bill 241, 243, 253, 268–9
Cloob-e-Meli 85
Cohen, Abner 101, 206
communist ideology and party 3, 81–5, 88–91, 94–103, 117, 152–3, 171, 201–2, 232; *see also* Khalq faction; Parcham faction

constitution, Afghan: 1923 version 63–4, 147, 228; 1931 version 67, 75; 1964 version 79–80, 147
Convention of St Petersburg 68
Cordovez, Diego 168–70

Daoud, Mohammad 21, 67, 70, 75–9, 82–96, 99, 108–12, 117–18, 143, 147–50, 167, 229–32
Dari language 8, 21–2, 81–2, 103–6, 176, 195, 200–1, 230–1, 237–8
Davis, Anthony 177–8
Dawlat Khan 44
'decade of the constitution' 79–82, 105, 229–30
'decade of Sovietisation' 130
Delhi Sultanate, the 28, 36, 199, 312
Democratic Women's Organisation of Afghanistan (DWOA) 161
Democratic Youth Organisation of Afghanistan (DYOA) 161
democratisation 75, 80–1, 85–6, 105, 239
depleted uranium weapons 260–3
Derwaza, Akhund 37
Dobbins, James 251–2
Doran, Jamie 187, 257–9
Dost Mohammad 53–4, 95, 227, 233
Dostoevsky, Feodor 122
Dostum, Abdul Rashid 115, 162, 174, 180, 185–8, 204, 213, 251–3, 258–9
Dubs, Adolpho 77
Dupree, Nancy Hatch 7, 51, 60, 64
Durakovic, Asaf 260
Durand, Sir Mortimer 61
Durand Line 24, 60–1, 69–70, 76–7, 227, 293–9
Durrani, Ahmad Shah 215, 226, 233
Durrani tribe 53, 200, 226–7
Durr-i-durran 44

ecological conditions in Afghanistan 225
economy of Afghanistan 8–9
educational system 190–3, 238
Edwards, David B. 6, 58, 227
Egypt 92, 126, 159, 236
Eid Conspiracy 120–1
Eisenhower, Dwight D. 84
Elmi, Yosuf 130
Elphinstone, Mountstuart 11–12, 37–8
Emad, Nurullah 147
Erikson, Thomas Hylland 30, 221

ethnicity and ethnic divisions 2, 5–7, 21, 29–30, 72, 81, 105, 195, 198–203, 213–18, 221–2, 227–33, 239

Fahim, General 245–7
Faiz Mohammad, Major 83, 86
Faizani, Mawlawi Ataullah 147, 149
Farooqi, M. 92
Farsi language 106, 221, 237
Fateh Khan 54
Fawzi, General 186
Federal Bureau of Investigation (FBI) 110, 241
Fetter, Steve 262
'fission' 22–3
five-year plans 77–8
Fletcher, Arnold 12, 43, 46, 53–4, 62, 65, 144
France 210–11, 239
Franken, Al 247
Frazer-Tytler, W.K. 47–8, 54
fundamentalism 145, 209

Gahiz, Minhajudin 146–7
Gailani, Sayed Ahmad 158
Gandomak treaty 60, 81, 227
'Gary' 245–6
Gellner, Ernest 25–8
Geneva negotiations and Accord (1982–88) 168–9, 306–9
Germany 268
Ghafar Akhundzadah 181
Ghafar Khan, Khan Abdul 107–8, 181
Ghilzais 46, 57
Ghobar, Mir Gholam Mohammad 98
Gigiani tribe 37
gilamjam 162
Glazer, Brent 29–30
globalisation 233
Gommans, J.L. 45–7
Gorbachev, Mikhail 165, 170
Gorgin (Shah Nawaz Khan) 39–40
Gortchakow Circular 68
Gran, Mohammad In'am 93–4
Gregorian, Vartan 11, 13, 37, 98, 56–7, 65
Grillo, Ralph 55
Gromov, Boris 210–12
Gromyko, Andrei 93, 124
Guantanamo Bay 256
Gulabzoy, Sayed Mohammad 86, 123
Gulistani, Abdul-Hasan 43
Gulliver, P.H. 12

Haday Mullah 145
Hager, Rob 17–18, 35, 49
Haji Jamal Khan 43, 53
Haq, Abdul 147–50
Haq, Mawlana Sami'ul 177
Haqiqat-i-Inqlab-i-Saur 154
Harakat-i-Inqilab-i-Islami 102, 158
Harakat-i-Islami Afghanistan 152
Harold, Marc 263, 266
Hashem Khan 67
Hass, Richard 248
Hazarah 7, 8, 21–2, 29, 43, 57, 62, 81–2, 106, 151, 167, 172–4, 183, 186–9, 200, 203–7, 210–13, 217–21, 223, 230–1, 302, 305
Hazarajat 58, 160, 184, 205, 220–1, 305
Hekmatyar, Gulbodin 90, 147–52, 172–84, 181, 205–6, 269
Herat uprising (1979) 127
Herawi 45
Herodotus 68
Herold, Marc 265–6
Hersh, Seymore M. 255
Hilferty, Bryan 255
Hippel, Frank 262
Hobsbawm, E.J. 50
honour, concept of 143
Hotak 39, 40, 41
human rights violations 204, 255–9
'Hunk' 245
Hussian, Mohammad Shah 41, 113
Hyman, Anthony 89–90, 105

Ibrahim, Muhammad 147
identity, Afghan 234, 239
'imagined communities' 24–7
imperialism 13, 18, 49
Inderfurth, Karl 244
India 1, 45, 61, 77, 92, 210, 226–7, 239, 267
individualism, Afghan 97
inflation 208
International Monetary Fund (IMF) 9
Ipi Faqir 145
Iqbal, Mohammad 136
Iran 1, 21, 84, 91–2, 127, 131, 152, 160, 169, 188, 192–3, 196–7, 202–10, 216, 221, 226, 231, 238–9, 247, 250, 267
Iraq 196, 252–6, 262
Isfahan 41
Islam and Islamism 10, 15, 30–2, 37, 39, 50, 71, 90, 144–52, 160–1, 164, 167, 170–4, 191–5, 229, 234–5, 242
Isma'il Khan 180–3, 186, 252

Isma'ilia 207
Itehad-e-Pashtunistan 85
Itihad-i-Islami Afghanistan (Islamic Unity of Afghanistan – IUA) 158
Ivanov, Igor 208
Ivashutin, Peter 133

Jabha Meli Padarwatan 128
Jabh-i-Nejat Meli (National Liberation Front – NLF) 158
Jahan Khan 45
Jahn, Amir 258
Jalaler, Mohammad Khan 91, 95
Jami'at Islami 203
Jam'iat Islami of Pakistan 152
Japan 268, 270
Jawanon-e-Afghan 98, 115
Jawanon-e-Musulman *90*
Jelalabad 161, 165
Jenkins, R. 231
jirgas 42–3, 71, 144, 214, 226
Jordan 236
Jowzjani 162
Jummah Khan 162
Junbish Shamal 203, 210
jurisprudence 277–9

Kabul Radio 161
Kabul University 146–7
Kafir 220
Kakar, Mohammad Hassan 121, 128
Kakar tribe 40
Kandahar 26, 39–47, 180–1, 199, 219, 226
Kargari Atla'ti Mo'sesah (KAMor Worker's Information Bureau) 130
Karim, Abdul 64
Karmal, Babrak 83–7, 94, 99–107, 111–15, 118–25, 130, 132, 137, 153, 157–8
Karzai, Hamed 168, 193, 215, 223, 240, 248–54, 265, 269–70
Katawazi, Kheyal Muhammad 124
Kayan 162, 207
Kemal, Mustafa 98, 220
Kerman 41
Keshtmand, Ali, Sultan 9, 120, 203
KGB 114, 120, 129–30, 137, 157, 232
KhAD 161, 162, 163, 195, 326
Khairkhwah, Khairullah 178
Khalis, Muhammad Yonus 90, 146–52, 205
Khalizad, Zalmai 215
Khalq faction 84, 93, 99–103, 115, 118–22, 125, 128–9, 132–5, 138, 152, 179, 194–5, 198, 202, 229–32
Khattak, Khushal Khan 27–8, 37–8
Khoja Khizer 44
Khomeini, Ruhollah 148
Khoram, Ahmad Ali 91, 94
Khorasan 26, 46, 49, 284, 333
Khruschev, Nikita 84, 91
Khyber, Mir Akbar 94, 114
kings of Afghanistan 20–3, 43, 45, 48, 61, 71
Klass, Rosanne 102, 104, 114, 143
Koh-i-Noor diamond 286
Kolesnik, Vasily 129, 133, 137
Konduz 258–60, 264
Koror, Amir 10, 20
Kosygin, Alexei 134
Krishnan, N.K. 92
Kuzichin, Vladimir 87, 114

Lali, Amir 180
landowners, treatment of 153
La'q, Suliman 119, 162
legitimacy of Afghan state and tribes 234, 240
Lenin, V.I. 69, 107, 111
Levi-Strauss, Claude 79
Liakhovski, General 210–12
'Liberal Parliament' (1949) 75
Lindh, John Walker 258
Lodi 36, 39, 312, 314
Logar 181
longue-durée of Afghan history 5–6, 224
Los Angeles Times 197
Loya Jirgas 42, 59, 63, 66, 71–2, 92, 138, 169–70, 173, 195, 201, 213–15, 223, 228, 233

McEntee, Andy 259
madrassas 145, 176–7, 191, 201, 232
Mahaz-i-Meli Islami (National Islamic Front of Afghanistan – NIFA) 158
Mahmud, Shah 65–7, 75–6, 218, 220
Mahmudi, Abdur Rahman 85, 98, 105
Mahrattas 45–6
Maiwandwal, Mohammad Hashem 78, 89–90
Majrooh, Baha'udeen 152–3, 170
Male, Beverly 111–13, 122–3, 129, 132, 135
Malik, Abdul 185–7, 204, 213
Marsden, Peter 172, 191–2
Masher, Mullah 182

Masoud, Ahmad Shah 90, 145, 147–50, 162, 167, 171–4, 181–92, 196, 206–12, 219, 231–2, 240, 245, 250
Mawdudi, Abul 'Ala 145
Mazari, Abdul Ali 174, 183
Mazdak, Farid 163
Mazdoryar, Sherjan 86, 123
Meli Mutahadah Jabah 128
Metrokhin, Vasiliy 102–3, 114–15, 120–1, 137, 232
Middelton, John 22
minefields 3, 106
Mir Abdul Aziz (Abdullah) 41
Mir Mahmud 41
Mir Wais (Amir Khan) 39–40
Miraki, Mohammed Daud 260, 264
Misdaq, Nabi 43, 214, 280, 314, 332
modernisation policies 13–14, 59–61, 64, 71, 75–8, 94, 98, 117, 219, 229, 232
Moghul Empire 36–9, 50, 199, 267
Mohammad Khan, Payendah 229
Mohammad Zaher, King 67, 75–9, 84–5, 95, 170–3
Mohammadi, Nabi 102
Mohammadzai tribe 37, 43, 227
Mohaqeq 186, 188
Mohmand tribe 37
Mohtat, Abdul Hamid 86
Momin, General 207
monarchy, Afghan, abolition of 82–3, 230
Mubarak, Hosni 242
Muhammad, Prophet 192
Muhammadi, Muhammad Nabi 158, 176
Muhammadzai clan 54
Muin-ul-Mulk 47
Mujadedi, Muhammad Ibrahim 147
Mujadedi, Sebghatullah 146, 158, 172, 250
Mujahideen 2–3, 124, 143, 156, 159–60, 165, 171–2, 175–9, 190–3, 203, 210–13, 216–21, 230–2, 236, 242–3, 252, 302–5
Mullah Mushk'alem 145
Mullah-i-Lang 64
Mu'min, Abdul 171, 174
Munshi, Mir 59, 61
Murad Bi, Shah 46
Musaheban family 106, 200, 201, 218, 229
Musharaf, Pervaiz 211, 248–9
Mushk Alam, Mullah 56

Muslim, Aslat 162
Muslim Brotherhood 113, 145, 152
Mustaghni, Abdul Karim 85
Muttaqi, Amir Khan 188, 193
Myers, Richard 248

Nader Afshar 41
Nader Khan, King (Nader Shah) 47, 65–7, 147, 218, 229; assassination 285–6
Naderi, Jafer 207
Naderi, Mansur 162
Nadershah 44, 45
Naim, Mohammad 79, 82, 96
Naim, Mustafa 96
Najibu Dullah 46
Najibullah, Dr Mohammad 3, 115, 162–4, 169–72, 185, 195
Naqib, Mullah 181
Naqshbandi Order 45, 153, 304, 321
'nationalisation' policy 59–60, 71
nationalism 13–14, 24–9, 37, 39, 43, 77, 99, 152, 173, 195, 200, 208, 222
nation-state, definition of 51
NATO 70, 84, 93, 112, 155, 159, 270, 320
natural gas supplies 8–9, 70–1, 164
Neda-i-Haq (Voice of Truth) 147
Neday-e-Khalq 85
Nekmal, Mullah 183
New York Times 265
newspapers 75–6, 85, 88, 98–9, 104–5, 148, 230
Niak, Niaz 244
Niazi, Ghualam Muhammad 90, 146, 149, 152
Nixon, Richard 84
non-aligned status 76, 84, 164–5
Norris, James 155
North Atlantic Treaty Organisation (NATO) 269–70
North West Frontier Province (NWFP) 15, 18, 36, 110
Northern Alliance 172–3, 195, 205, 211, 213, 243–50, 256–8, 269
Nurestani, Qadir 91

Olesen, Asta 31, 145
Omaid publication 213
Omar, Mullah Muhammad 175, 178–81, 186, 189–92, 235, 248
Orakzai tribe 37, 334
Organisation of Islamic Conference (OIC) 143, 156, 323, 329

Oruzgon 251
Ottomans 41

Pacha Khan 248
Pahlawan, Rasul 185
Pakistan 1, 61, 69–70, 76–81, 84–5, 90–2, 106, 124, 131, 143, 147–54, 157–8, 168–70, 174, 179–80, 187, 193–7, 202–7, 210–11, 216, 254
Paktia 10, 64–6, 132, 154–5, 182, 184, 201, 264
Paktiawal, Akhtar Muhammad 157
Paktika 68, 155, 182, 201, 261, 264
Panamarev, Boris 108
Panipat, battle of 46
Panjsher 150, 211
Parcham faction (and Parchamis) 83–95, 99–104, 113–15, 118–22, 125, 128–9, 132, 138, 149, 152, 179, 194–5, 198, 202, 216, 229–32
Pashto language 8, 10, 23, 81–2, 106, 201–3, 237–8
Pashtun society and culture 2–32, 36–9, 48–51, 55, 58, 171, 190–3, 199–206, 209–16, 225–9, 232–3, 236, 249–50, 270
Pashtunistan issue 76–9, 82, 90, 106, 143, 147–50, 170, 293–9
Pashtunwali 10–11, 32, 41, 188, 196, 204, 233–4, 243, 273–6
Patmanah 136
patriarchy 48
patrimonial system 19–23, 46, 48, 55, 229
patronage 81
Pavendah Khan 53
Pavlovskiy, Ivan 91–2, 129
Pazhwak, Ne'matullah 85
People's Democratic Party of Afghanistan (PDPA) 80, 83, 87, 91–4, 97, 100–5, 107–8, 112, 117–22, 130, 147, 149, 152, 154, 161, 164, 202, 216, 231, 300, 301
Peshawar 11, 13, 29, 37, 45–6, 151, 157, 161, 283, 313, 315, 332
Pir Roshan 36–7
Podgorny, Nikolai 91
Politburo, Afghan 118
political parties 81
Popal, Ali Ahmad 110
Popalzai 3, 53, 270
population of Afghanistan 7–8
Poulada, Leon 13
Powell, Colin 248–51

prisoners of war (POWs), treatment of 204, 206, 217, 223, 256–60
Pul-e-Charki prison 137
Pul-i-Alam 181
Punjedh 68, 69, 227
Putin, Vladimir 208
Puzanov, Alexander 101, 112, 123, 128, 131

Qader, Abdul 83, 86, 96
Qaderi Order 153, 322, 323
Qadhafi, Mu'ammar 148
Qadir, Abdul 37, 120–1, 149
Qadir, Haji 184
Qari Baba 181
Qays Abdur Rashid 10, 23
Qizelbash 21, 29, 43, 82, 151, 311, 312
Quran, the 148–9, 191, 232
Qutb, Sayed 147

Rabbani, Burhanuddin 90, 146, 149–52, 167–8, 171–6, 180, 182, 205–9, 231, 243
Rabbani, Muhammad 190
Rafi, Mohammad 105, 120
Rahman, Mawlana Fazlur 177
Rahman, Mawlawi Habibur 150
Rao, Raghunath 46
Rashid, Abdul 64
Rashid, Ahmad 175–80, 190, 211
Ratebzad, Anahita 83, 102, 114, 156
Raybchenko, Ivan 133
Reagan, Ronald 159
Red Cross 204, 256
refugees 154, 157–8, 203, 210, 218–19
Repacholi, Michael H. 261
Reshtia, Sayed Qasem 70
resistance, Afghan 143–67; against the communists 152–5; against Daoud 149–52; against Soviet intervention 155–6; against Soviet surrogate government 164–6
Rice, Condoleezza 247–51
Richardson, Bruce 203–4, 208, 212
Roberts, General 56
Robinson, Mary 256
Rohilkand 36, 45
Rohillas 36
Roshani movement 27, 36–9, 144
Rothstein, Hy 255
Roucek, S. Joseph 239
Roy, Olivier 145, 148, 150, 205, 234
Rubin, Barnet R. 150, 154, 159–60
Rumsfeld, Donald 246, 248, 251, 253

Russia 1–4, 13, 18, 56, 68–72, 76–8, 84–8, 91–6, 100–1, 109, 117, 121–3, 126–32, 168, 195–7, 202, 207–10, 215–16, 221, 226–7, 231, 236, 247, 290–2, 310; intervention in Afghanistan 132–9, 143–4, 155–7, 163–4; withdrawal from Afghanistan 165

Sabir Shah 44
Sadat, Anwar 242
Sadozai clan 41, 43–4, 53, 54, 219, 227, 233, 282, 313, 314
Safavid Empire 35–6, 39–41, 50, 199, 219, 226, 267, 281, 312, 333
Safi, General Rahmatullah 212
Safronchuk, Vasily S. 128
Salam, Abdul 120, 165, 181
Salangi, Bashir 187–8
Sarwar, Ghulam 86
Sarwari, Asadullah 123–4, 130
Sarwari, Mohammad Arif 245
Saudi Arabia 1, 92, 152, 158–60, 163–4, 187, 205, 210–11, 216, 242–3, 253–4
Sayyaf, Abdul Rasul 90, 146–9, 158, 161, 164, 172, 174, 180, 182, 205
Sazman-i-Jawanon Musselman (Organisation of Muslim Youth) 147
Sazman-i-Nasr-i-Islami 152
School of Oriental and African Studies (SOAS) 15
'segmentary state' concept 22–4, 52–6
separatism 195
September 11th 2001 attacks in the US 241–4, 253
Sergeyev, Igor 208, 249
Setam-i-Meli 80, 83, 105, 106, 115, 121, 229, 232, 320
Seton-Watson, Hugh 24
Sevan, Benon 171
Shafiq, Musa 80–1, 84, 146
Shah Ashraf 41
Shah Hussein 41
Shah Tahmaseb III 41
Shahadat (newspaper) 148
Shahi, Agha 131
Shah-i-Kabuli, Sabir 43
Shahrani, Nazif 213–14
Shami Mullah 145
Shari'ah law 31, 148–9, 193, 195, 244, 253
Shariati, Ali 145
Sharq, Mohammad Hassan 83, 95
Shi'ah groups 82, 105, 205–6, 238–9

Shir Shah Suri 45
Shola Jawed 80, 83, 105, 229
Shultz, George 169
Shura-i-Nezar 22, 58, 106, 171, 203, 205, 208, 213, 215, 217, 232, 331
Shura-i-Inqlab-i-Islami 152
Sihonauk, Norodom, Prince 170–1
Sikhs 13, 45, 287, 312
Silverman, Marlin 12
Smith, Anthony 24–5, 198
Somalia 126
South Africa 239
Southall, A. 18–19, 22–3, 55–7
Stalin, Joseph 77, 216
Stanekzai, Sher Muhammad 185
state, Afghan 17–20, 23–4, 27, 48–51, 96, 138, 195, 199–200, 219, 226–9; foundation of 57, 82, 227, 233–4, 285–6; fragility of 52–6
Stinger missiles 159–60, 165
Street, Brian 14
student demonstrations 102
Sudan 242
Sufi Orders 153
surface-to-air (SAM) missiles 159
Suri 28, 36, 39, 199, 314
Swat society 14
Sydney Morning Herald 259
Sykes, Percy 61

Tabibi, Abdul Hakim 126, 157
Tajiks and Tajikistan 1, 22, 81, 194, 202, 205–11, 222, 230–1, 237, 239
Taleban movement 2–5, 29, 32, 38–9, 146, 167–8, 174–97, 200–1, 204–6, 209, 213–19, 223, 230–40, 243–57, 264–9; conquests of 179–89; rise of 176–9
Tamerlane 199
Tapa-e-Tajbeg palace 135
Tapper, Richard 16–19, 49, 53, 222
Taraki, Nur Mohammad 85–7, 94–5, 99–104, 107–13, 118–28, 134–8, 153
Tarklauri tribe 37
Tarun, Sayed Daoud 124–5
Tarzi, Mahmud 62–4
Tehran 41
Tenet, George 245–6, 249
terrain of Afghanistan 224–5
Time magazine 243
The Times of London 170
Timur Shah 21, 52, 54, 226
Total Oil Company 93
traditional leaders 214

tribal society and tribal divisions 4, 9–10, 16–20, 24, 36, 43, 49–51, 60, 72, 138, 144, 166, 171, 225–6, 233–5
Tsagolov, Kim 165
Turabi, Hassan 242
Turabi, Nuruddeen 180
Turi tribe 37
Turk Atta 70
Turkey 1, 84, 149, 218, 236
Turki, Prince 88
Turkmenistan 205, 239

ulama 145–8, 152–3, 173, 192, 229, 234, 244
Ulfat, Gul Pacha 98
unitary states 57
United Arab Emirates 187, 243, 254
United Nations (UN) 9, 72, 156, 164–5, 168–73, 187, 190, 194, 196, 204, 209, 213, 215, 236–40, 242, 249, 253–4, 258, 268–9; Charter 126
United States 1, 9, 69, 72, 77, 84, 131–7, 143, 147, 155, 159–60, 163–4, 168, 187, 196–7, 215–16, 221–3, 241–70
Uranium Medical Research Center (UMRC) 261–4
Urban, Mark 85, 143
Ustinov, Demitri F. 129
Uzbeks and Uzbekistan 1, 194, 202, 205, 207, 210, 215, 231, 239

veils, wearing of 76
Verne, Jules 62
Voice of America 265
Voice of the Masses *see* Khalq faction

WAD 162
Wafadar, Pacha Gul 86, 96
Wahdat newsletter 213
Wahhabism 97, 148, 205, 321

Wais, Mir 26, 39–41, 45, 48, 226
Wakman, Mohammad Amin 126
Wali, Abdul 65, 85, 124, 131
Walliullah, Shah 45
'War on Terror' 266
Wardag, Muhammad Jan Khan 56
warlords 168, 171, 175, 178–83, 192–6, 199, 204–7, 217–19, 227, 245–6, 253–4, 269–70
Watanjar, Aslam 86, 123
Wazir Khan, Jahangir 255
Weber, Max 18–20, 30, 48, 54
Wilber, N. Donald 67
Wish Zalmyan 75–6, 85, 98, 115
women, status of 71–2, 190–3
Woodward, Bob 245–8, 249, 250, 252
World Bank 9

xenophobia 14, 223
Xinhua news agency 255

Yaqob Khan 82
Yar Muhammad, Mullah 165
Yepishev, Alexia A. 127–8
Yosuf, Mohammad 80
Yosufzai tribe 38

Zabuli, Abdul Majid 107
Zahir, Muhammad 148
Zahir Shah, King 146–7
Zairay, Salih Muhammad 128, 135
Zaman, Shah 53
Zaman Khan 44
Zari Khan, Malik 255
Zarif, Mohammad Javad 251
Zazi tribe 37, 65, 71, 313, 315
Zia Mohammad 83
Zia-ul-Haq 124, 131, 154
Zulfiqar 44, 68